For

Martin P Bonoan

Indeed the Wise Man's office
Is to work by being still;
He teaches not by speach
But by accomplishment;
He does for everything,
Neglecting none;
Their life he gives to all,
Possessing none;
And what he brings to pass
Depends on no one else.
As he succeeds,
He takes no credit
And just because he does not take it,
Credit never leaves him.

Tao Tê Ching
Lao Tzu

Philippine Vacations & Explorations

Jill Gale de Villa

Published by
Devcon I P Inc
PO Box 1843 MCPO
1299, Makati, Metro Manila
Philippines

Printed by
Raintree Publishing, Inc.

ISBN 971-91082-3-1

Acknowledgements

In 1982, when I first embarked on making the Philippines more accessible through producing information books, the first place I went for support was to **Martin Bonoan,** then Philippine Airlines' Executive Vice President. I am indeed most sad that he passed away before seeing this project come to fruition, for without his encouragement the book would not have been started. The cost of researching this book was made possible only with PAL's willingness to fly us all over the country, and assistance from their ground crews.

After Martin Bonoan's passing, **Leslie Espino** brought PAL back into the project, re–establishing support for the book. **Vic Bernardino, Manny Gutierrez, Poch Rilloraza** and **Freddie Alquiroz** of PAL all assisted and supported the project.

As the second printing got under way, **General Romeo David, Senen Lainez** and **Grace Ricafort** of PAGCOR extended their assistance and support.

I am grateful to my family, **Rico, Brian** and **Becky**, for putting up with long absences and more long hours when, although physically present, I was mentally elsewhere. Additionally, Rico checked maps, Becky typed and telephoned.

The number of people who have put time, effort and/or advice into this project seems almost endless. To all these people mentioned here, plus many whom I could not list, I, and, more importantly, the project, owe a huge debt of gratitude.

I had many long, happy hours with **Gretchen Hutchinson** and **Edgar (Bong) Ventura.** Initially we were working together to produce a single book which included land and diving information. When the project stalled due to delay in financing, Gretchen and Bong went ahead and published their dive material. The result is two books, each more comprehensive than would have been possible had we continued together.

Gretchen and Bong are responsible for most of the research and writing of chapters and sections on Boracay, Dumaguete, Kalibo, Romblon, and a large part of Puerto Galera; and their influence extends to many other areas of this book.

A few people have bent way over backwards to help, and deserve more than special thanks. These are **George & Gie Lao** of Bohol, **Baby Baldovieso** of Palawan, and **Gladys Montgomery Jones** for her constant support and encouragement, an initial edit, and for writing the history section. **Helen Huckle** did the final, thorough edit, and a marvelous job of eliminating my many gaffes and improving readability.

People who have assisted several areas of this book are **Malen Lim**, **Linda Lawyer**, **Bing Lim** and **Letty Nonoy**.

Gladys Jones, **Susan Gunn** and **Maureen Acox** have assisted with editing and proof reading.

Much of the Manila section is based on research done by **Maureen Acox**, **Carmen Jones-Clad**, **Terry Freixas**, **Susan Gunn** and **Gladys Montgomery Jones**. Maureen helped gather data and write portions of the introduction.

Photos were contributed by **John K Chua** (cover, Ivatan woman), **Maria Garcia Farr** (Boracay, Morion), **Jane Kempe** (Pagsanjan, Mt. Samat), **Gretchen Hutchinson** (marble carver), and **Leslie Ann Murray** (Morion).

Maps were created by **Valentino So** and **Tin Bautista**, Manila maps were based on work by **Jan Gaitan.**

Valuable assistance has been received from **Peter Bender** and **Franz Viana.**

People who have helped at the many places we visited include:

Bacolod: Adam Lawyer, Edwin Gatia, Maricar Cosculuella, Bing Leocardia, Cesar Peralta;
Basco: Vicente Bartolome, Ed Ballesteros, Marivic Lizardo, Jun Ugali, Myrna Ybay and Caridad Viola; Joan Beaumont;
Bohol: the Laos;
Boracay: Katy Asimus;
Cagayan de Oro: the Densing brothers, Ed Sytiongsa, Amy Neri, Chit Silva, Mrs Alfabeto;
Cebu: Maryanne Astillero, Gema Pido, Tom Casas and family;
Davao: Andrew Quinlan, Rosy Dayao, George Misa, Frank Villaraiz;
Dumaguete: Alan and Gail White; Sandy Swafford;
Iloilo: Bernadine Palacios, Edwin Trompeta, Pons Saldana, Jesse & Arlet Ledesma, Monray Mapa, Katy Asimus;
Leyte: Jene Parilla, Miguel Redono, Isagani Granali, Peter Cabrales, Roque Bacayo, Francisco Corales;
Luzon: Archie Vargas, Rowena Calica, the Baguio DOT staff, Gov Justiniano Cortez, Ching Santos, Josie Abbadu, Lucy Bantug;
Palawan: Vera Cohen, Dr John Mendoza, Ellen Hagedorn;
Puerto Galera: Helen Huckle;
Roxas City: Cesar Buyco, Jackie;
Zamboanga: Frank Lagniton; Butch Alvarez.

How to Use This Book

One of the major difficulties with traveling about the Philippines is communications. People in one area, even if they are in the travel trade, may know nothing at all about another area, and may answer questions inaccurately rather than say "I don't know".

I hope that the contents of this book will have enough information and tips to allow you to get around and see what you want to see, by filling in communications gaps. However, please do be aware that changes occur frequently, and it therefore is best for you to inquire about activities when you reach your destination, before setting out.

Those who wish to learn more about the country should refer to Recommended Reading.

Read the section pertinent to your travels and recheck transportation schedules before you set out. Allow plenty of time for everything. If you relax into this country, it is a great place. If you plan too much and are not constantly in a hurry, your trip will not be fun.

The book is in two main parts, with a short introductory section offering tips which will be useful throughout your stay.

The body of the book divides the country into major areas of accessibility. These are again divided into smaller areas. Most areas have a wealth of things to do, and instructions are given regarding how to go about them. "Nutshells" beneath each chapter heading encapsulate activities available in the area mentioned, and give references to transport and lodging listed in the back of the book.

Most prices are given in US dollars ($). Smaller amounts are listed in Philippine pesos (₱).

Plan several activities, and find out which is actually more easily available.

Most areas have a local or national tourism office. Some are well informed, others are not. They provide a starting point for information.

The sustenance columns list eating places. We have either eaten in these places or had them on good recommendation from people who either live at the destination in question, or visit frequently.

The reference section at the end of the book gives an at-a-glance picture of local facilities. The access chapter gives frequency of regularly scheduled air, boat and bus transport. Always recheck these schedules, as they vary seasonally and with availability. Information acquired at one destination regarding transport in and about another destination may not be accurate.

Lodging is described briefly, and approximate prices are given. Although these prices were valid when we got them, there is no guarantee they were valid the next day. Expect changes.

Also, as we were compiling information for this book, many telephone numbers were undergoing conversion, and will have changed in the near future. Refer to the newest phone book.

The glossary assists with the many non-English words in the book.

Introduction

T'Boli boys on an albino *carabao*

Contents

(wherever a significant portion of an area has been researched and written by someone other than the author, their names are appended in parenthesis to appropriate the section or sub-section title.)

Introduction

Seven years ago, when I commenced traveling the Philippines, I began a journey which continues to delight my senses, open my mind and please my spirit.

The variety of experiences the Philippines offers is truly amazing. Almost any tropical delight you fancy is available: tiny white sand-ringed islets and extensive beaches; spectacular reefs teeming with brilliant fish darting through coral gardens; azure waters to wind-surf, sail, swim, and relax in; *carabao* plowing, farmers planting, children playing; spectacular drives through farms, mountains, and along sea- side cliffs; caves to explore; hiking; rice terraces to walk; volcanoes to climb; a wide assortment of friendly, hospitable peoples, many of whom speak English; and a wide variety of accommodations and eating places to suit your budget and needs.

The ubiquitous coconut trees never allow you to forget you are in the tropics. Coconut milk to drink, meat to eat, wine to imbibe, heart of coconut for salad and *lumpia* (egg roll), and coconut oil for tanning and cooking. This is indisputably the Philippine's most important tree.

But there are many more plants to investigate. Nipa is important for roofing, rattan for furniture, mahogany for building and carving. A profusion of delicious fruits is available.

And there is a variety of fauna, too. Each September migratory birds visit on their way south from a chilling China. There are many indigenous birds and animals, the tamaraw (small, water- buffalo-like animal), sea turtle, mouse- deer, Philippine monkey-eating eagle among them. Unfortunately their habitat is being rapidly destroyed and most of these animals face extinction.

While the Philippine climate, and the people's need to eke a living out of small patches of land, necessarily limit the building materials most commonly used, the architectural style varies from north to south, both in response to varied environmental conditions and to local culture.

Much of the center of the country, from Luzon through the Visayas, has modest houses of nipa and cogon grass, often with GI sheet roofing; wealthier housing of brick, wood and more durable materials; and impressive, imposing Spanish churches and their *conventos*. But in the far northern Batanes, people combat six months of strong winds by building houses with meter-thick stone walls. And in Mindanao the graceful spires of mosques punctuate the skylines of Muslim villages, whose houses have steep, curved roofs reminiscent of the famed Moro *vinta*.

The Philippines' most outstanding feature is its people. Filipinos are Asian plus: plus Chinese, plus Spanish, plus American, plus uncounted other nationalities whose peoples have found their way here, been welcomed and stayed to add to the richly diverse cultures they found.

Filipinos genuinely want visitors to have a good time. Most of them not only are pleased to pose for photographs, they won't stop posing, making candid shots sometimes difficult to obtain. Visitors who come to get to know the people are seldom disappointed.

It is typical of the tropics that some things remain constant while other things grow and change rapidly. Resorts tend to come and go, and it is likely that some of the information contained in this book may have changed by the time you visit. Please let us know about these changes, and hence improve the accuracy of future editions, by writing to PO Box 1843, 1299 Makati, Metro Manila, Philippines.

The jeepney – the Philippines' most ubiquitous form of transport

Enjoying the Philippines

The Philippines is a diverse tropical nation with over 7,000 islands. Only about a dozen of the islands are large enough to support several communities.

The country divides roughly into three major areas: Luzon, the largest island, and islands around it; the central or Visayan islands; and Mindanao, the second largest island, in the south.

Manila, a metropolis of over 10 million people, is at the center of Luzon. It is by far the most important business center. Cebu in the heart of the Visayas, is the country's second busiest city.

Entry and Exit

All foreign nationals must have a valid passport. Provided you have onward or return tickets or proof of funds (credit card, etc), a 21-day tourist visa will be issued on arrival, except to citizens of countries not having diplomatic relations with the Philippines and stateless persons.

Because it is costly and time consuming to extend the 21-day tourist visa, it is best to obtain a multiple entry 60-day tourist visa from your nearest Philippine consulate prior to arrival if you intend a longer stay.

Tourists who have not over-stayed their visas do not require exit permits. Residents do.

Declare any amount in excess of the US$3,000 which travelers are permitted to bring into the country. Currency control is often strict. Keep receipts from foreign exchange transactions as you may be required to produce an amount in exchange receipts equal to double the amount of Philippine currency which you want to exchange upon exit.

Major hotels have representatives in the reception area just beyond customs at Ninoy Aquino International Airport (formerly Manila International Airport, and still referred to as MIA). Hotel cars are the easiest way to get to up-market lodging.

Taxis often ask for amazing fees. The real cost of a taxi ride to Makati or Malate should not exceed $3-5.

Buses leave from an area near the parking lot. Airconditioned Love Buses go to Makati, Ermita, and then to Quiapo (see map p 22). CBL and MMTC lines travel EDSA through Makati and Quezon City. DMTC goes to Ermita and Malate, then through Manila to Cubao.

Money

The Philippine unit of currency is the Peso - ₱, divided into ₱100 centavos. In early 1988, US$1 was about ₱21.

In Manila, most foreign currencies and travelers checks can be exchanged at banks, major hotels and authorized dealers. Don't use unauthorized dealers.

Outside Manila, only the US dollar is widely exchanged.

Major credit cards are accepted only at larger resorts, hotels, restaurants and shops.

Climate

The Philippines is divided into four climatic zones.

December through May is the best time to visit most of the north and central Philippines. December through February are cool while March through May are hot. Humidity is usually high, and temperatures are generally tropical (75-95°F or 24-35°C, with mid-day summer highs over 100°F and 37°C). Southern Mindanao is balmy year round.

Much of the Philippines is in the "typhoon

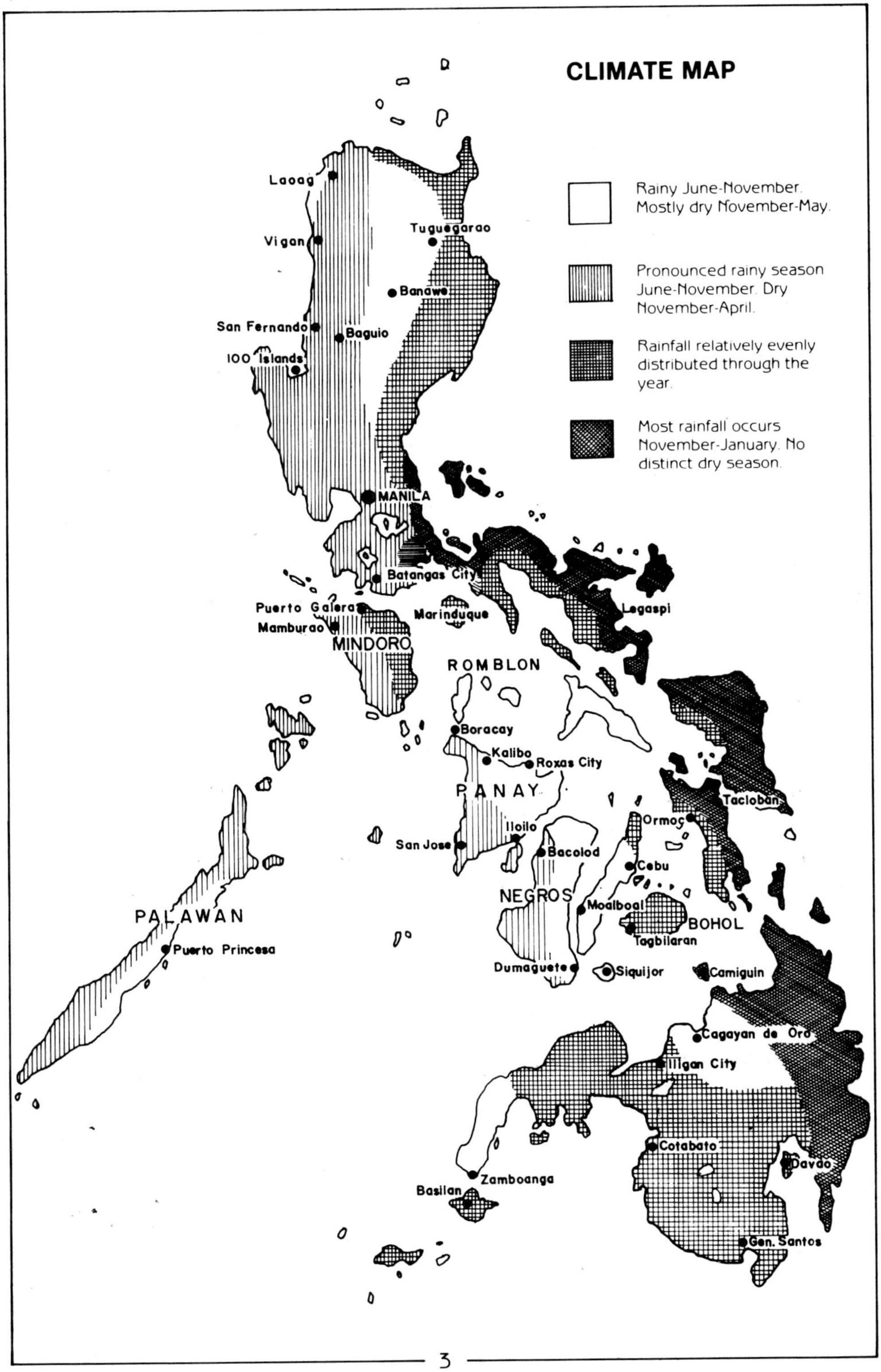
CLIMATE MAP
Rainy June-November. Mostly dry November-May.
Pronounced rainy season June-November. Dry November-April.
Rainfall relatively evenly distributed through the year.
Most rainfall occurs November-January. No distinct dry season.
Laoag
Vigan
Tuguegarao
Banawe
San Fernando
Baguio
100 Islands
MANILA
Batangas City
Puerto Galera
Mamburao
MINDORO
Marinduque
Legaspi
ROMBLON
Boracay
Kalibo
Roxas City
PANAY
Tacloban
Ormoc
Iloilo
San Jose
Bacolod
Cebu
NEGROS
Moalboal
BOHOL
Tagbilaran
PALAWAN
Puerto Princesa
Dumaguete
Siquijor
Camiguin
Cagayan de Oro
Iligan City
Cotabato
Davao
Zamboanga
Basilan
Gen. Santos

belt" and experiences several storms from June through November. During the height of rainy season as much as 18" of rain may fall in one day, and land and sea travel in many places is very difficult.

Clothing and Accessories

Light, natural fibre, loose-fitting garments are most comfortable. A jacket or sweater is useful in the mountain areas, especially December through February. Tennis shoes are useful if you plan on walking.

Shorts and skimpy tops should not be worn when visiting churches or mosques. Nude bathing is not acceptable on public beaches.

For formal occasions the *barong Tagalog* can be worn instead of a suit.

Hats provide helpful relief from the sun. Sun screen and block are essential. Insect repellant helps keep evenings pleasant. Baby oil thickly applied keeps sand fleas (encountered on some beaches) from inflicting lasting, itchy bites.

The Countryside

The Philippine islands were formed by faulting and folding along major fault lines and by volcanic processes. The country has several major volcanoes. Some of them, including Taal and beautiful Mayon, are important attractions.

Mt Apo, south of Davao City on Mindanao, is the country's tallest mountain, at 2950 meters. Apo is a dormant or extinct volcano. Mt Pulog, the country's second highest mountain (located in Benguet, on Luzon), is just a few meters shorter and was formed through crustal uplift. Both are enjoyable climbs.

Philippine highlands are of fairly recent formation, and tend to be precipitous. Much of the high altitude pine and mid-level rainforest which once carpeted the land has been logged, with farms taking over arable land.

Most valleys and lowlands are dotted with farms which grow coconuts, rice, sugar, corn, vegetables, fruits and tobacco. A wide variety of animals is raised as livestock, some as beasts of burden.

The strong water buffalo (*carabao*) is widely used for tilling the soil. Because the *carabao* have no sweat glands, they cannot work in the heat of the day. In areas where the heat is intense, farmers use zebu brahma cattle rather than *carabao*. In many areas ponies provide transport.

Mountains and lowlands which are not farmed often have a thick covering of cogon - a tough grass with razor-sharp edges. Many flowering plants, including jasmine (*sampaguita*), hibiscus (*gumamela*), bougainvillea, frangipani (*kalachuchi*), water lillies and water hyacinth enhance the beauty of the countryside. Wild orchids grow in mountainside rainforests.

Nipa palms, used as building material, grow in swampy lowlands. Much swamp land has been converted to prawn and fish ponds.

The Philippine shores and off-shore reefs, so long as they are left undamaged, serve as a breeding grounds for an incredible wealth of marine life, many of which feed a large portion of the population, and delight the visitor's palate. Coastal areas are usually fringed with coconut trees.

Transportation

Most travelers to the Philippines arrive by air to Manila. From there a vast network of air, land and sea transportation links the various provinces, cities, towns and *barrios*.

The Department of Tourism (DOT) Information Office (at the DOT Building, Rizal Park) has rate and schedule information regarding transportation throughout the country. Information for inter-island transport is provided on pp 266-73. Transport information within each area is provided in the text.

Air is the quickest, most efficient means of domestic travel. Airfares are reasonable.

Philippine Airlines (PAL) flights are reliable and usually on time, but the occasional flight cancellation can cause inconvenience. Passengers are given the next available unbooked seats on subsequent flights. Thus it is best to allow at least 24 hours in Manila before flights abroad. PAL offers good, inexpensive 2-day tour packages to several destinations.

A few small non-scheduled airlines, such as Pacific Air and Aerolift, offer charters and flights to places not served by PAL.

Inter-island **boats** operate regularly from Manila. Provincial boat services vary tremendously, from ships to *bancas*, small out-rigged craft.

There is **train** service from Manila to Legazpi. It is less expensive than the bus, takes 2 hours longer, seats are not as comfortable, but there is room to walk around.

Major **roads** surrounding Metro Manila are good, except after rainy season, when they are in need of repair. Luzon has a fairly good road system, and a highway which is mostly good extends through the Visayas to Davao, with some intervening ferries. Major towns throughout the country have paved roads, but roads beyond are often unsurfaced.

By **bus**, express services (1st class and regular) operate to all Luzon provinces and continue south to some Visayan and Mindanao points. There are connecting ferries to smaller areas. Regional and local services operate within each province. In addition, some travel companies offer special trips especially during dry season, holidays, and in May when there are many fiestas. There is 1st class (express, air conditioned) bus service between some provincial points.

Many buses proceed at amazing speed. 1st class buses are usually comfortable, express buses do not stop often, regular buses are crowded, sometimes uncomfortable, and stop for anyone along the highway wanting a ride. If there is no room inside, the roof may be filled.

Jeepneys and **minibuses** perform the same services as their larger relatives, will stop for passengers anywhere and pack very full.

Taxis are of varying degrees of cleanliness, road worthiness and cost. In Manila their fare is supposed to be regulated by a meter, but some meters are "doctored" to run at high speed. It is safest to hire a taxi at a hotel, where doormen note license numbers and hence can trace cabs if needed; and check that the meter is running.

Provincial taxis are often called "PU" after the "public utility" designation on their license plates. Trip cost is by arrangement. Some provincial taxi drivers are excellent guides - inquire from your hotel.

Tricycles, which are motorcycles or bicycles with a cab attached, are often the most convenient and inexpensive way to do short trips in the provinces.

Horse-drawn vehicles (*calesas* and *caretelas*) operate in many cities and provinces and are a relaxed way to get around.

Do take time out to watch these "lesser" forms of transport. The colorful jeepney is often decoratively and imaginatively painted. The driver and conductor sometimes manage to cram as many as 30 people in, around and on their vehicle. We have seen a dozen people attached to a tricycle.

Scheduled transport often runs late or early, departing when full rather than when scheduled. Arrive early, and be prepared to wait.

Toilet facilities along the way vary from acceptable to primitive to non- existent.

Food

Eating in the Philippines can be an outstanding experience, for all budget levels. In recent years a profusion of restaurants has emerged in major cities, many catering to European and Chinese tastes. There are some good Japanese restaurants, too, plus a smattering of Indian,

Korean, Thai and other cuisines. A few recommended restaurants are mentioned in the **sustenance** section of each area presented.

All major hotels have several good restaurants where you may have a good meal, often for under $20 (plus drinks).

American and American-influenced fast food chains have made inroads throughout Manila. McDonalds, Shakeys, Wendys compete with Chinese dimsum for the meal-on-the-run business, while sidewalk barbeque stalls also offer inexpensive fare.

The *turo-turo* is the Filipino version of a canteen. This can be a great experience as long as the food is fresh, and newly cooked.

While in the Philippines, be sure to experience Filipino cooking. Some of it is very good, especially the seafoods which are so fresh and tasty here that many westerners who never before liked fish are quickly converted to it. Filipino cooking, unlike most Asian cuisine, is not spicy.

Treats which the more adventurous eaters may want to try include bagoong (dried, fermented tiny shrimps or fish), used to flavor some dishes, and eaten with unripe mango slices, and *balut*, which is unhatched duck embryo.

Do not neglect fruits in season - mangoes, pomelo (*suha*), papaya, avocado, guava are among the well known ones; lesser known delights include *lanzones* (beige clusters of fruit), *chico* (brown fruits), jackfruit (langka), *atis* (custard apple or sweet sop), *santol*, *caimito* (star apple), mangosteen, *mabolo*, rambutan, the smelly durian and less odiferous *marang*.

Several establishments offer fruit shakes and/or daiqueries. Green mango, *buco* (young coconut) and *calamansi* (small green lemon-lime fruit) juices are among the favorites. Specify little or no sugar when ordering if you don't want the drink to come very sweet.

Filipinos eat hearty breakfasts which are often a combination of a western breakfast with anything left over from yesterday's meals. Meals are often multi-dish affairs. Snacks called *merienda* are eaten between

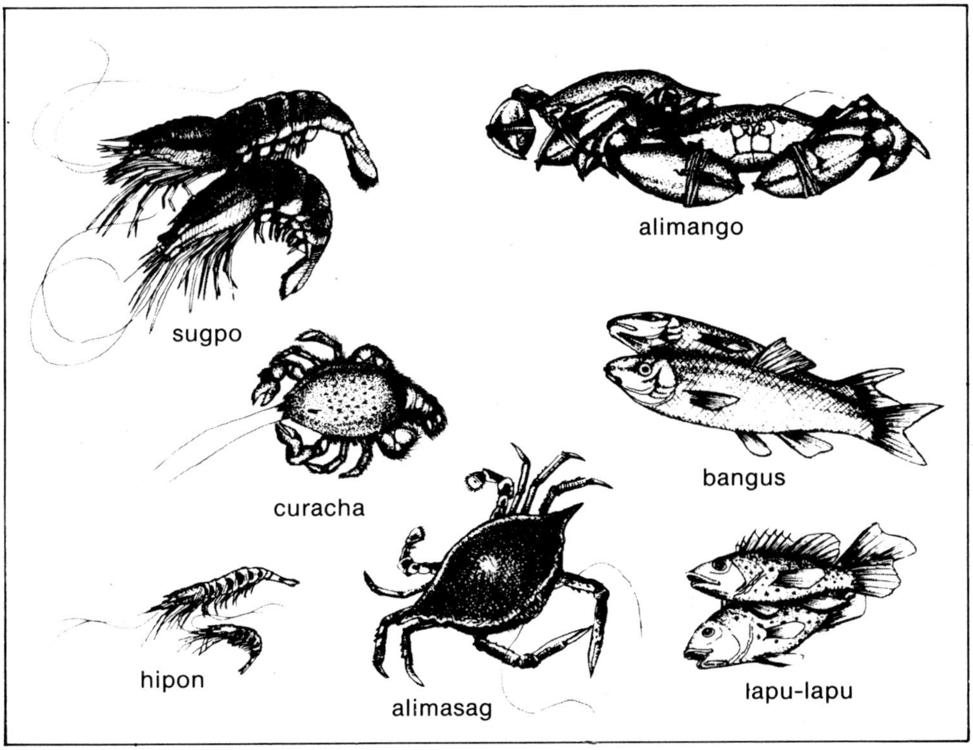

meals. Dinner is served around 7:30 pm. Several dishes and foods which you might like to try are listed below.

main dishes:

adobo — dishes cooked with vinegar and soy sauce, including *baboy* (pork) and/or *manok* (chicken), *pusit* (squid), *isda* (fish)
alimango — large shore-line crab - and
alimasag — the slender deep sea crab
bangus — milk fish, served stuffed, grilled or fried; specify boneless if you don't want to deal with many tiny bones
beefsteak *Tagalog* — thin slices of beef cooked with soy sauce and onions
calamares — fried squid rings
camote — sweet potatoes/yams
chop suey — (transplanted American food) vegetables
crispy pata — pork leg, boiled then fried
dinuguan — pork tripe stewed in blood
gulay — vegetables
inihaw or *ihaw-ihaw* — barbeque
kare kare — beef tripe
kambing — goat
kilawen — raw fish (or oysters, etc) soaked in vinegar, garlic, etc.
la Paz batchoy — noodle soup with meat
lechon — whole roast pig
lapu lapu — garouper
lumpia — egg roll; fillings include *shanghai* (meat); *sariwa* (fresh vegetables);
ubod (heart of palm); *gulay* (vegetables)
mechado — stewed beef roll
nilaga — boiled
pakbet or *pinakbet* — Ilocano vegetable dish with pork, shrimps and *bagoong*
pancit — noodles, which come in many varieties: *pancit Malabon* has a mixture of seafoods, vegetables and pork; *pancit guisado* is fried noodles with meat and vegetables; *pancit Canton* is similar;
singkamas — turnip, good peeled and eaten raw
sinigang — a delicious sour soup
talaba — oysters
tahong — mussels; very good baked
tapa — dried or marinated meat

tinola — chicken vegetable soup with lemon grass

sweets & snacks:

bibingka — rice cake, many varieties, some used as a sweet, others as a bread for merienda
guinatan — fruits boiled in sugar and coconut juice
gulaman — agar-agar (gelatin)
halo-halo — sweet beans and preserved fruits with ice and milk or ice cream
leche flan — custard
maja blanca — coconut milk and milk
pulutan — finger foods with drinks
puto — rice cake
siopao — dimsum, meat and gravy filling in a steamed bun

Health

Sidewalk vendors offer a tempting array of food, but it is safest to stick to those delicacies which have just emerged steaming hot from the pot or barbeque.

Water may not be sterile. Stick to bottled or canned beverages or coffee, tea or hot water.

Malaria is a problem only in the interior of more remote islands, such as Palawan, Mindoro and Mindanao. Start anti-malarials a couple of weeks prior to leaving for these destinations.

Should you become ill, seek medical advice before leaving the country. Philippine doctors may be more knowledgeable about tropical diseases than their temperate climate counterparts. Makati Medical Center has a good emergency room. Many embassies have a current listing of recommended physicians and dentists. Medical care is inexpensive in the Philippines. Most medicines are available, but under local brand names. Bring with you any medicines you anticipate needing.

Security

In general, the Philippines is pleasantly safe to travel. However, as in most countries, you should take reasonable precautions; don't display wads of money and expensive jewelry, etc; do not go off with people who promise you they know a better place to shop, where things are cheaper - you may be drugged or robbed.

There are of course areas to avoid. Some portions of Mindanao, most especially the southern islands of Sulu and Jolo, fall in this category at the time of writing. A few less remote areas of Mindanao have periodic problems which make it advisable for the visitor to ask before venturing afield. This is also true of some of the more remote mountain areas of Luzon. Caution must be exercised in and around public markets and transportation areas, where thieves traditionally operate.

In general, when visiting a rural area for more than a few hours, it is correct procedure to introduce yourself to the barrio captain, mayor or priest. Almost all will offer valuable assistance and advice, and many will take it upon themselves to look out for your welfare. Filipino hospitality is a wonderful thing indeed.

Recommended Reading

Travelers who intend to stay in the Philippines for extended periods of time will want to consider acquiring **Luzon by Car**, a driving guide to the Philippines' largest island, and **MANILA: The Traveler's Companion**, a 200-page guide to Metropolitan Manila.

Divers will want to have the informative and attractive **Philippine Dive Versions** (Hutchinson & Ventura).

Ins & Outs of Manila is a reasonably good book of maps, and there are two fold-out maps of interest - the **Manila Survival Map** and the **Metro Manila Landmarks map.**

History

Lid of a secondary burial jar, San Carlos University Museum, Cebu

Evolution of a Nation

The archipelago that came to be known as the Philippines was first settled perhaps 500,000 years ago. There is archaeological evidence of hunter-gatherers c 200,000 years ago in the Cagayan Valley. After the end of the Ice Age, trade developed with Indonesia and Borneo, then mainland Southeast Asia, Japan and India. Societies developed agriculture, became more complex and left their traces in gold and jade ornaments, pottery and burial sites.

By AD 500, the basis of a Filipino culture was in place. Over the next 1000 years, Filipinos smelted iron and mined gold; harvested rice, coconuts, sugar cane, cotton, hemp, bananas, oranges, and other crops; fished, raised livestock, cut lumber, built ships and wove textiles. Active trade developed among *barangays* and with China, Vietnam and Thailand.

They inscribed literature on perishable bamboo in script derived from Pali and Sanskrit. The local government unit, the *barangay*, consisted of 30 to 100 families. Disputes were settled by law and prompt public trial by a jury of elders. They were animists, practicing intricate religious rituals and ancestor worship.

A Succession of Rulers

From 200 to 1440, the islands were part of various Hindu-Malayan empires, the Javanese empire of Madjapahit, and Ming dynasty China. Then, until 1565, Northern Luzon was periodically controlled by Japan, Southern Luzon by Muslim Borneo and Brunei. From 1380 to the mid-1500s, **Islam** spread through Sulu and Mindanao to the Visayas and Luzon.

By the late 1400s, European countries began to penetrate the region. **Magellan**, funded by the Spanish king to find a new spice trade route, landed in Cebu, claimed the islands for Spain, and converted **Rajah Humabon** and his followers to Christianity. Magellan was killed in battle with **Lapu Lapu**, a chief of nearby Mactan Island.

Spain's conquest began in earnest in 1565 with the arrival of **Miguel Lopez de Legazpi**. After establishing settlements on Cebu and Panay, Legazpi defeated Rajah Sulayman, Manila's Muslim ruler, in 1571, and established a capital city better positioned for trade with China.

Apart from one short period (1855-73), Manila was the only Asian port open to the Spanish **Galleons**, which brought gold and silver from Acapulco to trade for porcelain, jade, bronzes, silk and velvet.

Land formerly owned by the community was given to the chief, who now owed his power and allegiance to the Spanish. The *barangay* remained the local government unit, but an oligarchy of mayors and higher officials was created whose abuses of power led to agrarian uprisings.

The Spanish found the islands were not rich in spices and yielded little gold. Muslims and mountain tribes resisted colonization, pirates harassed the galleons. The colony operated at a deficit. Spain stayed on at the behest of the Church.

Catholic friars first arrived with Magellan and promptly set about converting "the heathen". The local church became the center of community life, the parish priests were closer to the people than the governing Spanish. Church and state were the dual rulers, wrestling for power, both committing errors and excesses.

Manila became wealthy and gracious in the Spanish style (Britain took brief custody 1762-4 during the Seven Years' War).

In 1859, when the Spanish king reversed an earlier policy allowing Filipino priests to be in charge of some parishes, the Archbishop of Manila and Father **José Burgos** charged racial discrimination. In 1872, the government overreacted to a mutiny of Filipino soldiers and unjustly executed Burgos and two other priests, the first martyrs to the nationalist cause. Persecution of Filipino intellectuals followed; some fled to Europe to carry on a propaganda movement. Among them was José Rizal, whose written portrayals of government and church abuses galvanized his generation. In retaliation, Rizal's family's property was confiscated. He returned to Manila and was arrested. Andres Bonifacio and others reacted by forming an underground revolutionary organization, the **Katipunan**. In 1896, sporadic fighting erupted into rebellion. Rizal and hundreds of others were executed, fueling the fires of revolution.

Emilio Aguinaldo, a young mayor in Cavite, routed the Spanish. In 1897, a revolutionary assembly developed the first republican constitution in Asia, elected Aguinaldo President of the Philippine Republic, and declared independence. But the rebels were unable to match Spanish military response. Late in 1897, Aguinaldo surrendered and was exiled.

US Colonial Period

In 1898 the US declared war on Spain over events in Cuba. Commodore George Dewey's Pacific fleet defeated the few Spanish warships in Manila Bay.

The Americans enlisted Aguinaldo's aid by promising Philippine independence, but after the Spanish defeat by Filipino soldiers, Aguinaldo's envoy and army were barred from the city. Finally, Spain ceded the Philippines to the US for $2 million and Aguinaldo resumed hostilities against the new colonial masters; a brutal guerrilla war began. Aguinaldo was captured in 1901, but the war lasted until mid-1902.

The Americans introduced US-style educational and government systems. American markets opened to Philippine products; this favored large-scale agricultural production and inhibited land reform, perpetuating rural unrest.

Filipinos resumed positions of authority under the American governor. Political parties developed, generally around politicians with a personal following. This tended to assure long tenure in office.

The American intention to allow the Philippines to grow into self-government was delayed by two world wars and the Great Depression. Effects of the depression intensified Philippine agrarian revolts and discontent among the poor. In 1924, communists organized the Society of Workers of the Philippines.

In 1934 **Manuel Quezon** secured from the US promise of a Commonwealth by 1936 and independence in 1946. Quezon was elected the first President. He named General Douglas MacArthur, whose father had helped defeat the Spanish, his advisor.

World War II

Three days after Pearl Harbor, the Japanese invaded the Philippines. MacArthur and his Filipino and American troops retreated to **Corregidor** and **Bataan**, where they held up Japanese forces for months. The 48,000 survivors who surrendered were taken on the notorious **Death March** in the hottest season to internment in Pampanga.

Over 250,000 Filipinos engaged the Japanese in a guerrilla war. In Luzon, resistance was led by the Hukbalahaps (**Huks**), or People's Army Against Japan, which originated in the pre-war agrarian reform movement. To protect their families and homeland, some Filipinos cooperated with the Japanese, who established a new government with Jose P Laurel at its head. In late September, 1944, the US began its reconquest, which took a year and left Manila in ruins.

Independence

Immediately after the war, the US granted the Philippines independence. Rebuilding key infrastructures drained the treasury. The two major political parties represented only the wealthy elite. Corruption and the use of power to gain official positions became increasingly common.

The Huks turned their attention to agrarian injustice and insurrection. When **Ramon Magsaysay**, a young Congressman of working class origin was appointed head of defense, they controlled many towns in Luzon. Magsaysay reformed the military and offered the Huks pardons and land. His solution began to work. In 1953, with the support of the Church, US officials and Namfrel (the National Movement for Free Elections), he won the presidency.

Magsaysay championed the cause of the tenant farmer and sought to improve infrastructure. But economic planning was insufficient to implement his policies. Magsaysay was killed in a plane crash.

Succeeding governments regressed into corruption. Filipino businessmen bought out foreign investors. Manila acquired a swank new veneer, but economic growth did not compensate for population increase.

The Marcos Years

Ferdinand Marcos, a young congressman who had successfully appealed a conviction for killing his father's opponent in a local election, was elected President in 1966. On the stump, he sang campaign duets with his beautiful wife **Imelda**.

Marcos focused on construction of roads and other public projects. In 1969, he became the first president to be reelected, but his campaign sapped the treasury. The peso fell, the cost of living rose, strikes and protests flared. **Professor Jose Ma. Sison** founded the Communist Party of the Philippines, with its military wing the New People's Army (**NPA**).

In 1972, Marcos declared martial law, accusing the communists of fomenting unrest. He revamped the constitution, gained control of the National Assembly, major businesses and media, and jailed his opponents.

From 1972-75, economic growth averaged 7%. Some breathed a sigh of relief. Others joined the NPA. In 1972, the Muslim minority in the south began a rebellion that took over 50,000 lives and ended in 1976 with a treaty granting limited autonomy.

The political and economic situation deteriorated. The Marcoses increasingly isolated themselves. Their relatives and close associates became powerbrokers in new monopolies. The military became politicized and corrupt. Imelda chaired two dozen agencies, councils and corporations, and controlled budgets of more than $500,000,000 annually.

After nearly 8 years in prison, Senator **Benigno "Ninoy" Aquino**, Marcos' chief political opponent, was allowed to have heart surgery in the US where he spent three years in exile.

Cory & People Power

In August 1983, Aquino returned. As he stepped from the plane he was killed. The people turned against Marcos, and a reform movement in the military grew. The economy collapsed. By late 1985, Marcos was forced to call for an election.

His opponent in the February 7, 1986 election was Aquino's widow Corazon, backed by the Catholic Church and "People Power"

Marcos was declared winner of a fraudulent election. Aquino called for civil disobedience. Defense Minister Juan Ponce Enrile and Vice Chief of Staff Lt General Fidel Ramos defected and were followed within 48 hrs by most of the military. Thousands of civilians physically shielded them from government military action. The US withdrew support from Marcos and took him into exile in Hawaii.

Aquino restored a constitutional democracy. She faced her 6-year term with the challenge of improving a devastated economy, restoring the election process, and controlling insurgencies.

The Filipino

The Filipino

The Filipino is a delightful melange of the original Malay people who came to the islands, plus countless other nationalities who came to trade and stay. Most visitors were Chinese, others were Japanese, Arab, Indian, Spanish, American, Portuguese, English, French and many more people who came, stayed, and added their cultural and genetic input to the indigenous population.

Long before the Spaniards arrived the Filipinos divided themselves into approximately three classes: the upper, ruling class; the middle class which owed some allegiance to the upper class; and the serfs or slaves, who were to varying degrees owned by the ruling class. (There were regional variations on this theme.) The upper class had duties and responsibilities to the lower classes, and unpopular rulers risked being abandoned by their followers.

The Spanish installed themselves and their emissaries on the top rung, prohibited some forms of abuse of the lower echelon, and widened the distances between the classes.

The Americans attempted to introduce democratic institutions and expanded educational opportunities while still trying to maintain control.

The lowland Filipino was unavoidably altered by the colonial experience. He developed a sense that, because he was ruled by outsiders, his fate was not his own. But the "Yellow Revolution" of February 1986 may have changed all that. Millions of unarmed citizens took to the streets, and used Filipino behavioral principles to stop armed soldiers and tanks. With almost no violence they rejected an increasingly unpopular regime, brought in a new one. Nuns knelt in front of tanks. Tanks ground to a halt. People offered food to soldiers. The revolution was won. The world was amazed. So were the Filipinos. They regained the pride buried for so long under domination.

Filipino Culture

Visitors who make an effort to understand Filipino culture will find their stay greatly enriched.

Filipinos are possibly the most hospitable people in the world. Guests are honored, their idiosyncrasies tolerated even when found offensive. People arriving around mealtime are always asked to stay and share the repast, no matter how meager. Hence one should not arrive uninvited at mealtimes. In the provinces "my house is your house" is all too true. When an invitation is offered, you should tactfully refuse a couple of times before accepting - only when the offer is repeated can you be sure it was genuinely intended.

Filipinos have a refined sense of *delicadeza,* a sensitivity to the feelings of others. Getting along is the norm. The group will is all important. It is not nice to "rock the boat". Direct confrontations are avoided. Often a negative message comes through a third party. Efforts are made to keep communications smooth and courteous.

Consequently, if you ask a question, you may receive a positive response when in fact the correct answer is negative. If you are observant you can tell the difference between a genuine "yes", which is offered unreservedly, and a "yes" which essentially means no, and is offered with averted eyes and lack of enthusiasm. If you are unsure, ask the same question, or a similar one, again; or ask if the particular request is a difficult one. Should the answer, then, be "yes, it is difficult", you
know the response intended is "no"

The giving and receiving of favors comprise part of a network of debts of gratitude - *utang na loob* - which is at the core of most relationships. A favor given is to be reciprocated.

Tribal Roots

Filipinos divide themselves into many groups. Ilocanos are the frugal, hard-working people of Northern Luzon's coasts and valleys. Tagalogs are pragmatic people from the middle of Luzon. Bicolanos are from southern Luzon. Visayans are refined folk from the central islands.

All are subdivided into smaller groups. Many have emigrated to and mingled in other islands. These major groups may be descendants of later immigrants which displaced original peoples who are now known as tribal minorities.

The tribal groups, hidden in the interiors of some of the larger islands, escaped the impact of colonialism, but recently have been affected by the in- migration of lowland Filipinos.

Attitudes toward tribal minorities range from abuse to benign neglect to microscopic inspection. Often looked down upon by the lowlanders as inferior beings, some remain true to the tribe, clan, custom and law of their forebears.

They produce superb handicrafts, both utile and beautiful. Interpretations of their crafts (especially basketry and weaving) are now exported. Individual pieces are prized as collectors' items. The remoteness of their communities, the exotic appeal of their spirit and the uniqueness of their culture are an enticement to many travelers.

Tribes of Luzon's central mountains (pp 85-101) include the Bontoc, Ibaloi, Ifugao, Gaddang, Kalinga, Kankanoi and Tinguian. Theirs is a highly developed agricultural economy. Animists, they have numerous rites pertaining to the crops. They created extensive terracing and maintain a fierce independence. They produce superb utilitarian baskets and are excellent weavers.

The Mangyan of Mindoro (pp 133-137) consist of several tribes. Highly literate, they inscribe script on bamboo, telling of ancestral songs and poems known as Ambahan. They weave sturdy cloth.

Non-Muslim tribes, such as the T'Boli, Tiruray, Bagobo, Subanon, Bukidnon, Mandaya and Manobo inhabit Mindanao's mountains (pp 226, and 252-253).

The Muslims of the south are considered the largest cultural minority (pp 226-263). Some seek autonomy for Mindanao (which is now predominantly Christian) and Sulu. Tausug, Maranao, Maguindanao, Samal, Badjao and Yakan are all distinct Muslim groups.

The Negritoes (pp & 165), variously called Aeta, Ati, Eta, Ito, Batak, live in small groups in remote areas throughout the Philippines. Sometimes timid, they are distinguished by short stature, dark skin and kinky hair. Masters of life in tropical rainforests, some Negritoes are regularly employed by the US army to teach its soldiers how to survive in the jungle. Considered the original owners of at least one island, they are the object of the Philippines' most famous festival, the Ati-atihan (p 165).

Language

Most Filipinos are multi-lingual, speaking at least the national language (Filipino or Tagalog) and their own regional dialect (of which there are a profusion). Many also speak some Spanish and a version of English, or, more accurately, American. They often find English accents difficult to comprehend. In some areas of Luzon's central mountains and Mindanao, however, English is as widely spoken as the national language.

The literacy rate in the Philippines is high. Filipinos value education highly.

In Filipino, the b and v, f and p are interchangeably pronounced and used. Vowel sounds blend into one another: a and e, e and i, o and u may be indistinguishable. Communications are enhanced if the traveler will speak slowly and distinctly.

Double vowels are pronounced

separately, eg. *Ta-al* Volcano; i is pronounced "ee"; ay is pronounced as the "y" in by; and j is pronounced as "h"

While it is not necessary for the traveler to speak Filipino, a few words are much appreciated. The honorific *po* or *ho*, meaning "sir" or "ma'am", should be used whenever talking with an older person, or someone in a position of authority or respect.

Hello, how are you .... *Kumusta ka or kumusta po kayo*
I am fine .... *Mabuti (po)*
Thank you .... *Salamat (po)*
Thank you very much .. *Maraming salamat (po)*
Yes/No .... *O-o/Hindi*
Good morning/afternoon/evening .... *Magandang umaga/hapon/gabi po*
May I ask .... *Puede (po) mag tanong?* is the correct way to commence a conversation asking for assistance or information

Where is the .... *Nasaan (po) ang*
Toilet .... CR (comfort room)
City hall .... *Municipio*
Bus or jeepney to .... *Bus o djipney sa*
Where is (a person) .... *Nasaan (po) ba si* (name)
What time is it now? .. *Anong horas na ba?*
What time does the *(bus, jeep, etc)* leave for *(destination)* ... *Anong oras aalis ang* (bus, jeep, etc) *para sa* (destination)
How much is this? .... *Magkano (po) ito?*
It is too expensive .... *Masyadong mahal naman*
Time to eat .... *Kumain na (po)*
Delicious .... *Masarap*
Water .... *Tubig*
Large/Small .... *Malaki/Maliit*
Hot/Cold .... *Mainit/Malamig*
Good or kind/Bad .... *Mabait/Masama*
Man/Woman/Child .... *Lalake/Babae/Bata*
Okay .... *Sigue*
Good-bye .... *Paalam*

Fiesta of San Isidro Labrador, Lukban, Quezon, May 15

Fiestas

Filipinos love a good party, and have them often, celebrating the harvest, births, and anything else worth a celebration. The Spanish overlaid their religion on existing rituals, celebrating a saint's birthday on dates formerly associated with animistic rituals.

Celebrations are found in every ethnic group, as people gather for essentially spiritual events which bring them together in a sharing of drama, excitement, food, music and renewal of relationships. Fiestas may be large, organized, regional events or small barrio happenings.

Visitors are welcome at festivals, and you should make an effort to attend one during your visit. Descriptions of some specific festivals are given in chapters pertinent to the area where they are held. Activities always center around the church, from where they proceed into the community.

January	
1	**New Year's Day** — early mass after a night's revelry
1st Sunday	**Three Kings** — last day of Christmas celebrations & gift giving
2nd Tuesday	**Black Nazarene** Quiapo, MM (p 31) — the black Christ is carried forth from Quiapo church in a huge procession. People try to touch his palanquin in hopes of having their sins forgiven.
movable	**Appey** Bontoc, Mt Prov — planting rites
3rd weekend	**Ati-atihan** Kalibo, Aklan — spectacular festival (p 164)
	Sto Niño de Cebu Cebu City — 5pm procession from the Basilica
4th weekend	**Dinagyang** Iloilo — a choreographed version of Ati- Atihan (p 170)
February	
movable	**Hariraya Hadji** — pilgrimage of Moslems to Mecca
1-3	**Feast of Our Lady of Candles** — blessing of candles, which are then taken home to protect the house against danger
1-7	**Armadahan Regatta** — gathering and racing of sailing *bancas* in Laguna de Bay
11	**Feast of Our Lady of Lourdes** Quezon City
March & April	
movable	**Sarangolahan** — kite-flying contests
	Ulpi Banawe, Ifugao — thanksgiving rites (p 98)
Friday before	**Feast of the Virgin de Turumba** Pakil, Laguna (p 58) — a throwback to ancient rites
Palm Sunday	Vigan, Ilocos Sur — a procession makes 14 stops following the stations of the cross
Holy Monday	Paete, Laguna — a procession in which the images of Christ & saints are moved and worked to appear life-like (p 58)
Holy Thursday	Navotas & Malabon, MM; Arayat & Floridablanca, Pampanga; Bocaue, Bulacan; Bagac, Bataan — flagellants and penitents move down the

	roads to churches
Good Friday	processions for the dead Christ
Easter Sunday	dramatizations of Mary's meeting with the risen Christ, processions, flagellants, penitents
	Moriones Festival Marinduque (p 38)
March 10-16	**Araw ng Dabaw** — Davao City fiesta (p 241)
April 9	**Bataan Death March** — reenactment in Bataan & Tarlac (p 53)

May	THE month for festivals
whole month	**Santacruzan** — processions in honor of Sta Helena of Constantinople
	Flores de Mayo — floral processions
1	**Labor Day**
6	Pilgrimages to Corregidor (p 52)
8	**San Miguel de Mayumo** San Miguel, Bulacan — folk art decor, local food & confectionery, procession (p 55)
14-15	**Carabao Festivals** Pulilan, Bulacan (p 55) & Angono, Rizal
15	**Pahiyas** Lukban & Sariaya, Quezon — fabulous folk art decor (p 63)
17-19	**Kasilonawan** Obando, Bulacan — fertility rites (p 55)
24-25	**Bale Zamboanga** — Zamboanga City festival

June	
12	**Independence Day**
24	**St John the Baptist** San Juan, Rizal — everywhere water throwing is possible Balayan, Batangas — parade of roast pigs
28-30	**Fluvial Parade** Apalit, Pampanga — Sts Peter & Paul are borne down the Apalit River

July	
movable	**Apuy** Banawe, Ifugao — harvest rituals
	Pisit Bontoc, Mt Prov — harvest rituals
1st Sunday	**Bocaue Fluvial Festival** Bocaue, Bulacan, (p 55)
29	**Fiesta of St Martha** Pateros, Rizal — in memory of the occasion when the apparition of St Martha saves the town's ducks from a crocodile

August	
movable	**Lesles & Fagfagto** Bontoc, Mt Prov — harvest rituals
26	**Cry of Pugad Lawin** — commemorating the first uprisings against Spain

September	
10	**Sunduan** La Huerta, Parañaque — bachelors escort formally dressed young ladies around houses, with bands
3rd weekend	**Peñafrancia Festival** Naga, Cam Sur — Virgin of Peñafrancia rides down the Naga River accompanied by many decorated boats (p 116)

October	
3	**Feast of Our Lady of Solitude** Porta Vaga, Cavite — commemorates finding the image floating at sea
2nd Sunday	**La Naval de Manila** Sto Domingo Church, QC — commemorates the defeat of the Dutch fleet in 1646
19	**Nuestra Señora de los Dolores** Pakil, Laguna
last Sunday	**Christ the King** — all male processions
November	
movable	**Hari Raya Poasa** — marking the end of Ramadan, 30 days fasting for Muslims
1	**All Saints Day** — during the preceding week people clean and paint the graves of their ancestors. On the 1st, they hold a 24-hour vigil and leave offerings of flowers and candles at the graves.
15-30	**Yakan Harvest Festival** Basilan
23	**Feast of San Clemente** Angono, Rizal — fluvial parade
December	**Christmas** lasts from Dec 1 through the 2nd Sunday of Jan, except in Vigan, where it starts a week earlier.
8	**Feast of Our Lady of Immaculate Conception** Malabon, MM & Vigan, IS — in Malabon, a nocturnal fluvial parade along the Malabon River
8-9	**Feast of Our Lady of Caysasay** Taal, Batangas — fluvial parade (p 61)
12	Pagsanjan town fiesta
16-25	**Misas de Gallo** — literally, mass of the cock, as everyone wakes at dawn to go to church
24	**Lantern Festival** San Fernando, Pampanga — judging of giant lighted lanterns (*parol*)
	Maytinis Kawit, Cavite — reenactment of Joseph and Mary's search for a room
last Sunday	**Bota de Flores** Ermita Church, MM — girls toss flowers to Nuestra Señora de Guia
28	**Holy Innocents Day** — a day of pranks
30	**Rizal Day** — commemorating Dr José Rizal, national hero
31	**New Year's Eve** universal — incredible noise

Metropolitan Manila

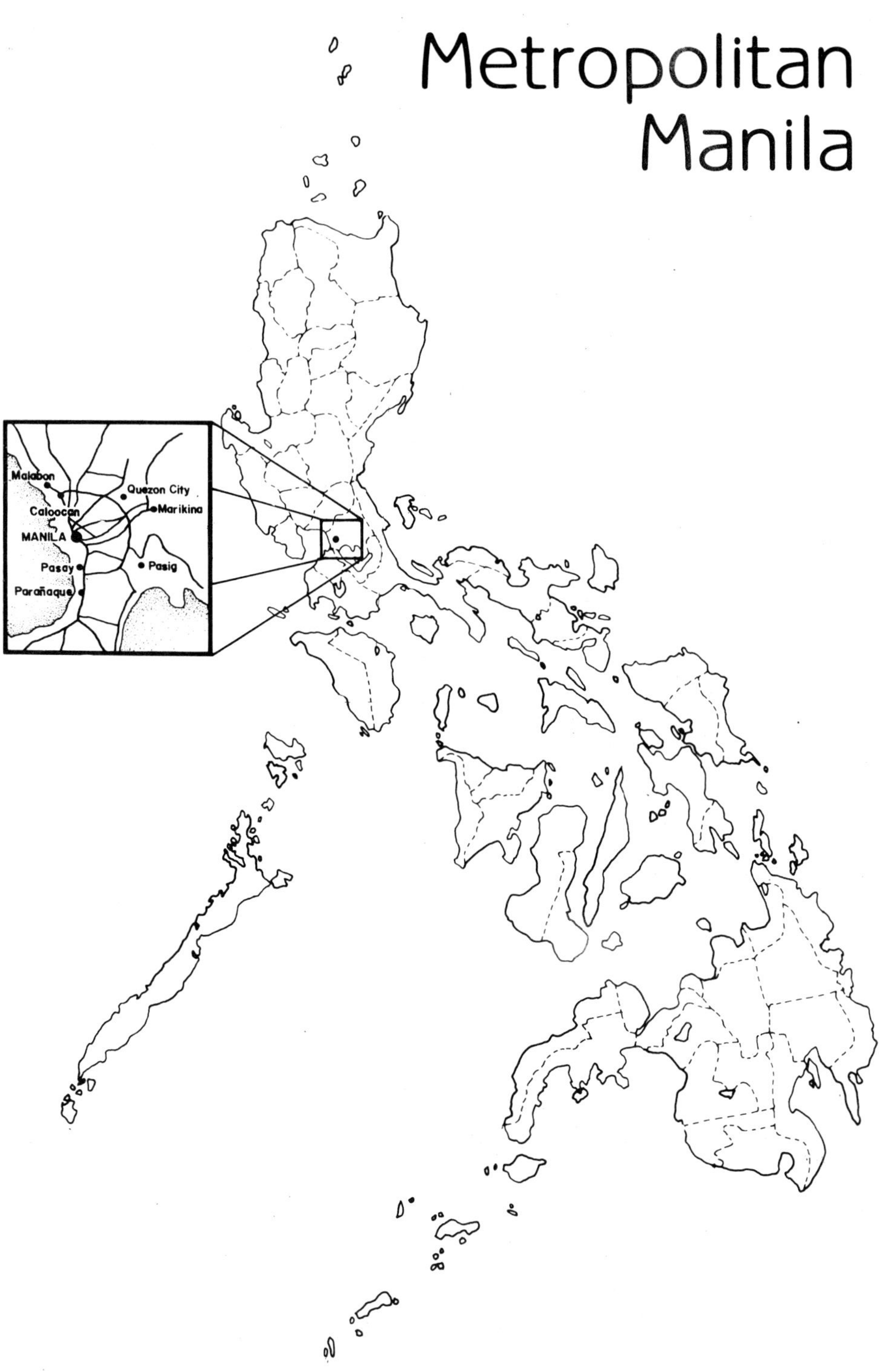

METROPOLITAN MANILA

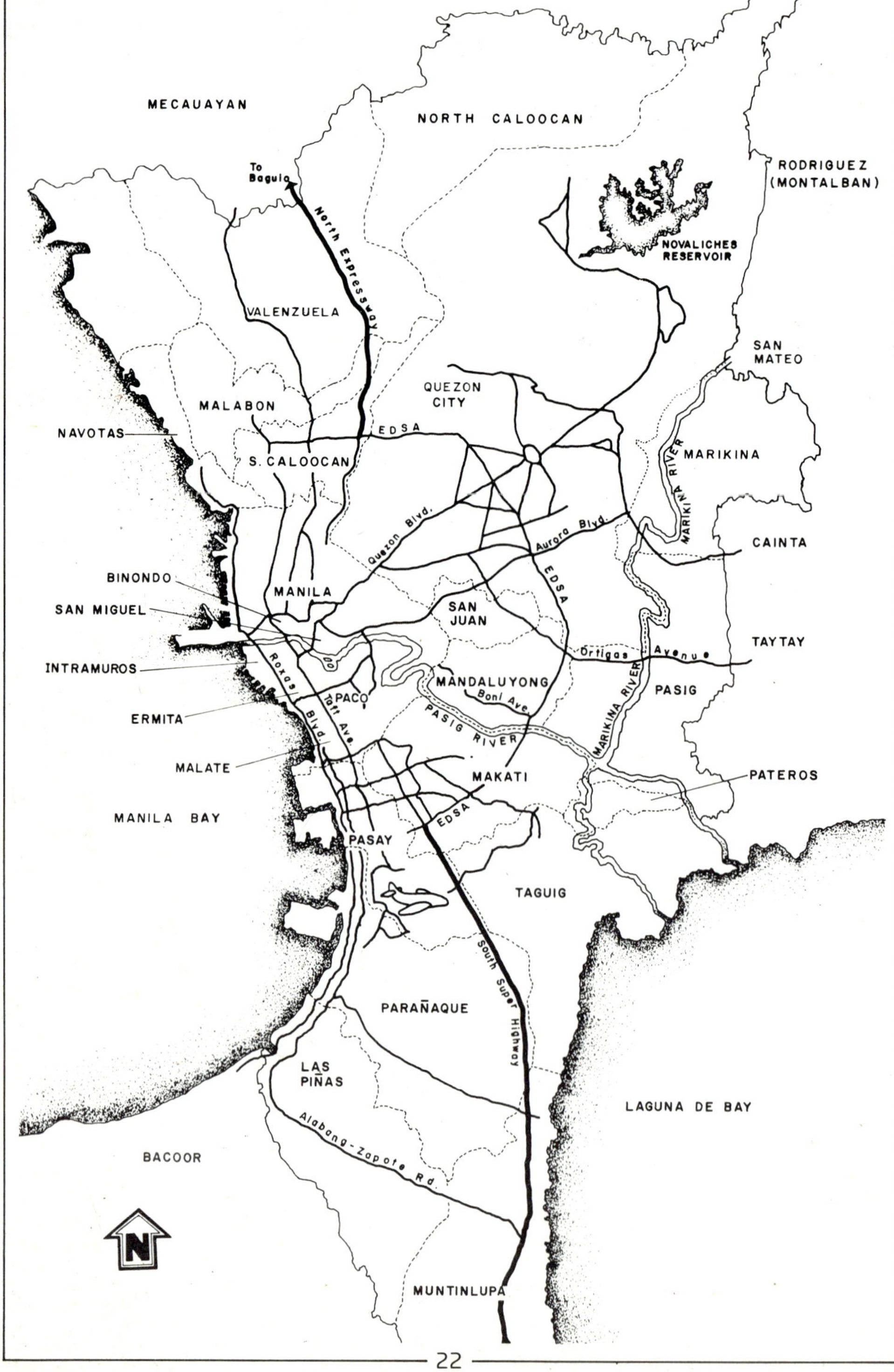

Metropolitan Manila

zal Monument, Rizal Park, Manila

Metropolitan Manila

Manila, the capital of the Philippines, began as a small settlement on the eastern shores of Manila Bay and grew into Metro Manila, encompassing 17 cities and towns with a combined population of around ten million people.

The metropolis is divided by the Pasig River, which arcs and curves as it carries water from the interior lake, Laguna de Bay, to Manila Bay. To the north are Navotas and Malabon, fishing towns, then Caloocan, with its many fish ponds. Quezon City, in the northeast, is gathering the overflow as government and education institutions out-grow their Manila premises. Marikina is a new industrial area.

To the east are Mandaluyong, a residential-shopping area with two large military camps, Pasig, an industrial town, and San Juan del Monte, site of Philippine resistance to Spanish and American colonialism.

Makati, the new business center, is just south of San Juan. To the south, Pasay City, Parañaque, where the airports are located, and Cavite fringe Manila Bay.

Manila is an eclectic study in contrasts. Its history antedates the 14th century. Its citizenry sports the latest fashions. The wealthy ride unobserved in limousines with tinted windows. Its poor live on the sidewalks. Once known as "the Pearl of the Orient", Manila now suffers from economic down- turn. Yet few of Manila's expatriot residents want to be transferred to Hong Kong, where the pace of life is frenetic, or Singapore, where everything is clean and too regulated, or Tokyo, where everything costs an arm and a leg, and so on. Manila may need a face lift, but beneath the scratchy surface, it is a vibrant, alive, fascinating city.

Airport

Please see p 4 for the international airport. All domestic flights leave from the terminal on Domestic Road. Minimal airport taxes are included in the price of the ticket. Arrive an hour ahead of flight time. When arriving at the domestic airport, baggage delivery is usually quite prompt. Taxis outside the arrivals gate may charge high prices. If so, walk out to the street in front, where you can get normal prices.

Sightseeing

Guided tours leave from some hotels - inquire at the desk. Most of the larger hotels have chauffered car rental services. Street signs often aren't, so if you don't know your way around, a chauffeur is a good idea, and isn't very costly.

But sooner or later you are going to want to get out and about on your own, to experience the city first hand and at your own pace.

Main Routes of Access

Roxas (once Dewey) Boulevard starts at Del Pan Bridge, the bridge which spans the Pasig River closest to its mouth. It follows the coast of Manila Bay southward through Ermita, Malate, Pasay City and Parañaque, and is recently extended to Cavite.

Epifanio de los Santos Avenue (mercifully shortened to EDSA, and pronounced Ed-sa) is the circumferential highway which starts in Caloocan and circles through Quezon City's new government center, Cubao shopping area, divides military camps Aguinaldo and Crame, (pronounced crah-may) goes

LRT

LRT Stops and Points of Interest accessed from them are, from north to south:

1. Monumento – EDSA, Bonifacio Monument, Araneta U, Victory Liner terminal;
2. 5th Avenue – Caloocan City;
3. R Papa – Baliwag Transit, buses to Bulacan;
4. Abad Santos – Chinese Cemetery;
5. Blumentritt – Chinese Cemetery;
6. Tayuman – San Lazaro Race Course;
7. Bambang – University of Santo Tomas, Sampaloc;
8. Doroteo Jose;
9. Carriedo – Sta Cruz Church, Quiapo Church, Ilalim ng Tulay, Globo de Oro, Binondo, Escolta;
10. Central – Manila City Hall, Central Post Office, Metropolitan Theater, Immigration, Intramuros;
11. UN Avenue – Paco Park, Paco Hong Giam Taoist Temple, Rizal Park, Department of Tourism, Malate;
12. Pedro Gil – Manila Midtown, Robinson's, Malate;
13. Quirino – San Andres Market, Manila Zoo, Ermita, Remedios Circle;
14. Vito Cruz – Rizal Coliseum, De La Salle University, Sheraton, Harrison Plaza, Metropolitan Museum, Fort San Antonio Abad, Cultural Center, Hyatt;
15. Gil Puyat (Buendia) – buses for Makati, Cartimar Market; 16 Libertad – Libertad Market;
17. EDSA – buses for Makati and Quezon City;
18. Baclaran – Baclaran Market, Redemptorist Church, Seaside Market; buses and jeeps for the airport, Cavite, Tagaytay.

Gateway to Fort Santiago

through Makati, and terminates on Taft Avenue.

Quezon Boulevard starts from the heart of Manila and runs out, like the spoke of a wheel, through EDSA to the Quezon Monument in the new government area. From it the North expressway exits, leading to points on northern Luzon.

South Expressway, known also as South Superhighway, begins near Paco, cuts through Makati's southern reaches, hops over EDSA and continues to newly developed residential areas and points south.

Transportation

Manila is fairly easy to get about in, once you have a good map and some directions. Public transport is cheap and readily available, and the general public can help with information on which bus, jeepney, etc to take.

Hire cars are available at major hotels and at the international airport.

Taxis are everywhere, except during rush hour. Doormen at hotels take down license numbers of departing taxis, thus providing a guard against abuses by taxi drivers picking up passengers at hotel doors.

Blue **Love buses** are airconditioned. Their routes are: from the terminal in Greenbelt, Makati, along Puyat to Harrison Plaza, along Mabini to Rizal Park and Plaza Lawton, across the Pasig to Binondo and back; from Ayala Ave, Makati (in front of Rustan) along EDSA, Boni Ave and Ortigas to Cubao and back; from Binondo (Escolta) along España to Quezon Ave to Elliptical Circle in Quezon City, then to Cubao before returning.

Major **bus routes** include:
Baclaran - vehicles go south to Cavite (Saulog Transit) and the airports (DMTC), and north to most major points of Manila; buses running along Ayala Ave, Makati, go to the Cultural Center (DMC and MMTC), Quiapo and Cubao via Taft Avenue through Ermita-Malate; from the corner of EDSA and Ayala Ave, Makati, buses travel south to Baclaran (CBL, DMC, FIL, JD, MMTC, Pasvil, YBL), to Nayong Filipino and the airports (CBL, MMTC), Alabang (DMC, FIL, MCBC, MCL, MMTC, YBL), the Cultural Center (DMTC, MCBC, MMTC); from the corner of EDSA and Ayala Ave, Makati, north-bound buses go to Cubao, some continuing to the UP-Government center area (DMC, MMTC, Pasvil).

Plaza Lawton, fronting Manila City Hall, Cubao, Plaza Santa Cruz and Baclaran are major hubs of transport.

Buses and jeepneys often pick up and discharge passengers in the middle of the road - take care when alighting.

Jeepneys and **tricycles** serve points not accessed by buses.

The **Light Rail Transit (LRT)** system is the most painless, smogless way to traverse Manila from Monumento, Caloocan in the north to Baclaran, Parañaque in the south. The LRT runs atop Taft Avenue, south of the Pasig, and atop Rizal Avenue, to the north. Rides, no matter how far you go, cost ₱3. You need to know your departure terminal - there are no maps in the trains or in stations.

Manila's History

By the fifteenth century, Manila and environs were peopled by Muslim communities. A small settlement on the banks of the Pasig River, which connects the large interior lake Laguna de Bay with Manila Bay, was carrying on active trade with Chinese and other visiting merchants.

Legazpi's men arrived in 1571, overcame what little resistance the ruler, Rajah Sulayman, could raise, and commenced construction of a European- style walled city. Initially, only Spaniards were allowed to live inside the walls. Natives were removed elsewhere. Chinese were required to live outside, but within gun range.

The original wooden palisades were replaced by massive tufa walls. In 1609 a moat was added. In the early 18th century it was drained by the Americans, who considered it a health hazard. It has now been converted into a municipal golf course.

Within the walls of the old city were churches, a hospital, schools, government offices, barracks, and homes which only the Spanish and their *mestizo* offspring could occupy. The city's seven gates were closed by drawbridges at night.

At the middle of Intramuros was **Plaza Royal**. Around it were the **Manila Cathedral**, **Governor General's Palace**, and government buildings. In the evenings concerts were held amid the Plaza's gardens and fountains.

In 1762 the British took Manila. Although they were ejected two years later, the Spanish realized that Intramuros was not invincible, and began moving outside the walls.

In 1863 the Governor General's Palace was destroyed by earthquake, and the seat of government was moved to Malacañang.

At the outset of WW II, General MacArthur moved to Corregidor to spare Manila from the ravages of war, but, in 1945, when the Americans returned, their bombs reduced Intramuros to rubble. For many years much of it was inhabited only by squatters and freight forwarders

Intramuros & Vicinity (map p 29)

In the 1970s, the tremendous task of restoring the old walled city to its previous grandeur commenced. Low on funding, the Intramuros Administration has been able to make a start.

Manila Cathedral was rebuilt after the war. The Governor General's Palace has been reconstructed.

San Agustin Church, 2 blocks south from the Cathedral, along Real St, has beautifully painted ceilings, and an impressive collection of religious art.

A reconstructed 18th century building across from the church houses a small restaurant, called Muralla, several curio and antique shops, and the **Casa Manila** museum. Casa Manila has been refurbished as the home of a wealthy 18th century urban family, and brims with furnishings and paraphernalia they may have used. Casa Manila is closed Mondays.

A couple of blocks further along Real is **El Amanecer**, a 4-storey building containing one of the finest collection of handicrafts available in Manila, at good prices.

Real St exits Intramuros at **Puerta Real**, the main entrance used by officials during ceremonies. Turn here for a stroll along the wall. To the right is the newly excavated **Bastion San Diego**. To the left are **Bastion San Andres, Aurora Gardens** and the ruins of **Bastion de San Fernando Dilao.**

Parian Gate was the exit to the Chinese settlement. Behind it stands the Lyceum of the Philippines.

Nearby is **San Juan de Letran College,** founded in 1639, and one of few establishments still occupying its original location.

From **Bastion San Gabriel** Intramuros' guns were pointed in silent threat at the Parian (Chinese quarter), attempting to frighten the Chinese residents into submission.

Puerta Isabel, with a statue of Queen Isabel II outside, houses a small museum.

Fort Santiago, at the northwest corner of Intramuros, is located on the original site of Rajah Sulayman's settlement. It was used to control traffic flowing along the Pasig River. Two centuries ago all access to Laguna de Bay's coastal towns was by water.

The Fort has been headquarters to several occupying armies, many of which have committed atrocities. Prisoners were left to drown as the tide rose in the Pasig and filled the lower dungeons; 600 bodies were found in the powder magazine chamber at the end of the Japanese occupation.

At present, the fort is an attractive park with several points of interest other than the original dungeons and walls. The old barracks have been converted to the **Rajah Sulayman Theatre**, where open-air performances are held. Historic cars and an old wood-burning railroad engine used during the Fil-Am war are kept beneath the western ramparts.

The **Rizal Museum** houses memorabilia of Dr José P Rizal. A non-militant poet, physician, artist, and intellectual, Rizal wrote two novels which denounced the abuses of the Spanish friars, and founded a society which pressured for reforms. Initially imprisoned in Ft Santiago, he was exiled to Dapitan City, on Mindanao, before being brought back and shot. Rizal's execution, instead of deterring the uprising against Spain, served to further agitate the population.

South Harbor, seawards of Intramuros, is the arrival point for ships from abroad.

The **Commission on Immigration**, on the north side of Intramuros, is the place to go for visa extensions.

Manila's **City Hall** and other government buildings are across Taft Avenue, near LRT's Central Station.

The art-deco **Metropolitan Theatre**, on the banks of the Pasig, was built in 1935. It holds plays, concerts, etc.

Rizal Park & the Luneta

When the Spanish settled in Intramuros, they moved the natives to Bagumbayan - literally, "New Town". Later, for security, they removed the natives further. The area was cleared for a park which was named Luneta after the semicircular redoubt near P Burgos St.

On Sundays and evenings Manila's society came to Luneta in carriages, wearing their finery. It was "the" place to be seen.

In 1896 the Spanish executed Rizal at the Luneta, hoping to use his slaying as a deterrent to popular uprising. Rizal's body was buried in a mis-marked grave in Paco Cemetery, then moved to his mother's house before finally returning to Luneta to rest under a monument which is the focal point of the park.

The park continues to draw crowds who come to enjoy the greenery on Sundays and holidays and to attend political rallies. Over a million people came to see Ninoy Aquino's body as it passed; the same number later came to listen to his wife campaign against President Marcos.

The park is a good place to walk about, watch people and get a feel for Manila.

Bordering the Luneta are the **Manila Hotel**, which served as MacArthur's headquarters, several government offices, the **Department of Tourism** (apply for information and assistance), the **National Museum**, and the Army Navy Club.

A large relief map of the Philippines and children's playground are near the tourism offices. Snacks are available from a cafe run by and for the deaf. The Rizal Monument and the huge Quirino Grandstand are at the western end.

INTRAMUROS & LUNETA

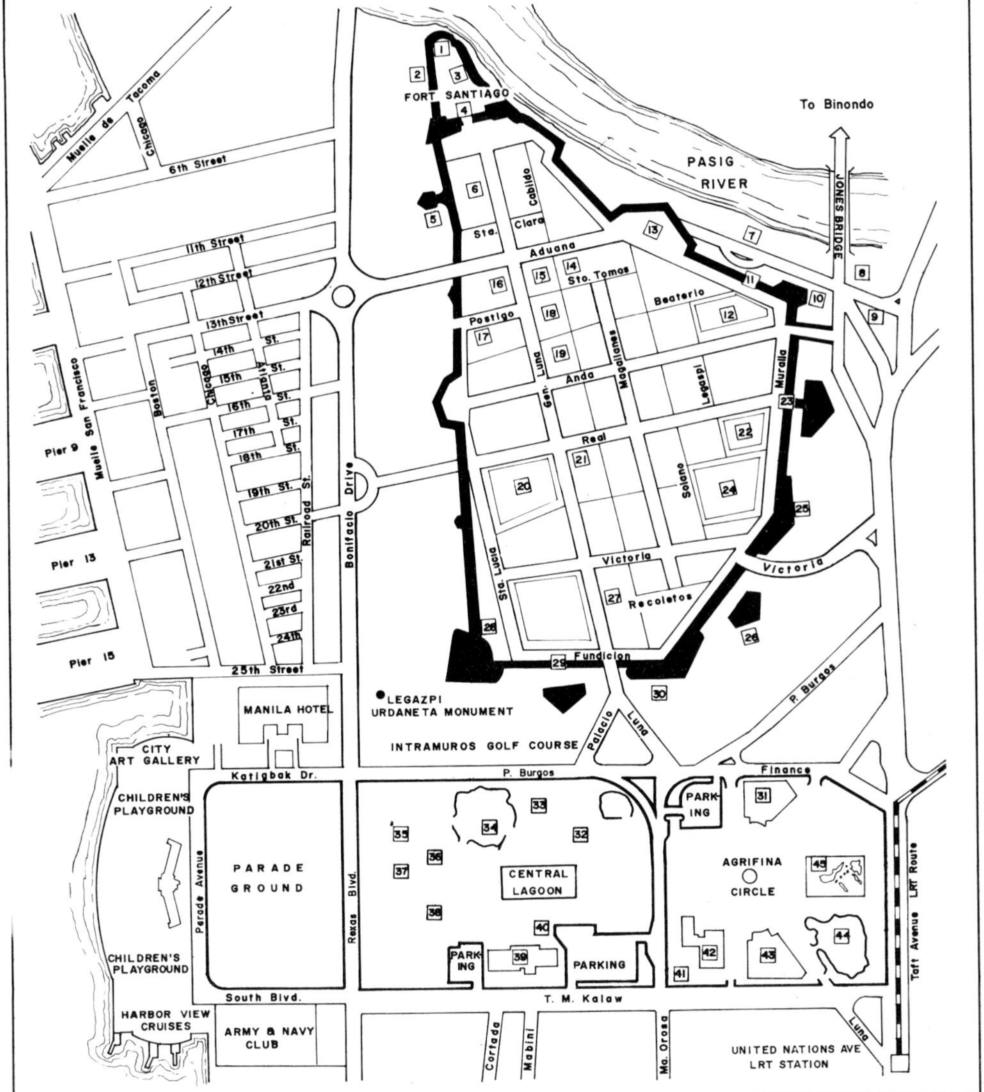

1 Bastion San Lorenzo & Bateria Sta Barbara
2 Rizal Museum
3 Plaza de Armas
4 Main Gate
5 Bastion San Francisco
6 Plaza Moriones
7 Commission on Immigration
8 Post Office & Liwasang Bonifacio
9 Metropolitan Theater
10 Bastion de San Gabriel
11 Puerta Isabel II
12 San Juan de Letran College
13 La Intendencia
14 Ayuntamiento Ruins
15 Plaza Roma
16 Plaza del Gobernador
17 Archbishop's Palace
18 Manila Cathedral
19 Plaza Sampalucan
20 San Agustin Church
21 Barrio San Luis & Casa Manila Museum
22 Lyceum of the Philippines
23 Parian Gate
24 Mapua Institute of Technology
25 Bastion de San Fernando Dilao
26 Revellin de Recoletos
27 El Amanecer & Silahis Crafts
28 Bastion de San Diego
29 Puerto Real
30 Bastion de San Andres
31 Dept of Finance
32 Outdoor Stage
33 Planetarium
34 Chinese Garden
35 Site of Rizal's Execution
36 Monument to Frs Gomez, Burgos & Zamora
37 Rizal Monument
38 Madre Filipina
39 National Library
40 Cafe run by the Deaf & Dumb
41 Garden for the Blind
42 Park Administration
43 Dept of Tourism
44 Children's Park
45 Relief Map of the Philippines

Chinese Cemetery

San Nicholas (map, p 32)

Six bridges cross the Pasig, connecting Manila south with north. **Del Pan** bridge brings you from the end of Roxas Blvd to **San Nicholas**, Manila's commercial center during the years of the galleon trade. Many warehouses still line the riverbank. Colonial era houses which were not damaged during the war are falling into disrepair.

North Harbor, where inter-island vessels depart for Philippine points, is to the west.

To the north is **Divisoria**, a vast, teeming market where anything and everything is wholesaled and retailed in shops and on the sidewalks.

Tutuban Station, where you catch north-bound trains, and **Seng Guan Buddhist Temple**, with its golden stupa- like roof, are just beyond Divisoria.

Northward is **Tondo**, once home to artisans and craftsmen, now a teeming, steaming slum housing many who came to the city in hopes of increasing their income.

Binondo (map, p 32)

Binondo is the heart of Chinatown and, with **Escolta**, is the older of Metro Manila's two business centers. Originally home to the Chinese who moved out of the Parian district just beyond Intramuros, during the 18th century, the Spanish built warehouses and mansions here. In the 19th century, it became a shopping and residential district.

Severely damaged during WW II, the Spanish residents moved out. By 1960 Binondo reverted to being a predominantly Chinese area, again a business hub.

Jones Bridge brings vehicles from Taft Avenue across the Pasig, directly to an imposing **Filipino-Chinese Friendship Arch,** and into the heart of the banking area.

Quintin Paredes St continues to Plaza Calderon de la Barca, with **Binondo Church** on the right. Originally built in 1596, Binondo Church was damaged several times. Of the current structure, only the octagonal bell tower is original.

Directly across from the church, a bridge, so distinctly Chinese that it appears to have been transported here from Beijing, leads across a canal and past a pagoda-style fire station.

Ongpin St, with its many jewelry dealers, is known as "24 karat street".

Several nearby Chinese restaurants, among them the Mandarin and the President, serve delicious meals, and bakeries serve snacks.

Binondo's narrow streets, made narrower still by parked trucks, *calesas* and cars, twist and snake past hardware shops (Gandara area), Chinese apothecaries and groceries, clothing and material shops, almost anything is available. One interesting way to tour Binondo is by hired *calesa*.

Santa Cruz & La Loma

Continuing west near the Pasig through Manila's mazed streets, you reach **Sta Cruz Church**. The original church was built in

1608 by the Jesuits for Chinese converts. Damaged twice by quake, then destroyed during WW II, the church was rebuilt in 1957.

Plaza Locsin, fronting the church, has many Chinese-owned fastfood outlets, among them Chow King, Dunkin Donuts and McDonalds.

MacArthur Bridge brings traffic from the Manila City Hall area to Sta Cruz Church.

Inland is Santa Cruz district, a farm in 1640. Bilibid Viejo, once the National Penitentiary, now lies unused. **Central Market**, filled with textiles, clothes, dry goods, spills into the streets.

Chinese General Hospital is conveniently located beside the North and the Chinese cemeteries, and San Lazaro Hospital isn't far away either.

North Cemetery is the resting place for many rich and famous Filipinos and Spaniards. Their families have built some incredible mausoleums, (including 2 pyramids and a sphynx) complete with kitchens and bathrooms (useful during visiting days). It has also become home to a large squatter colony. Do not visit alone.

Because the Spanish would not permit the Chinese to be buried at La Loma, in the mid 1850s Lim Ong and Tan Quien Sien (now known as Don Carlos Palanca) founded the **Chinese Cemetery**. Several Chinese mausoleums are as interesting as those of North Cemetery. Pictures of Christ, Buddha, the Virgin Mary and Kuan Yin may all decorate one mausoleum, as the flexible Chinese turn to whatever proves useful and advantageous.

Quiapo (map, p 32)

Quiapo, named after the water lily *kiyapo*, is the geographic center of Manila. From Quiapo all other points are accessible by public transport.

Two bridges cross the Pasig into Quiapo: Quezon Bridge from Manila City Hall, and Ayala Bridge from Taft and Ayala Aves.

While crossing the Pasig, Ayala Bridge touches down on **Isla de la Convalencia**. Once a rest and recuperation station for Spanish soldiers, the island now has a hospital with a turn-cradle for unwanted babies.

Below Quezon bridge is **Quiapo Market** and **Ilalim ng Tulay**, literally "under the bridge", a handicrafts market which is frequented by pickpockets.

Brass and Muslim handicrafts are available at **Rajah Sulayman Market**. Next to it is **Globo de Oro** mosque.

Quiapo Market area

Quiapo Church, a Mexican Baroque Cathedral until it burned in 1928, was reconstructed, and is again undergoing renovation. Its primary attraction is the life-sized Black Nazarene which came from Mexico by galleon. On January 9 the Black Christ is carried forth on his gilded palanquin, drawn by barefoot men through crowds crying "Viva Señor" and trying to touch the image in hopes of having their

MANILA NORTH OF THE PASIG

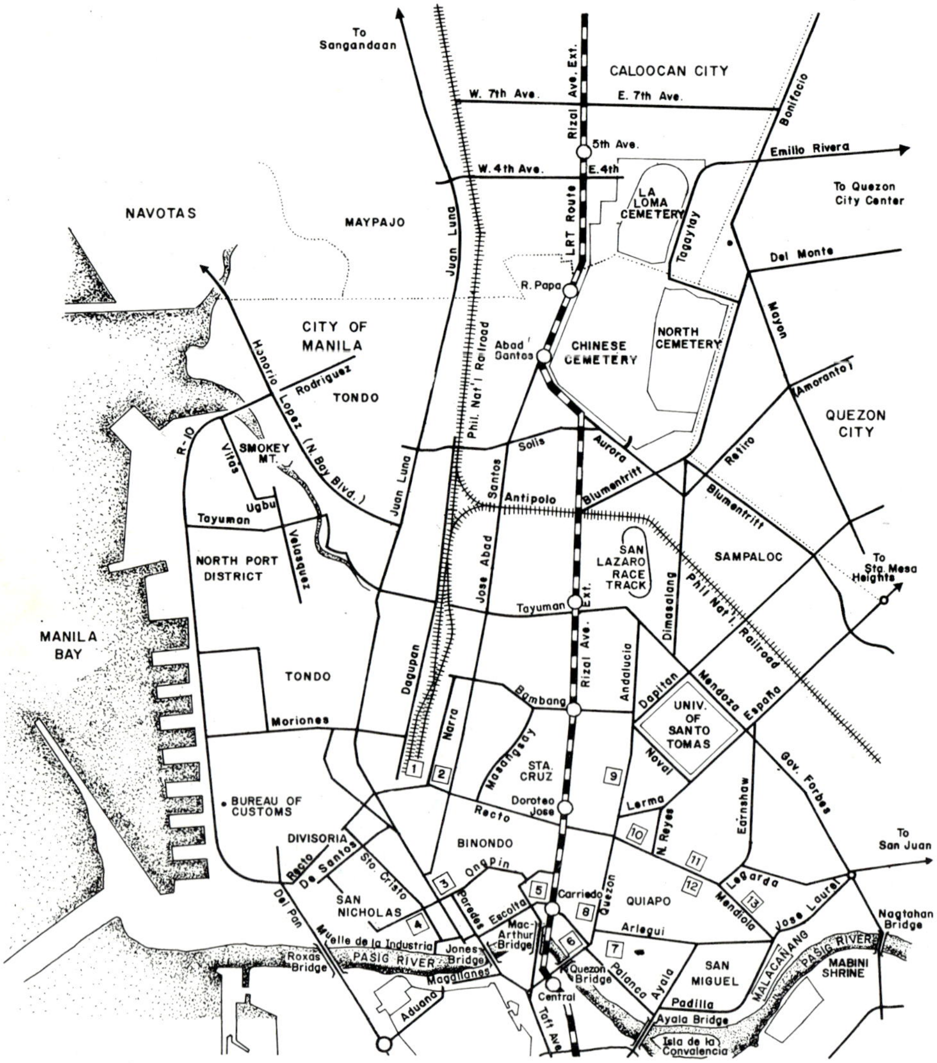

sins forgiven.

Every Friday devotees flock to the church. Stalls around the church and plaza do a good business in herbal medicines, *anting-anting* (amulets), religious items, snacks, and flowers.

Plaza Miranda, fronting the church, was the scene of many heated political rallies, one of which was bombed, before Marcos declared martial law.

Quiapo's other church of note is the very beautiful **San Sebastian Church**. Three churches built on this site were destroyed by quake, so the Agustinian/Recollect parish fathers decided to build one which would endure. The current gothic church is built totally of steel which was prefabricated in Belgium and imported piece by piece in eight ships. The church has lovely stained glass windows and interior work which earn its sobriquet "the little jewel box".

San Miguel

During the 18th century, San Miguel was the resort district of Manila, where wealthy families built summer homes. The grandest of these, **Malacañang**, was built by Don Luis Rocha in 1802. It was purchased by the Spanish Government in 1825, for ₱5,100, raised by taxing the Chinese traders. The name derives from the Tagalog phrase, *may lakan diyan*, or "there are powerful people there". After many renovations, little remains visible of the original structure.

Malacañang has been the seat of the Philippine Presidency since Independence. It, and the entire area around, were closed to the public during the Marcos regime.

Tours are offered ($10) daily except Sunday and Wednesday through parts of Malacañang, now maintained as a museum where much Marcos memorabilia, including some of the 1,000 pairs of shoes Imelda left, continue to be of interest to the curious.

Not far from Malacañang is the pretty gothic **San Beda chapel**, the Abbey of Our Lady of Monserrat, founded in 1926. Interior work includes lovely paintings, murals and carved wood. Ring the bell on the door to the right of the chapel to ask for admittance.

Malacañang's grounds span both sides of the Pasig. Beside its grounds on the south side of the river, near the end of Nagtahan Bridge, is the **Mabini Shrine**.

This was the home of Apolinario Mabini. Known as the brains of the revolution, Mabini advocated independence from Spain. He was a law student and advisor to the revolutionary Katipunan organization and, later, to General Aguinaldo.

The house in which he and the Katipunan wrote their constitution was declared a national shrine. Originally situated on the north banks of the Pasig; the house has been moved twice. Beside the house is a replica of the hut in which Mabini was born.

University of Santo Tomas

UST, the oldest University in Asia, was founded by the Dominicans in 1611 in Intramuros. In 1927 the University moved to Sampaloc, into a massive new quake-proof 4-storey building.

Atop the building is a huge clock and statues of Faith, Hope, Charity, St Vincent, St Agustin, St Raymond, Aristotle, St Albert, Plato, de la Barca, Sophocles, Shakespeare, Lope de Vega, Aristophanes and Moliere.

1 Tutuban RR Station
2 Seng Guan Buddhist Temple
3 Binondo Church
4 Bureau of Coast & Geodetic Survey
5 Sta Cruz Church
6 Ilalim ng Tulay
7 Globo de Oro Mosque
8 Quiapo Church & Plaza Miranda
9 Central Market
10 Far East U
11 U of the East
12 San Sebastian Church
13 San Beda Church

Until the 19th century, students were of Spanish parentage. In 1927 UST first admitted women. Many of the Philipines' well known historical and current figures were educated here.

For 3 years during WW II Santo Tomas was an internment camp for allied nationals who remained in the Philippines during the war.

UST has extensive archives and relics, but space allotted to the museum continues to shrink as the student body grows.

The university, designed for 5,000 students, now has 40,000.

Paco, Ermita & Malate (map, p 36)

When the Spanish arrived they found 3,000 Japanese living in Paco. Some were fishermen or traders, others were escaping from the law or society at home. The statue at the center of Plaza Dilao (Yellow Plaza), fronting Paco train station, is **Lord Wukon Takayama**, a Christian Samurai who preferred to relinquish his life rather than his religion.

By the mid 19th century, Intramuros' Spanish and *mestizo* populations were spilling out from the walls, north across the Pasig and south into Ermita and Malate.

Opened in 1822 to provide a burial place for victims of a cholera epidemic, the cemetery provided niches in its circular wall. These niches were soon filled, and another, inner wall was built to provide more spaces.

The central chapel once held the bodies of the famous who lay in state. Behind the chapel is a small area with little niches for children.

Immediately after his execution, Jose Rizal was interred here in a mis-marked grave, his initials reversed. His remains now rest at Rizal Park, and a large white cross marks the spot of his burial at Paco.

Paco Park, away from it all, was spared the destruction of the war. A small admission fee allows you a peaceful get-away from the city's hustle and bustle.

Paco Hong Giam Taoist Temple is located behind the cemetery. It has three main buildings, fish ponds and fountains. Ring the bell if you wish to enter. The main temple, ornately decorated, is in the center.

Ermita, named after a hermit who had moved there to get away from the worldly city life, is now a district of bars, massage parlors, tourist traps, art galleries, money changers, travel agencies, middle and low budget hotels and restaurants. The large new American consulate building dwarfs an older, more pleasing structure which nestles in the trees behind.

Bars and shops line Mabini and MH del Pilar Sts. A few Muslim shops with items from Mindanao are located on Cortada St, near Ermita Church.

Ermita Church, a low-budget post-war reconstruction, houses **Nuestra Señora de Guia**. On her festival day, the last Sunday of December, girls who are hoping to marry come to Ermita Church and toss flowers at the icon.

Malate is similar to Ermita, although seemier aspects appear to be more contained behind closed doors. "Motels" in the Philippines are only used for "short time" stays, and many rooms also have their own garages with doors, so even the car may be concealed. Massage parlors give way to some folk bars and more up-beat night spots.

The **Flea Market** and **Pistang Pilipino**, located between Roxas Blvd and Mabini St, have many small shops which sell handicrafts, often at good prices. There is a restaurant and cultural show. A shop at Pistang offers packing and mailing service.

Malate Church is an interesting structure, mixing Mexican baroque, Muslim, Spanish and Romanesque motifs. Dedicated to Nuestra Señora de Remedios (Our Lady of Remedies), the first structure dated from the end of the 16th century.

Malate Church and Rajah Sulayman

The British used the church to stage their invasion (1762) of Intramuros. The current 19th century structure is interesting only on the outside.

Fronting the church is **Rajah Sulayman Park**, with a statue of May-nila's Muslim ruler dancing with his sword. A statue of Nuestra Señora de Remedios stands behind.

South along the boulevard, in front of the Central Bank and Finance Ministry, is **Fort San Antonio Abad**. In 1584, when it was built, it was right on the water's edge. Occupied by the British in 1762, shelled by Dewey and then occupied by the Americans in 1898, and used as a bomb shelter by the Japanese during WW II, the fort still has an original powder room and bears the scars of its many encounters.

The **Metropolitan Museum**'s austere exterior gives way to a good interior housing several excellent galleries, a good shop, and the Central Bank's extensive numismatic collection.

The **Manila Yacht Club** and **Philippine**

ERMITA-MALATE

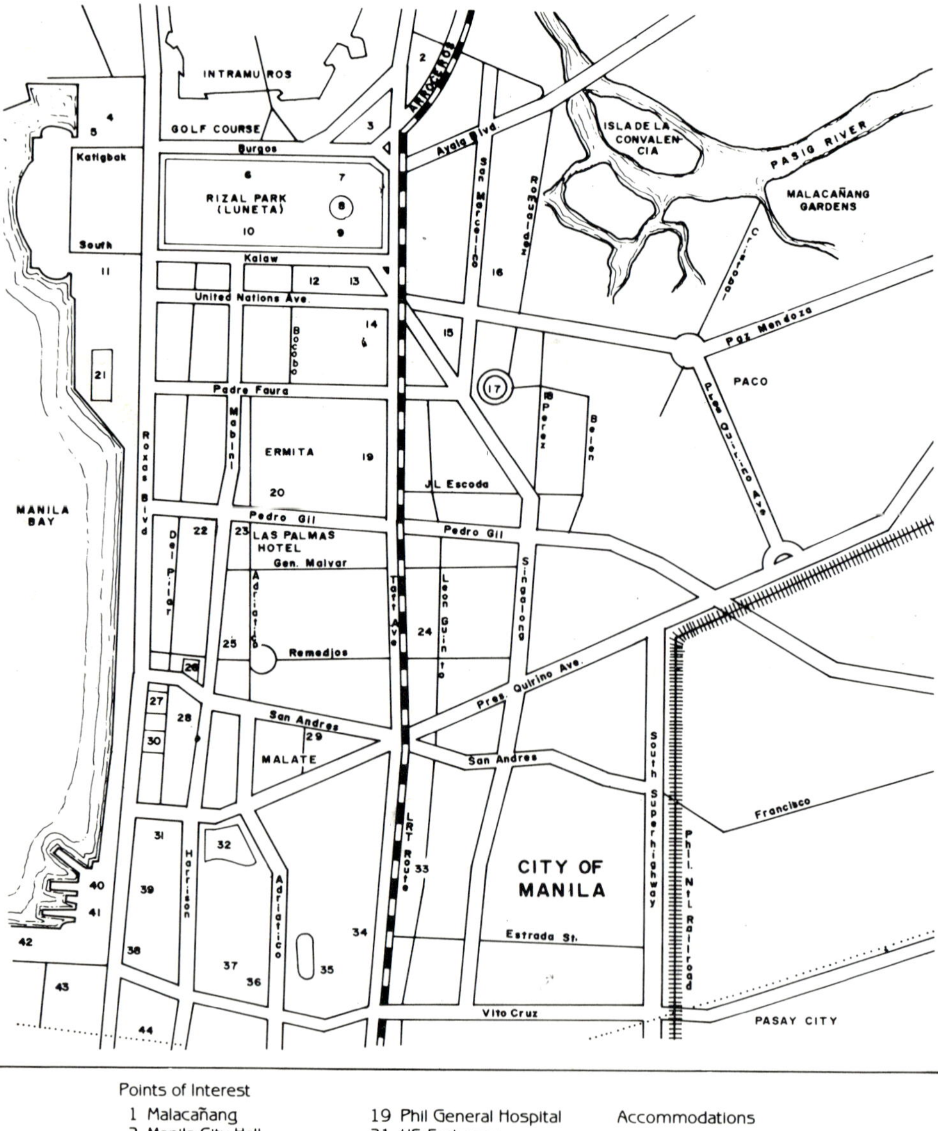

Points of Interest

1 Malacañang
2 Manila City Hall
3 National Museum
5 City Art Gallery
6 Planetarium
7 Department of Finance
8 Agrifina Circle
9 Department of Tourism
10 National Library
11 Army-Navy Club
13 Manila Doctor's Hospital
14 World Health (WHO)
15 Manila Medical Center
17 Paco Park
18 Paco Hong Giam Taoist Temple
19 Phil General Hospital
21 US Embassy
22 Pistang Pilipino
25 Carfel Shell Museum
26 Malate Church
29 San Andres Market
31 Ospital ng Maynila
32 Zoo
34 De La Salle
35 Rizal Stadium complex
38 Central Bank
39 Metropolitan Museum
40 Manila Yacht Club
41 Philippine Navy
42 Boats to Corregidor
43 Cultural Center

Accommodations

4 Manila Hotel
12 Hilton
16 Hotel Mirador
20 Manila Midtown Hotel
23 Las Palmas Hotel
24 Casa Solanie
27 Silahis Hotel
28 Ambassador Hotel
30 Admiral Hotel
33 Kanumayan Inn
36 Sheraton
37 Harrison Plaza
44 Holiday Inn

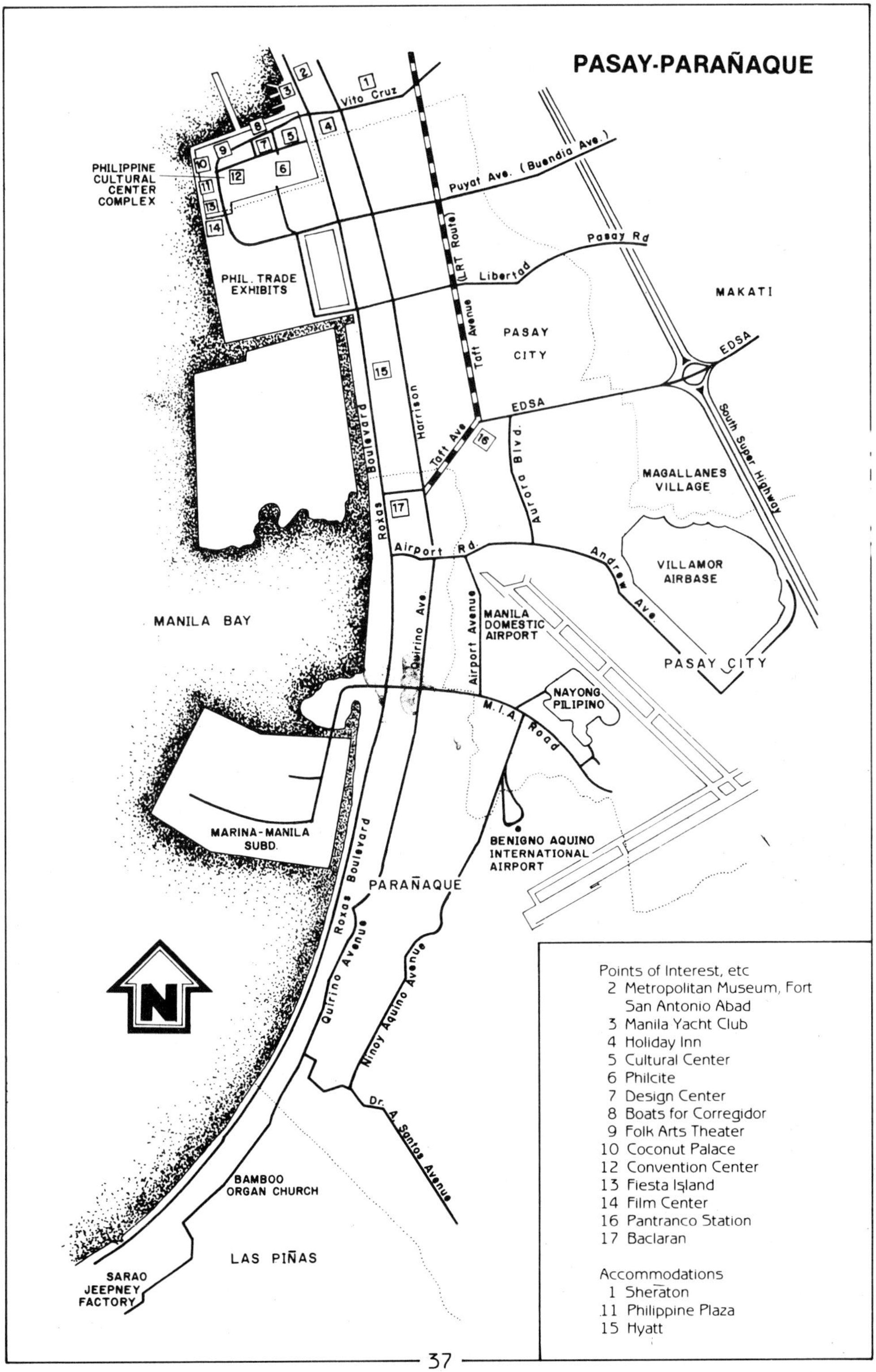

Points of Interest, etc
- 2 Metropolitan Museum, Fort San Antonio Abad
- 3 Manila Yacht Club
- 4 Holiday Inn
- 5 Cultural Center
- 6 Philcite
- 7 Design Center
- 8 Boats for Corregidor
- 9 Folk Arts Theater
- 10 Coconut Palace
- 12 Convention Center
- 13 Fiesta Island
- 14 Film Center
- 16 Pantranco Station
- 17 Baclaran

Accommodations
- 1 Sheraton
- 11 Philippine Plaza
- 15 Hyatt

Coast Guard HQ are across the Boulevard, both with restricted entry. During Easter on even years, scores of sailing boats from around the world come to the club after finishing the South China Sea Race.

San Andres Market, close to the Quirino LRT exit, has perhaps the best collection of fruit available in Manila. Nearby antique shops sell santos and other relics, some of which may be imitations.

Rizal Coliseum, where sports events are held, is accessed from the Vito Cruz LRT exit.

Pasay and Parañaque (map, p 37)

The vast **Cultural Center Complex**, on reclaimed land just over the boundary with Pasay City, holds numerous recent buildings. Many were built in great haste at the bidding of Imelda Marcos, who paid no heed to advice about the length of time the refilled land needed to settle before being built upon.

The Cultural Center of the Philippines, Imelda's most imposing structure, hosts many ballets, concerts and other performances in its main theater. Smaller performances are held in the **Little Theatre**, downstairs, and there is an upstairs museum and gallery.

Boats for Corregidor leave from a wharf beside the CCP.

The **Folk Arts Theater** is used for performances which expect huge crowds.

The **Design Center of the Philippines**, erected to encourage improved product design, often has interesting displays. The **Philippine International Convention Center**, the **Philtrade** building, and the **Philippine Plaza Hotel** are all here, as is the **Coconut Palace**, which Imelda built to house Pope John Paul during his visit. The Pope, however, stayed at the Papal Nunciature and advised Imelda to spend her money on the poor.

The **Manila Film Center**, rushed to completion for a film festival, looks like a forlorn Parthenon. Not only is it suffering from subsidence of the fill beneath, it also contains bodies of workers who perished in

American Cemetery, Fort Bonifacio, Makati

Makati Skyline

an accident during rushed construction, and who could not be exhumed from the quick-drying cement.

New Central Bank and GSIS buildings are nearing completion.

As the boulevard continues south it passes a few handicrafts shops and restaurants, and the Asian Development Bank.

Baclaran and Seaside Markets are located at the entrance to Parañaque.

Baclaran Church is dedicated to Our Lady of Perpetual Help. The icon is venerated by thousands of people, who come here on Wednesdays to worship. Tiny stalls with excellent bargains open up, traffic is clogged for kilometers around, and pickpockets come to make their weekly earnings.

Where the boulevard once ended, a road exits to the airports.

Although the Domestic and International **Airports** share the same runways, they use separate terminals.

All of PAL's domestic flights depart from the **Domestic Terminal**. Taxi drivers picking up incoming passengers may try for high rates. If you can't get an attractive price, walk out to the main street, where the price will be right.

The International Airport, once called **MIA**, has been renamed the **Ninoy Aquino International Airport**, after Corazon Aquino's husband, who was assassinated here.

Nayong Filipino, a park near the airport, was conceived as a mini- Philippines which would allow the visitor who only had a short stay to catch the flavor of the provinces. There are several provincial-style buildings, many shops, jeepneys to ride around in, a mock Mayon volcano, and a restaurant. As of this writing Nayon is suffering from lack of funds.

Makati

The Makati which most travelers see is the new face of high rise buildings and parks put up on land sold centuries ago by the Agustinian friars.

In the mid 1950's, the Zobel de Ayala family began construction of a new city,

MAKATI

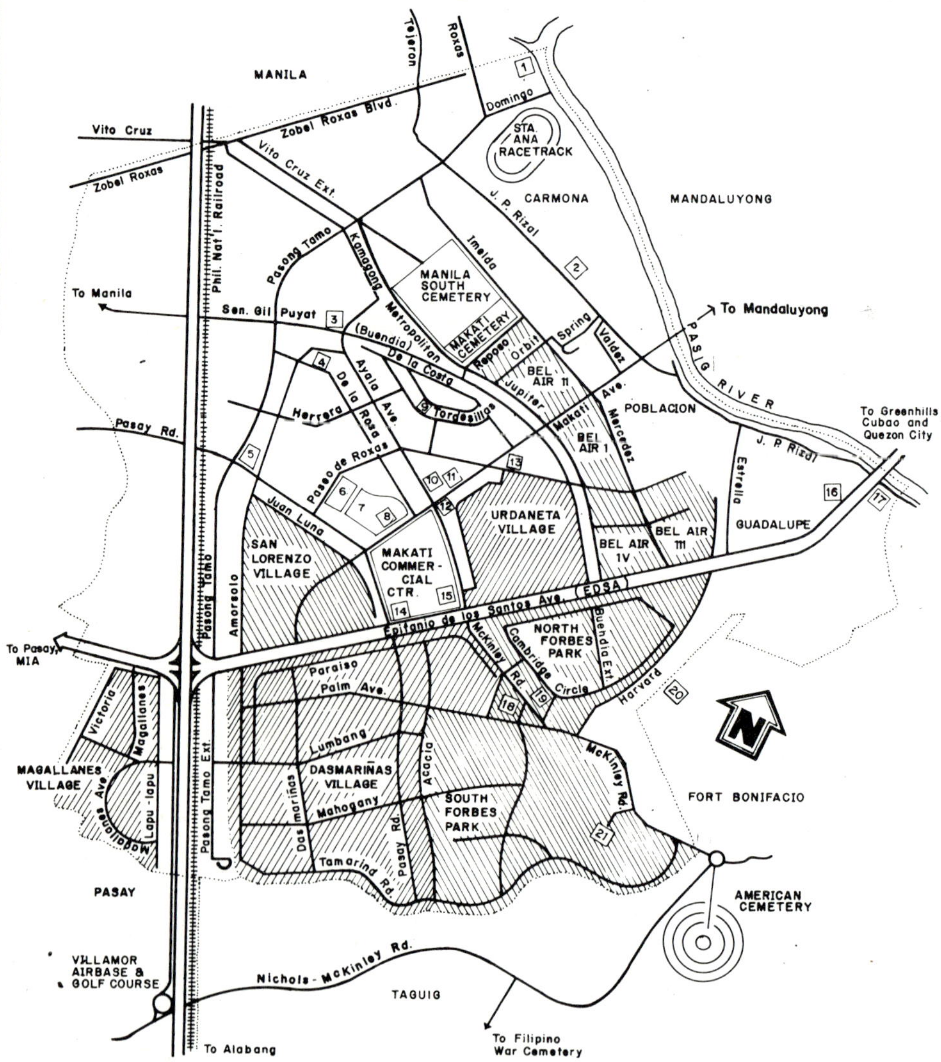

Points of Interest
1 Manila Boat Club
2 Makati City Hall
·3 Post Office
4 Makati Medical Center
5 Sunvar
6,7 Greenbelt
8 Ayala Museum
9 Makati Sports Club
10 Makati Stock Exchange
11 Nielson Tower
16 Guadalupe Church
17 Guadalupe Market
18 San Antonio Church & Plaza
19 Holy Trinity Church
20 Manila Golf Club
21 Manila Polo Club

Accommodations
12 Peninsula Hotel
13 Mandarin Hotel
14 Manila Garden Hotel
15 Intercontinental Hotel

putting their resources to full use by leasing the land, which would return to them in a decade with vast improvements.

Makati's business district is as busy as Escolta and Binondo, has its own stock exchange, and a bank every few meters.

Several top hotels are located here, including the Intercontinental, Peninsula and Mandarin, plus the Manila Garden and several pensions. Scores of restaurants offer various international cuisines.

Makati's Commercial Center and its shops offer a more western buying atmosphere than Manila's markets and bazaars.

Major department stores, such as Shoemart and Rustan, offer a wide range of goods. Clothing is inexpensive.

The commercial center area is intersected by two major thoroughfares, Ayala Avenue and Makati Avenue, parts of which run atop what once were the runways of Manila International Airport. Neilson Tower, now a restaurant, was the terminal of that airport.

The commercial area is bounded on the north by Gil Puyat (Buendia), on the east by EDSA, on the south by Arnaiz (Pasay) Rd, and to the west by Amorsolo, which runs around Makati Medical Center and along a canal. There are new shops and restaurants beyond the canal, and a minigolf course.

Residential villages in new Makati are definitely high rent, enclosed and guarded.

The **Manila Polo Club**, McKinley Rd, Forbes Park, is private, has facilities for most sports. Polo Games are held on Sundays during the dry season.

The **Manila Golf Club**, also private, is nearby.

McKinley Road continues into **Fort Bonifacio**, which has a public golf course and driving range, and the American and Filipino Cemeteries.

The American Cemetery contains remains of over 17,000 allied forces who died in Asia during WW II. Visitors first go to the reception area immediately inside the gate, then continue past picturesque concentric circles and parallel lines of white crosses.

A memorial in the center lists the names and states of 36,000 who were missing in action.

Deeper into Bonifacio, one finds the **Libingan ng Mga Bayani**, or National Heroes Cemetery, where many Philippine statesmen and soldiers have been laid to rest.

The Philippine Airforce base is in **Villamor**, across the South Expressway from Bonifacio. Here, also, there is a public golf course and driving range.

Old Makati reflects the more normal state of affairs about the country.

Makati Avenue leads from the newer area past many restaurants and bars. A few blocks away is the **Church of Sts Peter and Paul**, a lovely stone church with a small acacia-shaded plaza in a crowded area. On June 30th, during the Feast of the Virgins, beautifully bedecked young girls join the procession from the church.

Makati Avenue crosses Rizal Ave, and then continues over the Pasig to Mandaluyong.

Rizal Avenue follows the Pasig River, leading seawards past the municipal hall and **Santa Ana Race Course**, a dirt track where locally bred horses run Tuesdays, Wednesdays and weekends.

Continuing, you may wind your way to **Manila Boat Club**, where members set out to skull on the Pasig, and over the border into Manila to **Santa Ana**.

Remains of over 200 graves were unearthed beneath Santa Ana Church (named, aptly enough, Our Lady of the Abandoned). In 1986 the finds were relocated to the National Museum. These remains indicate that the settlement, called Namayan, was trading with China some 400 years before the May-nila community was settled.

Makati's third ancient church is **Our Lady of Grace** in **Guadalupe**. The original building dates from 1601. In 1839 the church served as a sanctuary for Chinese escaping

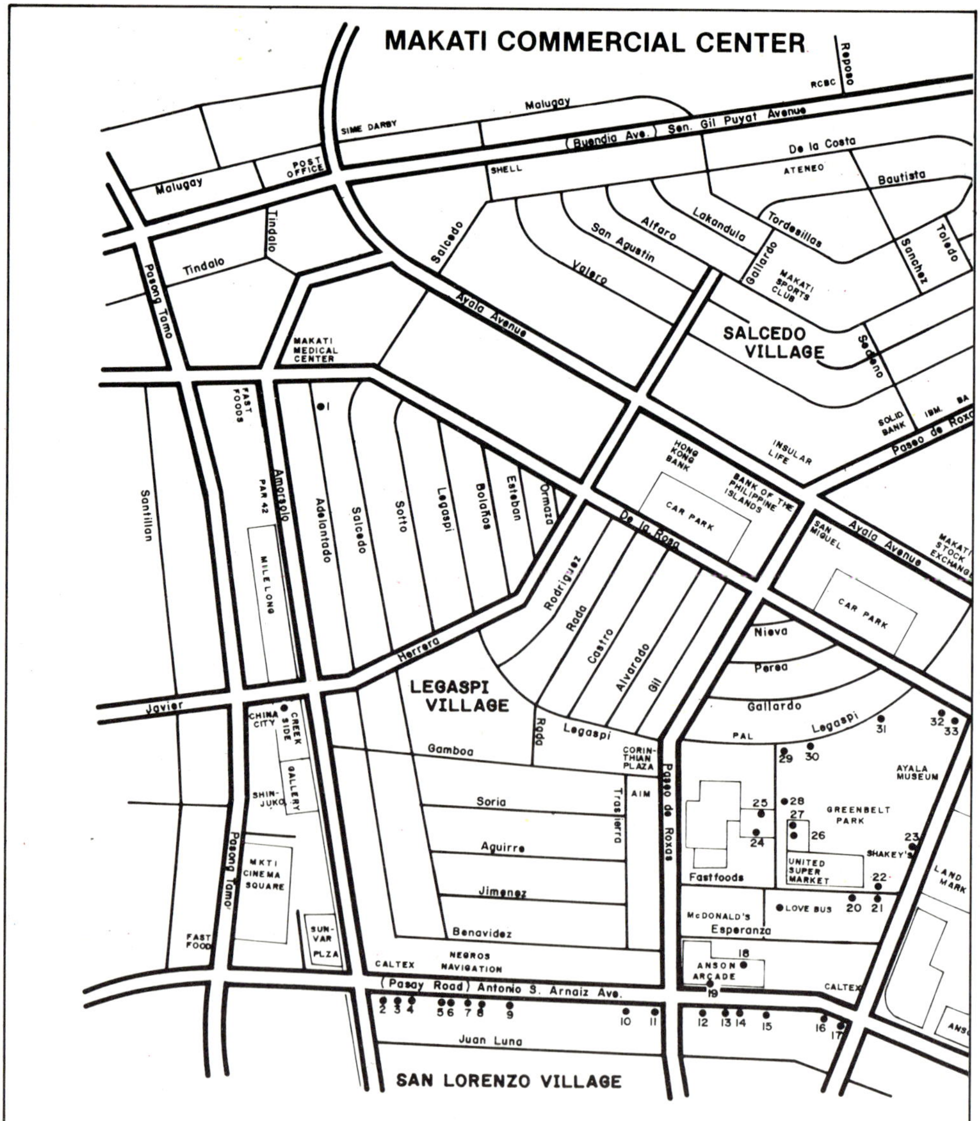

1 Indonesian Embassy & Restaurant
2 Sinugba
3 Oshio
4 Probinsiya
5 El Cielito Tourist Inn
6 Bulgogi
7 Pinausukan
8 The Grove
9 Ville de Saigon
9 Pension Virginia
10 Bistro RJ
11 Joni's
12 Swiss House
13 El Meson
14 MOPC
15 Youngbin
16 Vintage

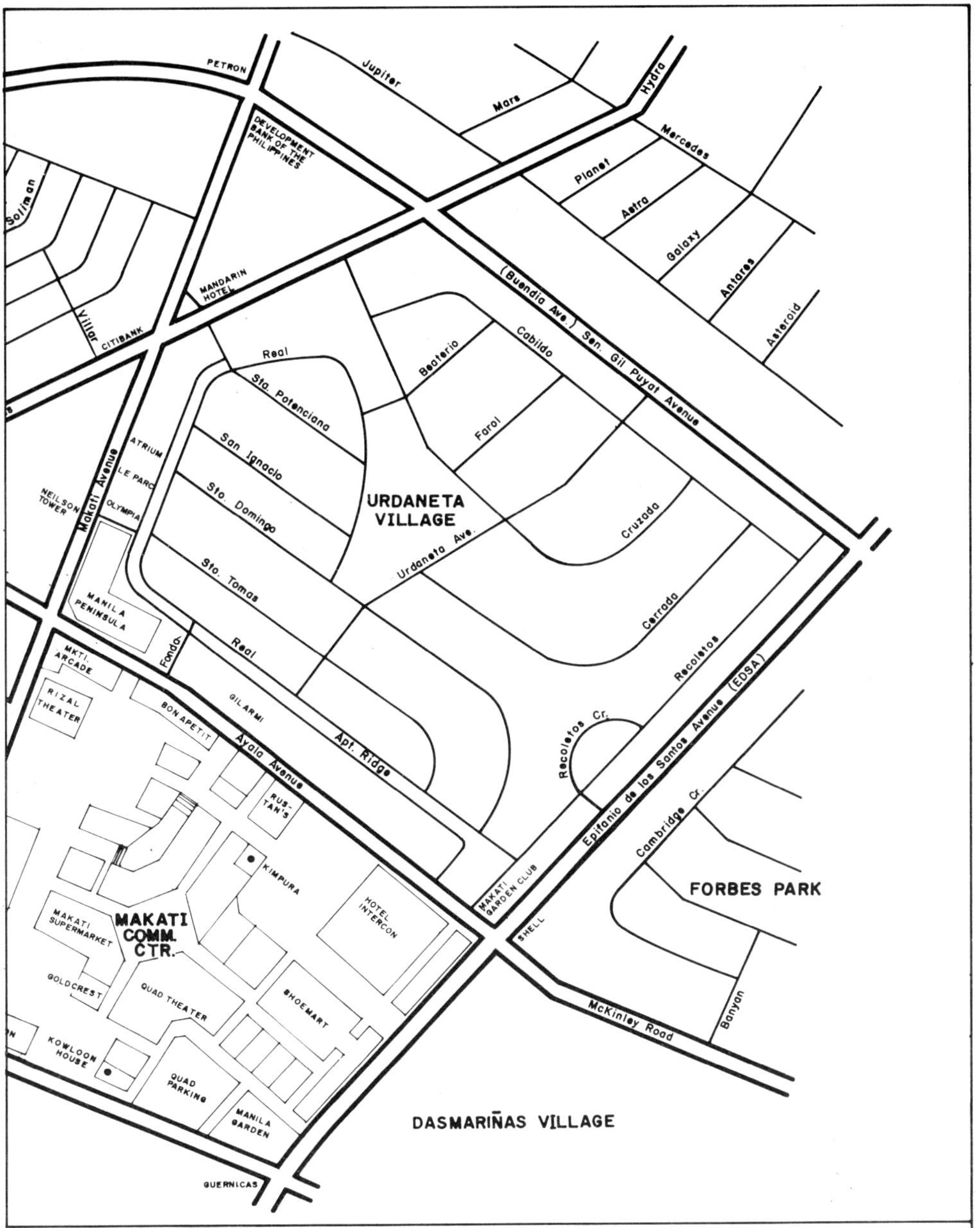

17 Faces
18 Saisaki
19 Sing-ya
20 Bookmark
21 Pancake House
22 Josephine's
23 Shakeys
24 Aling Asiang
25 Sugi
26 Fruit stands
27 Real Fresh Seafoods
28 Flavours & Spices
28 Beverly Hills Deli
29 La Primavera
30 La Tasca
30 San Mig Pub
31 Nandau
32 Takayama
33 Schwarzwalder

SAN JUAN, MANDALUYONG & QUEZON CITY

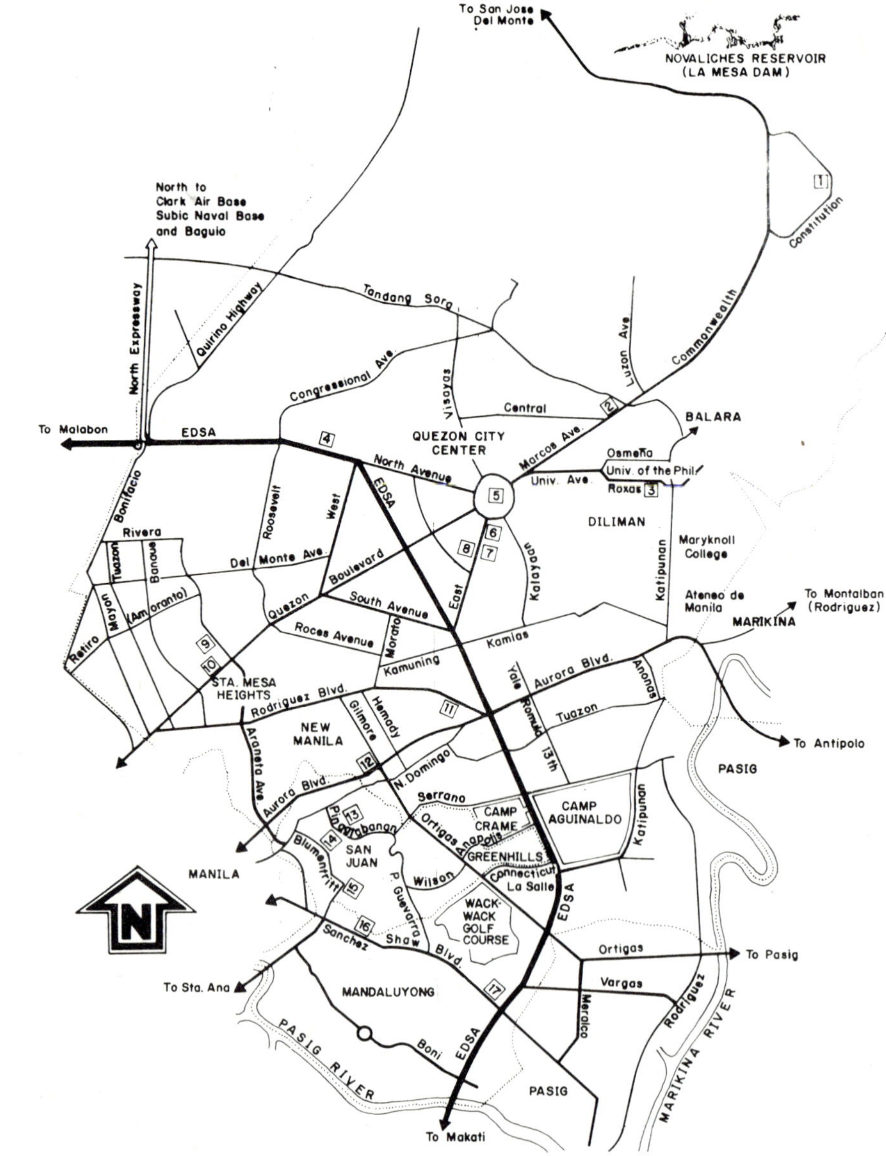

1 Congress
2 Iglesia ni Cristo HQ
3 Vargas & UP Museums
4 Iglesia ni Cristo Church
5 Quezon Monument
6 Quezon City Hall
7 Heart Center
8 Central Bank Mint & Museo ng Buhay Pilipino
9 Buddhist Temple
10 Sto Domingo Church
11 Heritage Gallery
12 Goethe House, Philippine Motor Assn
13 Pinaglabanan Shrine
14 Pinaglabanan Gallery
15 San Juan del Monte Church
16 Vargas Gallery
17 Gallery Genesis

reprisals after an uprising. The church roof collapsed during the earthquake of 1880. After repair, the building served as an orphanage and school.

Mandaluyong & San Juan

Two bridges access Mandaluyong from Makati: Guadalupe bridge on EDSA, and Marcos Bridge at the end of Makati Ave. San Juan was the base of activities of the Katipunan resistance to both Spanish and American rule.

EDSA passes through the western portions of San Juan, then crosses Shaw and Ortigas Blvds, which lead seawards to San Juan and inland to Pasig.

San Juan's twisting streets pass by many houses hidden behind high walls. Its major points of interest are the **San Juan Del Monte Church**, the **Pinaglabanan Shrine**, and several galleries, most notably Genesis on Shaw Boulevard, Galeria Vargas, on Papa Rd off Shaw Blvd, and Pinaglabanan Gallery on Arellano (Tuberias) St.

In the 19th century, the San Juan del Monte Church, known as the Santuario de Santo Cristo, served as a meeting place for members of the Katipunan resistance.

Pinaglabanan Shrine on Pinaglabanan St commemorates the battle fought here in 1896 against the Spanish.

Ortigas Avenue passes Greenhills commercial center, a large mall with many shops, then continues into New Manila past small rattan shops and fruit stands.

Quezon City

EDSA continues into Quezon City, dividing the two military Camps Aguinaldo, Army Headquarters, and Crame, PC Headquarters. These camps were the scene of much of the important action during the revolution which overthrew President Marcos, as millions of unarmed people gathered to protect defecting Minister Enrile and General Ramos from reprisal.

Next is **Cubao**, another shopping area. At its heart is the Araneta Coliseum, where circuses and other events requiring indoor facilities and seating for thousands are held.

On the other side of EDSA from the shopping center, on a side street, is the **Heritage Art Gallery**, off Lantana St, where you may see an eclectic collection of Philippine art. The collection is contained in three old houses which are connected by a maze of walkways.

East Avenue leaves EDSA for the **Quezon Monument**, at the heart of the new city President Quezon believed would eventually become the center of government.

Many government offices are located near the elliptical road around the Quezon Monument.

The remains of President Quezon rest beneath the monument, which also has two small museums, one of Quezon memorabilia, the other about Quezon City.

The **Heart Center** is on East Avenue, as is the **Central Bank Mint** building which contains, aside from the mint, the **Museo ng Buhay Filipino** (Museum of Philippine Life). Originally kept in a native house in Parañaque, the collection was acquired by the Central Bank and moved to Quezon City with plans to build a new house for it. These plans have not come to fruition, but the collection is well maintained within the mint. Visits are during office hours only.

The University of the Philippines' main campus is at Diliman. The **Vargas Museum**, with an extensive collection of Filipiniana, has recently been moved to a new building on campus.

EDSA continues to circle Manila, passing through Balintawak, where the North Expressway exits, and Monumento, Caloocan, the northern terminus of the LRT.

Shopping

Good buys in the Philippines include many handicrafts produced from natural materials, hand woven fabrics, quilted and embroidered articles and clothes. Many shops (except the larger ones) will give discounts when asked. In smaller shops, sales persons may stick close to you. In markets you are expected to haggle.

Native **handicrafts** and clothes are available in Intramuros at El Amanecer; in Malate-Ermita at many places, most notably the Flea Market off Roxas Blvd and Pistang Pilipino between Mabini and MH del Pilar; Tesoro's on Mabini, Robinson's on Adriatico; Ricardo Baylosis and Tribal Arts in the Padre Faura Mall, cor Padre Faura and del Pilar; Terry Baylosis, Likha and Via Antica in the 1400s block of Mabini; T'Boli Arts and Crafts, 1362 Mabini has an excellent collection of Mindanao tribal crafts; SC Vizcara, 464 UN Ave; Small shops along Cortada sell Muslim brass and other crafts; in Makati at major department stores (Shoemart, Rustan), Susanacrafts, Tesoro; Nardas, 5781 Felipe St near Bel Air has hand woven articles.

More adventurous souls will want to venture into the city's many **markets**, especially Ilalim ng Tulay, under Quezon Bridge, and the stalls around Quiapo church. Be aware of your belongings when in and around public markets. Keep wallets in front pockets, bags held in front.

City markets of note are: Divisoria (p 30) for anything, Central market (p 31) for fabrics and clothes, Quiapo (p 31) for handicrafts and amulets, Baclaran (p 39) for clothes and handicrafts.

Shoes and clothes and other supplies are available in many shops, large and small. D'Paul's and King Philip are among the many tailors who will make men's clothing at short order. For better suits, with a longer waiting time, try Giovanni Sana on Arnaiz Rd.

Carfel, on Mabini, sells **shells** and has a shell museum.

Ox carts from Pangasinan travel all over Luzon to sell their baskets. The trip from Pangasinan to Manila may take three weeks.

Sustenance

It is easy to get happily fat in Metro Manila's vast array of restaurants and food places which suit any budget and taste. All major hotels have restaurants. The Manila Hotel's Champagne Room is the place to be seen; good Chinese food at Hilton's Toh Yuen; Hilton's Rotisserie gets good reports; Plaza's Abelardo's and Mandarin's Tivoli and L'Hirondelle are well worth a visit; Prince Albert, Intercontinental, is also good. The Sheraton has many restaurants and a very good delicatessen.

In **Intramuros**, try Muralla at Casa Manila.

In **Ermita**, at and around Rotary Circle are a number of good places - Prego (Italian), Bistro Remedios (Filipino), Cafe Adriatico (great after theatre), Guernica's (Spanish, music), Nonesuch beside Malate Church. Steaktown at 1738 Adriatico does steak and seafood.

The Aristocrat, cor Roxas and San Andres, serves a wide variety of dishes, some very inexpensive.

And there are many fastfood places, especially on Padre Faura near the Midtown. The Seafood Market receives high praise.

At the **Cultural Center** are Gloriamaris for Chinese food and Karehan Karetela (Philtrade) for Filipino dishes.

Further south, along Roxas in **Pasay**, are Furusato, the excellent Japanese Restaurant; Nandau and Pinausukan Restaurants for Filipino and seafoods. While visiting **Chinatown**, eat at the Mandarin Villa Seafoods Restaurant (789 Ongpin) or the nearby President (769 Ongpin).

In **Makati** there are literally hundreds of places. All the major hotels have good restaurants, plus:

General - La Tasca (Greenbelt); Bistro Burgos (5007 P Burgos); Neilson Tower, evenings only, in the terminal building of Manila's first airport (Makati Ave across from the Peninsula); Gasparelli (Greenbelt); Don Juan for French-Japanese Cuisine (1016 Arnaiz);

Chinese - South Villa (Greenbelt); Jade Garden (Makati Commercial Center); China City (Creekside, Amorsolo); Peacock, (Greenbelt);

European - Schwarzwalder (Makati Ave nr Ayala Museum); Mario's (7856 Makati Ave);

Filipino - Kamayan (47 Arnaiz), Nandau (Legazpi St, Greenbelt - great blue marlin, *adobong kang kong*, much more), Kusina ni Maria (108 Jupitur St, Bel Air), Pinausukan (810 Arnaiz);

Korean - Young Bin (916 Arnaiz .. various prices)

Mongolian Barbeque - Mongolian Grill (Mile Long, Amorsolo); Mongolian-Korean Barbeque (Creekside, Amorsolo);

Spanish - Patio Alba (Doña Narcissa Bldg, Paseo de Roxas);

Japanese - Sugi (Greenbelt), Takayama (Arnaiz);

Italian - Primavera (Greenbelt);

Thai - Thai Room and A Taste of Thailand

Quezon Monument

(Mile Long Bldg, Amorsolo St), Flavors and Spices (Greenbelt);
Vegetarian - Cosmic Plate (The Gallery, Amorsolo St); Mother Sachi (Puyat near Pasong Tamo)
Vietnamese - Ville de Saigon (816 Arnaiz)

For inexpensive meals try Pancake House, Tokyo Tokyo across from McDonalds, Young Bin (Korean, a range of prices), Realfresh (a fish shop that serves sushi) beside United Supermarket, Mother Sachi. Shakeys serves noise, also Pizza, Wendy's does baked potatoes as well as other fare. The coffee shop near Tesoro is very pleasant.

Many hotels have cake shops where one may have a sandwich, roll, coffee.

Fruit in season is often available from stalls near transportation hubs. San Andres Market, Malate, always has a superb selection, as do the shops behind United Supermarket in Greenbelt, Makati. Try the refreshing juice of the young coconut (*buco*), straight from the green, unhusked nut. Vendors will open a hole in the *buco* and poke a straw through the young meat.

Nightlife

Manila society bores easily, so nightspots come and go from fashion and are replaced quite rapidly.

In Ermita-Malate there are a number of girlie bars which cater to the baser tastes.

Several places are nice for drinks and music: Weinstube on Mabini; Hobbit House on Mabini (folk music, service by dwarfs); Guernica's, in Mabini on Rotary Circle and in Makati on the corner of Arnaiz and EDSA, has nice Spanish atmosphere, good music; San Mig Pub, Greenbelt, Makati and Padre Faura, Ermita, serves meals; as does Prince of Wales, also in Greenbelt. Bistro RJ, Arnaiz Rd, Makati, has 60's music; jazz at Club 690, T Morato, Quezon City.

Makati Discos, for those who like it loud, are Kublai's Rock (also serves Mongolian barbeque at lunch and dinner), Zigzag, Faces, Rumors.

Cocobanana, Rotary Circle, Ermita, is a great gay bar where straights go sightseeing.

Miscellaneous Entertainment

There are sometimes open air performances at the Luneta, Ft Santiago and other places. During dry season there are concerts at Paco Park on Friday evenings at 5 pm.

Philippine **folk dancing** may be seen at Josephine's, on Roxas Blvd; Maynila Restaurant, Manila Hotel, with dinner, 7-10 pm Mon-Sat, tel 470011; Pistahan, Plaza Hotel, 6-9 pm, tel 832-0701; and Sulo Restaurant, Makati, tel 818-5011 & 816-1350.

Sundays and holidays there are **cock fights** where you may watch the action, which includes much betting, with men (called "Jesus") who somehow keep mental records of everybody's bet.

The largest arenas are the Pasay Cockpit Arena, Dolores St, Pasay City; the Elorde Cockpit, Santos Ave, Sucat, Parañaque; and the La Loma Cockpit, 68 Calavite, La Loma.

Minigolf is available at Par-42 Mini Golf, Amorsolo St Makati, and Par-44 Mini Golf, Greenhills, Mandaluyong. There is horse racing Wednesdays and weekends, alternating between the Santa Ana Race Course in Makati and the San Lazaro track in Manila.

There is a public **golf** course and driving range inside Fort Bonifacio, Makati.

Day Tours

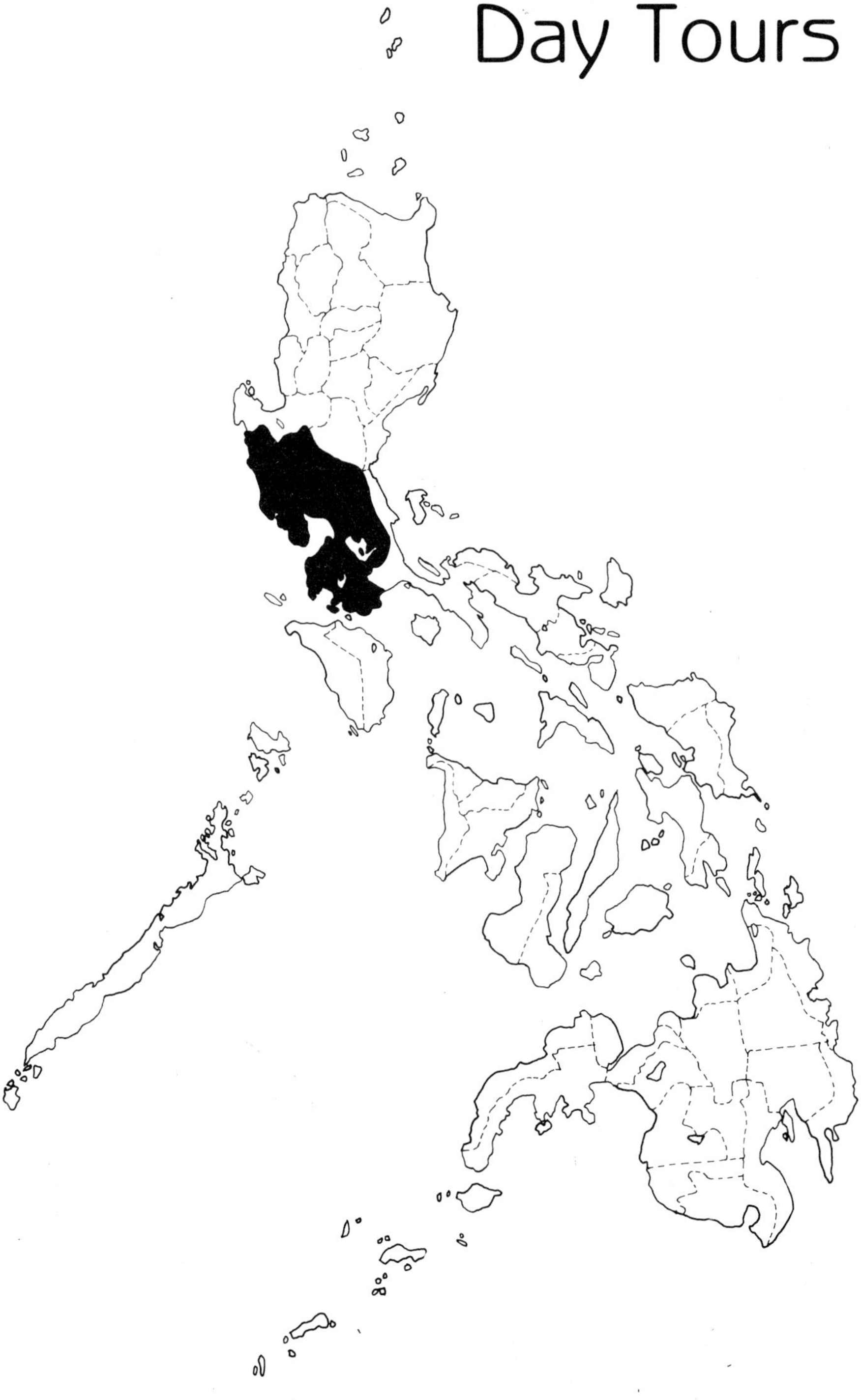

DAY TOURS AREA MAP

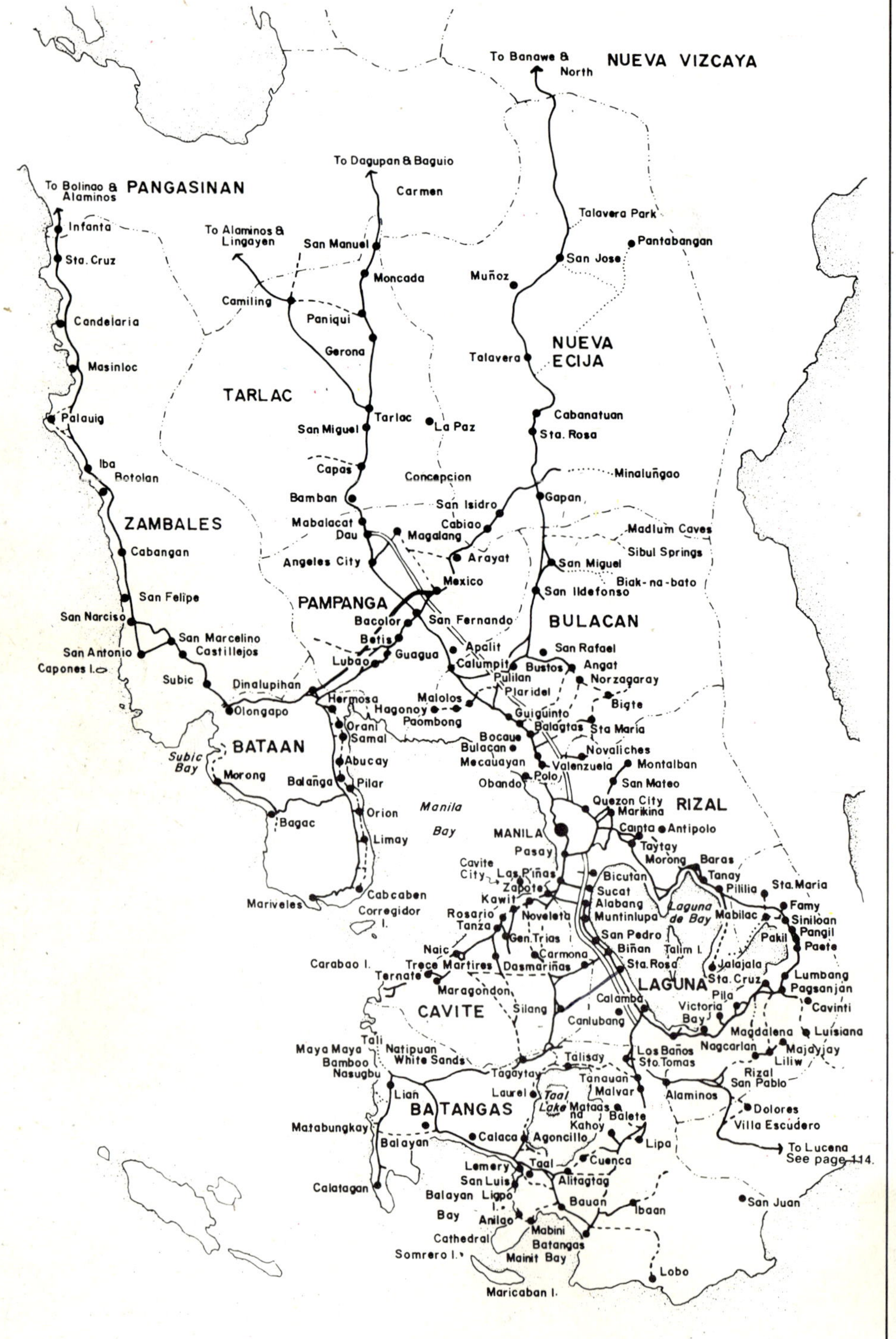

Day Tours

Taal Volcano

Day Tours from Manila

A wide range of sights, experiences and opportunities are available in day outings from Manila. Some offer overnight possibilities.

If you plan to spend several days in this area, we recommend you get **Luzon by Car**, which has more extensive coverage, maps and detailed directions for getting to places mentioned below.

Transport and sustenance information is given in each area. The most pleasant way to do land tours is by car. Bring a packed lunch unless a recommended resort or restaurant is on the schedule, at about lunch time.

Corregidor

Corregidor, a small, tadpole-shaped island comprising only about 15 square kilometers of land area lies at the entrance of Manila Bay. It is strategically located for controlling sea traffic entering Manila Bay.

Limahong, the Chinese corsair, used Corregidor as a base before trying to enter Manila in 1574. During the years of the galleon trade, Moro pirates hid there, waiting to intercept laden ships.

The island was first fortified by the Spanish in 1795. The fortifications did not deter Admiral Dewey's entry to the bay in 1898. The Americans also fortified the island, and it was to "**The Rock**", as Corregidor is called, that the Philippine government and allied forces retreated before advancing Japanese forces, leaving Manila in the hope that it would be spared much damage.

Philippine President Manuel Quezon, Generals Douglas MacArthur and Carlos P Romulo, and a few other officials were taken off Corregidor by submarine prior to the final surrender. The Japanese, who lacked facilities for a large number of prisoners of war, marched the rest 184 km to a camp in Capas, Tarlac (see p 53).

At **Malinta Tunnel** Filipino-American forces planned the efforts which succeeded in delaying the Japanese takeover. The tunnel, almost 1 km long, plus side tunnels adding up to nearly another 4 km, served as home to the 12,000-man resistance forces for nearly 5 months.

Huge canons are still emplaced on **Battery Way**. You may walk through ruins of **Topside Barracks**, and visit a Buddhist shrine at **Suicide Cliff** where, when the tides of war reversed, many Japanese soldiers chose to jump to an honorable death in the sea below rather than surrender.

Tristar Corp has boat tours to Corregidor. The boat leaves from the dock beside the Cultural Center. The tour includes boat fare, coach tour of the island's points of interest and lunch.

Architect Francisco Mañosa is revamping Corregidor into a war memorial complete with trams and tourist resorts, intended to be operational by 1990.

At present, a small, rustic lodge has a few rooms to let for those who wish to explore the island further.

Bataan and Zambales

The Zambales mountains line the western shore of a spur of land which protrudes from Luzon and forms the northern border of Manila Bay and the southern reaches of the Lingayen Gulf. Originally the area was thickly forested and inhabited by Zambals and Negritoes. These populations were displaced by later Ilocano immigrants. The forests began to decline when great quantities of wood were used for the galleon building, although some wood had earlier been used by the Chinese for their

CORREGIDOR ISLAND

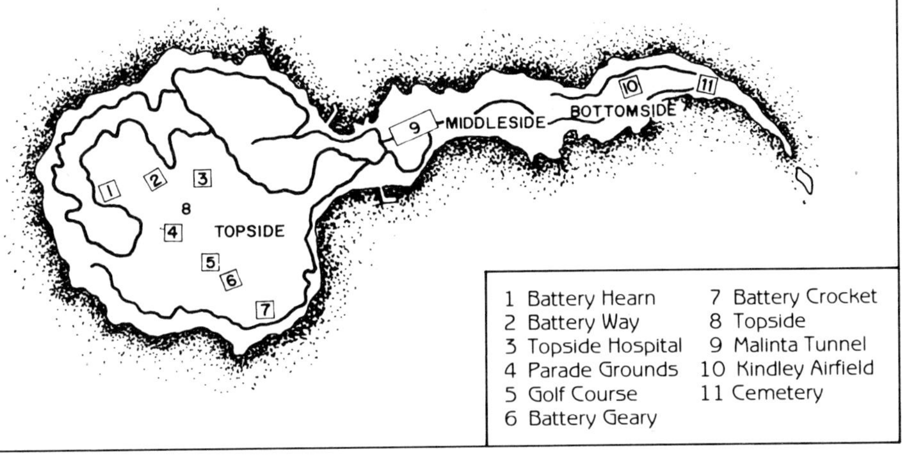

boats.

Today much of the Zambales Mountains has been denuded. There are a few mining operations. Bataan, too, has lost much of its forest cover. Valleys are cultivated to rice and other crops, but these are seasonal as little irrigation has been installed. During the latter half of dry season both Bataan and Zambales are extremely hot and dry.

At the outbreak of WW II, American and Filipino soldiers on the fortress island **Corregidor** held off Japanese invaders as long as they could. After surrendering they were force-marched 184 km through Bataan to Capas, Tarlac, where they were kept prisoner for the remainder of the war. 7,000-10,000 men perished along the march, many more died during their incarceration. The infamous Death March, as it is now known, is re-enacted yearly by boy scouts on April 9. Memorial markers show the way.

Victory Liner has hourly buses to Olongapo and occasional buses to Morong and Bagac. These stop on the highway in Bagac. Tricycles and jeeps meet the buses.

Several restaurants on the road through Bataan do acceptable lunches and snacks.

All manner of fastfoods and American-influenced restaurants are available in and around Olongapo.

Sand Valley Resort, Iba, Zambales, has good food.

A good road leads from Manila to Mariveles Port at the tip of **Bataan**.

Cabcaben, on the coast before Mariveles, is a jump-off point for Corregidor (see p 52), has a beige sand beach and rustic overnight facilities.

Mariveles Port town has an export processing zone and points of interest pertinent to the Death March.

About half way down the Bataan peninsula, a road diverges from the route to Mariveles and crosses to Bagac and Morong.

A tall cross tops Bataan's **Mt Samat**, 7½ km from the road to Bagac. Views of Manila Bay and of Zambales from Samat are spectacular, even better if the elevator inside the cross is working and you can ascend to the arms. Known as **Dambanang Kagitingan**, or Shrine of Valor, the area is a memorial to those who fought and died in Bataan.

There are a few pretty beaches in the **Bagac** vicinity, but not much in the way of facilities. You may hire a *banca* from Bagac to go exploring, or proceed to Sun Moon Beach - grey sand, very rustic facilities, bring all food. This is a good spot for camping. Montemar next door has nice facilities, but is a private club. Make arrangements in Manila before visiting; a private vehicle is needed for access.

The Philippines' controversial nuclear plant is on the way to **Morong**, where a large refugee camp holds Vietnamese refugees.

Much of **Zambales**' economic life centers around **Subic Bay Naval Station**, a huge American facility in **Olongapo**. Two cultures come together at the base fringes, which hum with bars, folk joints, discos, "good time" places.

Zambales coast above Olongapo and Subic is dotted with pretty coves and beaches along a lovely alternative route to Pangasinan and the 100 Islands. Women by the roadside in **San Narciso** sell delicious *bibingka* (rice cake), and sometimes lovely little white *singkamas* (jicama) are available in **San Marcelino** - just peel and eat. **San Miguel**, where the Americans have a smaller base, is a take-off point for diving, but the locals are not always honest, so you should go with people who know the area.

Villa Loreta Fishing and Beach Resort, on the approaches to **Botolan**, has a pretty white sand beach, nice basic facilities, often used by Americans from the bases to go fishing.

Iba is Zambales capital. The highway detours around its impressive church. Baskets and the fine salt made in Zambales are among items available at the market next door. Sand Valley Resort offers adequate accommodation on the beach.

If you would like to stay on a little island ringed with white beach, offshore snorkeling, small cottages, common bathrooms, everything basic (like camping in a small nipa hut) but clean, head seawards to **Potipot Island** in Candelaria. At the seashore ask for Lolita Alvarez and wait while a *banca* comes for you. Unless you have made prior arrangements, bring all supplies.

There are several basic beach resorts further along in **Sta Cruz**, before the road crosses into Pangasinan.

Inlaying furniture with carabao bone; Baliwag, Bulacan

The Pampanga River Valley

The vast Pampanga River carved out a wide flood plain which is extensively cultivated. Two centuries ago galleons sailed up the river, coming from Mexico, Central America to Mexico, Pampanga. Extensive agriculture and aquaculture have since tapped much of the river's water, diverting it to farms, fish ponds and a profusion of rivulets so that the remaining channel is shallow and small.

Two major roads cut through the valley. The North Expressway carries traffic to Baguio and the central mountains and the Ilocos coast. The Cagayan Valley Road diverges from it, carrying vehicles to the headwaters of the Pampanga River, then over the precipitous Balete (Dalton) Pass into the Cagayan Valley. The two roads meet again across the top of Luzon. The road to Bataan and Zambales also diverges from the North Expressway.

Baliwag Transit serves Bulacan.

Many buses to the Cagayan Valley, including Sarkies, Inland Trailways, Dangwa, pass through Bulacan and Nueva Ecija. Buses to Ilocos (Fariñas, Pantranco, etc) and Baguio (Sarkies, Dangwa and others) pass through Pampanga and Tarlac. Aircon buses stop less frequently than others at intervening towns.

Cafe Valenzuela, at the end of the North Expressway, is a popular stop for Filipino foods. There are several American-style eating places surrounding Clark (try Los Amigos, on the peripheral road south of the base, for Mexican food in large helpings).

Bulacan's 4 famous festivals, all within an hour's drive from Manila, are fun for visitors and residents alike.

San Miguel holds its colorful fiesta, **San Miguel de Mayumo**, on May 8. Residents display folk art decor, local food and confectionaries are available, and there is a religious procession.

Pulilan's **Carabao Festival** is held on May 14-15, the feast day of San Isidro, who used oxen to plow his fields. On the morning of May 14, the *carabao* and oxen

JANE KEMPE

Cross on Mt Samat, Bataan

are cleaned and decorated; some have their hair shaved in assorted patterns. During the afternoon they parade into town. Some pull carts laden with families, their produce and saints. A few are forced or coaxed to kneel in front of the church in obeisance to San Isidro (a practice which is very hard on unpadded knees). May 15 is a day of games and races.

Obando's **Fertility Rites**, held May 17-19, have obvious animist origins with Christian overlay. Pre-Christian roots have left recent memory. The rites gained popularity when a childless couple, after dancing before the image of San Pascual, had a baby. Sta Clara was the town's original icon, but fiesta rituals switched to San Pascual when he proved the more efficient benefactor. The third saint is Our Lady of Salambao (fish net), a statuette of Mary which came as part of a fisherman's catch.

Celebration dates for all three of the town's patrons were merged to permit one long fiesta. During festivities, townspeople of all ages perform rhythmic, somewhat suggestive dances in the plaza and a good time is had by all.

Bocaue's **Fluvial Festival** takes place on the first Sunday of July, when the Holy Cross of Wawa is enthroned on a gaily decorated boat and tended down the Bocaue River by many smaller *bancas*, hundreds of faithful holding candles line the river banks.

Bulacan has produced many men of note in Philippine history and is replete with historical points of interest. In recent years Manila's industrialization has spread into Bulacan's farm lands, and there are cottage industries in many towns which may be visited.

Malolos, the capital, was a center for political activity in the 19th century. **Barasoain Church**, now reconstructed, was the site of the First Philippine Congress, where the nation's first constitution was written. Balagtas, one of the Philippines' early poets, was born in Barasoain. Writing in the native dialect, he castigated the Spanish rulers for their abuses, but carefully disguised his works with amusing anecdotes so he could not be accused of subversive activities. **Casa Real** is a reconstructed turn-of-the-century house with displays of historic memorabilia and art works.

Hiyas ng Bulacan, along the MacArthur Highway, is a handicrafts display center where you may see and purchase local products ranging from leather wallets and bags to inlaid furniture, rattan furniture, clothing and more.

Baliwag is a center of inlaid furniture industries. Several shops welcome visitors. You may watch *carabao* ribs cut, soaked in bleach to soften them, and inserted in the wood. The finished products are stained and varnished. The dry varnish is scraped off the bone, leaving it white. Baliwag is also famous for its *buntal* hats, which are available at the market.

Biak na Bato National Park is on a rough road outside San Miguel. Here President Aguinaldo of the short-lived First Philippine Republic, was captured by the Americans. A small river flows by beautiful limestone formations and creates an underground swimming pool. The Sibul Spring area, which is accessible from the highway north of San Miguel, has caves to explore.

San Miguel is also famous for its *pastillas de leche*, candies made from sugar and *carabao* milk.

Calumpit, on the border with Pampanga, has one of the oldest churches in the Philippines, built 400 years ago. Fr Garcia, the present parish priest, has been restoring the interior to show some of its brick and limestone block construction. Originally tunnels beneath the church led to the river, providing the priests an avenue of escape for themselves and the treasury if threatened by attack. A school is beside the church, and there are always friendly children whose curiosity about strangers overcomes their shyness.

During the 13th century, refugees from the Madjapahit Empire sailed up the then deep Pampanga River and settled, infusing the local population with their customs, dietary predilections and language. Consequently Pampanga, like an island in the middle of the Tagalog area, has its own dialect and cuisine.

When the Spaniards took the Philippines, the Capampangans, like the rest of the people on Luzon's lowlands, converted to Christianity. Spanish blood was added to the local population. Outside infusion now continues at an even greater rate from the American airbase near Angeles City.

The expressway ends in Mabalacat, **Pampanga**, near Clark Air Base. **Angeles City** throbs with the activities which inevitably surround large concentrations of soldiers - bars, discos, the loose life. Good Philippine handicrafts are available in many shops. There is a thriving black market in

American goods brought off the bases and sold in nearby stores to anybody craving these articles. This is also the place to stop to stock up on American junk food as you continue north. Shakey's, McDonald's, Dunkin' Donuts are all near the end of the expressway.

In Mabalacat the route rejoins the MacArthur Highway, the original north road. General Douglas MacArthur's troops marched down this road in 1944 to retake Manila.

Before terminating at the MacArthur Highway, the expressway passes **Mt Arayat**, Pampanga's dormant volcano, which stands alone among flat cane and rice fields. Once forested, then re- forested with teak by President Manuel Quezon, Arayat now only has trees on its steeper slopes. Mt Arayat National Park has swimming pools fed by free-flowing spring water, picnic areas and trails leading to the top of Arayat (climb up one day, spend the night, come down the next).

Pampanga has several very ornate churches which attest to its Spanish heritage. Beautiful, sturdy, extensively decorated churches are found in Arayat, Sta Ana, Betis and other towns. **Betis Church** is a particularly outstanding example of the baroque, ornate workmanship which has gone into these structures.

In Mexico, at the **Golden Palayok Pasaoya**, Mrs. Lilian Lising Borromeo makes an assortment of delicious cookies and biscuits. Some are manufactured the way they were two centuries ago, using identical copies of the original cookie presses which have been retired for display purposes.

Artisans make intricate **wood carving and furniture** which you may see (and purchase) along the road through Bacolor, Betis and Guagua.

Not really a tourist destination, **Nueva Ecija** is the northern gateway of the Pampanga River Valley.

A rugged road goes over the Sierra Madre from Cabanatuan to **Baler**, on the Pacific Ocean. There are lovely beaches and excellent fishing. Locals are friendly and hospitable. There is little in the way of lodging.

Pantabangan Dam, inland from San Jose over dirt track road which fords a couple of streams, supplies water for much of the valley's farmlands.

Travelers continuing north may stop to stretch their legs at **Talavera Park**, just beyond San Jose, and to enjoy the views of the valley behind and the hills into which the road continues.

Around Laguna de Bay

Laguna de Bay, a large inland body of water, was once part of Manila Bay. When the land between Makati and Marikina rose, the inner basin was isolated and became a fresh water lake supplied by run-off from surrounding mountains.

Once infested with huge crocodiles, the bay has now been taken over by fish farmers and duck raisers. The crocodiles are gone, and the once steaming jungle has been pushed back from the lake shores. For centuries the only access to most bay towns was by *banca*. Boats sailed up the Pasig into the lake to pick up and deliver passengers and cargo.

A good road now circles the Bay. A day's outing takes one to many scenic spots and past lovely views. The newer road has been built around town centers. It is pleasant to get off the main road and investigate a few of the quieter towns.

If you wish to circle the lake in a day, hire a vehicle. Buses and jeepneys ply these routes, but most stop at Antipolo in the north, Sta Cruz in the south. Transport between these points is infrequent. Buses for Antipolo leave near the corner of Aurora Blvd and EDSA; those for Sta Cruz stop on the South Expressway in front of the South Supermarket to pick up passengers. Jeepneys and an occasional bus continue from Sta Cruz to Pagsanjan or Majayjay.

Liliw Resort offers some food. It caters to Filipino travelers. Several hotels in

Magdapio (Pagsanjan) Falls

Pagsanjan offer lodging and food, the best known being Pagsanjan Tropical and Pagsanjan Resort Hotels.

Top of the line resorts in Calamba/Los Baños are Club Solviento, Country Air Hot Springs, Crystal Springs and Villa Pansol. All serve food.

Montalban (Rodriguez) is not on the bay, but is close enough to be included here. No facilities, but scenic hiking and some mountain climbing are accessible. Go to Wawa Dam and walk upriver from there.

Antipolo has long been a destination for travelers. The church icon, Nuestra Señora de la Paz Y Buen Viaje (Our Lady of Peace and Good Voyage) is credited with miraculously saving several galleons from the deep. Consequently, for many years, anyone intending to travel made a pilgrimage to her to ask for safe passage.

Morong, which is directly downhill from Antipolo, has a remarkable 17th century church which was constructed wholly through donations by the townspeople. Chinese artisans who built the church added many touches reminiscent of their own culture. Towards the close of the Spanish era, when the Katipunan actively resisted the colonizers in this area, several rebels were caught and executed beside the church's side door.

Baras has another 17th century church.

Daranak Falls are inland, along the road to Sampaloc. Vehicles can approach the falls during dry season, but at other times you must hike 3 km through lovely farm land. Water drops into what apparently once was a cave, then flows downstream. The pool at the base of the falls is a qood place to swim. Bring food if you intend to stay the day.

Tanay church has lovely stations of the cross painted on wood. A restaurant called Fisherman's Wharf serves good fish on the bay. From Tanay the road around the Bay continues through a valley, then rises steeply into the mountains for spectacular views before ascending to the lake shore communities beyond.

Mabitac's solid 18th century church rests high on a hill, overlooking the bay and the flatlands. A very rough road goes into the Sierra Madre, crossing to Infanta which has beautiful beaches and great fishing but very limited accommodations.

Pakil is a sleepy town once famous for its *catalonas* (female shamans). An ancient *catalon* ritual is still performed on the Friday preceding Palm Sunday, when townspeople do the *turumba*, a strange rhythmic dance. During Lent special homemade cookies shaped like the Virgin Mary are sold here.

Paete, the next town, is famous for its wood carving and *papier mache*. During dry season *papier mache* horses, carabao and other figures are made, gaily painted and sold at fiestas in many communities. There are two remarkable antique paintings in Paete church.

Beyond Paete, a road goes steeply uphill

to man-made **Caliraya Lake**. There are a few resorts on Caliraya's fringes. Reservations should be made in Manila. Wind surfing, swimming, relaxation are available, and this is a lovely area for hikers.

Lumban has a tradition of superb embroidery. Ask directions to Lolly Aquino's house to see fine work.

Pagsanjan is Laguna Province's most famous town. Many visitors come to ascend the Pagsanjan River as it flows through a lovely canyon from Magdapio Falls. Here you may change to a raft and go under the powerful falls. Expect to get soaked. Then everybody shoots the rapids on the way back downstream. Be sure to wear appropriate clothing and have your camera and watch secure in a waterproof bag.

During and just after rainy season it is not possible to go all the way to the main falls, and *bancas* will turn at a smaller one. Towards the end of dry season, when the river is low, "shooting the rapids" becomes "carrying the *banca*". Passengers are hefted over rocky areas by boatmen who, in hopes of getting a good tip, loudly proclaim how hard they are working.

The Pagsanjan Rapids Hotel is one good departure point for the river ride, and serves a tasty lunch.

Majayjay, Liliw and Nagcarlan at the foot of Mt Banahaw all have nice churches and scenery. You may see buri palm leaves being dyed along the poor road to Majayjay, and some rice terracing. There are good views of Laguna de Bay from Liliw's bell tower. Shoes and slippers are manufactured here, and several biscuits. Try the uraro (arrowroot) biscuits.

Queso puti, salty cheese made from carabao milk, is sold by the road in **Sta Cruz**.

Pila has a small museum containing some Chinese pottery unearthed in this area.

Los Baños is a large town where the International Rice Research Institute carries on work to improve rice and disseminate information about its culture throughout the world. An information office and guided tours are provided for visitors interested in the program.

Taal Church

The University of the Philippines has a large campus in Los Baños, having relocated its forestry, veterinary, animal science and several other departments away from Metro Manila.

It is possible to climb **Mt Makiling** and to hike to natural **hot springs** on its slopes via the access road through UP campus. A trail continues to Makiling's summit. Ask permission to access the forest from the Forestry Department. You may also visit the UP Arts Center for good views over the Bay.

Several resorts in Los Baños and **Calamba** have harnessed hot water from volcanic Mt Makiling and channeled it into baths where people come for medicinal cures.

Philippine national hero Jose Rizal came from Calamba. The house where he lived has been beautifully restored and opened as a museum with Rizal memorabilia, period pieces, and labeled fruit trees and plants in the garden.

Biñan has many fascinating old houses still with heavy tiled roofs, but none are open to the public.

From Calamba it takes about 45 min to return to Manila via the expressway.

Cavite and Batangas

Cavite and Batangas line the coast south of Manila. Taal Volcano, Batangas' eruptive heart, easily accessible from Manila, often receives visitors. Anilao, Batangas is the first destination many divers and snorkelers head for, and Batangas City is the departure point for visits to Puerto Galera.

Many buses and jeepneys ply the south coastal road to Cavite City. Occasional vehicles continue to Naic and Maragondon. but private hire would be simpler. Do not travel the Cavite roads at night. The road from Tagaytay to Naic often has bandits.

Many tour operators do excursions to Taal. Buses leave Baclaran Market, Pasay for Las Piñas, Tagaytay, and other points in Cavite. Although possible via public transport, the Taal Circle is best done with private hire. Philippine Experience Tours do a lovely day outing to the area.

Anilao area may be reached via bus (BLTB Co) to Batangas City, then jeepney to Anilao. Many resorts are reached via *banca* from Anilao ($4), most of the closer ones are served by jeepney.

Cavite is famous for its seafoods, and many people feel that the best is available at the original Josephine's in Cavite.

Taal Vista Lodge, Tagaytay, has meals, rooms and cottages.

When heading for destinations which do not have up-market resorts, it is better to bring a picnic.

Roxas Boulevard continues past the road to Manila's international airport down the coast. The inland road is congested with traffic but passes some points of interest. Jeepneys and buses constantly ply the route.

Sarao Jeepney Factory, where Metro Manila's colorful jeepneys are made, is along the inland road, as is **Las Piñas Church** and its **Bamboo Organ**. The organ, built in 1795 by Fray Diego Cera de la Virgin del Carmen, was damaged several times and fell into disuse until, in 1975, it was restored in Germany.

Today the organ is fully functional and open to visitors daily 9-11 am and 2-4 pm, except Sundays. There is usually an organist who can demonstrate the instrument. The gift shop downstairs in the *convento* sells souvenirs and good tapes of bamboo organ music.

The **Aguinaldo Shrine**, further along the road, is worth a visit.

General Emilio Aguinaldo resisted the Spanish colonizers until exiled, and then supported American entry because he had been led to believe they would give the Philippines its independence. When it became clear he had been tricked, Aguinaldo rebelled and fought the new overlords as President of the First Philippine Republic until he was caught at Biak-na-Bato, San Miguel.

His house and its remarkable furnishings

have been made into the Aguinaldo Shrine. The ceiling of the dining room has a bas relief map of the Philippines, with Cavite painted red to symbolize the Province's resistance.

Aguinaldo's remains are entombed behind the house.

Cavite City and Sangley Point are located on a narrow spit of land which protrudes like a tongue into Manila Bay. Part of the spit is only wide enough to accommodate the road. Both sides of the road are lined with salt beds in some places, and there are many beach resorts for day excursionists.

Houses in Cavite are nice wood structures with pointed finials and carved wood under the eaves. The carvings are decorative, and allow hot air which gathers under the roof to exit.

Cavite's coast is lined with resorts. Puerto Azul and Marbella are posh, pricey, have many facilities. Many less expensive places are further north.

Maragondon, at the other end of Cavite, is accessible either via the Cavite Road, or via the South Expressway, exit at Carmona. Maragondon was settled in 1663 by Indonesian Christians. The town has a nice old church with good views from the bell tower. Historical markers line the roadsides, for Maragondon has figured prominently in Philippine history.

Although **Taal Volcano**'s lake and central islands are in Batangas, the best vantage point for viewing the volcano, Taal, is in **Tagaytay**, Cavite. People come to Tagaytay for the view, as well as for fruits, pony rides for the children, a 45-min drive to where the air is fresh and cooler than in Manila.

Tagaytay is situated on the huge rim of what once may have been one of the world's largest volcanos, perhaps 14,000' tall. Taal exploded, a crater lake was formed, then another crater formed within that. Yet another lake is within that crater, and it, too, has a small island inside.

Should you wish to go to **Volcano Island**, easiest access is from the other side, through Tanauan to Talisay. Because the lake tends to be rough in the afternoon, I recommend you continue to a closer departure point in barrio Leynes, where Mrs Gloria de Castro takes very good care of visitors wanting to go to the island, and several other people also provide *banca* hire services. The trip to Volcano Island takes about 45 min. The new crater is a 15-min uphill walk from the shore. The old crater and interior lake is a further hour. You may swim in the lake's sulphurous waters. Bring drinking water, and, if you are going to the interior lake, start very early, wear sturdy shoes, and be prepared for some dust and sliding about.

It is possible to visit Volcano Island from Talisay and Balete, but the *banca* ride is longer.

Taal City, on the southeast side of Taal Lake, is a gracious old town. Residents once became very wealthy when the coffee they planted brought good prices. When coffee declined as a source of income, the fortunes of the townspeople also declined.

Taal Church is an unusual structure, more like a government building than a place of worship. Climb to the "bell tower" for superb views of the town below and Batangas Bay beyond.

A few houses near the church have been nicely restored. The nearby market is a good place to buy embroidered fabric, clothing, accessories and table linens at reasonable prices. *Balisong*, or fan knives, are available here or in nearby barrio Balisong.

There are a few coastal resorts in San Luis, but most beach-bound people head for **Anilao**, where there are a number of resorts, wind surfing, hobie cats, snorkeling, and good diving. Anilao's beaches are not remarkable, but some nearby islands, such as **Sombrero** and **Maricaban** have good beaches. Ligpo Pt has a nice little beach with good snorkeling. Always take care with currents.

There are some beaches also on the **Calatagan Peninsula**, and a few resorts, most notably the Punta Baluarte

Intercontinental Inn, which has many facilities, including golf, tennis, swimming pools, diving, snorkeling and more. Hotel Intercontinental in Manila has bus service to Punta Baluarte.

There are accommodations also in Matabungkay.

South from Manila

The road south from Manila which leads to Bicol cuts through several towns that are worth visiting.

Philtranco, Sarkies, BLTB Co buses are among the companies that serve this route. Jeepneys connect from the highway to other towns.

Hidden Valley Resort, in Alaminos, is a coconut plantation with a crater-like area where spring water of varying temperatures is piped into natural- looking pools where you may bathe and relax. Numerous fruit trees and lush tropical growth make the area attractive, and you may walk to a waterfall. There are overnight cottages and food is served. The entrance fee ($8) includes lunch.

Kristalino Falls, Mt Banahaw

San Pablo has 7 picturesque little crater lakes. The most accessible, Sampaloc, is directly behind the City Hall. Palakpakin is beside a provincial road. Mojicap and Calibato are short walks. Yambao and Pandin are a hike into the coconut plantation, and a guide is necessary. Bunot is accessible through a resort.

Mt Banahaw is a dormant volcano. Its last very violent eruption occurred long before anyone living can remember, but the mountain has retained its power in another way. Many people come to worship and to meditate on its slopes. Some believe that Christ walked here, and that Jose Rizal was one of Christ's re-incarnations. Healers, *albularios* and priestesses abound in scattered communities. One group comes to contact UFOs.

Banahaw's slopes have lovely falls and streams. It is an exhilarating 2-day climb, and you may ascend to Lukban or a number of other towns. Shorter hikes are also possible, and can at least get you to the beautiful Kristalino Falls. You'll be tempted to continue to Suplina Falls.

Forays onto the mountain start at Sta Cruz, Dolores, from where an incredibly rough road continues to Kinabuhayan. For a guide, ask at the BFD office, or see the barrio captain or Cuyo Jose, one of the religious leaders. Discuss the route ahead of time, as the locals are much more agile than most visitors.

Villa Escudero, on the border between San Pablo and Tiaong, is a functioning coconut plantation cum resort, where you may see demonstrations of how coconuts are processed and used, enjoy the surrounds, have a ride in a cart pulled by a *carabao* while being serenaded by local folk singers. Explore the Escudero Museum, which has collections of everything from silver altars to plastic spoons, and then eat

Lukban, Quezon on the 15th of May

a delicious lunch overlooking the lake, or while sitting at shaded tables with your feet dangling in the stream below.

Bibingka (rice cake) stands line the highway near Villa Escudero, and are operating at *merienda* times. Banahaw and Mazapan Restaurants, on the way into Sariaya, serve *turo-turo* meals.

The road south continues through Candelaria to **Sariaya**, where coconut planters once waxed rich from their produce and built ornate, imposing mansions in which to live. Coconuts are no longer so profitable, but many of the houses are still there, the most spectacular being the Gala house on the highway beside the church.

San Isidro Labrador is the patron saint of Sariaya, Tayabas, Lukban, Lucena and a number of other towns. Town fiestas are always fun, but the **Pahiyas** festivals of Lukban and Sariaya in May are very special events. Make every effort to attend.

People of both towns decorate the main procession. The decor erected in **Lukban** is folk art at its acme. Uncounted millions of *kiping* leaves are hung as *pabitin* (chandeliers), placed along house fronts, worked into imaginative designs along with coconuts, rice, *palay* (unhulled rice), vegetables, bread, fruits, table mats, hats, and items related to the family's livelihood. *Kiping* is made from colored rice flour paste which is pressed onto a leaf and dried.

The people of Lukban finish decorating on the morning of May 15th. By noon the town is indescribably beautiful. Vendors anticipating the influx of visitors set up shop near the church plaza, selling food, plants, handicrafts and local products.

The afternoon procession, headed by Lukban's century-old *gigantes* (giant mannequins), progresses along the decorated streets back to the church.

Sariaya's decor is not as remarkable. Houses along the procession route erect large bamboo stems with packages of sweets and other things hanging from them. House fronts are decorated with fruits. Several houses have costumed mannequins and children on their roofs.

Late in the afternoon San Isidro ventures forth from the church, high on his palanquin, and pandemonium breaks loose. People lining the procession route are supposed to wait until San Isidro has passed before tearing down the decorations and carting them away, but many jump the gun. People on the street clamor for out-of-reach decor until someone throws it down. Twenty minutes after the procession has passed, residents have swept the debris away and Sariaya is once again a stately old town.

Further south, beyond Lucena and Pagbilao towns, two falls are each a short walk from the highway. It takes about half an hour to hike to pretty **Iringan Falls**, and you may swim in the pool at its base. **Malicboy Falls** are closer. Ask for local guides.

Pagbilao Island is usually accessed through Burgos, which is along a rough road east from the highway. Fare on regular *banca* trips to the island is very inexpensive. *Bancas* may also be hired. Tulaybuhangin, the picturesque town on a small, low sand spit, is for some reason never troubled by high waters. Houses are built almost down to the sea. There are several pretty beaches.

Quezon National Park is a small but good park where you may investigate the foliage and perhaps spot some wildlife. A trail leads northwest from just above the parking lot. The 1½-hr climb to the summit of **Mt Mirador** leads to superb views of both sides of Luzon and the impressive limestone formations below.

From the parking lot, find the path which goes through a dip, then uphill and through some limestone boulders. When you come to a cement sign the path drops down to the left, then continues through more limestone to some stairs built in the 1930s by the Americans. Ascend the stairs, then proceed on the other side of the hill among totally different foliage, following the now more difficult path to the summit.

Pinagbanderahan, the flag pole, marks the summit. Three triangles at the base mark where Katipunan members who actively resisted Spanish rule met to plan their moves.

The road continues south through the coastal towns of Atimonan, Gumaca, Lopez, all of which have some basic overnight facilities by the sea.

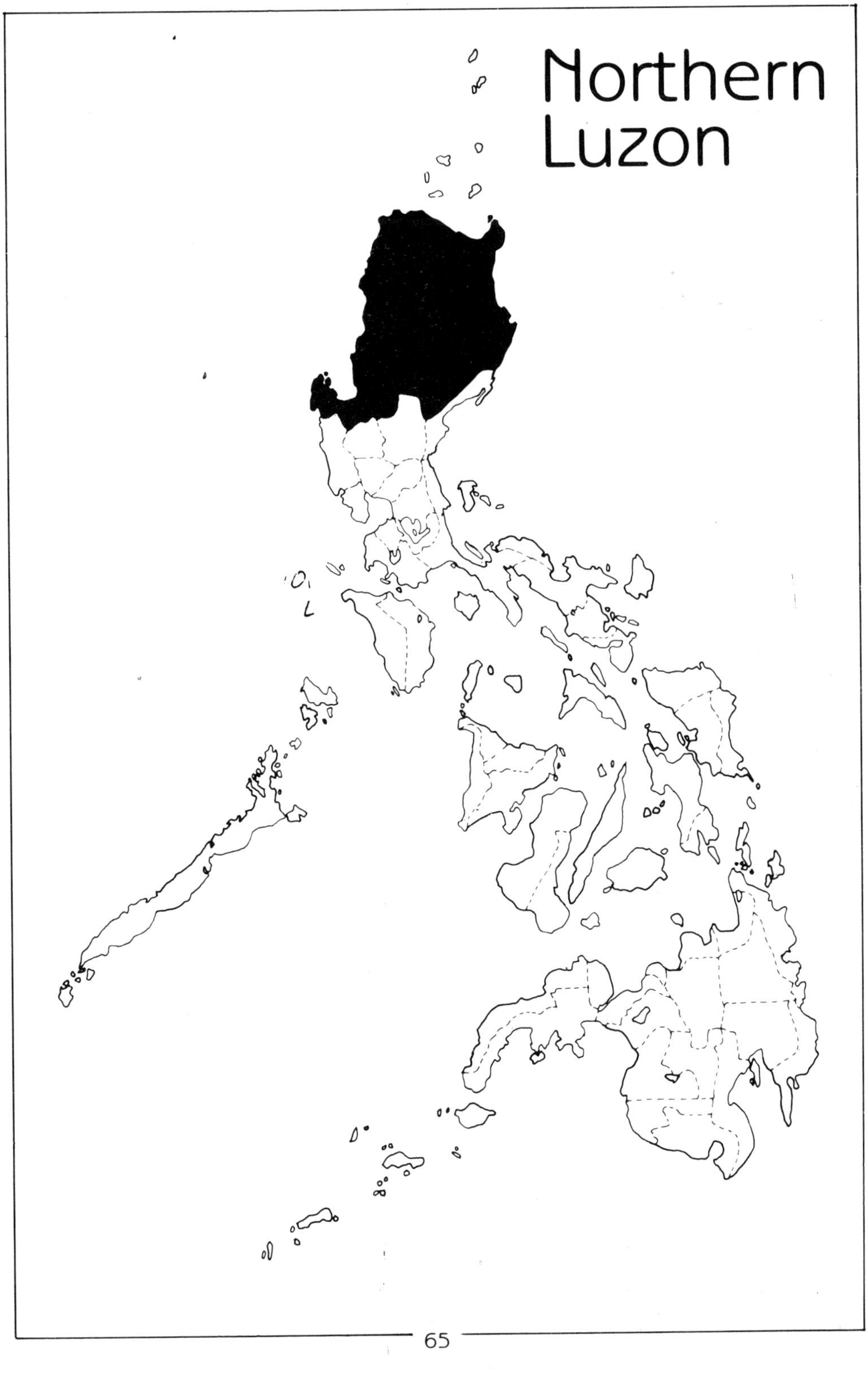
Northern
Luzon

NORTHERN LUZON

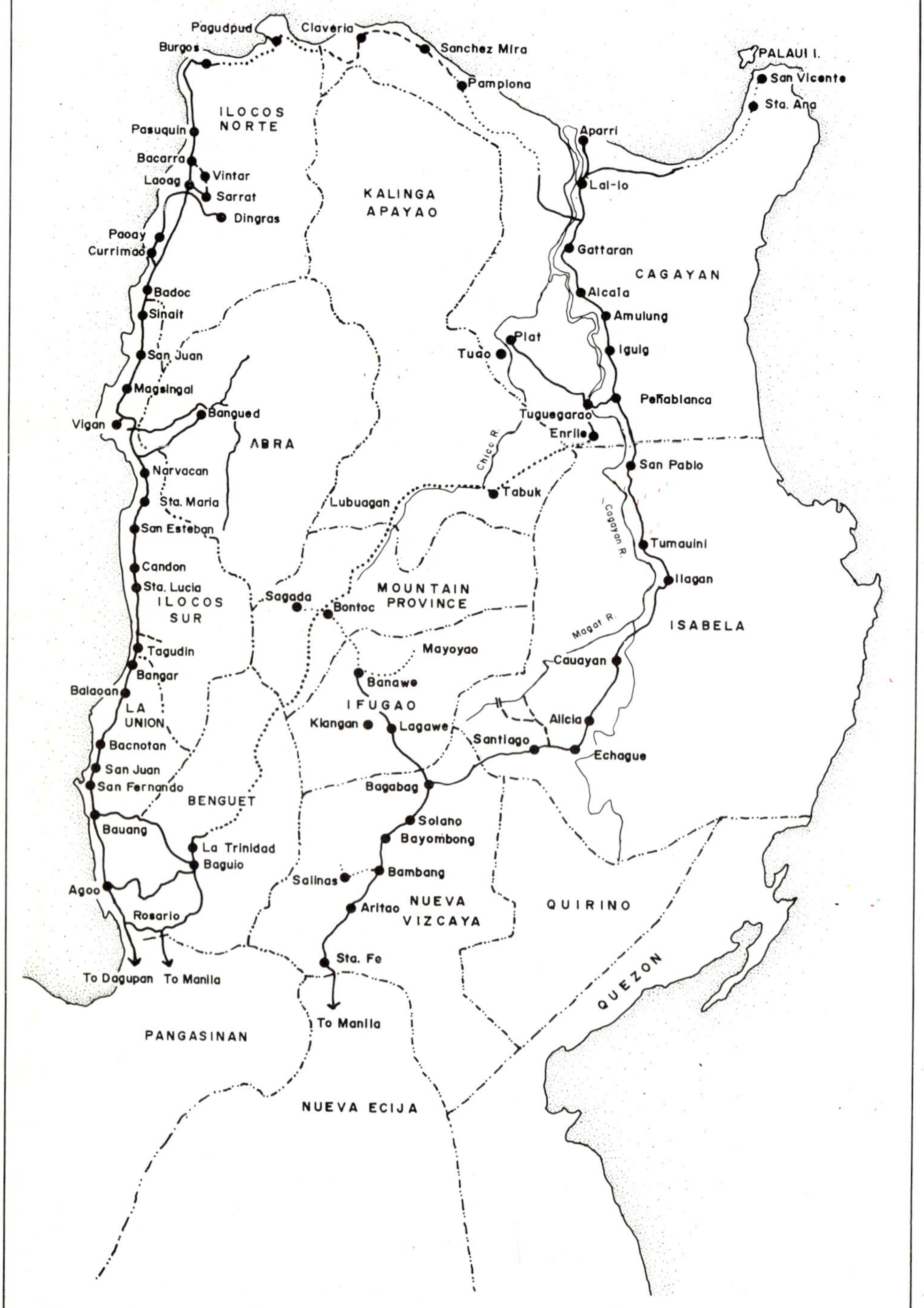

Pangasinan & La Union

Hundred Islands, Alaminos, Pangasinan

PANGASINAN AND LA UNION

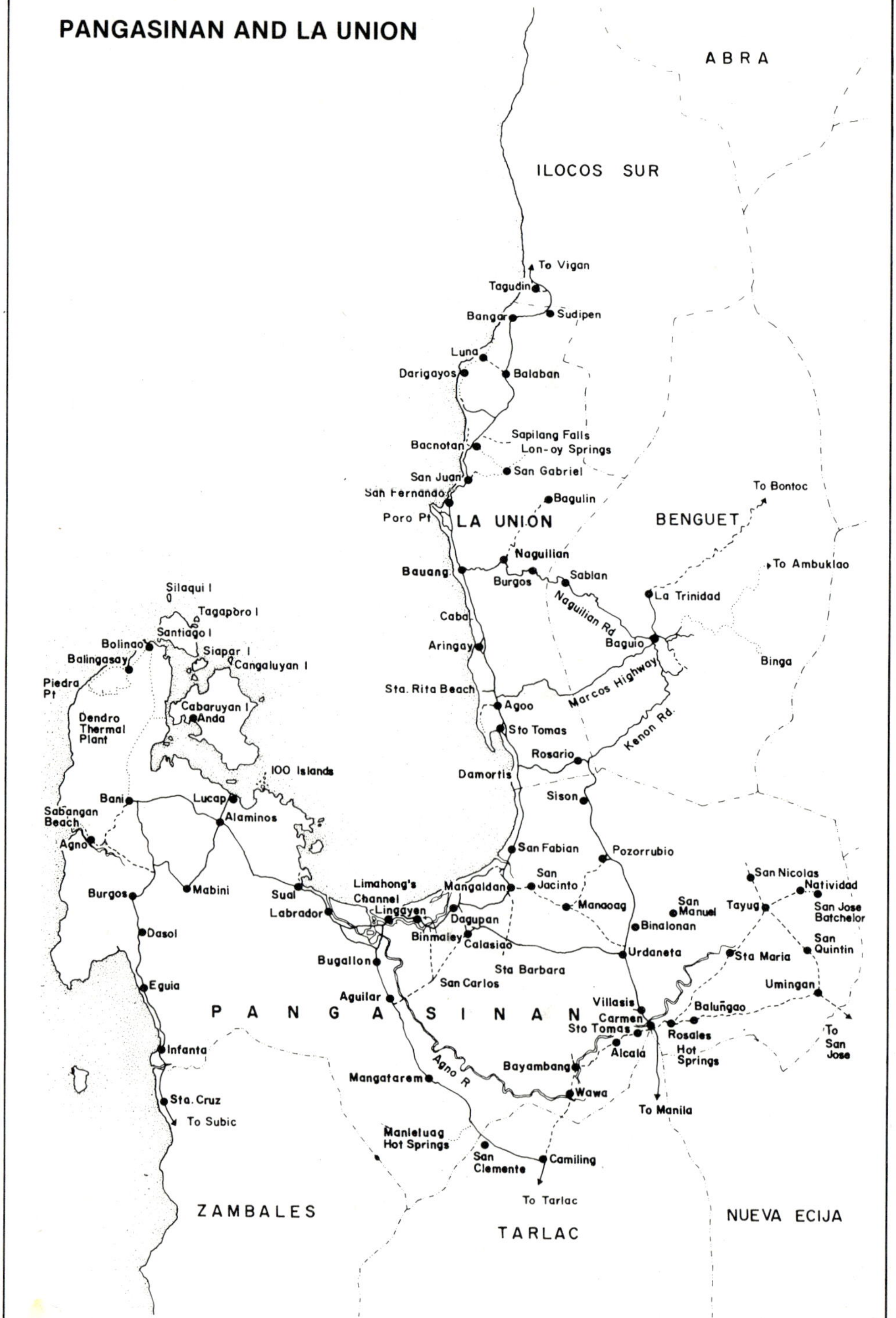

Pangasinan & La Union

access: by land, 4-5 hrs from Manila, 1- 1½ from Baguio, p 267

climate: dry Nov-May

to do: beaches, islands, dive, caves, museums, tennis, golf

facilities: beach resorts, lodges, camping, p279

Pangasinan and La Union are the southernmost Ilocos provinces.

Pangasinan's best-known attraction is the Hundred Islands, although there are other islands and beaches, and some caves to explore.

Lingayen Gulf curves from Bolinao, Pangasinan, through southern La Union, with its northernmost extremity at San Fernando, La Union's capital city. All of the arc consists of long stretches of attractive brown sand beaches which offer good swimming. Resort areas and beach cottages dot the coast.

Pangasinan has had extensive contact with Chinese traders. Bolinao has yielded very early remains. Sual Port has been used since prehistoric times as a ship's haven in times of stormy seas.

Lim Ah Hong, together with 3000 followers who were fleeing from the Ming Empire, tried to enter Manila in 1574 and was repulsed by Salcedo. He and his ships retreated to Pangasinan, came ashore in Lingayen and settled into the hills to establish a colony. Salcedo sent an army after them. The Spanish army arrived, bottled Lim Ah Hong's people up near the mouth of the Agno River and burned their ships, but were unable to overwhelm them. During a period of several months, Lim Ah Hong's men built new ships and set about digging their way out from seige, creating a new mouth for the Agno and escaping out to sea. Behind them they left the Limahong Channel, a tribute to their endeavor. They also left many men and women who, unable to go with the reduced fleet, remained in Pangasinan and became a part of the local population.

In 1850 La Union Province was created in an effort to end years of border struggle between Ilocos and Pangasinan. The result, in the short run, was one more political entity to squabble about its borders, but these matters have finally been laid to rest. La Union is now the principal gateway to the mountain provinces.

For centuries Igorots walked down from the Cordillera into Pangasinan and La Union to trade gold, honey and cloth for supplies they needed, following a trail which still exists.through Tuba and Sto Tomas Pangasinan, or the Naguilian trail which terminated in Bauang, La Union.

Pangasinan

Except during the busiest holidays, you may find your own little white sand beach on your own coral islet for a day, have a relaxing swim, tan, and escape from the rest of the world at the Hundred Islands. They are a pleasant 20 min *banca* ride from Lucap, a barrio of Alaminos. Overnight camping is permitted on Children's Island.

During holidays, enjoy the crowd or head for less frequented spots such as Bolinao; Umbrella Rocks, Agno; Cacupangan Cave, Mabini; Cabalitian Island, Sual Bay; or San Fabian.

Only the Hundred Islands, Cabalitian Island and some beaches near Bolinao have white sand.

Bolinao, on the northwestern tip of Pangasinan, was once a thriving trading community. Human remains from the 11th and 12th centuries have been exhumed, some with gold face masks indicating their possessors were wealthy.

Bolinao Museum, open weekdays and Saturday mornings, has a few relics unearthed nearby. Most finds have been moved to the National Museum in Manila.

Bolinao's impressive Spanish church, **St James fortress church**, was built to be useful in time of attack, for this area was frequented by many types of sea-going vessels. The first Spanish settlement was located on Santiago Island, but was moved to the mainland in 1609 for safety.

The church's façade has remained unaltered since the 17th century. Its Aztec-like decor reminds one that the Philippines' links with Spain came through Mexico. On Saturday mornings people throng to the plaza surrounding the church selling handicrafts: bags and mats woven from *buri*, handbags, shell ornaments, knives, and bamboo cake, which is cooked in large bamboo segments and will last several days.

Bauang, La Union

Piedra Point lighthouse is a ½-hr tricycle ride away, past lovely little beaches and a few forges where *bolos* and axes are made. Climb the lighthouse for wonderful views. Nearby Dendro Beach is spectacular, great for swimming and snorkeling. An underground river emerges near the northern end of the beach. About 6 km inland, a dendro thermal plant produces electricity from harvested *ipil-ipil* logs. There is a very pretty waterfall nearby.

If you wish to explore the **islands near Bolinao**, get a *banca* from Picocobuan, Bolinao's port. Ask for Rodolfo. **Cangaluyan** is ringed with a squashy white beach, with some good snorkeling offshore. **Tagaporo**, or Dewey, has produced archaeologically noteworthy finds. **Silaqui** has beautiful beaches, good snorkeling and diving, and is being used by marine biologists for coral transplant experiments. There are several good white beaches on the western side of **Santiago Island**, and land explorations are possible.

Travelers not wanting to hire a *banca* may take the ferry to Santiago and make their way to the beaches.

Umbrella Rocks are at Sabangan Beach, Agno, off the beaten track. Lodging is available during summer months. Agno is accessible only to those who have their own transport or are not pressed for time. The Balincaguin River flows gently to the sea at a pretty dark sand beach where several mushroom-shaped limestone formations provide shade at all hours of the day for those who need it. Agno has a pretty 18th century church.

A day's respite from the sun could well be spent exploring **Cacupangan Cave** in **Mabini**, Pangasinan. Inquire at the Mayor's office for guides and assistance. Bring powerful flashlights and be prepared to get wet. Mabini's water supply comes from the stream that flows from Cacupangan Cave.

Clamber up a small waterfall at the cave's mouth, then walk beside and in the stream past lovely formations. The cave isn't large but it is long. Its formations are delicate. You will have to crawl neck-deep in water to go the full length, and be prepared to spend the day at it.

At nearby **Binmatya Springs** water flows into a rocky depression where you may bathe.

Hundred Islands (map p 72)

The take-off point for the Hundred Islands is Lucap, a barrio 2½ km from Alaminos. Administrators at the office of Hundred Islands National Park charge a ₱2 entry fee, a small price to pay for having the *banca* traffic and tariffs regulated and reasonable. If you wish to do extensive island hopping, you will have to negotiate with the *banca* people.

Take cover-ups and sun block as it is easy to get burned before you realize it. Bring food and refreshments, and, if you are sensitive to the sun, ask the boatman for a beach with shade. If you intend to leave the beach and explore the islands, bring sturdy sneakers or shoes. There are snakes on several of the islands. Arrange the pick-up time, and pay when you return to Lucap.

Snorkeling is great off some beaches. Diving is not very good. If seas are rough the crossing to the islands may be unsafe. Sea conditions occasionally render some islands inaccessible while others are easily reached. A few islands are described below:

Carias: nice long beach.
Cathedral: domed rock formations with a cave which is home to large fruit bats.
Children's: camping areas, bathroom facilities, well maintained walks, guards and good views. Some camping gear is available; best to bring your own.
Clave: difficult to land on during rough weather; pretty little cove with good snorkeling, not much shade.
Duque (Roque): nice beach.
Governor's: one of the larger islands, steps lead to a panoramic view of the park, beaches on both sides, house for the governor.
Kagaw (Devil's): the best diving, good beach with morning shade.
Lopez: good beach, no shade.
Marcos: nice beach with helipad on the smaller dome. Imelda Cave, in the larger dome, is full of bats. A trail leads from the beach to the cave.
New Scout: small beach with pretty cliffs behind.
Quezon: the largest island, with canteen, eating pavilion, concrete walks and decor

Darigayos Cove; Balaoan, La Union

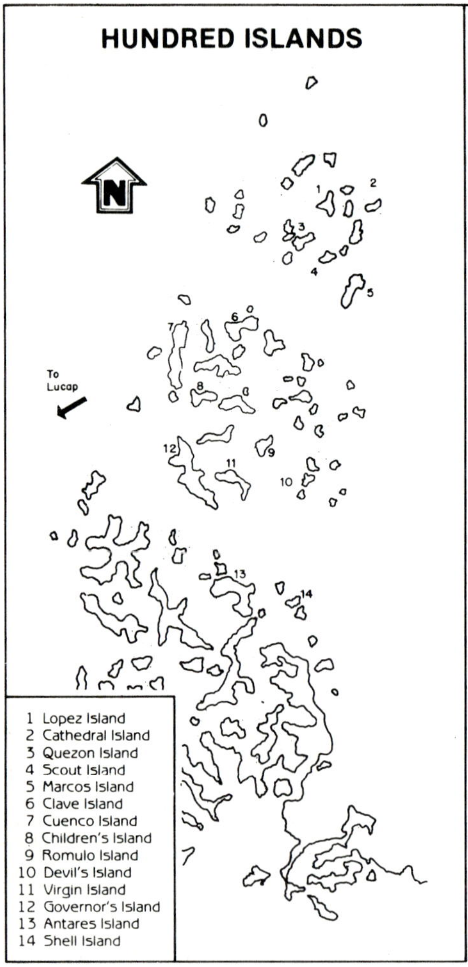

used for local movie productions. Good views of other islands from the statue of Manuel Quezon, the Philippines' first president.
Quinco (Cuenco): 2 small beaches and a cave through its center, great fun for exploration.
Raganza: beach with afternoon shade.
Romulo: good beach with morning shade and a cave at low tide.
Scout: good snorkeling, nice beach.
Shell: many shells in a charming tide pool; when seas are rough waves crash between

Hundred Islands National Park is a preserve. It is illegal to take corals or shells away with you.

the broken halves of this island, creating beautiful cascades down the limestone.

Large oceangoing vessels take refuge from storms in **Sual Bay**. Nearby Cabalitian Island has pretty beaches, residents don't pester visitors, rustic accommodations, bring everything. Sea Breeze Resort on the mainland has less rustic lodging.

At the close of WW II, the Americans first chose **Lingayen Beach** as a landing site. In order to flush out the Japanese (who had already left), they levelled **Lingayen**, Pangasinan's capital, with bombs - then decided to land further along the coast, to Bonoan Blue Beach in Dagupan. After the war the Americans rebuilt Lingayen in southern colonial style. The church, fortunately, was not ruined during the bombing.

Lingayen beach has a strong undertow and is not safe for swimming.

Dagupan is Pangasinan's business hub, a busy city. There is a busy market. Photographers can get good supplies at Fred's. Bonoan Blue Beach, the site of the return of US Forces during WW II, has a statue commemorating this event.

Beaches along the **San Fabian** waterfront have several small resorts and cottage facilities.

La Union

La Union's beaches have long attracted people from Baguio and Manila who come for relaxation and a change of pace. In the past few years several beach resorts have been leased to Australian managers. Many resorts can arrange tours.

Beaches dot all of La Union's coast, but resort development has for the most part confined itself to Agoo and Bauang. The beach at Agoo Playa Resort is not good, but facilities are. **Agoo** has a lovely museum, and the Agoo-Damortis National Seashore is a nice place to walk, although there are no longer facilities available for visitors.

Marcos Park, along the Marcos highway to Baguio, has an 18 hole golf course open to the public, and a huge Mt Rushmore-like bust of Marcos.

Bauang is a resort town, its shores lined with an assortment of places suitable for almost any budget. Most places do meals quite adequately. The long, brown sand beach is safe for all ages except during rough weather. There is a stretch of white beach towards Poro Point with one hotel, the Acapulco, on it. Diving, boating, wind surfing, water skiing are available, if not at your establishment, at another. Some people go game fishing, but you really have to know how to get a boatman who knows what he's doing, or be prepared for a pleasant day bobbing about in the sea getting a tan but not much else.

Watch the fishing folk drag the shorelines for small fishes. Skilled older men swing nets at schools of fish. In the morning bancas come ashore with their nightly catches. On dark nights the fishermen's lights glimmer on the horizon just below the stars.

Naguilian town, on the road to Baguio, has a basi-making industry where, when they are operating, you may watch liquor being made from sugarcane.

Pindangan Ruins, north of Bauang, off the seaward side of the highway, beside a Carmelite monastery. The remains of a small church lie covered with vines.

San Fernando, La Union's capital, has a tourism office where you may get information, a museum with displays of Ilocano life and a loom on which Ilocano cloth is woven. Great views from the tourism office and from the Pagoda nearby. The market is fun to wander.

Bacsil Ridge, behind San Fernando, was the scene of much bloody fighting during WW II, as the Japanese captured it and then dug in. From this ridge they controlled the entry to the largest port in the north. Eventually the Americans recaptured the ridge from the valleys behind.

Ma-cho Chinese temple, just north of the city, is a religious center for the local Chinese population. Every year the Virgin of Caysasay makes the 7-hr journey from Batangas to be worshiped here for a day.

Pottery is displayed along the highway in **Tabuc, San Juan**, the next town north. Delicious smoked fish is occasionally available at Mona Lisa Resort by the highway in San Juan.

Darigayos Cove is a lovely inlet off the main highway in Balaoan. No facilities.

Bangar, the northernmost town, is a center for Ilocano weaving and 3 or 4 weaving places line the highway. You may watch the women work the looms and listen to the bamboo counterweights' melodic clinking as they weave. An assortment of items, especially lightweight blankets, is usually available.

Sustenance

Good seafood is available cheaply in Dagupan at D'Original Dawel, very rustic setting. Good seafoods also at Siapno, more expensive.

Eating at Hundred Islands is not exciting, probably best at Last Resort. Bring snacks.

Good home cooked meals at A&E Garden, Bolinao.

In La Union, very good food at the Agoo Playa Resort in Agoo.

Most resorts have restaurants and the food is quite good at Anchorage, Bali Hai, Cabañas, Long Beach, Cresta del Mar. Carlos, at Driftwood beside Acapulco, provides wonderful meals, great Caesar Salad, and baked mussels among other temptations.

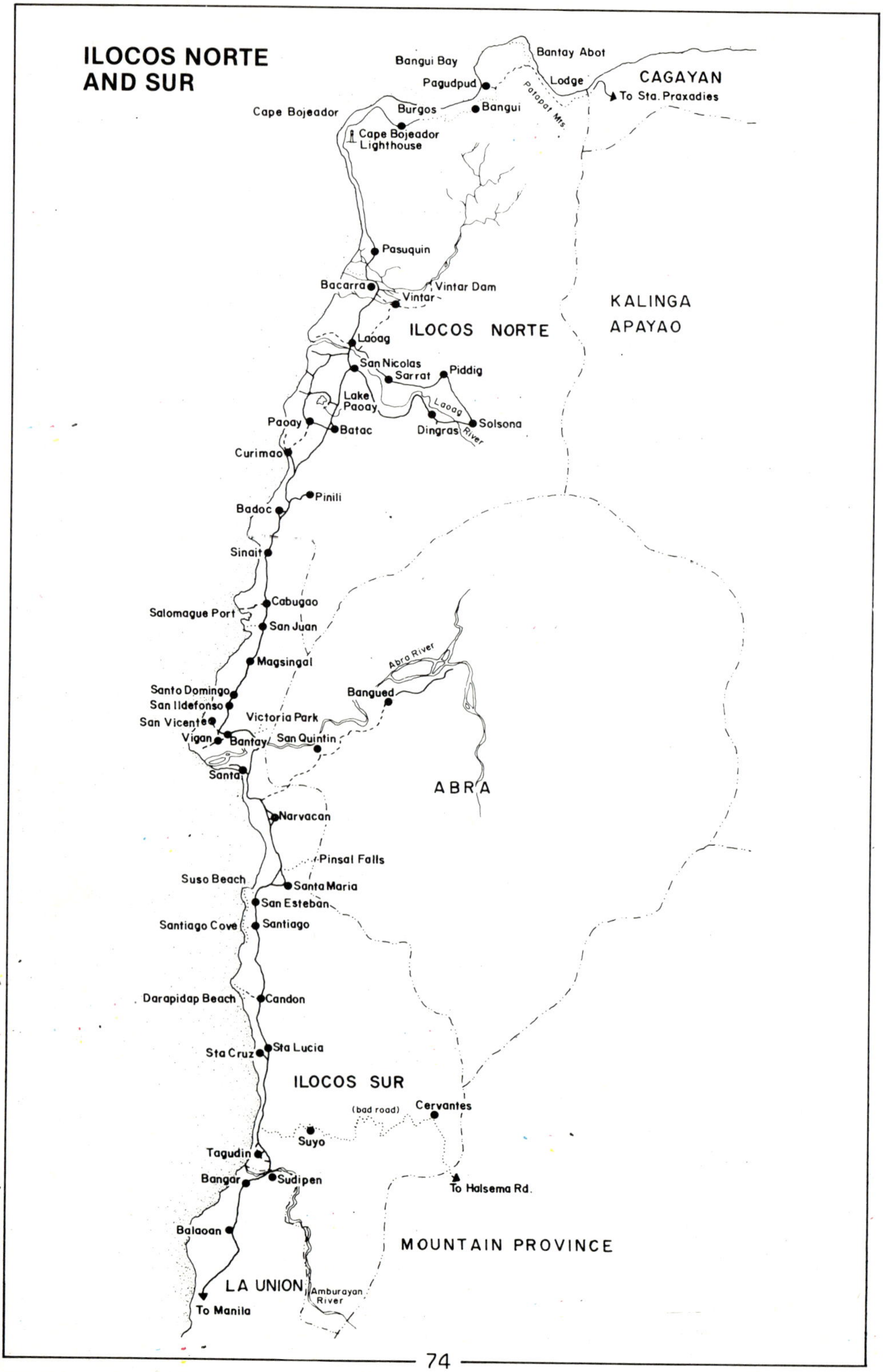
ILOCOS NORTE
AND SUR
Bangui Bay
Bantay Abot
Pagudpud
Lodge
CAGAYAN
To Sta. Praxadies
Patapat Mts.
Bangui
Burgos
Cape Bojeador
Cape Bojeador
Lighthouse
Pasuquin
Bacarra
Vintar Dam
Vintar
KALINGA
APAYAO
Laoag
ILOCOS NORTE
San Nicolas
Sarrat
Piddig
Lake
Paoay
Laoag River
Paoay
Batac
Dingras
Solsona
Curimao
Pinili
Badoc
Sinait
Cabugao
Salomague Port
San Juan
Magsingal
Abra River
Santo Domingo
San Ildefonso
Bangued
San Vicente
Victoria Park
Vigan
Bantay
San Quintin
Santa
ABRA
Narvacan
Pinsal Falls
Suso Beach
Santa Maria
San Esteban
Santiago Cove
Santiago
Darapidap Beach
Candon
Sta Cruz
Sta Lucia
ILOCOS SUR
(bad road)
Cervantes
Suyo
Tagudin
Bangar
Sudipen
To Halsema Rd.
Balaoan
MOUNTAIN PROVINCE
LA UNION
Amburayan
River
To Manila

Ilocos Norte & Sur

Bantay, Ilocos Sur

Ilocos Norte & Sur

access: 1 hr by air, 9 hrs by bus from Manila, p 267
climate: driest Nov-May, coolest Nov-Jan
to do: tour countryside, churches, museums, swim, sun
facilities: hotels, lodges, resort areas, p280

The provinces of Ilocos Norte and Sur line the edges of Luzon's northwestern shores.

The climate of the Ilocos area is dry and increasingly hot from November through April. Rains start in May, and increase to torrential downpours during August and September. November through January is the best time to visit Ilocos, for these are the coolest dry months.

Vigan's Holy Week celebration is the area's most notable festival. The Easter Monday procession makes 14 stops, following the stations of the cross. On Good Friday another interesting parade takes place.

The original settlers were probably Dumagats (Negritoes) and Tinguians (of Malay ancestry). These tribal people were pushed inland by succeeding waves of immigrants. The next settlers lived in coves, or *locos*, along the shore and consequently were named *y-locos*.

Ilocanos are hard working, pioneering people who have settled and resettled many areas. Much of the Philippines now has immigrant Ilocano populations.

In the 17th century, Juan de Salcedo established the northern diocesean seat of Nueva Segovia in Lal-loc, Cagayan. But Ilocanos proved easier to deal with than the people of the valley, so the seat of the diocese was moved to Vigan in the mid 18th century.

The Spanish introduced tobacco culture and, finding the soil and climate of Ilocos highly amenable to this crop, not only banned farmers from growing anything else, but made them sell all their tobacco to the government. This one-sided deal created great problems for the Ilocanos, who, understandably, resisted and circumvented the law wherever they could. Finally, in 1881, King Alphonso XII repealed the tobacco monopoly in the face of determined rebellion.

Ilocos Norte

Laoag, which means light in Ilocano, is the capital of Ilocos Norte. It is primarily a commercial city, but the cathedral, bell tower and Ilocos Museum are well worth a visit. The Tobacco Monopoly Monument, just beyond the bridge over the Laoag River, in the plaza fronting the provincial capitol building, was erected to thank the King of Spain when he rescinded the tobacco monopoly.

The **Cathedral of St William** was built in the latter half of the 18th century, a squat, solid Italian Renaissance example of earthquake baroque. The attractive façade has two layers of columns dividing it visually into two storeys.

The **bell tower**, a later addition, was built a block away, on sandy subsurface, ignoring the Biblical injunction not to build upon sand. When construction of the tower was completed, the door was so high that a man could ride a horse through it. Since then, however, it has been constantly sinking. At present, half of the lower door is below ground level.

Wednesdays and Sundays are market days, and aside from a good assortment of handicrafts from the coastal as well as inland mountain areas, you may find *herbolarios* (herbalists) selling cures for many ailments.

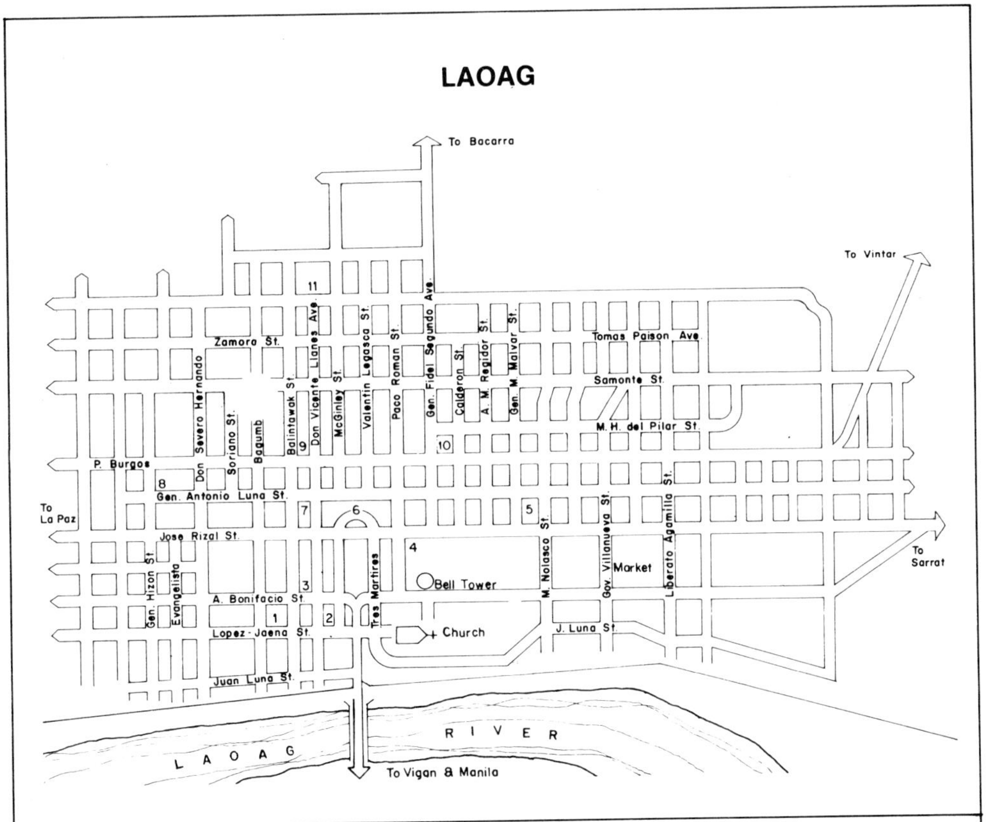

1 Buses to Manila
2 City Hall, Post Office
3 Peppermint Brickside
4 City Tourism information
5 Barrio Fiesta Restaurant
6 Provincial Capitol
7 Ilocandia Museum
8 Texacano
9 Casa Llanes
10 Buses north
11 Pichay Lodge

During the Marcos era Ilocos Norte's west coast road system was well built, many roads cemented and even small barrio roads were asphalted. Consequently travel is pleasantly comfortable.

The best way to get around is to hire a vehicle for the duration of your travels. If funds do not permit this, local transport is available from one town to the next. Ft Ilocandia Resort can assist you in hiring a vehicle, or you may ask the people at the city tourism office, or see Francisco Baquiran or Chris Pascual at PAL.

Half day trips from Laoag include a circle through Paoay, Currimao and Batac back to Laoag; an excursion to Dingras, and to Sarrat. You may also get to the lighthouse at Cape Bojeador and back in a half day, but allow more time to go on to Bangui and Pagudpud. Vigan may be a day trip from Laoag, or allow more time to enjoy Ilocos Sur.

The Paoay Circle takes you past **Lake Paoay** and the Malacañang of the North to **Paoay town**, with its impressive church. The Malacañang of the North, or *Balay ti Amianan* in Ilocano, was President Marcos' northern base. Its extensive grounds are well kept and visitors may use the adjacent golf course and sports facilities. Lake Paoay is currently used for aquaculture. The lake is said to have appeared in the 18th century after a cyclone. Legend says that the area was inhabited by very materialistic people. God warned them to change their ways, but they did not, and were punished by having their town sunk beneath the lake.

Paoay Church is one of the few Spanish Churches of the Philippines which was designed by Filipinos. The influence of the Indonesian Madjapahit Empire, which held sway before the Spaniards, is very obvious in the design of the church.

Saturday mornings, beside the church, there is a market where you may see and acquire beautiful woven products and a few handicrafts.

The coastal road from Paoay to **Currimao** passes a sugar cane press where, during harvest season, you may watch a *carabao* mill the cane. The juice is collected and boiled in an underground oven fueled by the cane waste. It is then cooled and used for molasses or fermented into *basi*, potent cane wine. During rainy season the press is

Potter; Vigan, Ilocos Sur

dismantled and put away.

The road continues through farms to Currimao, a fishing town, with two resorts. La Playa Blanca has rooms on a nice beach, is run by Swagman Tours, an Australian group. D'Coral Beach Resort has an assortment of rooms and cottages further around the beach.

From Currimao return via the inland route to **Batac** to see the reconstructed **Aglipay Church** where Bishop Aglipay, along with many followers, broke away from Roman Catholicism.

Most traffic in the Ilocos area follows the coast, but in 1598 the Spanish decided to establish an outpost for trade at **Dingras**, 22 km inland from Laoag through San Nicolas. While establishing their presence they built a truly monumental church, which was damaged several times by quake and fire. The church is as magnificent in ruins as it must have been when completed, a truly moving sight. A smaller church nearby serves the community, which never became the large center envisioned. It is possible to continue to Sarrat through Solsona, or you may return to Laoag.

Sarrat, which is east of Laoag, has the last Spanish church built in the Ilocos. The church of Sta. Monica has been destroyed twice by quake, and is again being restored from massive damage. Its impressive *convento* once served many purposes, and even had a basement jail where rebellious natives were held by the Spanish. The *convento* is attached to the church by a very attractive brick stairway.

Going further north from Laoag you pass **Bacarra**, which has a magnificent church. Its bell tower, after many years as an attraction, was finally toppled by the quake of 1984.

Several small beaches north of town have signs indicating their presence and names. Continue through Pasuquin to the lighthouse on **Cape Bojeador**. There is a magnificent view of the shores and fields below from the base of the tower.

Continuing north one ascends the hills then arrives at the **Bangui Valley**, a beautiful view indeed. **Pagudpud** is just the other side of Bangui, and has one of the most beautiful beaches anywhere. There is one cottage available, and miles of golden white sand to walk, offshore corals to snorkel over, a casual traveler's paradise. The cottage is at Villa del Mar, owned by Mr & Mrs Rogelio Benemerito.

Refer to the Ilocos Sur section for excursions south. You may want to stop en route in Badoc to see the **Juan Luna Museum**. Juan Luna is a National Artist. The house where he was born has been

Paoay Church, Ilocos Norte

restored and furnished with period pieces and reproductions of his art paintings.

Ilocos Sur: North of Vigan

Pug-os Beach in **Sinait**, the northernmost town of Ilocos Sur, has a spectacularly beautiful beach: no facilities, just a cove where fishermen haul their nets into white sand bracketed by green hills. This is a place for surreal sunsets.

Cabugao, the next town, has a massive, low church. Its Salomague Port is a major fishing pier. You can sometimes buy fish here and have it cooked while you wait under shades by the beach. The port is a 10 min drive seawards from the town, through bamboo-covered hills and farms.

There is a cotton buying station in Cabugao. Cotton was once an important crop in Ilocos. Some of the ships in the Spanish Armada wore sails made of Ilocano cloth. But as synthetics and imported materials became available cotton went into decline. Recent efforts to revive cotton raising have met with limited success.

Magsingal has a huge church which dates from 1827. The impressive *retablos* are beautifully carved. Let your eye rise to the two mermaids which flank the top of the main *retablo*. They have suspiciously protruberant bellies. The sculptor used his wife as a model, and she was pregnant at the time. Walk out to the area between the church and convento, which is also striking.

Remains of two previous churches are situated north of the present structure. Mr Angel Cortez has made a park and museum in the ruins of the second church, beside the new one. Walk in and stroll around the houses, see the roots of two huge banyan trees. At the eastern entrance of the park there is a stone phallus which Mr Cortes unearthed nearby and which he believes to be a remnant of pre-Hispanic religion. This museum once contained much more but has not been maintained in recent years.

The **National Museum** maintains a branch next door, in the restored remains of the small second church. Restoration has been beautifully done, and there are great views beside the church, looking out to the attractive bell tower. The museum contains exhibits of Ilocano artifacts with explanatory signs, and a collection of pottery and porcelain. It is well arranged and maintained, a must-see for anyone interested in the area's history and culture. The museum is open every day, 9-11 am and 1-5 pm. Arrangements can be made in advance to have it opened on holidays.

Continue through San Ildefonso and San Vicente to Bantay, where you turn left to Vigan. **Bantay Church** has a strikingly restored façade which contrasts with the simpler sides. Its bell tower stands on a mound nearby, commanding a good view of the surrounding countryside. *Bantay* means "watch", and this tower is perfectly sited to provide a lookout for intruders from any direction.

Vigan

Juan de Salcedo, grandson of Miguel de Legazpi, settled in Vigan in 1572, renaming the area Villa Fernandina after his king's son. Salcedo set about building Vigan much like his grandfather had initiated construction of Intramuros.

In 1755 the seat of Nueva Segovia, the diocese for northern Luzon, was moved from Cagayan to Vigan. The Cathedral was built between 1790 and 1800, and remains Vigan's most noticeable point of interest. The city around was constructed by wealthy Chinese merchants and artisans who were the ancestors of today's aristocracy.

Manila's Intramuros suffered extensive damage over time, especially during and since WW II, but Vigan's **mestizo quarter** has remained relatively unscathed by the passage of time. Today most of the commerce has moved to Manila, Laoag, San Fernando, leaving Vigan a genteel reminder of the not-always genteel past.

Anti-Spanish activities were always overtly or covertly on-going in this area. Diego Silang was one of many who rose in open and violent revolt against the colonizers. After he was assassinated, his wife, Gabriella, carried on the battle until she was captured and executed.

The Ayala Museum, in the Burgos house, houses dioramas, paintings and artifacts from the area's history. The ground floor contains articles used by the Tinguians who once inhabited the area. Part of the first and all of the second storey details the past since the arrival of the Spanish, not sparing the gory details of the more violent portions. The house belonged to the family of Padre Burgos, one of three Filipino priests garrotted by the Spaniards as a warning to natives contemplating action against Spain.

The **National Museum** maintains a branch in the Flor Crisologo House, where you may view exhibits of artifacts, documents and other items from Vigan's past.

Walk down the streets of Vigan to get the feel of the square buildings which were designed to serve as living quarters on the upper storeys, warehouses on the ground floors. Antique shops sell lots of "instant" (newly manufactured) antiques and artifacts, and an occasional real old piece.

Hi-Q, 27 Salcedo St, sells a wide assortment of woven goods; more may be available in the market.

Burnay ware is pottery made from very resilient clay found in this area, fired at a high temperature, and sold throughout the country for water containers and other purposes. Visit RG Pottery to see the process. Once or twice a week the *carabao* come to mix the clay by walking around in it. Chunks of clay are then thrown on foot-powered wheels. The resulting jars are fired in an ancient, almost horizontal kiln which uses heat so inefficiently that quite a number of the pieces being fired collapse, and are then sold as unique items. RG Pottery can arrange for shipment of larger purchases to Manila.

Communities around Vigan have their own charm. Traveling south, you will pass a number of interesting towns. Santa has a nice little church and some interesting houses. Its steep Rancho Beach was a landing site for Japanese forces during WW II.

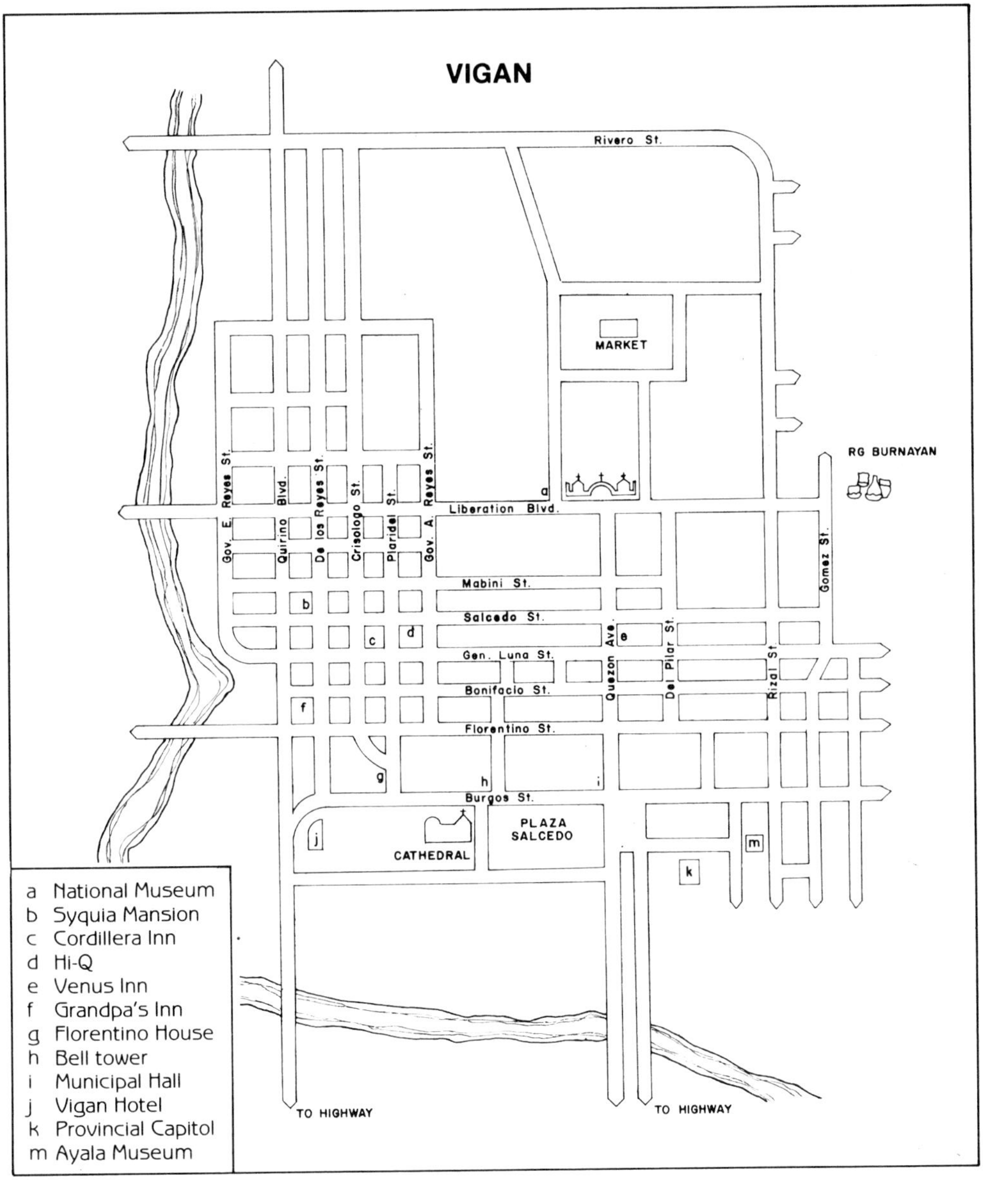

South of Vigan

A long bridge takes the highway across the **Abra** ("gap") **River**, past **Paraiso ni Imelda**, where swimming and snorkeling are good. The Bagong Lipunan Lodge sits on a protrusion of lava which issued from Mt Narvacan in prehistoric times. Guests may spend time looking into the crevices at sea creatures, swimming at the nearby beach or in the pool. **Solvec watch tower** is around the corner, just prior to the junction with the road inland to Abra.

Tinguian tribespeople were pushed inland to **Abra**, and still live there. Because they literally now have their backs against the wall, and have, for the past century or more, had to fight to re-tain the little land left to them, it is necessary to inquire about the political situation before venturing into their territory. They have learned not to welcome strangers.

Narvacan town has a nice old church and *convento*, as well as several attractive Spanish houses. It was here that Diego Silang held the Bishop of Vigan captive during his revolt of 1662. Foundations of the church date from 1587, but the present structure was erected in the early 17th century.

Beautiful Pinsal Falls are inland from **Sta Maria** (get a tricycle from the town). The church was built high on a hill, 250 meters above sea level. It is a massive building with tiled floor and walls and an attractive façade surrounds the whole. In the afternoons there are sometimes women selling delicious *bibingka* (rice cakes) near the steps to the church. The ground subsided under the bell tower as it was being constructed, and the builders curved the tower to compensate.

San Esteban, the next town, has a lovely beach, and you often see limestone mortars and grinders along the road, along with more touristy items such as ash trays. San Esteban has a very attractive watch tower, and several beaches along a dirt road which goes to Apatot Beach, where American forces landed during WW II.

Sta Lucia's attractive, early 19th century church is right on the main highway. The small, dark, pretty image of Sta Lucia resides in a glass house in the church.

Candon's church has a massive, attractive curvilinear façade. Darapidap Beach nearby offers good swimming and some resorts. Tirad Pass is 5 hours inland by jeepney, (very rough road). Here the young (22-year-old) General Gregorio del Pilar was shot by the Americans as he delayed them to cover President Emilio Aguinaldo's retreat.

Tagudin is the southernmost town of Ilocos Sur. A very poor road goes inland through the Bessang Pass to the Mountain Province. About 1,500 men lost their lives retaking this pass during WW II.

A bridge spans the mighty Amburayan River which marks the border with La Union (see p 72).

Sustenance

Food is good at Fort Ilocandia, nicely presented and served. In Laoag, locals like Peppermint Brickside, Garden Restaurant and Barrio Fiesta. Good snacks at the Magic Bunny, across from the PAL office. Cafe Guingoni serves food in a nice setting.

Vigan Hotel does a good buffet at about $3/person. Grandpa's Inn and Venus Inn also have restaurants, the latter being popular. Short orders are available at cafés near the cathedral. The air-conditioned Magnolia Plaza is a good place for a snack, especially on a hot day.

Central Mountains

Miner's Prayer Box from Mountain Province

CENTRAL MOUNTAINS

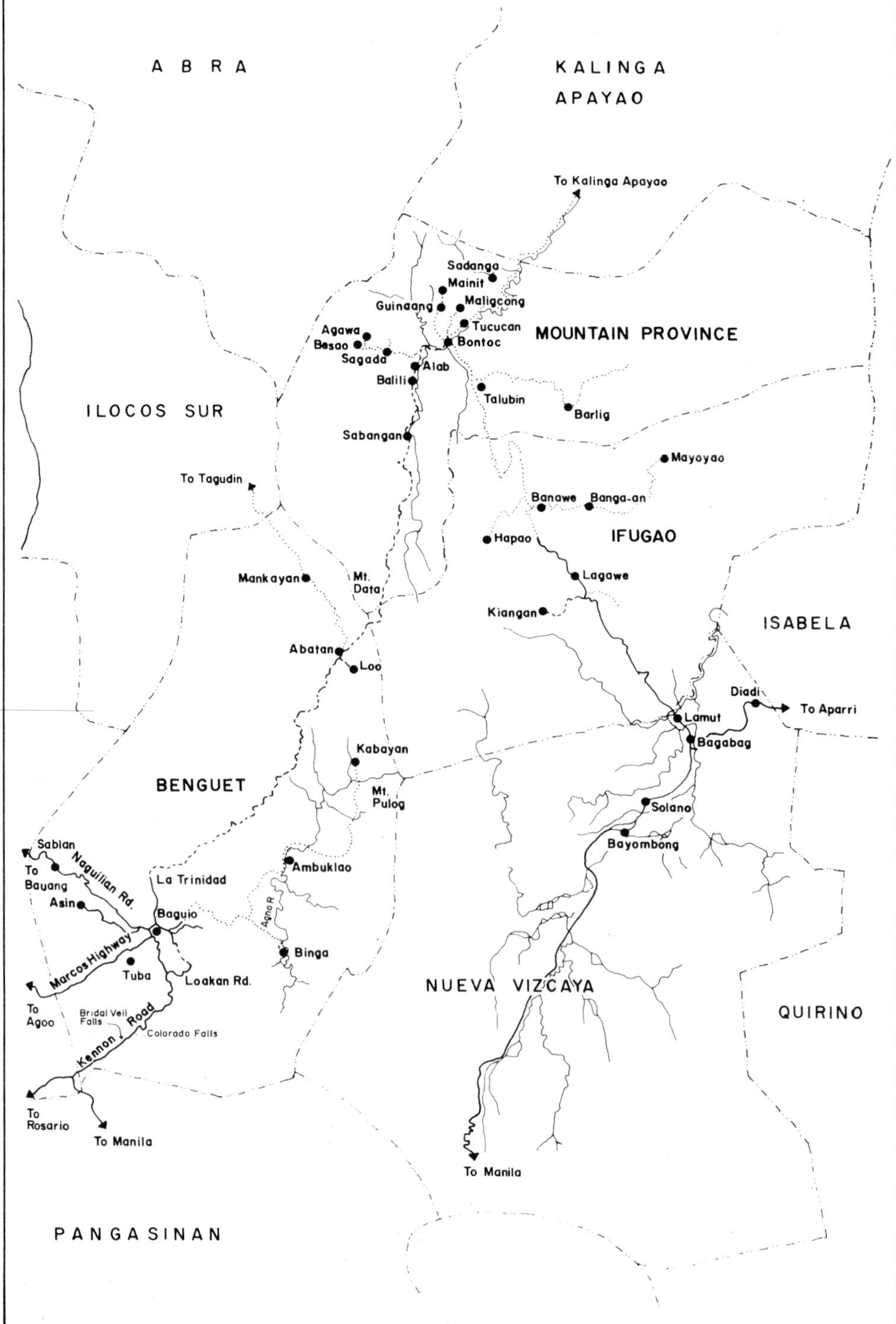

Luzon's Central Mountains

access: to Baguio: 1 hr by air, 5 hrs by land from Manila, p ; to Bontoc, 8 hrs from Baguio; to Banawe, 10 hrs from Baguio or 7 hrs from Manila, p 267
climate: dry Nov-June, chilly Nov-Jan; rice harvest in Banawe, end March - beginning of April

to do: in Baguio: golf, hiking, casino, pony rides, many activities for kids, healers; Bontoc & Banawe: hiking

facilities: in Baguio, many & varied; in Bontoc & Sagada, lodges; in Banawe, one hotel, many lodges, pp 281-3

The central mountains offer visitors not only a change of scenery and climate, but also a whole different cultural experience. The mountain areas are inhabited by people who for centuries have had a separate culture from the lowlanders. They are collectively called Igorots, but prefer their individual tribal names: Ibaloi, Kankanoi, Ifugao, Bontoc, Kalinga, Gaddang, etc.

These peoples traditionally made their living slash-and-burn farming in the rocky hills, augmented by mining gold and harvesting honey which they took to the lowlands to trade for articles they needed. The women weave colorful, strong fabric from bark and cotton fibers, each community having its particular pattern. Women wear the material as skirts, men as g-strings and blankets. Today many of the mountain people wear jeans and western attire. Some of the old people still wear traditional costume, but only in the most inaccessible areas do women still forego tops.

Mountain architecture varies from place to place. The Ifugao build grass and wood structures on tall stilts. The Bontocs build houses close to or into the ground. Attractive grass roofs are rapidly giving way to unappealing, hot tin which is preferred because it doesn't catch fire easily.

All the tribespeople are skilled basket weavers; some are skilled wood carvers. Unfortunately much of the carving is monotonously repetitive. Tribal people only part with antiques and family heirlooms in times of dire necessity, and, when they do give these precious items up, they must placate the spirits with rituals.

Many tribes still practice their ancient religion, with its pantheon of spirits and rites intimately tied to the land and planting and their ancestors.

Prior to the Spanish arrival, the mountain tribes developed and maintained distinct cultures, and lived a constant cycle of war, peace, or intermediate transitional stages, with their neighbors. They were almost always at war with the lowlanders, whom they considered fair game at any time except when trading with them. The taking of heads was considered an honorable pursuit. Some tribes required a man who wanted a woman's hand to prove his prowess by presenting her with a head. If a person lost his head, he was considered to have died in disgrace and was not accorded the intricate burial rituals of those who died of natural causes. It was incumbent upon his relatives to avenge his death, for, until this was done, his spirit would not rest in peace but would return to his people and make mischief. Hence the internecine wars were bound to recur.

Terrace building probably commenced prior to Spanish arrival. The remarkably extensive area of terracing is considered to be one of the world's 8th wonders. It is said that if these terraces were placed end on end they might stretch around the world. All were built by painstaking manual labor: people carrying rocks, digging down to bedrock and building walls up from there. In places where bedrock could not be reached, the exceptionally hard trunk of the tree fern was buried and used as a base for the wall.

The walls and the irrigation system which channels precious water from the highest terraces gradually into lower and lower ones are indeed a product of genius.

The Spanish arrival did little to change mountain culture, except to give the people a new and more dangerous enemy to resist. The Spaniards tried to get into the mountains, primarily to get the Igorots' gold. But they were successfully resisted. Every foothold they achieved in the mountains was eventually retaken. And, although they claimed to have come to civilize, they avenged head taking with reciprocal decapitation.

Not until the Americans arrived at the turn of the century did outside culture begin to have an impact on mountain life. The Americans who went into the mountains were a rough and ready lot, willing and able to live with the mountain people in their own style, marry mountain girls, raise mountain families, and administer justice in the accustomed way. They brought hospitals, schools and road building with them, and hence were accepted and respected.

Head hunting was officially banned, and the incidence of it declined, but one still sees many people with tattoos indicating that they or close family members have honorably completed a head hunt, and the occasional personal vendetta may still result in one of the offending parties having his head separated from the rest of his anatomy. Elsewhere he might have been merely shot.

But none of this need concern the traveler in areas which are quiescent. Travelers frequent Benguet, Mountain Province and Ifugao, but not Kalinga and Apayao. Thus it is sensible to contain your explorations to the former three provinces until you have reliable advice that the tension in the other two has abated.

Stalls on Kennon Road, Baguio

Benguet

Benguet is the southernmost mountain province. La Trinidad is its capital, Baguio is its best-known tourist destination.

Baguio is a relatively new town, built at the turn of the century by the Americans. They also constructed the Kennon Road, the first route over which vehicular traffic could pass into the Cordilleras. Baguio soon became the summer capital, where the government and Manila's wealthy citizens retired to escape the oppressive summer heat.

Thus Baguio is a mixture of many folk, yet it retains mountain flavor.

The average yearly temperature is a pleasant 68°F or 20°C. Except during the peak holiday seasons of Christmas and Easter, it is a relaxing place to stroll and shop. A Grand Cañao (festival) is held in November. Animals are sacrificed, the resulting omens read, gods are asked for assistance and thanked for past favors, and everybody eats well, drinks much.

A number of agencies offer tours, and can be recommended by your hotel or by the DOT. Additionally, some taxi drivers double as tour guides.

Botanical Gardens, Baguio

Inroads

There are now 3 access roads to Baguio. **Kennon**, the oldest, provides constant reminders of its American builders, who named points of interest along the way after spots in the American West. **Bridalveil Falls** is 6 km from the beginning of Kennon Rd. Cross the suspension bridge to have a better look. **Colorado Falls** are a further 2½ km, and a short walk upstream. A lion's head, carved from a huge limestone rock, marks the entrance to Baguio City's perimeter.

Naguilian Road follows one of the oldest trails which has been used since time immemorial to enter the mountains through La Union, and is less precipitous than Kennon. It is also the best route to the beaches and to northern Ilocos.

The newer **Marcos Highway**, built from Agoo, La Union to Baguio, is not so frequently used as the others, but is also a very nice drive and takes one to the Marcos Park, a country club where golf and other sports are available. The gigantic head of ex-president Marcos which is the visual focal point of the park has long been a controversial monument.

Baguio City

There is a wealth of things to do in Baguio, much of it within walking distance of the city center. Refer to the map for locations of points mentioned. The first stop should be at the **DOT Offices** on Gov.Pack Road. Here you can get information about the Mountain Provinces and travel assistance and advice. The second storey of the adjacent building houses a **museum** with

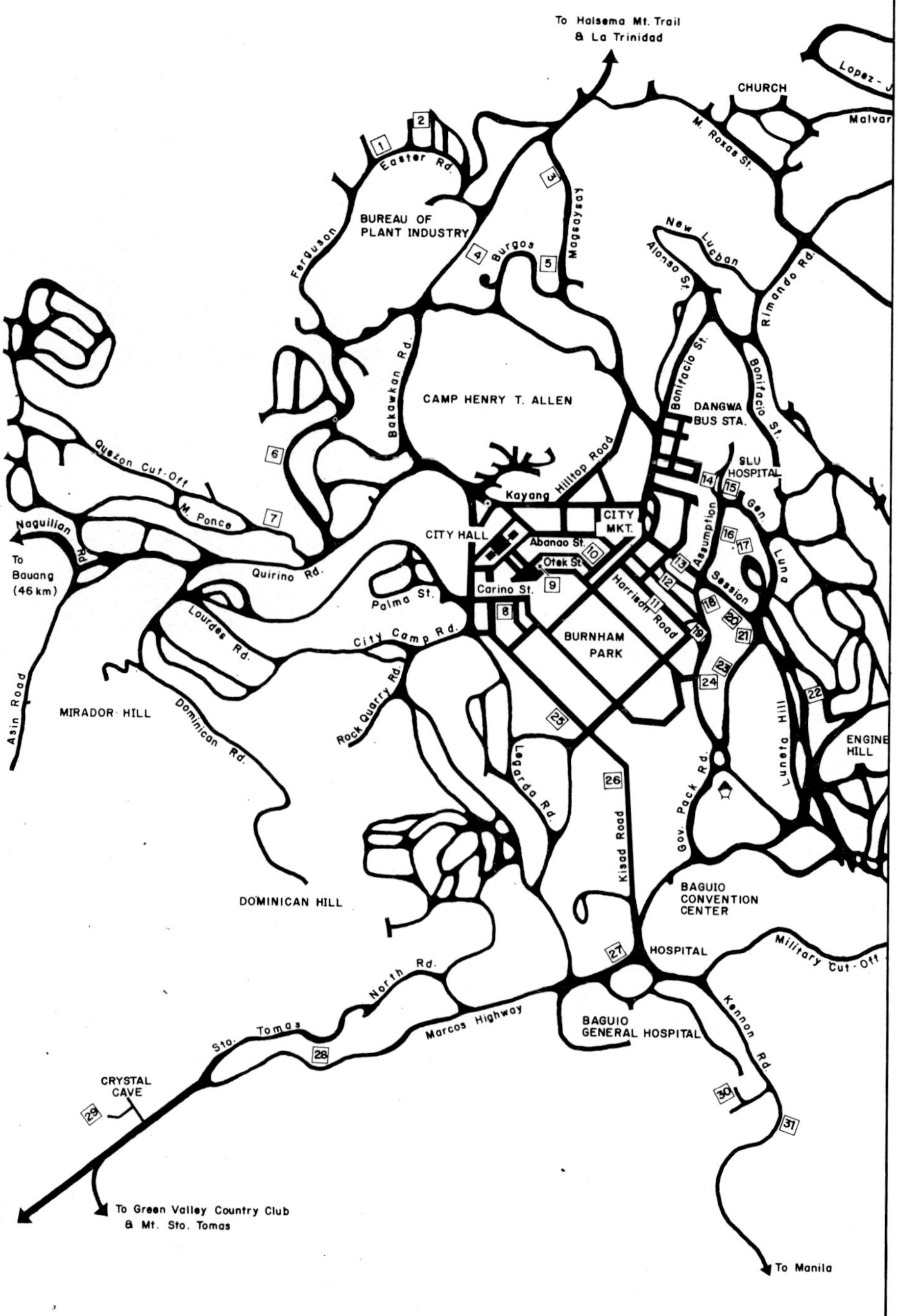
To Halsema Mt. Trail
& La Trinidad
CHURCH
Lopez-J
Malvar
M. Roxas St.
1
2
Easter Rd.
3
Magsaysay
Ferguson
BUREAU OF
PLANT INDUSTRY
4
Burgos
5
New Lucban
Alonso St.
Rimando Rd.
Bakawkan Rd.
CAMP HENRY T. ALLEN
Bonifacio St.
Bonifacio St.
DANGWA
BUS STA.
SLU
HOSPITAL
6
Quezon Cut-Off
Hilltop Road
Kayang
14
15
Gen.
M. Ponce
7
CITY
MKT.
Naguilian Rd.
To
Bauang
(46 km)
CITY HALL
Abanao St.
10
Assumption
16
17
Luna
Otek St.
9
Quirino Rd.
13
Carino St.
12
Session
Palma St.
Harrison Road
11
18
20
8
19
21
Lourdes Rd.
City Camp Rd.
BURNHAM
PARK
23
24
22
Asin Road
MIRADOR HILL
Rock Quarry Rd.
25
Dominican Rd.
Legarda Rd.
Gov. Pack Rd.
Luneta Hill
ENGINE
HILL
26
Kisad Road
BAGUIO
CONVENTION
CENTER
DOMINICAN HILL
27
HOSPITAL
Military Cut-Off
North Rd.
Marcos Highway
BAGUIO
GENERAL HOSPITAL
Kennon Rd.
Sto. Tomas
28
CRYSTAL
CAVE
29
30
31
To Agoo,
La Union
To Green Valley Country Club
& Mt. Sto. Tomas
To Manila

BAGUIO CITY

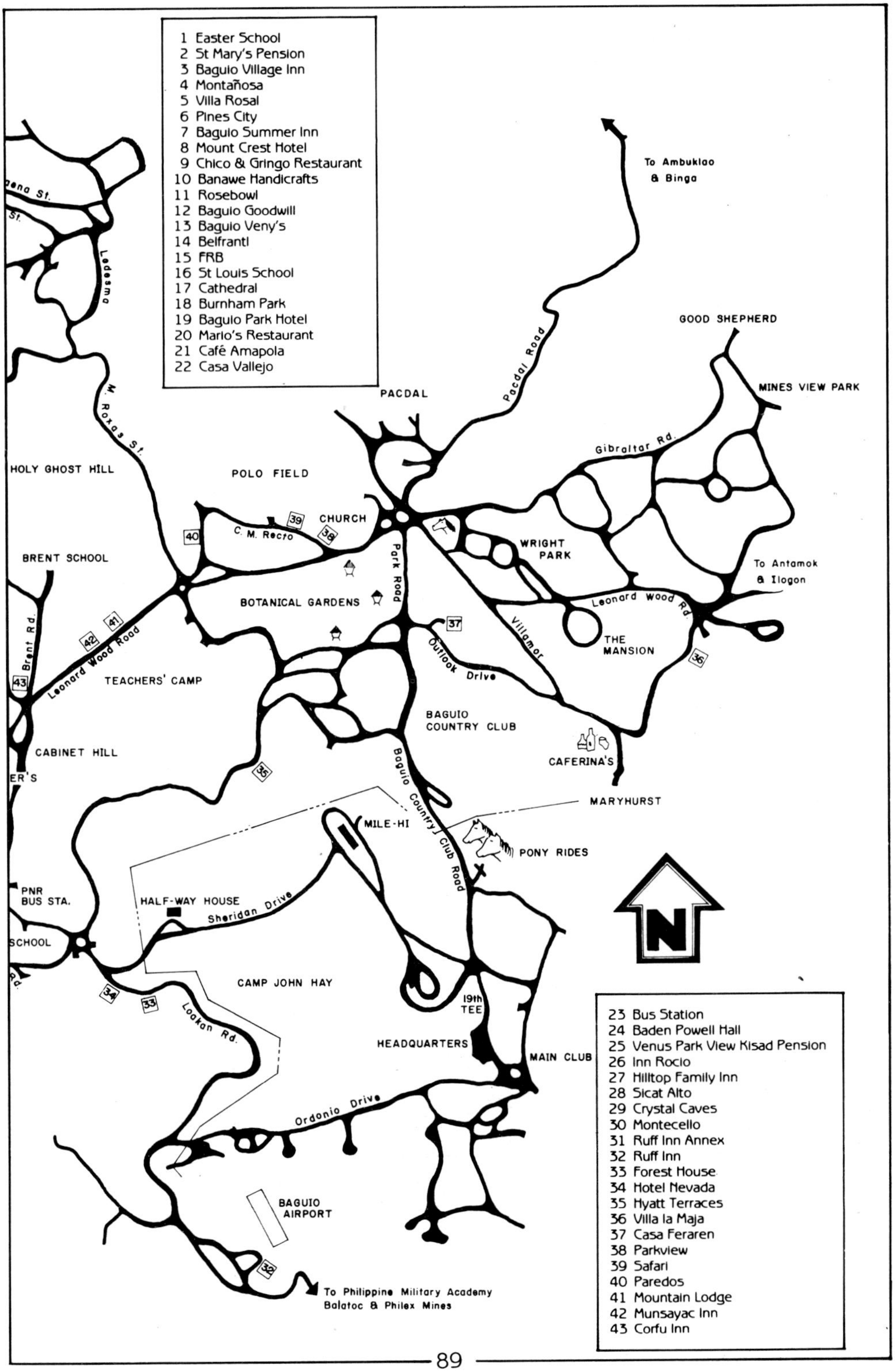
1 Easter School
2 St Mary's Pension
3 Baguio Village Inn
4 Montañosa
5 Villa Rosal
6 Pines City
7 Baguio Summer Inn
8 Mount Crest Hotel
9 Chico & Gringo Restaurant
10 Banawe Handicrafts
11 Rosebowl
12 Baguio Goodwill
13 Baguio Veny's
14 Belfranti
15 FRB
16 St Louis School
17 Cathedral
18 Burnham Park
19 Baguio Park Hotel
20 Mario's Restaurant
21 Café Amapola
22 Casa Vallejo
To Ambuklao
& Binga
Ledesma
M. Roxas St.
Pacdal Road
PACDAL
GOOD SHEPHERD
MINES VIEW PARK
Gibraltar Rd.
HOLY GHOST HILL
POLO FIELD
CHURCH
C. M. Recto
Park Road
WRIGHT
PARK
To Antamok
& Ilogon
BRENT SCHOOL
BOTANICAL GARDENS
Leonard Wood Rd.
Villamor
THE
MANSION
Brent Rd.
Leonard Wood Road
Outlook Drive
TEACHERS' CAMP
BAGUIO
COUNTRY CLUB
CABINET HILL
CAFERINA'S
Baguio Country Club Road
MARYHURST
MILE-HI
PONY RIDES
PNR
BUS STA.
HALF-WAY HOUSE
Sheridan Drive
SCHOOL
CAMP JOHN HAY
Loakan Rd.
19th
TEE
HEADQUARTERS
MAIN CLUB
Ordonio Drive
BAGUIO
AIRPORT
To Philippine Military Academy
Balatoc & Philex Mines
N
23 Bus Station
24 Baden Powell Hall
25 Venus Park View Kisad Pension
26 Inn Rocio
27 Hilltop Family Inn
28 Sicat Alto
29 Crystal Caves
30 Montecello
31 Ruff Inn Annex
32 Ruff Inn
33 Forest House
34 Hotel Nevada
35 Hyatt Terraces
36 Villa la Maja
37 Casa Feraren
38 Parkview
39 Safari
40 Paredos
41 Mountain Lodge
42 Munsayac Inn
43 Corfu Inn

artifacts from the tribes, all labelled and displayed nicely - an excellent introduction to the mountain area.

St Louis School's silver shop makes and sells items of sterling silver. Except on Sundays, you may watch delicate filigree work in progress at the workshop. The nearby **cathedral** is very attractive inside.

Burnham Park has long been the focus of activities. You may rent boats to row, paddle or sail in shallow Burnham Lake, and hire bicycles for use in the park. Bicycle boys are masters at the art of teaching children how to maneuver two-wheelers. A nearby children's playground provides further amusement.

During peak season, stalls from the nearby **city market** overflow into part of Burnham Park. A wide range of handicrafts are available in both places: woven fabric, blankets, knitwear, baskets, *bulol* (granary gods), silver, brass, jewelry, wood carvings, jars. Stroll into the vegetable section of the market (flowers and fruit available along the way) for a feast of greens and many other edibles. Carry- your-bag boys will pester you constantly until you hire one. Be very careful with your belongings in and about the market. If you are interested in woven goods, visit nearby Banawe Handicrafts also.

Baguio Vicinity (maps pp 88-89 & 93) Other points are accessible by taxi and/or jeepney. **Camp John Hay** has a golf course, tennis courts, skating, mini- golf, hiking trails. Designed as an R&R center for American military personnel in Asia, many of its facilities are open to the public.

Restaurants at the Halfway House and 19th Tee are open, steaks are sometimes good at the steakhouse (19th Tee), there's Bingo Friday nights at the Officer's Club, and pony rides outside the Country Club gate take riders into the area surrounding the camp.

Mines View Park has another collection of souvenir shops, and the nearby **Good Shepherd Convent** derives partial support for its assistance to unwed mothers by making and selling very good peanut brittle and jam. **Ceferina's Bamboo Crafts & Rattan Shop** is a good stop for handicrafts.

Backstrap weaving at the Easter School, Baguio

Wright Park is a nice place to stroll, or rent ponies for children.

The Mansion, the Philippine President's summer home, has gates designed to look like those of Buckingham Palace.

The **Botanical Gardens** is yet another collection of souvenir shops, plus some native houses which you may inspect. There are usually a few Igorots at the park posing for photos and expecting a peso for each snap. There is also a "Japanese cave" to investigate.

Easter School, run by the Episcopalian and Philippine Independent churches, has two weaving rooms. Women use the upright looms to produce colorful blankets on the entry floor. Downstairs the traditional mountain cloth is produced on back strap looms. The work is like a meditation, very peaceful to watch and listen to.

La Trinidad, Benguet's capital, has several points of interest. **Bell Temple** is where the area's large Chinese community practices an amalgam of Daoism and Christianity. You may request the priest to tell your fortune. **Narda's** produces very fine weavings and tapestries and items ranging from bags to dresses to linens. **La Trinidad market** is a smaller, and occasionally cheaper, version of Baguio market.

The ground floor of the **Provincial Capitol Building** has a good pictorial exhibit of provincial activities. The museum and gift shop across the driveway is open Mondays through Fridays. It has some antique articles of clothing and mining displays.

Three **mummies** from Kabayan are displayed in glass cases in the governor's office. You may view them if the governor isn't busy at the time. A century ago deceased mountain people were seated in a special chair and smoked for several days. The smoking and herbal treatment mummified the remains. This art has been lost with time, although some of the original burial practices are still extant.

Hikers will want to walk up **Mt Sto Tomas**. Start from the road beside Green Valley Country Club, and continue 7-8 km to the summit for good views all around. Mt Sto Tomas is a huge, soft mountain stretching almost to the shores of Lingayen Gulf. Much of it is soft limestone which slowly erodes, causing landslides and damage to roads.

Silver filigree, St Louis School, Baguio

The mountain is riddled with caves. Crystal Cave, just off the Sto Tomas Road, is accessible and fun for children.

Asin, a wood carvers' village, is down a rough road which exits from the Naguilian Road. Much of the carving is also available in the market, and is pretty routine, but occasionally you may find a good piece.

The town of Asin at the end of the road has a couple of mini-hydro projects and a hot springs resort.

Shoppers will want to poke into the Baguio, La Trinidad and Asin town markets, as well as stores in hotels and lodges, especially at the Terraces, Munsayac Inn (see the shop upstairs at the inn), as well as shops in the building adjacent to Baguio's market.

Good **golf** is available at Camp John Hay, where the steep course is designed to keep you in excellent shape (greens fees $10 weekends, $8 weekdays), at Marcos Park, an hour down the Marcos Highway (greens fees $4 weekends and $2.50 weekdays) and at Baguio Country Club, through a member.

Ambuklao & Binga, Pulog & Kabayan

Arrangements to tour **Ambuklao and Binga** dams can be made through the NPC offices in Baguio. Don't arrive during lunch hour, unless you're prepared to wait.

The drive to Ambuklao and Binga is lovely, although not very forested any more.

Mt Pulog, Luzon's loftiest peak, is an easy and enjoyable climb. Make arrangements with DOT for a guide recommendation. Allow 3-4 days, bring hiking gear, ground cloth, food.

Kabayan is known for the many mummies found in burial caves, along with skulls and bones ritually placed. Unfortunately many of the mummies have been stolen.

Sustenance in Baguio

Almost every hotel and lodge has a restaurant, and eating places in Baguio tend to come and go. Fast foods are readily available, Shakeys does the usual pizza, small restaurants serve an assortment of dishes at reasonable prices.

Delicious dining available at Mario's, great Caesar salad, linguini, fettucini, steaks, saté, and many other dishes, luncheon menus available also. Cafe Amapola, just up Session Rd, does some things very well, and you may enjoy them on the sidewalk tables or inside - the whole place is furnished with antiques. Wonderful baked mussels, marinated mussels, salads, native dishes, walnut pie, *kamote* (sweet potato) bread, much more, and folk music in the bar evenings. Julio's does reasonably well, is a bit pricy. American food available at the 19th Tee and Halfway House in Camp John Hay, steaks at the Steak House at the 19th Tee. Rose Bowl does good Chinese food; try Mexican food at Chico and the Gringo.

Good, inexpensive meals at the stalls known as Slaughter House on Magsaysay Blvd, just beyond the market.

For a real treat go to Forest House, by reservation only and you have to order a day in advance, tel 442-2624. It is most definitely worth the effort, everything prepared and cooked to perfection, served very well, a gourmet delight in a lovely old house.

Mountain Province

Mountain Province is at the center of the Cordilleras. It is inhabited by Bontoc people.

While Banawe's terraces are best known, and many feel are the most beautiful, Mountain Province is also extensively terraced.

Bontoc, the capital of Mountain Province, nestles deep in a valley at the confluence of two rivers which meet and form the mighty Chico. Because it is in a valley, Bontoc tends to be hotter and more humid than the surrounding highlands: one reason many travelers head for Sagada.

Traditional community patterns are maintained in many villages.

Traditional Bontoc houses have stone and/or grass walls and cogon roofs. Pigs live in holes in the ground near their owners' house.

In the past tribes had a community in which married couples and very young children lived together, older unmarried children lived in separate housing for boys and girls, houses were provided for the elderly and indigent, and special constructions were made for religious rites and for normal community necessities such as granaries, storage, etc.

Many people in Mountain Province object to having their photographs taken. Respect their wishes or risk unpleasant consequences.

Unfortunately many people, from children to the aged, expect gifts from visitors. Bring matches, trinkets, small items to give away and, if you are planning to stay overnight in a village, bring food to share. When venturing into the more remote areas, leave watches and valuables behind.

BAGUIO VICINITY

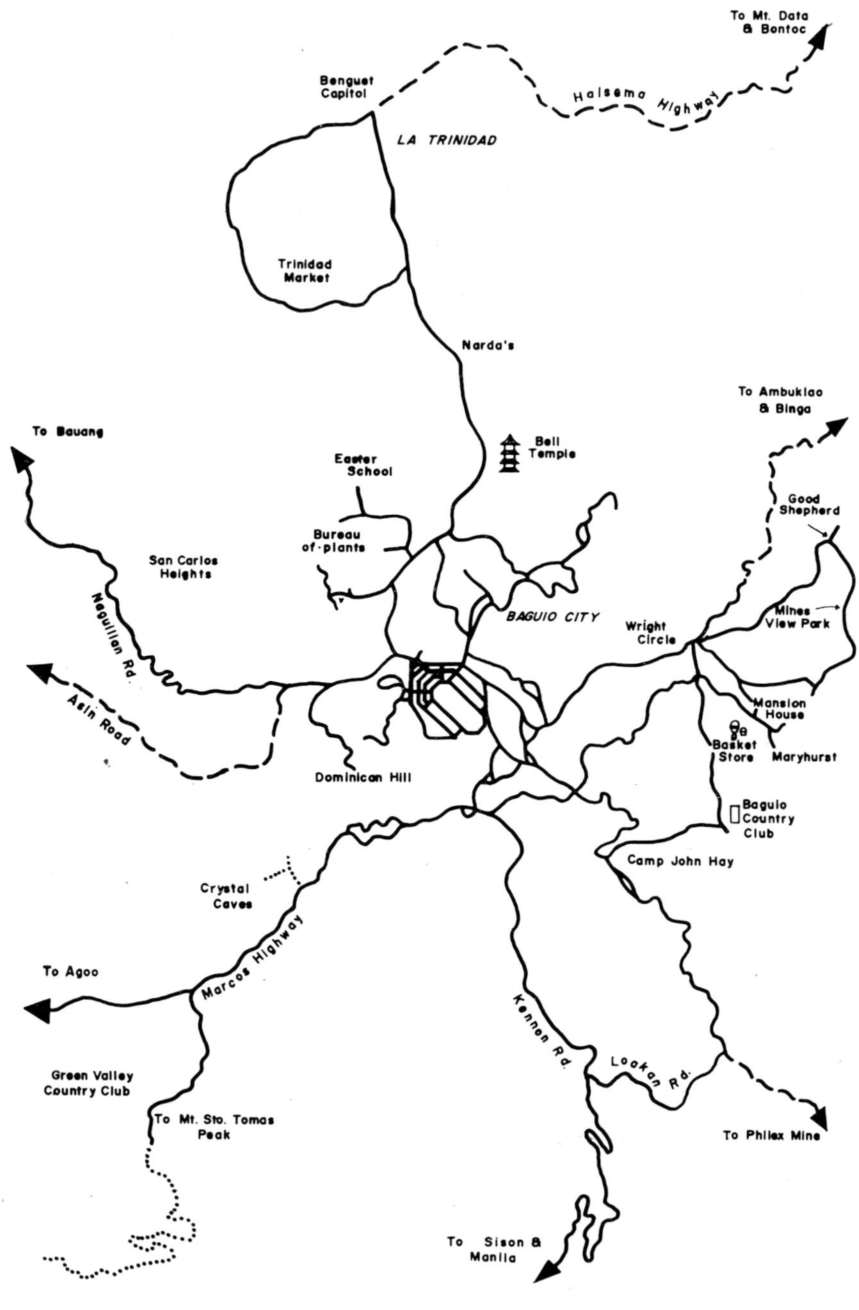

Sagada (map, p 96)

Sagada is 600 m and 18 km above Bontoc, cool (cold at Christmas), a whole different world. Food in Sagada is good and cheap. Most lodges do tasty meals. Julia's has a hearty, set vegetarian menu. Good meals at St Joseph's, Mapiyaaw, Daoa's and the Moon House, which is also a gathering place for drinks. Good, inexpensive meals at the Shamrock, another meeting place.

Unfortunately many visitors have come to "hang out", and not shown respect for the culture. Consequently ill feelings between the local people and travelers have occasionally arisen. Nevertheless, Sagada remains a very popular destination, with several good places to stay and eat and a weaving room, but the main activity is hiking out into the environs to see the terraces and falls and villages. Once you get away from the town itself, people are friendly.

Sagada area is riddled with caves, and caving is one of the main activities travelers come for. Many of the caves are burial places for residents' forebears, so treat the sites with respect - you never know when some skull's grandson is right beside you.

In the center of town, Christina Aben has a small, unobtrusive museum called **Ganduyan** (once Sagada's name), with antique artifacts. You may have to wait until it is open. Ask about items you would like to know more about.

Echo Valley is near Sagada center, past the church and Mt Calvary. Several burial caves, and a nice place to sit.

The **Sagada Weaving Shop**, on the road to Bontoc near Crystal Caves, is a good place to buy the beautiful, closely woven Bontoc cloth.

Matangkib Caves and Latang Underground River are 10 min from the town center, just past Sagada Weaving. The caves are off to the right, contain some burials and some pretty sparkly formations. Bring torches, and a guide if you want to explore the underground river.

Bokong Falls are close to Sagada, a 25-min walk through terraces to a small

Traditional Bontoc houses; Sagada, Mt Province

Terracing along the road to Sagada

falls and pool where you may swim and relax.

Masferré's Studio (see Bontoc) has a branch in Sagada, at the corner of the roads to Banga-an and Bontoc.

There are literally dozens of hikes you may do from and about Sagada, and many lodging houses have maps with activities painted on the walls. Because many paths close to town criss-cross, you will have to ask residents for directions from time to time.

There are several caves you may investigate. **Lumiang Cave**, a 30-min walk, past Ambasing, has many burials. Nearby **Sumaging**, or **Latipan**, is for spelunkers. On the way you will walk through some interesting limestone formations and past the **hanging coffins**, perched high on a rock face.

The beautiful **Keltepan Terraces** are a 2½ km walk from the Bontoc road, about 4½ km along the way to Bontoc.

Fedilisan is an interesting village 3 hrs from Sagada, or you could take the jeepney to Banga-an and hike 30 min downhill from there. Fedilisan Falls is a further 30 min. The last part entails some scrambling over rocks and it would be helpful to have a guide. Once there you may be ready for a refreshing swim in the pool while water cascades down from above. Another, even taller waterfall is accessible along a trail which crosses the river downstream, but it is not safe to swim at this one. Only do this trip in groups - do not go alone for security reasons.

Hikers with an interest in the ancient ways here will want to head for Agawa, Besao by jeepney, then take the 40-min walk to **Gueday** where there is a primitive Stonehenge-like arrangement of rocks which once was used to tell when planting should begin. Even if you're not interested in **stone calendars**, the walk is lovely and you pass coffins placed high into precipitous rock faces. Only the months of January through March are dry here - expect showers at other times. In April the men of Gueday mill sugar cane using manual presses.

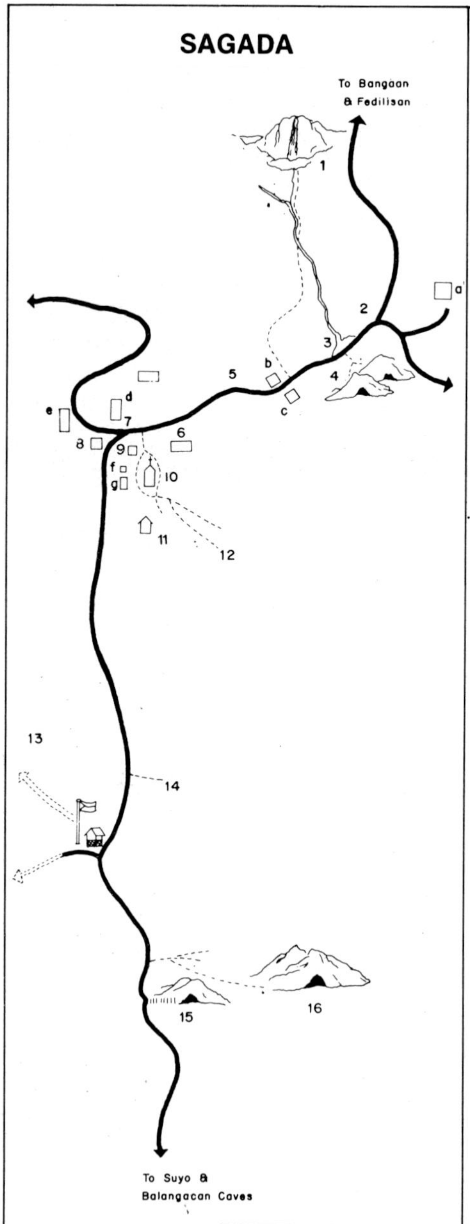

1 Bokong Falls & Pool
2 Masferré's Studio
3 Latang Underground River
4 Matangkib Cave
5 Sagada Weavers
6 Hospital
7 Ganduyan & Christina's Store
8 Town Hall
9 Market
10 Church
11 School with Mural
12 Echo Valley
13 Vegetable fields
14 Hanging Coffins
15 Lumiang Cave
16 Sumaging Cave

a Mapiya-aw Sagada Pension
b Traveler's Inn
c Cangbay's Place
d St Joseph's
e Daoa's Sagada Pension
f Shamrock Café
g Julia's
h Moon House

Bontoc (map p 97)

The high-points of a visit to Bontoc are the Bontoc Museum and Masferre's studio.

The **Bontoc Museum**, founded by the Belgian Sister Basil Gekiere, houses a collection authentic artifacts and photos from the mountain tribes, all well labelled and displayed.

Eduardo Masferré is a Spanish *mestizo* who has lived and worked in Bontoc for over 75 years. A talented, avid photographer, Mr Masferre spent 50 years documenting Mountain life with his camera, and has a large collection of excellent black and whites. Prints of his work are available at his studio, along with a few artifacts and maps.

Handicrafts are also available at Basco's Antiques, the Tourist Information Center and other shops, but perhaps the most interesting collection is at the Kalinga Information Center.

You may see weavers at the All Saints Elementary School, or in **Samoki Village**, where simple pottery, patted together and fired in burning rice straw, is also made.

Food is available in Bontoc at Pines Kitchenette and other inns.

North of Bontoc

In the past many travellers went north from Bontoc to Tucucan to see the "monkey bridge", a precarious pine sapling affair over the Chico River. A couple of years ago it was replaced with a much safer construction, which is of little interest.

Sadanga is almost at the Kalinga border, a 26 km (2-hr) ride through lovely terracing. There is a hot spring nearby. **Sacasacan** is a 30 min hike from the Sadanga junction, and **Anabel** is a 25-min hike across the Chico River. Because of the proximity to Kalinga you should ask about the peace and order situation in this area before visiting.

West of Bontoc

Hikers may be interested in heading into the mountains above Bontoc to go to Malegkong or Mainit Hot Springs.

Malegkong Village is a 3 to 4-hr hike from Bontoc (you may also hire a jeepney) and is surrounded by attractive terraces. Beautiful views of Bontoc from the road to Malegkong.

Mainit Village is so named for its hot springs, and you may also watch gold panning. Mainit is a 4 to 5-hr hike from Bontoc, or you may catch the jeepney to Guinaang and then have a ½-hr hike to Mainit.

Between Bontoc and Baguio

The drive from Baguio to Bontoc is a very scenic but rough 10-hr bounce, at least until the "highway" is repaired. It often hugs the walls high above the river, giving spectacular views of terracing and mountain life along the way. If you take public transport you will find yourself whizzing by these scenes and around corners at amazing speed, so it is well worth the money to hire a vehicle if you can afford to do so.

Alab, 9 km south of Bontoc, is a pretty riverside village. You may see panning in the river. There is a 3-hr climb to Ganga, above the village and past burial caves to petroglyphs, ancient writings that have not been decyphered. You will need a knowledgeable guide.

Balili, 12 km south of Bontoc and a short hike into the mountains, is known for jewelry making.

Mt Data Lodge, which is about two thirds of the way from Baguio, nestles in the few pines remaining from a once extensive forest. It is still a nice place to stop for an evening rest, and they sometimes have evening cultural shows put on by residents. It is interesting to compare the dances and

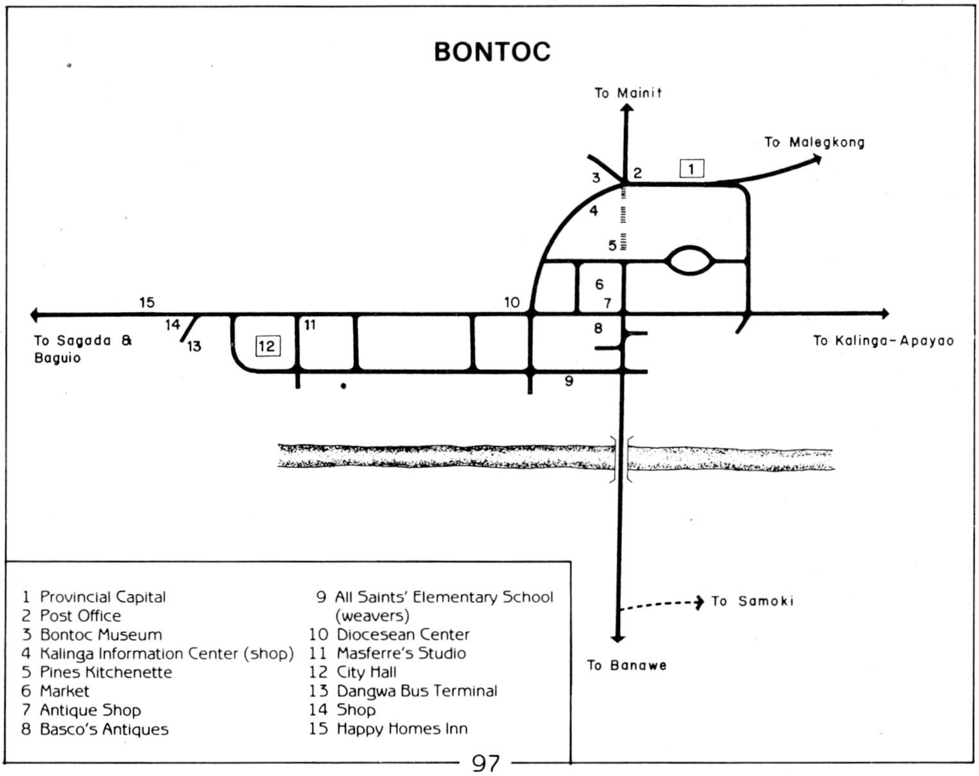

Viewpoint, Banawe

rituals of the Bontocs of this area with those presented by the Ifugao at the Banawe Hotel.

Bontoc to Banawe

The delightful 2 hr (50 km) trip to Banawe passes impressive terracing and even goes through a bit of remaining forest - a real treat. **Bay-yo**, which is 18 km along the road to Banawe, has impressive, fortress-like terrace walls, then the road continues to rise into forest and the check-point at the border. From here you descend, with a few more rises, to Banawe.

From Manila, the easiest access route to Banawe is through the Cagayan Valley (see p 104).

Banawe & Ifugao

Banawe's rice terraces are indeed both beautiful and amazing. The Ifugao labored for several centuries, carving terraces out of the mountains, carrying rocks, building walls to make the terraces permanent, perfecting the art of wall-building and irrigation. Ifugao houses, built of cogon and wood, stand high on stilts in village clusters among the terraces. Village women weave under the houses, the blacksmith makes jewelry, and, these days, products for tourists also.

Although Banawe has become a clutch of boxy tin buildings, the surrounding villages retain their timeless ways. Unlike many Ifugao areas which have exchanged their ancient ways for more modern ones, the people of Banawe retain their customs. They have learned to keep their ways to themselves, having been subjected to lowlanders' scorn and Spanish lectures about paganism. Many people feel that the continuing practice of ritual sacrifice keeps practitioners poor, but it is this adherence to the old ways which gives Banawe a special atmosphere to complement the special scenery.

Banawe

The town itself (map p 100) is nothing special, but there are numerous shops with woven goods, baskets, carvings.

H Ottley Beyer, the anthropologist whose studies made Banawe and the Ifugao culture known to the outside world, worked, lived and died here, becoming very much a part of the culture he studied. His bones are kept, Ifugao-style, wrapped in a blanket under a special house behind the Municipal Hall.

When the Banawe Hotel has enough guests, a **cultural performance** is arranged. Ifugaos from nearby villages come to the hotel. Their native costume and some artifacts are described and demonstrated. Some of their dances, rituals and songs are portrayed. The whole presentation is good precisely because it is the real thing, not a professionalized, choreographed show.

Banawe has great, and very inexpensive eating. Try Las Vegas, at the market, the Terrace, and Stairway Lodge and Halfway House.

Banawe is a hiker's paradise. You can walk for minutes, hours or days, depending upon your desires, but it presents problems to those with acrophobia, for much of the hiking is along terrace edges.

It is easiest to get around if you have a guide, and the children here are very eager to offer their services - for as high a fee as they think they can get. Ask at your hotel what a fair rate should be, and have the rate agreed upon before you go off with the guide.

Tam-an, down steep steps behind the Banawe Hotel, has some weavings and handicrafts. If your are a good walker, you may continue through old Tam An, across terraces to **Poitan**. It is somewhat easier to take the 1½ km walk along the road through town.

Poitan has weavers, carvers, blacksmiths and a special stone which is idolized, plus a dug-in area where the village elders gather to discuss village problems. The nearby waterfall is also respected as a spiritual place, and a rock formation part way up the fall looks like a rice god from certain angles.

Matang-lag and Bocus are on the other side of Moyoyao road from Poitan. The Abul family of Matang-lag make bronze fertility, good luck and tribal symbols, *bulol* (rice gods) and other popular items of bronze through the lost wax process. A model of each item is first made in wax, and the wax surrounded by clay. Then molten bronze is poured in, the wax melts and runs out (hence is "lost"), the bronze hardens and becomes a unique item. There are several houses with smiths, the Abuls having the best quality and highest prices.

You may continue from Matang-lag to **Bocus** (or vice versa) to see weavers and carvers. One area of Bocus has several houses decorated with a profusion of skulls from sacrificed water buffalo and other animals. Mine and Josef Blas live in lower Bocus. Joseph is a very talented wood carver whose work is unique. He and his wife give good explanations of their works.

Banawe's **viewpoint** is 4 km along the road to Bontoc, a spectacular spot where natives come dressed in full regalia and expect payment for each photo taken.

Banawe's famous terraces

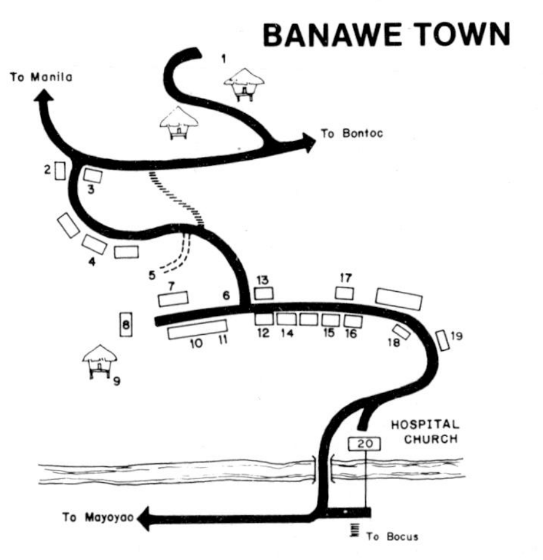

1 Banawe View Lodge
2 Adespa Lodge
3 Historical marker; bus stop
4 Basket shops
5 Folk house
6 Market
7 Happy Homes Inn
8 Town Hall
9 Beyer's Tomb
10 Las Vegas
11 Sanafe Lodge
12 Valgreg
13 Wonder Lodge
14 Green View Lodge
15 Stairway Lodge
16 Halfway House
17 Cozy Nook
18 Lodge
19 Traveller's Inn
20 Clinic

Guihob Natural Pool is 4½ along the road to Mayoyao, a good place to stop and bathe on the way back from Batad. The pool is just off the road.

Batad Village nestles at the foot of steep terracing placed on a rock face so that it resembles an amphitheater. To get there you may hire a jeepney. From the Banawe-Mayoyao road you walk (unless the jeep will take you) up to the "saddle", from where a trail continues to downhill Batad - in all, a steep 4 km walk: allow 2-3 hours, each way.

On the outskirts of the village it is useful to accept the services of a guide. Set prices in advance, don't pay until you're through. There is a waterfall beyond town. Coffee, soft drinks, beer are available at the saddle and Batad's viewpoint. There are 2-3 primitive places where you could stay over night. Bring food if you are at all concerned about your diet, and drink only boiled water.

Banga-an is a very picturesque village 2 km further along Mayoyao road. Between March and May you can often see rainbows in the sunset over the terraces from

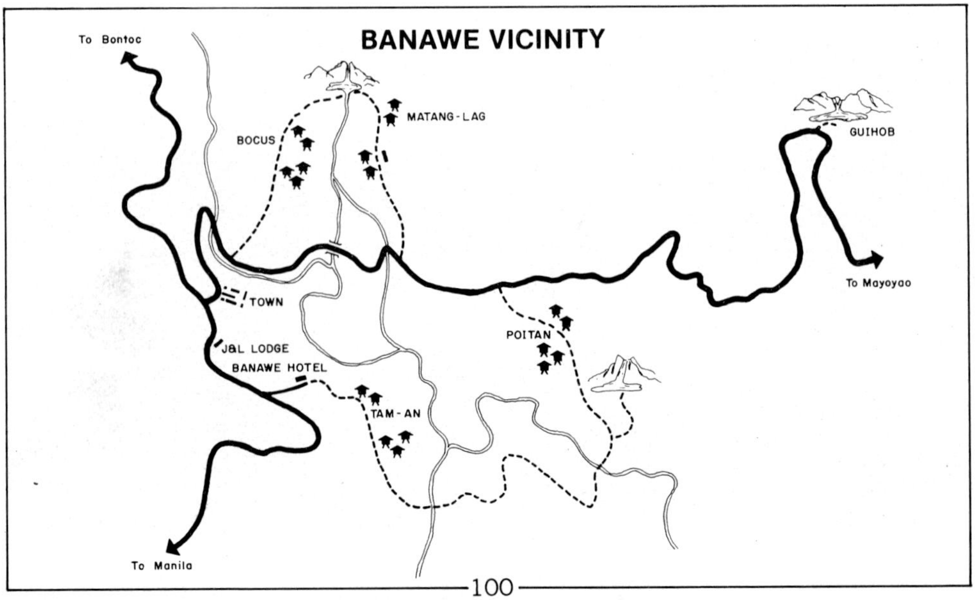

Banga-an viewpoint.

Mayoyao is a long but lovely 3-hr ride from Banawe, on a road which dips and climbs among terraces and hills, through forests and villages. You may stay overnight at Traveller's Lodge, or, if you hire a vehicle, do the trip in a day. Houses in Mayoyao have a huge roofs, and are different from those of Banawe; the whole town is more spread out, neater.

Trekking in the area of Banawe is fine, as long as you are prepared for very primitive sanitary facilities. Water may need treating. Bring food. Arrange for a guide who knows the area and is liked, as he can accompany you to villages for the nights. Bring gifts - matches, candies, vitamins, etc for the villagers who will host you along the way. And take your guide's advice should he declare any areas unsafe to visit.

The Ifugao Calendar

Ifugao Month	Approx Equiv	Events	Climate
Amda-doyong	Jan	beginning of planting season	cold; sometimes rainy
Litong	Feb	celebration of Ulpi, thanksgiving rituals; men repair terraces; women transplant rice	foggy mornings; clear; mornings
Bisbis Luya Oeeh	Mar April May		sunny, clear summer days
Ludo	June	beginning of harvest season	clear mornings; rainy afternoons
Bacaco	July	performance of Apuy, harvest rites; Bulol (rice god statues) are bathed with the blood of sacrificial animals	unpredictable; rainy
Et-eti Manaba	Aug Sept	performance of Gotod, rites for ancestors	rainy, but may clear in the afternoons
Chawe Chattu Ocar	Oct Nov Dec	repair of terraces; sowing of rice seedlings	cold; sometimes rainy

*this is the tradional calendar used when one rice crop is harvested per year. New strains of fast maturing rice have allowed two crops per year in some areas, such as the vicinities of Banawe and Bontoc, where the first crop may harvested in April and May, and another planted to be harvested in August and September.

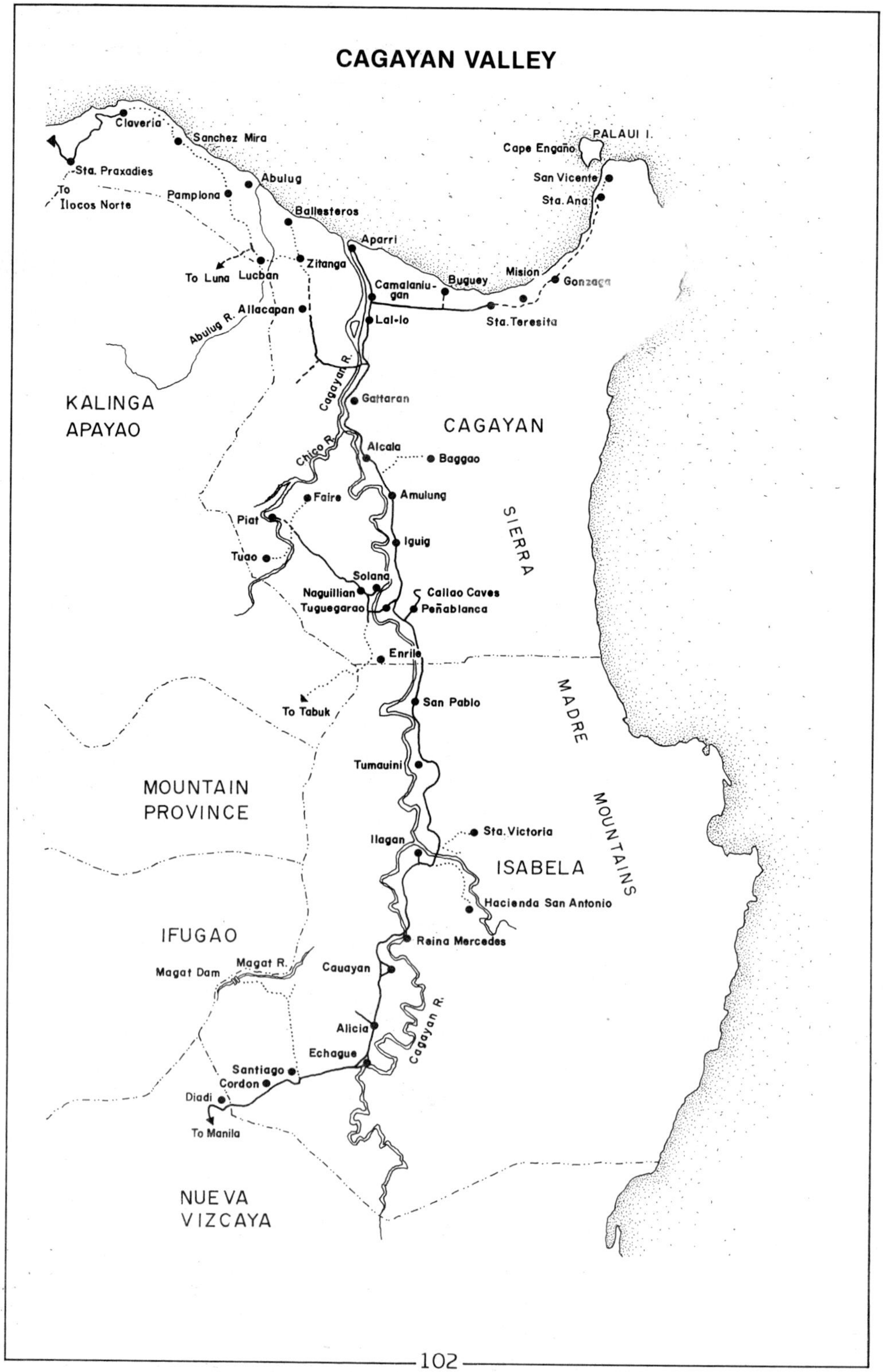
CAGAYAN VALLEY
Claveria
Sanchez Mira
Sta. Praxadies
To Ilocos Norte
Pamplona
Abulug
Ballesteros
Aparri
Zitanga
To Luna
Lucban
Allacapan
Abulug R.
Camalaniu-gan
Buguey
Mision
Gonzaga
Sta. Teresita
Lal-lo
PALAUI I.
Cape Engaño
San Vicente
Sta. Ana
KALINGA APAYAO
Cagayan R.
Gattaran
CAGAYAN
Chico R.
Alcala
Baggao
Amulung
Faire
Piat
Tuao
Iguig
SIERRA
Solana
Naguillian
Tuguegarao
Callao Caves
Peñablanca
Enrile
To Tabuk
San Pablo
MADRE
Tumauini
MOUNTAIN PROVINCE
MOUNTAINS
Sta. Victoria
Ilagan
ISABELA
Hacienda San Antonio
IFUGAO
Reina Mercedes
Magat R.
Magat Dam
Cauayan
Alicia
Cagayan R.
Echague
Santiago
Cordon
Diadi
To Manila
NUEVA VIZCAYA

Cagayan Valley

Callao Cave, Penablanca, Cagayan

The Cagayan Valley

access: 1 hr by air, 8 hrs by land from Manila, p 267
climate: driest Feb-June; coolest Nov-Feb
to do: museums, churches, forge, caves, sports fishing, untraveled areas, swim
facilities: moderate hotels, lodges, Callao Caves resort, places to eat, p 283

The Cagayan Valley isn't a heavily touristed area, but it is a very interesting one, with an assortment of historic and scenic spots to see, and things to do ranging from hiking, swimming and fishing to visiting churches of architectural and religious significance. It is also the gateway to the famous Banawe Rice Terraces.

Please refer to p 99 for Banawe, which is more easily accessed by land from Manila than from Baguio owing to the poor condition of the mountain roads. Hence information about the lower Cagayan Valley will interest travelers taking this route to the mountains.

The **Cagayan River** is the Philippines' mightiest watercourse. Small streams originating from the Balete Pass, the Cordillera Centrale and Caraballo Sur, which comprise Luzon's central mountain ranges, and the Sierra Madre which line the western coast, meet other streams and rivers and eventually flow into the Babuyan Channel at the north of Luzon. By the time it emerges at Aparri, the mighty Cagayan is truly an impressive expanse of water. The first time I stood at its mouth I thought the distant land I sighted was an island. Later I realized it was the river's opposite bank.

The Balete Pass

Both the Pampanga and Cagayan River Valleys trace part of their origins to the Balete (Dalton) Pass, a rugged piece of terrain where a spur of the Caraballo Sur reaches out and joins the Sierra Mádre. This pass long prevented commerce and contact between the peoples of the two valleys, and they developed different cultures, different dialects. Even today, with the Pan-Philippine Highway breaching the pass, it is a long winding pull to the top.

Because of its strategic importance as the only access between the two valleys, the pass was the scene of much bloody fighting during the final stages of WW II. Japanese soldiers tried to hold their positions while Filipinos and Americans determined to dislodge them. By the close of hostilities, the blood of almost ten thousand combatants mingled with the soil. White markers commemorating their sacrifice stand by the road's highest point, with good views into the headlands of both valleys and snack stands nearby.

Hiking trails cut through the hills on the ascent to the Cagayan Valley. A nearby BFD (Forestry) Office can give information to those interested in exploring the trails.

Perez Park, on the descent, is a good place to stop for information and a picnic under a lovely balete tree. If you wish to spend a night, continue to **Sta Fe**, where there are a few basic roadside lodges and restaurants.

Stalls full of interesting baskets line the roadside in Sta Fe. Most wares are from the Cagayan Valley and the Cordillera tribes, but pieces from all over the country manage somehow to find their way here. Hammocks, brooms, bread baskets, waste baskets, chicken baskets, chairs, cradles, wallets, bags, the assortment seems endless. Some of the quality is excellent.

Salt Hills

Salinas Salt Dome is a short (20 min by car, one way) side trip from **Bambang**, Nueva Vizcaya. Turn west in the center of Bambang, cross a bridge and continue through fields and pastures bordered by wide flat mesas on the left and steep hills on the right, very pretty country indeed. After spotting the dome, take your second right, through **Salinas** barrio and continue 1½ km uphill to a parking area. A brief walk through some trees brings you to a large white dome that stands out distinctly from the surrounding green flora and grey rocks around.

Mineral rich water percolates up, depositing sparkling white precipitate and constantly enlarging the dome. Climb the dome to see the springs and great views of the valley below. Knock on the surface; it's hollow. Turn around and look uphill to find a succession of higher mounds. The springs once formed these hills, then found lower exits. When their springs ceased to flow, the older domes oxidized grey and now blend in with the rest of the landscape.

During the first week of August Negritoes come down from the hills to celebrate **Bayombong**'s fiesta. They dance in front of the church and around the houses, re-enacting the welcome originally accorded the patron saint. There are two or three mountainside resorts outside Bayombong - Villa Luz, Villa Margharita among them. They are off-the-beaten-track get-aways.

If you like *kaimito* (star apples) and yellow *kamote* (yam), stop at the roadside stalls in barrio Tuao Norte. A few km further the highway splits, the left spur rising into Bagabag, the mountains, to Ifugao Province, Banawe and beyond.

Magat Dam

The right fork rises slightly through Diadi, past a reforestation area, then descends into Isabela, through Cordon to Santiago. Green View Lodge, along the highway north of **Santiago**, offers fair accommodation and meals. A dusty road goes 26 km west from Santiago to the Magat River, where an impressive irrigation dam provides water for farms, some electricity and fantastic views. The immensity of the dam gives the feeling of the great power nature can provide.

Continue through **Alicia**, pausing to see its pretty church, and through Cauayan. The airstrip is outside of **Cauayan**, and there are several hotels which cater to traveling businessmen. The Isabela Hotel, north of town on the highway, looks nice and appears to be the best of them. Continue past Reina Mercedes to Ilagan, which also has a few basic lodging places.

Sta Victoria Caves & Hacienda San Antonio

Fuyot Springs National Park has over a dozen caves, lots of mosquitoes and is a malaria area. Park land was donated to the government in the hopes that its caves and springs would be preserved for posterity. However, the lone forester in charge cannot keep squatters from encroaching, and *kaingeros* are fast reducing the park forest to farms, while nearby logging concerns eat away at more remote forest areas. Nevertheless, the caves are very nice.

Mr Eugenio Ansa, whose father gave Fuyot to the government, lives near Sta Victoria. Contact him at his office in the Isabela Electric Cooperative, Ilagan, if you would like to make arrangements to visit the caves. Use plenty of bug spray and cover up well.

To get to the caves, turn east 10 km above Ilagan. 1 km later bear left beside a logging company and slightly right at the next junction. One half km further there is a village. Ask for Mr Florendo, the officer in charge of the park, and see if he can accompany you to the caves or if he can give you a guide.

A short walk from the end of the trail through woods brings you to the main cave, which has its formations intact.

The **Hacienda San Antonio** is an old Spanish estate owned by Tabacalera, the tobacco corporation. Its antique furnishings have been removed, but the magnificent old main building remains, with lovely views from the rear verandah across fields which now belong to the farmers.

Permission to enter the hacienda may be gained with the help of Mr Ansa, who should be contacted in advance of your visit.

Salinas, Nueva Vizcaya

Tumauini & San Pablo

The long cemented road between Ilagan and Tuguegarao winds gently through farms and over rivers. Tobacco grown in the Cagayan Valley is used for cigars. When mature, it is picked and hung to dry, but not smoked in kilns, as Philippine Virginia tobacco of the western Ilocos provinces.

Tumauini is 30 km north of Ilagan. You need to get off the highway a block or two to see its unique 18th century church, one of the most beautiful in the Philippines. The bell tower is round, with wedding-cake decor around its exterior. The edifice and extensive plaza walls repeat and emphasize the motif. Look closely. The raised designs were baked onto the bricks before the church was built, a feat requiring much forethought. The current priest is doing an excellent job of restoring the inside of the church in keeping with its exterior.

24 km further north the highway passes **San Pablo**, a small community with the remnants of a large, once elegant church that may have rivaled Tumauini in beauty. Because the bricks used to build San Pablo church are not as highly fired as those used in Tumauini's, it is assumed that San Pablo is the older structure.

A cyclone destroyed the church several years ago, and the priest is gradually covering more and more of the ruins with GI sheeting so his parishioners have a place to worship.

There are lots of opportunities for great pictures, and do climb the bell tower for views across the valley and farms below.

Carabao Milk and Bolos

Catingtingan is a village of grass huts on the left just before the Cagayan border. Its inhabitants were displaced from the mountains by the troubles there.

Once we stopped to picnic nearby and struck up a conversation with Purissima Ruiz, a petite woman who often sits by the road and sells *carabao* milk. She said her children were small because she could not afford to buy vitamins for them. She wished she could afford to send them all through school, and do something about birth control so she didn't have any more.

Although we decided that her children's stature was largely hereditary, we bought some vitamins and gave them to her the next time we came by. She was very grateful, and we met her husband, a carpenter, and came away with presents of milk.

Just before the next large bridge a dirt road goes west. Follow it if you would like to go to **Barrio Larion Baho** and see the forges where knives, bolos, axes and some decorative pieces are made. The first time I came here we purchased so many things that my car was armed to the hilt by the time we left.

Callao Caves

Beyond the bridge, the road divides. The right fork goes to **Peñablanca** and the Callao Caves. There are cottages at the cave area, and a new dormitory built by ex-governor Justiniano Cortez. The dorm has 2 bunk rooms, as well as several individual rooms which can sleep 2-4 people, is ideally located on a hill, a great place to stay. Ask at the governor's office. You may bring food or arrange for it at the small store at the bottom of the Peñablanca resort's driveway.

Years ago the caves area was inhabited by the wonderful *kalaw*, or hornbill. But, as more and more people came to farm and cut the forest, the birds retreated inland and no longer visit the area. When the Spanish came they hispanicized the spelling, from kalaw to callao, but the original pronunciation remains.

The main cave is a short *banca* trip across the river, then a good puff up about 250 steps. Ex-governor Dupaya removed formations from the huge first chamber to accommodate a chapel. Stroll on through the 7 chambers, and ask the caretaker to turn on the lights in the 1st chamber.

When Teddy Roosevelt was Governor of the Philippines he visited Callao. He arrived on horseback, then scaled the steep hillside clinging to roots and vines to get to the mouth of the cave.

Nearby there are other caves of interest to spelunkers and those with exploratory urges. Some have yielded very ancient remains.

Take a *banca* upriver past **Mororan**, a place where water showers into the river from an underground stream in the cliff above. Relax on a small white beach and stay for sunset when the bats stream out of a cave high on the cliffs. They hunt insects at night and return individually to roost in the morning. A good swimmer could easily float back downstream to the cottage area.

A hundred meters or so further upstream fishermen dig trenches in a rocky river bend, and create traps for *ipon*, the tiny fish fry that are making their way upstream. Because they hug the river's rocky edge

Alcala, Cagayan

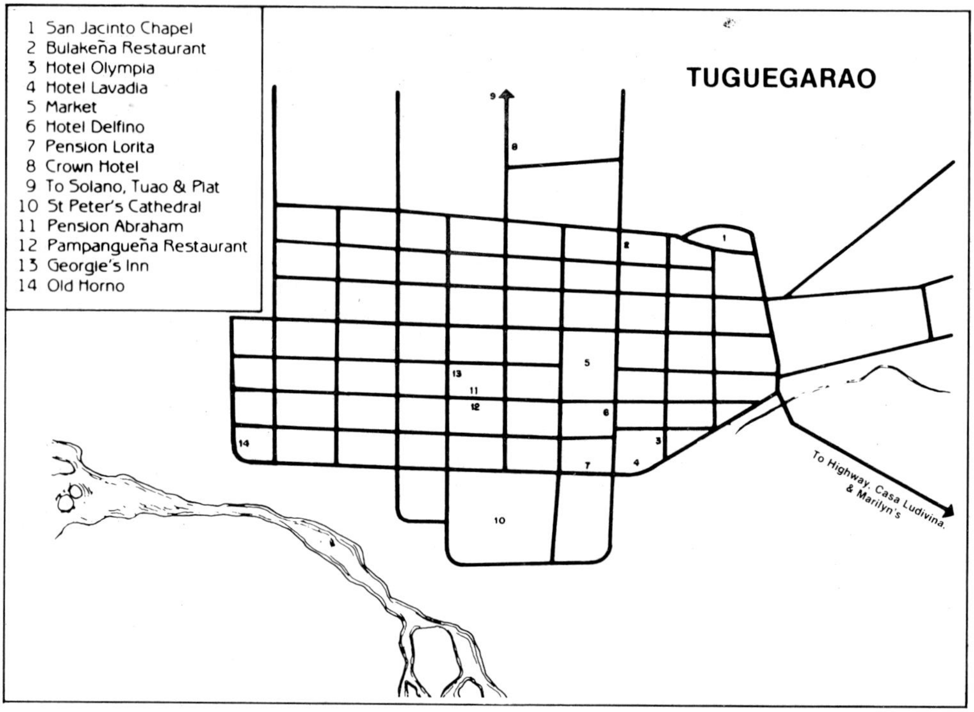

they swim up the trenches. Fishermen construct tiny dams and channel the fish into banana trunk tubes. The swift current washes the fish into collecting cans.

Try these for a meal, as well as *mori*, the tiny hatchlings caught in the Cagayan River and fried in omelettes. Both delicacies are seasonal.

Capital Sights

Cagayan's Provincial Capital is on the highway just north of the junction with the road to Peñablanca. Visit the site to arrange for accommodation at the caves, and to see the museums.

The **Provincial Museum** houses a collection of Spanish-era religious artifacts, archaeological finds, and a display of the tribes of the Cagayan Valley. A small shop on the first floor sells baskets and other articles made by some of the Valley's minorities. The Aeta basketry is especially attractive.

A branch of the **National Museum** nestles behind the building opposite the Provincial Museum. It houses a display of some of the geological and archaeological remains found in the valley, arranged so that they explain the area's history. A million years ago the area was inhabited by pygmy elephants, rhinoceroses and other now extinct fauna and flora.

Tuguegarao

Tuguegarao is a busy city, humming with commerce and with students who come from all over the valley to attend colleges. Except for the cathedral, the adjacent ruins and the remains of the Old Horno (kiln) beside the Cagayan River, the architecture isn't interesting. During Spanish times, bricks for all the valley's churches and other buildings were baked in the Old Horno.

Piat and Tuao

Religious folk will want to go through

Tuguegarao and continue east to Piat. Our Lady of Piat is attributed miraculous powers and attracts thousands of visitors annually.

The image came to the East from Acapulco and first went to Macao, then arrived in Lal-lo in 1604. In 1630 she was evacuated to Piat, and the warlike Ytawes people in the vicinity immediately became peaceful, a feat with which she is credited.

Jeepneys leave for Piat from a corner near the Crown Lodge.

Tuao, another pretty town, lies across the Chico River. There is now a bridge, but 3 years ago access was by ferry. I arrived in my Toyota station wagon to have a look at the river, with no intention of going across. But the ferry operators didn't get many tourists. Four American women were indeed rarities. They decided we should take their ferry. We acquiesced. The wagon got on with a jeepney, and we were off to the other side. We drove the few km to Tuao, looked at the pretty cemetery. The priest came for a chat as we looked at the church, and soon we were surrounded by school children who spoke very good English.

Then we remembered that the ferry made its last trip before 5 o'clock, and hurried back to the river.

We arrived to find a huge dump truck already on board. Because the proper ferry had been washed away in a storm, the current construction consisted of 3 large *bancas* with planks across their decks, the whole powered by 2 outboard motors. One dump truck appeared to be quite sufficient load for this vehicle. I told the ferry people we'd wait for the next trip. They told us we could do this trip. We didn't like that idea, but neither did we want to be left in Tuao for the night.

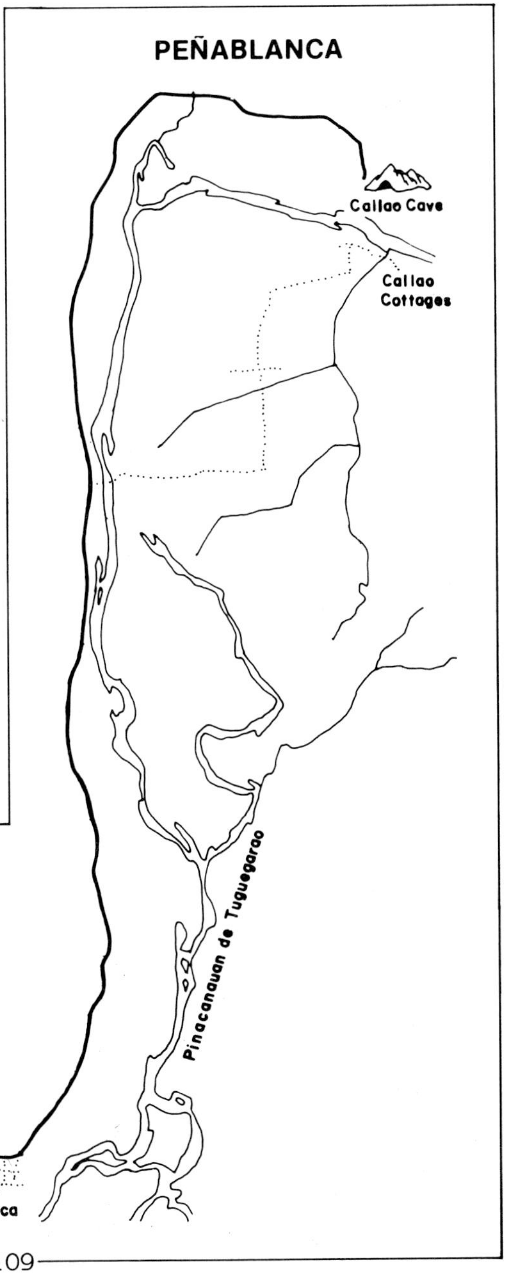
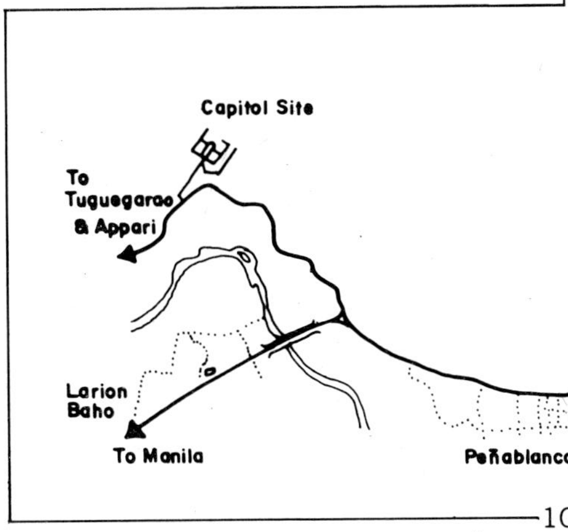

So, with the wagon's nose tucked under the dump truck's posterior, we nervously crossed the Chico, shucking and eating delicious boiled peanuts, silently hoping we'd make it.

As we approached the other side, the head ferry man told me to get in my car and start the engine. I wondered what for, then found out. When the truck drove off, the ferry suddenly reared and bucked from its relief of weight. My car, with blocks under the wheels, didn't move, but the ferry man wanted me at the wheel ready to drive forward just in case Our Lady of Piat wasn't watching over us.

Ybannag, Ytawid, Ilocano

A long, almost straight road traverses the final 126 km from Tuguegarao to Aparri, through towns with mixed Ilocano, Ytawes and Ybannag populations. For centuries these peoples have lived side by side yet often they have remained in separate communities and retained their different dialects.

Ybannag people originally inhabited the Cagayan Valley lowlands. Their name derives from Bannag, the Cagayan River's pre-Spanish appellation. Ytawes people come from hilly areas of southern Cagayan and are a subgroup of the Ybannag. They were less subject and more resistent to Spanish colonialism than the lowlanders.

When the Spanish arrived they brought Ilocanos and Tagalogs with them, eventually encouraging Ilocanos to immigrate because they were considered more cooperative than the natives. Ilocanos immigrants named barrios they founded for towns they had left, and road signs along the highway give the driver flash-backs to places on the other side of Luzon. Most town poblacions are still inhabited by Ybannag and Ytawes people, with the Ilocanos settling in the surrounding areas. Occasionally, Ilocano mayors have even rebuilt the town hall outside the central districts, in Ilocano barrios.

Stations of the Cross

Iguig (an Ytawid word pronounced Hig- ig), is 17 km north from Tuguegarao. Attractive Iguig Church was built between 1765 and 1787. It has unusual flying buttresses protecting its posterior from soil erosion. Larger-than-life-size stations of the cross have recently been installed on the hills beside and behind the church.

Upon first impression they seem a rather gaudy intrusion, but as you walk with them over the rolling hills their impact grows until you reach the last moving sculpture of Christ on Mary's lap with the vast river, valley and distant mountains behind.

Pastillas & Hiking

Continue through Amulong to **Alcala**, an Ilocano town with a large attractive church. 1½ km before the poblacion a sign on the right announces, "Milk Candy". Stop here for delicious *pastillas* made from *carabao* milk. People in this area fish the river, and you may see huge fish traps called *pattig* under sheds just north of Amulong's central district.

To get to **Mapaso Hot Springs** and **Tanlagan Falls**, you turn right a little more than 1 km before **Gattaran** poblacion. The road will get you to the hot springs, but there is some hiking involved in getting to Tanlagan, and rivers to cross. Ask for Mr Agatep, in Gattaran, for a guide.

A simple boarding house behind Gattaran town hall serves good food. There are several furniture-making industries in and about the town, and an incipient weaving project. From Gattaran's Freedom Hall you can see the Cagayan River below and Lasam on the other side.

The Magapit bridge, which allows traffic to cross the mighty Cagayan River at one of its few narrows, is 9 km north of Gattaran.

Sanchez Mira, Cagayan

Nueva Segovia

Lal-lo is 16 km further north. Its parish dates frôm 1595. The church, the earliest in the Cagayan Valley, is of somewhat later construction. Ruins of an old fort built for defense now lie in grass and weeds on private property.

Eight km north of Lal-lo, a road goes right to San Vicente, and the northernmost tip of Luzon. The intersection with the east-bound road is a good place to gas up for trips over the top (last premium gas before Laoag) or San Vicente.

The River Exits

Camalaniugan (another Ytawid word) was once the ferry departure point for the other bank of the Cagayan. The church's unremarkable bell tower houses the oldest European bell in the Orient.

The next, and last town, is **Aparri**, where mountains of logs await shipment and the Cagayan finally joins the sea. Winds often come howling in across the Babuyan Channel. Houses near the waterfront have their roofs securely lashed down with large bamboos. Even in good weather, large rollers push onto the wide, sloping beach, and the power of the sea is awesome.

Equally awesome is the extent of the mouth of the vast Cagayan by the time it reaches Aparri. Walk out onto the jetty at the juncture of the river mouth and the sea. Stand, wind-blown, experiencing the beauty and power of this place. Large and strong as the jetty may have seemed when it was constructed a few years ago, the sea is quickly humbling and destroying it.

There aren't many places to stay in Aparri, just a couple of basic hotels. Aparri's unusual, 4-wheeled tricycles are enclosed all around and look a bit like space capsules.

Cape Engaño

To visit **San Vicente** you need to return to Camalaniugan and turn east for the 1½-hr ride to the end of the road.

The road bypasses Buguey, where the Spanish first landed in Cagayan, then goes through St Teresita and Mision. It is thought that the Cagayan River once had its mouth in Mision, later shifting westward.

Forty km and some interesting bridges further, you reach **Sta Ana**, then continue to barrio San Vicente.

Ex-mayor Ernesto Borja has a guest house where visitors may sleep dorm-style, and he can help arrange *banca* trips to **Palaui Island**. This is a big game fishing area, and most of Mr Borja's guests come in search of marlin and other large prizes of the sea.

Palaui is a volcanic island. Lava flows twist dramatically down to the coast. Small sand or pebble beaches nestle in coves. Dumagats inhabit the island. Mainlanders come to fish, often staying several days in huts by the shore, and some keep cattle on the island.

Near Palaui's northwestern tip a beautiful white sand beach curves gracefully against pasture. **Cape Engaño lighthouse** stands high on a hill above. We landed on the beach and climbed to the lighthouse for terrific views beyond, to the Babuyans, and back and down to the cove, its glistening beach and azure waters.

Over the Top

The top of Luzon is remote, beautiful. Buses make the journey from Tuguegarao to Laoag and back, across flat paddy lands, over wide rivers, then into the mountains and along the cliffs where the Cordilleras plummet into the Babuyan Channel. The area is only dry from February through late April. Roads are impassable during heavy rains.

Camp Carillo, in **Sanchez Mira**, is a great place to picnic, and you can walk down to the nearby fishing village for photos. **Pamplona**'s old church continues to deteriorate for lack of funds needed to reinforce its massive frame against the elements, yet it remains a moving presence. Stop in **Claveria** for a swim at the beach. Take care, the current may be strong at times. Very basic accommodation may be had at the municipal waterfront cottages, other lodging may be available at Taggat Industries' lodging house in the next barrio.

Rise through forested **Sta Praxadies**. A pretty waterfall lies a few hundred feet off the road. Cross into **Ilocos Norte**, then descend to **Pasaleng Bay**. Good accommodation may be had at the cliff-side lodge in Pansian. The lodge is beside a waterfall, and there are lots of trails to hike in this area. **Pagudpud** offers beautiful beaches. Accommodation may be available at Villa del Mar, on the **Saud Beach**, which is one of the world's finest stretches of golden sand. From here it takes only about 1½ hours to get to Laoag. Please refer to the Ilocos section for more details.

Sustenance

Small rustic cafés are in every town along the main road, especially at bus stops.

La Pampangueña, The Bulakeña, and Marilyn's serve the best native food in Tuguegarao. Hotel Delfino has a Chinese restaurant on the 2nd floor. The canteen at the capital site serves lunch and snacks.

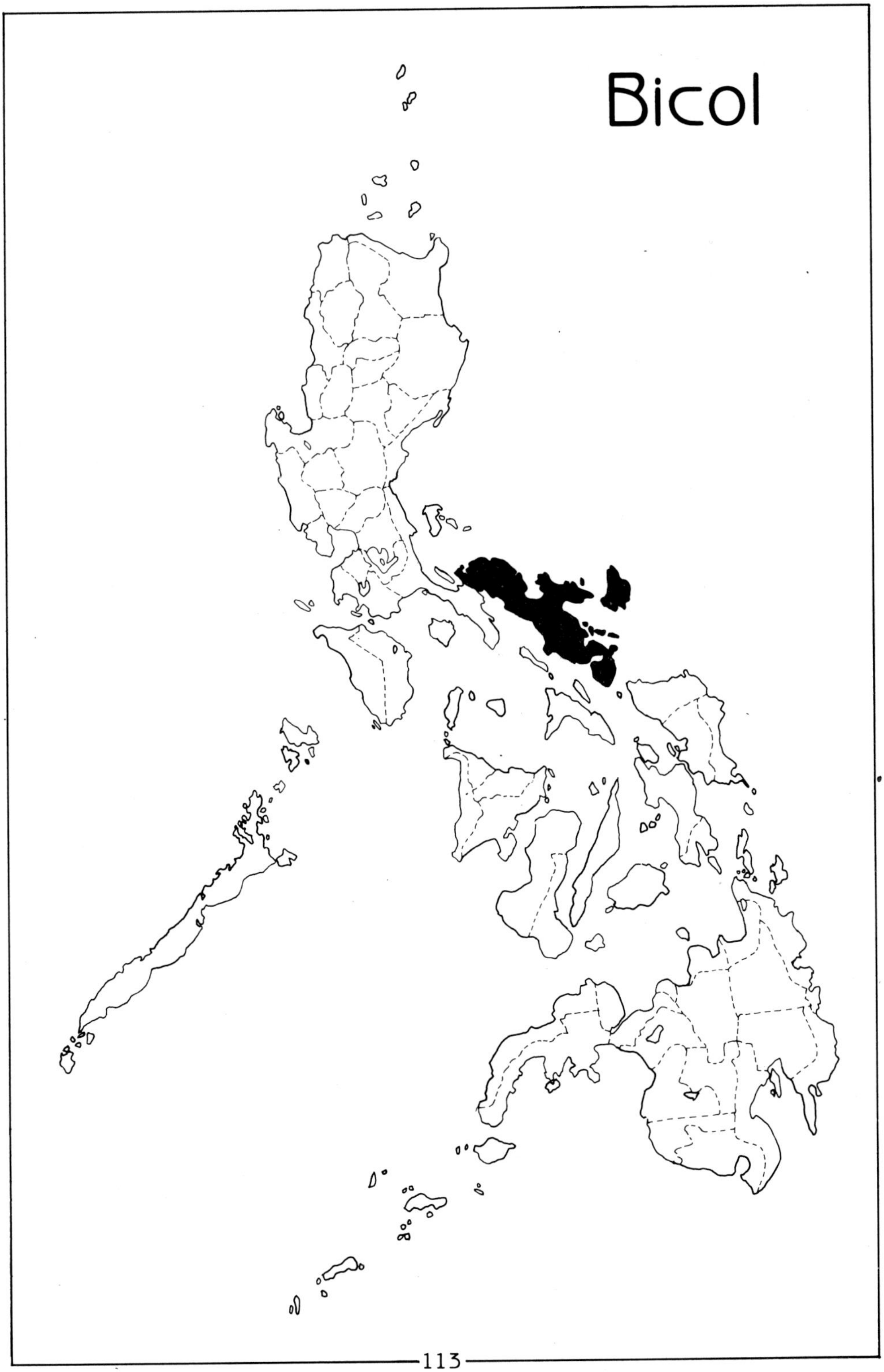
Bicol

BICOL

Alaminos
To Batangas City
San Pablo
Tiaong
Dolores
Lukban
Mt. Banahaw
Candelaria
Tayabas
Sariaya
Lucena
Pagbilao
PAGBILAO I.
Padre Burgos
Atimonan
ALBAT I.
Gumaca
Sta. Elena
Lopez
Calauag
MARINDUQUE I.
QUEZON
Labo
Vinzons
Mercedes
Daet
CAMARINES SUR
Sipocot
San Miguel Bay
Pasacao
Naga
Carolina
Milaor
Mt. Isarog
Sabang
Lake Balo
Nabua
Mt. Asog
Iriga
Lake Buhi
BURIAS I.
Libon
Tiwi
Lagonoy Gulf
Polangui
Malinao
Tabaco
Guinobatan
Camalig
Mt. Mayon
Bacacay
CAGRARAY I.
Daraga
Legazpi
Bascaran
Manito
BATAN I.
RAPURAPU I.
Bacon
Sorsogon
Gubat
Rizal Beach
Mt. Bulusan
Bulusan
Irosin
Matnog
Sta. Magdalena
SAMAR

Bicol

Mt Mayon at sunrise, through the window of an airplane

Bicol

access: 1 hr by plane from Manila; 10-12 hrs by bus, train, p 267
climate: OK Feb-July; best Mar-May
to do: handicrafts, tour, hike, swim, dive
facilities: hotels, lodges; p 283-4

The Bicol Region comprises Luzon's southernmost provinces, Sorsogon, Albay, Camarines Norte and Sur plus the islands of Masbate, Romblon, Tablas and the Catanduanes. Bicolanos are well known for their artistry with abaca and other fibers.

Mt Mayon, which soars gracefully to a peak 2420 m above Legazpi, is Bicol's best known attraction.

According to legend, long ago a girl named Magayon (which literally means "beautiful") had many suitors, and fell in love with a Tagalog named Ulap. Her father agreed to their marriage, but Pagtuga, one of her Bicolano suitors, refused to accept his rejection. He kidnapped and threatened to kill Magayon's father unless she reconsidered and agreed to marry him. To save her father, she consented. Ulap appeared at the wedding ceremony and slew his rival, but he and Magayon were slain in the resulting fight.

Magayon's father buried the lovers together in one grave. The grave shook and grew until it became Mt Mayon. When Mayon quakes, it is said that Pagtuga is trying to retrieve his wedding gifts. When the top is covered with clouds it is said that Ulap and Magayon are kissing.

Bicol has a number of other volcanoes, most notably Isarog, Asog, Masaraga and Bulusan. Like Mayon, Bulusan is active.

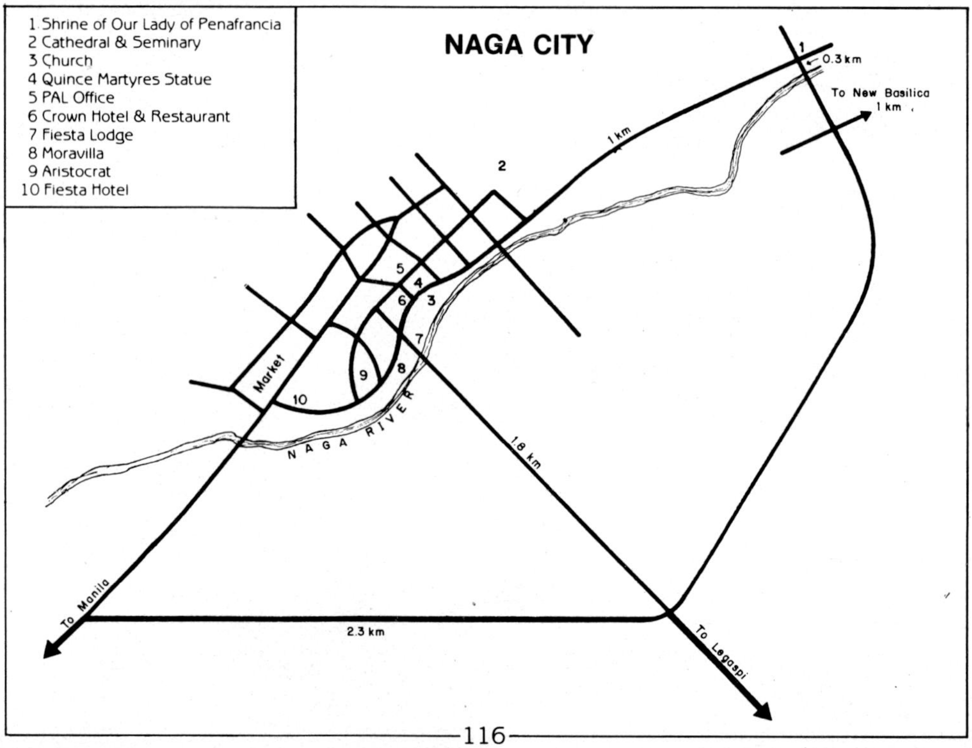

Masaraga's latent energy is used to power the Tiwi Geothermal Project.

Bicol has some lovely, remote beaches, hiking and excellent diving.

Camarines Sur

Camarines Sur's twin hubs are Naga, the business center, and Iriga, its quiet, pretty capital.

Although Naga City is geared primarily to local business needs, there are places of interest and relaxation outside the city, and the Virgin of Peñafrancia draws thousands of faithful to her annual fluvial procession.

Our Lady of Peñafrancia originally came to Naga via Macao during the 17th century. Miraculous cures are attributed to her, and people flock to Naga for week-long festivities during the third week of September. The activities climax in a fluvial parade held on the 3rd Saturday as 10,000 people gather to watch the image transferred from the new basilica in which she is housed to gaily decorated floats and tended down the Naga River by boats with all-male crews.

At other times the city has little to offer the tourist except the pretty Peñafrancia church, where the icon used to be housed, and a few hotels intended mainly for tourists. Outside the city, however, there are a couple of relaxing resorts, beaches and interesting towns. Hire cars wait for business in the plaza beside the Crown Hotel, and jeepneys and buses leave from the market for places mentioned below.

Carolina is a mountain resort area 9½ km from Naga on the base of Mt Isarog, an extinct volcano. The volcano has several pretty waterfalls. About 4 hrs of hiking and climbing are needed to reach the striking Panigwasan Falls, which can sometimes be seen on the volcano's right face as you approach Carolina.

Good accommodations available at Peñafrancia Resort in Carolina; adequate accommodation at the New Kayumanggi, further downhill.

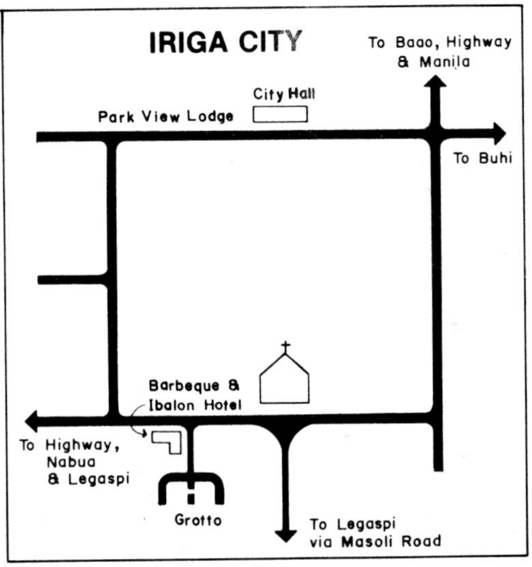

From Naga you may make your way around the volcano to **Partido Beach,** Sabang, San José, where Mrs San Jose runs a different Peñafrancia Beach Resort: nice spacious cottages with good tiled bathrooms on a long dark sand beach. You may take a *banca* out to Rosa Island if white sand and snorkeling are your interests.

Pasacao beach is closer to Naga, less than an hour's drive. Golden-beige sand, and you may be able to buy fish to roast on the beach. Very primitive overnight facilities are available at Pongol Beach Resort. Refugio Island's white sand beaches are about an hour away by *banca.*

Magarao town, which is about 15 min from Naga, is famous for its *parahilots,* or healers. Roadside signs announce them and adjectives claim each one's attributes: "the famous"... "the popular"... "always strong" Bonbon's attractive church, which is 10 min further along the road, is flanked by a curiously **leaning bell tower.**

Iriga is a postcard pretty town, its white church centrally located in the spacious city plaza, with the town nestling around the whole.

Its one hotel, the Ibalon, has a small museum of artifacts and documents antedating the Spanish coming. Simpler accommodation is available across the plaza, at the Park View.

Because the Spaniards systematically and effectively destroyed everything they associated with pagans which could not be incorporated into their religion, almost nothing is known of the ancient Filipino beliefs. Attorney Reyes of the Ibalon discovered one of few surviving documents detailing myths prior to the Spanish era. These documents are housed in the museum, along with paintings of the mythical beings associated with the papers and some ethnic artifacts.

Climb the grotto behind the Ibalon Hotel for a great view of Mt Asog behind the town.

A tribe of **Aetas** (Negritoes) live on the slopes of Mt Asog, on land owned by Attorney Reyes. If you wish to visit them, ask at the Ibalon for assistance. Bring small gifts - matches, T-shirts, enamel cooking utensils, medicines would be helpful, but cigarettes and candy are also appreciated.

Buhi town sits on the shores of a small crater lake which once was home to the smallest freshwater fish in the world. Very pretty views at sunset of the lake, fish pens and surrounding hills. Unfortunately the tiny fish (called *tabios* or *sinarapan*) were replaced by other species introduced to increase the people's income.

Sinarapan are still, however, cultivated in even smaller lakes in surrounding barrios. If you would like a pretty walk and a look at these fish, go to San Vicente, then turn off for Makangay, where the road ends. Ask the barrio captain here for a guide to go to Danao - tell them you're just sightseeing. The walk goes along a steep hillside with lovely views, then through an abaca plantation to Danao town, from where it is a couple of min walk to Danao Lake. *Sinarapan* are cultivated in and around the lake.

During abaca harvesting season you will see *carabao* hauling heavy loads of abaca along the trails, and people cutting the plants and stripping away the pulpy matter to expose the tough fiber inside. This fiber is dried and sorted according to grade, the whiter abaca being the better quality.

Stripping abaca, Danao

Mt Asog with Iriga City in the foreground

Legazpi, Albay & Sorsogon

You may plan several days of activities in and about Legazpi, always in view of Mayon. Its once perfect conic symmetry has been slightly knocked akilter by recent eruptions, but it remains one of the most beautiful volcanoes in the world, a captivating, powerful presence.

Check with the DOT desk upon your arrival at Legazpi airport or at their head office in Albay District for information and requests for special arrangements, such as caving, hiking, etc. Even if the office is closed the guard can give maps and some other information and, in an emergency, will contact one of the staff.

Accommodations in Legazpi are reasonably priced and there are several restaurants. Beaches near the city are not safe for swimming.

If you wish to climb Mayon, be in top shape. Allow 3-4 days and contact DOT Legazpi in advance, requesting them to make arrangements with Eduardo Arnaldo or Ricardo Dy for guides, porters and equipment.

Legazpi City

Legazpi, Albay's capital, (map p 120) was built on mangrove swamps which once fringed its excellent deep water port. The Spanish arrived in 1567 and introduced Christianity. Prior to 1635 Albay, Sorsogon, the Catanduanes and much of Camarines Sur comprised a single political entity called Partido de Ibalon. Legazpi suffered raids by Muslim and Dutch pirates, and was the scene of much bloody fighting during the Fil-Am war and again during WW II.

The city is now a relaxed place to stroll about. The monument at the junction of Quezon and Rizal Sts commemorates the defeat of Filipino freedom fighters by American forces in 1900. **San Rafael church's** massive altar is an impressive 10-ton block of lava.

The city's **market** and many small handicrafts shops are great fun for bargain hunters. If you are interested in seeing handicrafts produced, drop in at the NACIDA exhibit on Peñaranda near the Executive Inn, and inquire for assistance. Some handicrafts activities, such as abaca twine

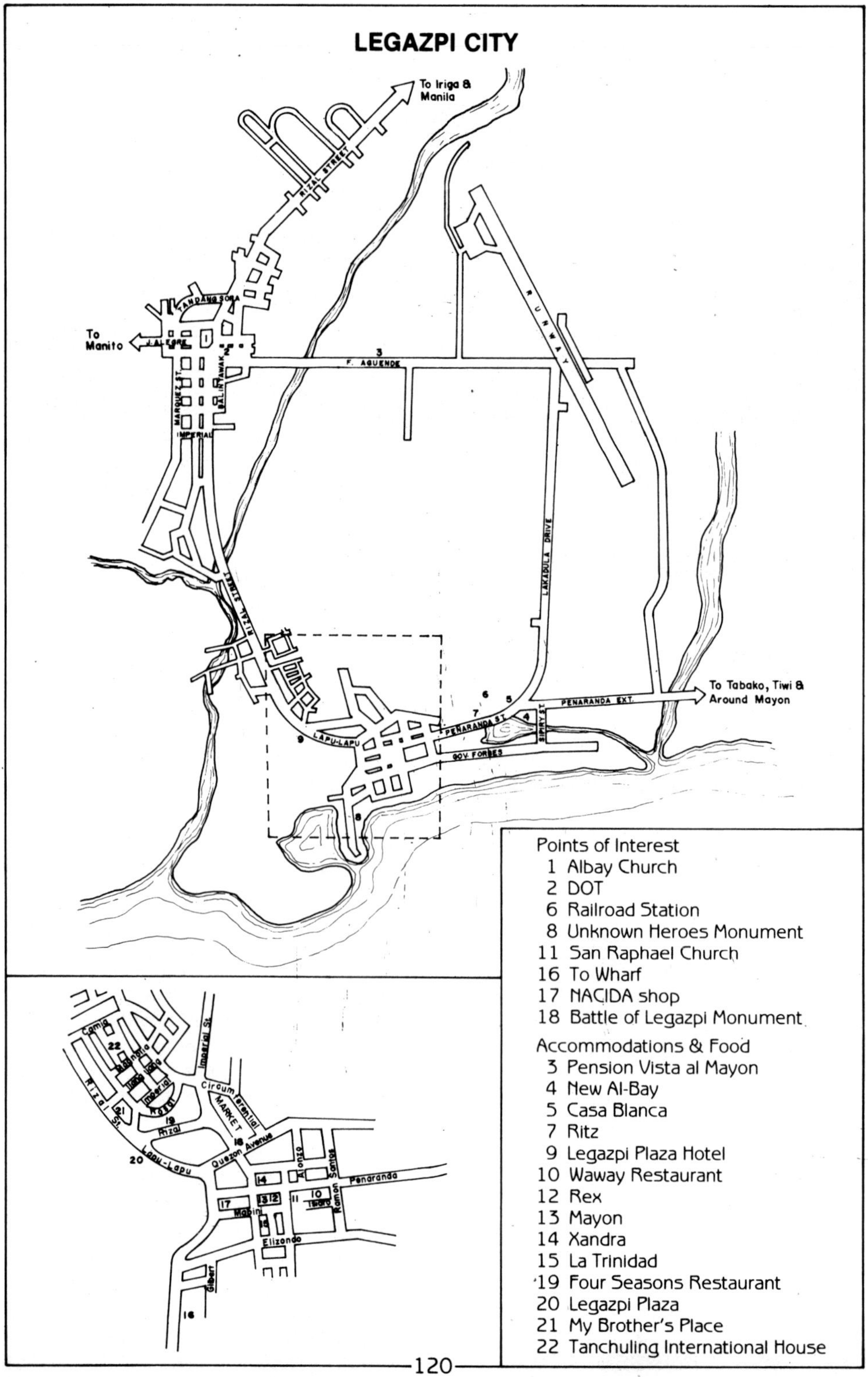
LEGAZPI CITY
To Iriga & Manila
RIZAL STREET
TANDANG SORA
To Manito
J. ALEGRE
MARQUEZ ST.
BALINTAWAK
IMPERIAL
F. AGUENDE
RUNWAY
LAKADULA DRIVE
RIZAL STREET
PENARANDA ST
PENARANDA EXT.
To Tabako, Tiwi & Around Mayon
GOV. FORBES
LAPU-LAPU
Camia
Imperial St.
Circumferential
MARKET
Rizal St.
Rizal
Lapu-Lapu
Quezon Avenue
Alonzo
Ramon Santos
Penaranda
Mabini
Elizondo
Gilbert
Points of Interest
1 Albay Church
2 DOT
6 Railroad Station
8 Unknown Heroes Monument
11 San Raphael Church
16 To Wharf
17 NACIDA shop
18 Battle of Legazpi Monument
Accommodations & Food
3 Pension Vista al Mayon
4 New Al-Bay
5 Casa Blanca
7 Ritz
9 Legazpi Plaza Hotel
10 Waway Restaurant
12 Rex
13 Mayon
14 Xandra
15 La Trinidad
19 Four Seasons Restaurant
20 Legazpi Plaza
21 My Brother's Place
22 Tanchuling International House

spinning, are seasonal, and many items are produced on a small scale in homes. Visitors are usually welcome, but you may need assistance locating the homes.

Albay

Day trips in the Legazpi vicinity include a circle around Mayon, a visit to Rizal Beach, Sorsogon and circling Bulusan Volcano. These trips may be done by public transport (while Rizal Beach is relatively accessible by bus, the Bulusan circle will in this case take 2 days), but it is far simpler to rent your own vehicle. Ask the DOT or your hotel to assist with arrangements.

Tricycles and jeepneys meet each incoming flight and go to Legazpi's center. A constant flow of jeepneys ply the route from Legazpi to Daraga.

Tricycles are available at Daraga market for short trips. Jeepneys frequently leave Legazpi for Tabako, where you change for Tiwi or Ligao. Ask the driver to let you off at your intended stops on the way around the volcano, and start early if you are going by public transport. Jeepneys and tricycles go from Camalig to Hoyophoyopan, but it is best to take a jeepney. Buses leave the market for Sorsogon. JV Liner goes through to Rizal Beach.

To get to Danao (see p 118) you will have to go to Polangui, take a jeepney for Buhi, then a tricycle from San Vicente to Makangay.

There are frequent departures for Iriga and Naga. If you want to go to Iriga you may have to get off at Nabua and switch to a jeepney.

Around Mayon

Allow anywhere from half a day to several days to explore Mayon's attractions, depending upon what you enjoy seeing, and of course your time and budget. Visit ancient churches, swim at a coral islet, dive, watch scissors and knives forged, traverse recent lava flows, hike to falls, visit the functioning volcanology station on Mayon's slopes, walk through caves and see the ruins of a community buried by Mayon's 1814 eruption.

Points of interest are presented below in order around Mayon starting at Legazpi and progressing northeast to Tiwi, then back-tracking and going inland. If the circle is done as a day trip, proceeding this way will keep Mayon at her photographic best. Mayon is often shrouded in cloud except during March, April and May.

Sto Domingo's picturesque twin-towered church is made from lava blocks. Reyes and Sirangan Beach Resorts offer rustic accommodation by the sea. From Reyes Beach Resort it may be possible to hire a *banca* to visit the Batan Islands or the galleon wreck off **Buhatan**, a simple fishing village 8 km from Sto Domingo.

Bacacay is another beach area, with resorts for daylight visitors and wood furniture industries. Sometimes you can see abaca twine being spun along the road in **Malilipot** and other towns.

Mr Ignacio Mapa, Bacacay's tourism officer, can assist people interested in the off-shore islands. **Batan Island's** wilderness is disappearing rapidly, but one may still explore Minarosa Cave.

There is good diving around Rapu Rapu Island. Rapu Rapu town has no cars or tricycles, but does have paved walks. It is charming, right on the water. The people are friendly, unused to seeing foreigners. They keep well tended gardens.

Tabako is famous for hand-forged scissors, knives, axes, etc. Cobo Bliss, a government-backed foundry project, is west of the main road on the approaches to Tabako. Here you may see steel bars, truck springs, etc turned into scissors and other articles. The whole community rings to the "cling, cling, cling" of hammers on steel, and you can watch as the raw material is heated, melted and formed with amazing speed and dexterity. The products are sold very cheaply at the cooperative store.

From Tabako you may head inland and

around Mayon or do the side trips to Tiwi Geothermal Springs, Malinao and Palale Falls.

Malinao church has an interesting façade: St Anne holding baby Mary, riding a cow, chasing pirates. The relief work was done after St Anne was credited with saving Malinao from a pirate attack.

Tiwi town is the departure point for **Coral Island,** a white sand strip with good snorkeling but no vegetation or shade. Arrange *banca* prices and sensible pick up times in advance and bring refreshments.

Tiwi Geothermal Plant is 2½ km further along the road. Visits should be prearranged through the DOT. If you're there at lunch time, eat at Table Talk Restaurant, where the food is usually good and the garden is lovely.

Palale Falls are an hour's hike through 7 rivers and streams and an abaca plantation to a secluded spot where a stream plummets 80' in a lacy ribbon to a pool below. Ask the barrio captain in Labnig for a guide.

You may picnic at Roca Monte (even if it is not operating as a resort, the caretaker usually allows people to come in and rest), or continue to **Mayon Rest House** and the **Volcanology Station** which is located at the end of an access road, about 1/3rd of the way up Mayon's slopes. On clear days there are great views of the volcano above, the bay below. You may watch the seismograph and tilt meter operating and see displays about volcanism.

Continue through scenic farms and villages to Ligao. Only about 8 km of the road between Tabako and Ligao is unpaved.

Hoyophoyopan Caves are about 10 km southeast of Camalig. 4000-year-old remains have been unearthed from Hoyophoyopan and nearby Calabidongan. During WW II the caves served as a refuge for residents hiding from Japanese atrocities and, later, American bombs.

"Hoyophoyopan" is an onomatopoeic Bicolano word meaning "blow, blow". The cave is named for the sound of wind whistling through the entrance.

Mr Fred Nieva, owner and caretaker of the caves, heads a newly-formed spelunking society. He guides visitors through and tells the caves' history during a leisurely ½-hr stroll. Serious spelunkers will want to contact Mr Nieva in advance to make arrangements for a day's exploration of **Calabidongan Caves.** Be prepared to get wet in the underground river.

Remains excavated at Hoyophoyopan are stored in Camalig church, which unfortunately doesn't have the funds to display them properly. The church's bell tower was used as a lookout post during

Toddlers warm themselves in a hot spring, Masacrot, Sorsogon

Sta Magdalena, Sorsogon

WW II.

In 1814 Mayon erupted violently, peppering the community of **Cagsawa** with hot boulders. Over 1000 townspeople took refuge in the church and were buried alive in cinders and lava. Camalig church was originally built in 1587, burned in 1636 and rebuilt in 1724. It now stands a ruined and poignant reminder of the 1814 tragedy. The site has been turned into a lovely park where you get the traditional photo of Mayon behind Cagsawa bell tower.

Survivors of Mayon's 1814 eruption left Cagsawa and moved to **Daraga,** where they built the present very attractive church. Shoppers will want to pause in Daraga to see the many little handicrafts shops along the road.

Sorsogon

Long known as cowboy country, Sorsogon, with its precipitous volcanic peaks, green valleys and pretty beaches, is reminiscent of Hawaii. Sorsogon does not get a lot of tourists, and isn't set up for them. It's ideal for travelers who like out-of-the-way places. Those who don't mind rustic accommodation may find lodging in Sorsogon City and at Rizal Beach acceptable, but people who need their creature comforts at night will want to plan excursions into Sorsogon as day trips from Legazpi.

Roads to Rizal Beach and to Matnog are very good, but the road around Bulusan volcano is sometimes only negotiable by jeepney or similar sturdy vehicle.

There are frequent buses from Legazpi to Sorsogon City, JV Liner goes through to Gubat, from where you need to get a tricycle or jeepney to Rizal Beach. Jeepneys ply the route around the volcano. Buses continue from Sorsogon City through to Matnog, where some await the ferry and continue the journey in Samar.

Before entering Sorsogon province you will go through **Bascaran, Albay,** where the road is lined with anahaw fans drying in the sun. Small ones are used as fans. Large ones serve as shades. All are used for decorations.

If you have extra time, or are staying in Sorsogon City, you may want to visit **Bacon,** a pretty old town of solid stone houses where baskets dry in the sun by the road. Continue to **Tolonggapo Beach,** for dark sand, good swimming, and some very rustic facilities.

Rizal Beach in Gubat is one of the prettiest beaches anywhere. Miles of golden sand ring an extensive cove. Swim near the resort area. Portions near the center of the cove are unsafe due to undertow. Walk to the end to look for shells. Spend a day enjoying the sun and sand.

Rizal Beach Resort has rooms with bath. There are a couple of very rustic places nearby.

The trip **around Bulusan** goes through a remote area of hot springs, forest, picturesque coastlines and a crater lake. Take the south highway to Irosin, where you may stop briefly at **San Mateo Hot Springs** for a healing bath in waters of varying temperatures, stroll along the forested walks of the resort and look at the nearby **Bulusan Volcano Observatory.** The observatory monitors Bulusan's activity and has a good display of illustrations explaining volcanic activity.

Turn westward through Irosin to **Masacrot Hot Spring** where, for a small entry fee, you may bathe. Several springs flow beside the road, and I once saw children huddled neck-deep in the warm water on a cool day.

The road climbs through forest where people gather pandan and caragomoy for weaving into mats and other articles. A few km past Masacrot a road bears left, into **Bulusan's crater lake.** The emerald green lake nestles in tropical growth lining steep walls. There are picnic shades and a walk around the lake's edge. Bring insect spray.

Bulusan town is the next stop after the lake. You descend through trees into a town where every house seems draped in a profusion of shrubs and flowering plants. Very pretty indeed. From here the road continues past spectacular coastal views through Barcelona to Rizal Beach. Barcelona's shores are lined with ruins of buildings erected too close to the sea. Its church is quaint and attractive, with twin bell towers typical of this area.

If you go even further south from Irosin, to **Sta Magdalena** and **Matnog** you will find remote, lovely beaches. Matnog is the departure point for ferries going to Samar. **Tiklin Island** off the pier is very pretty indeed, and, although privately owned, the caretaker, Mang Eli, sometimes allows campers to stay.

Sta Magdalena is 5 km from the main highway, and has a very pretty beach - great for swimming and picnicking.

Sustenance

In Camarines Sur, Crown Hotel does the best food in **Naga**, and there are some Chinese Restaurants near the market. Good barbeque can be had at the *ihaw* (barbeque) place near the Ibalon in **Iriga**.

You won't find *haute cuisine* in **Legazpi** but tasty Filipino and Chinese dishes are readily available. Waway, on Peñaranda, does good Filipino food *turo-turo* style. Salo-Salo and Family Restaurants, also on Peñaranda, do good fried chicken and seafoods, and are especially well appreciated for their clams. Sa Bay Bay does seafoods and Spanish dishes. Four Seasons on Rizal St and Shanghai do the best Chinese food.

Local dishes worth trying include *laing,* a mixture of shrimp and pork rolled in *gabi* (taro) leaves and stewed in coconut milk, and the Bicol Express, a ground beef tartare with chili peppers, guaranteed to clean out any cobwebs you may have in your mouth. Legazpi's best appointed and priciest pub is the Magic Pan. Try also the Melon Patch and My Brother's Place for beer and music.

Islands Near Luzon

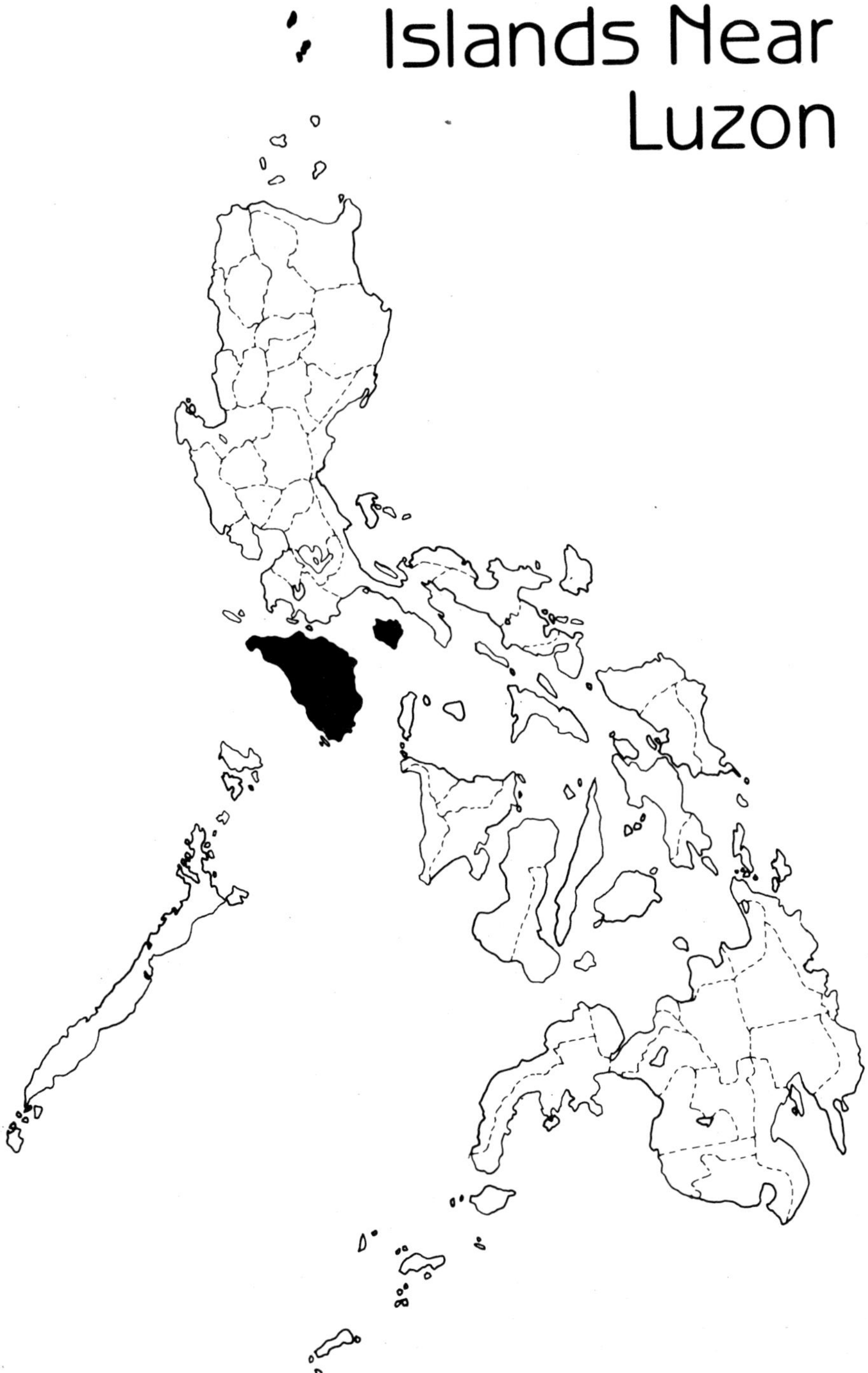

BATANES

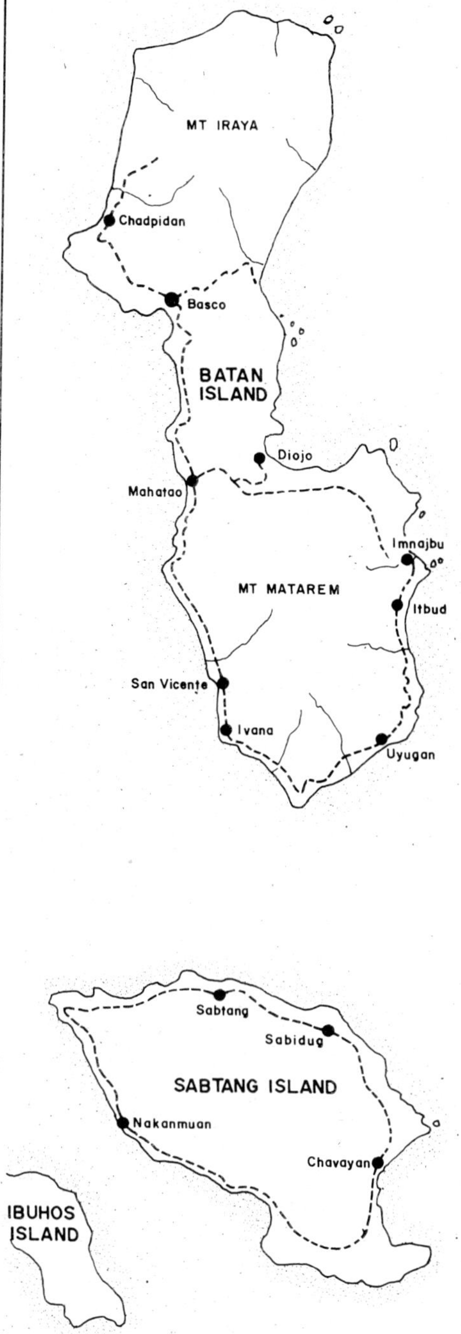

BASCO

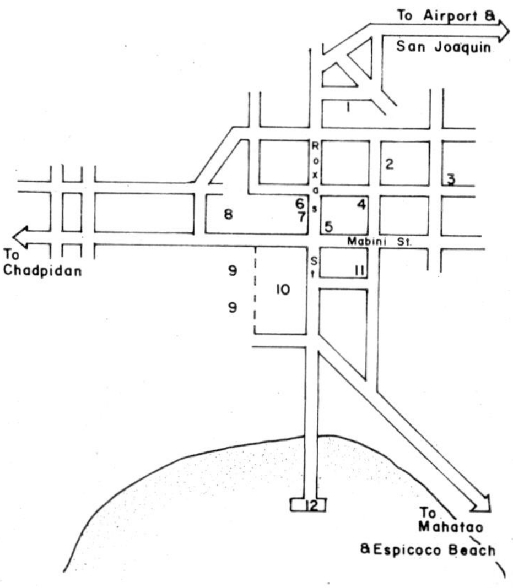

1 Elcano's
2 Post office
3 PAL
4 Store
5 Casa Tolentino
6 PNB
7 Capitol
8 Church
9 School
10 Plaza
11 Amboy's – jeeps to Mahatao
12 Wharf

Typical Batanes houses with a woman in her *so-ot*, the all-weather hat (inset by John K Chua)

The Batanes

access: 3 hrs by air from Manila, p 267

climate: best March-May

to do: hike, camp, swim, birds, get well away from it all

facilities: a few rooms, p 285

The far northern reaches of the Philippines, the Batanes Islands, are distinctly and beautifully unique. Lashed by gale force winds 6 months of the year, the early inhabitants lived in low dwellings and subsisted on root crops, goats and pork. Calm seas permit fishing only during the short summer - March through June - and 2 weeks of Indian summer in late October. Flocks of birds migrating south for the winter stop in the Batanes for a brief respite during the Indian summer, then continue their journey.

In recent years cattle production and a few hardy crops have been introduced. Much of the year everything must move in and out by air, as seas are too violent to allow shipping.

From July through December the Batanes are a bleak inhospitable place, with rain sand cold wind soften continuing through February. But from March through June they transform into a veritable paradise for travelers who like places off the beaten track, spectacular scenery, a people who are peaceful and friendly in a reserved, unobtrusive way, hiking, camping, swimming, and true serenity.

The original inhabitants were probably mostly Malay with Chinese and Japanese admixture. Their language is a combination of several Philippine dialects, including Tagalog, Ilocano, Pangasinan and Ibannag from Cagayan. Y'Ami, the uninhabited northernmost Batanes Isle is only 50 miles below Lanyu, the southernmost Taiwanese Island, and it is said that people from Lanyu originally came from the Batanes.

The first Spanish missionary arrived in 1686 and found an illiterate, impoverished people oppressed by the climate yet hungry for a new religion. After many fits and starts, during which missionaries and government officials alternately tried to accommodate the Islanders' wishes and then acceded to climatic exigencies, the Spanish finally moved in to stay in 1855.

The people learned to build solid houses of mortar and stone in addition to the indigenous grass and cane huts. Current buildings are a combination of the two architectural styles. Many small houses have meter-thick walls and foot-thick thatched roofs. Even the boats the Ivatanes use are different, being more like European wooded dorles than Eastern craft.

It's hard to say what is most striking about Batan Island: its hardy people who look strong, and must be to survive; its neat little houses, many painted white; its clean villages, not a scrap of trash in evidence nor the odor of close living and the animals which are everywhere; or its spectacular scenery.

The island is peaceful, you can camp safely anywhere. The people are honest.

There's only one place to stay and eat - Mama Lily's, with 2 clean rooms, good food, $6.25/day for room and board. Or you may inquire from St. Dominic's College about the possibility of dormitory space. Food shortages in the Batanes are not uncommon. Bring snacks and any other needed items.

Basco

Basco, the capital, is a picture-book-pretty community of attractive, solid buildings somewhat reminiscent of the wind-swept

Isles off England. The church stands white and strong in the middle, looking towards the harbor and bay below. The spacious plaza fronting the capitol building is ringed by hills quilted by fields and pastures with steep volcanic Mt Iraya for a back-drop.

There are a few small shops with basic necessities and of course some junk food, a modest NACIDA handicrafts outlet in the capitol building, a lovely church, many photogenic buildings, seascapes and landscapes and lots of people ready to say "Good morning", "Hello", or "Good afternoon", in response to a greeting, and no market. Householders arrange for their needs by negotiating directly with fishermen, farmers and butchers.

There are no industries, and few souvenirs to buy. You might try asking Mama Lily or the Elcanos to help you acquire a *soot* (the grass headdress Ivatan women use to protect their head, shoulders and back from rain, wind and sun), or some baskets.

The first stone church, built in 1787-96, was destroyed by typhoon. Its current replacement utilizes the front and north wall of the original. Its rear and south walls have been erected inside the original ruins, a thrifty and sensible adaptation.

Some places in Basco have private generators, which they use to provide a few evening hours of electricity.

Natives of Basco often say they meet the planes at the airport just to have something to do, even if they don't know anybody arriving or leaving.

There is a tennis court, and many residences have nightly betamax showings for 25c a head, but no movies, no bowling, just peace, walking, looking and beaches. Snorkeling is great. There are no diving facilities.

Walks can be as short or long as you like, from a few minutes about town and down to the wharf to days spent rounding the south of the island (about 30 km).

Stroll past the cemetery, up the **Naidi Hills** where three abandoned pre-war telecommunications houses sit. Great views. It is said that the rocks are still home to the spirits of Basco's ancestors, who used to live on highland plateaus and gather piles of rocks for self defense. If the spirits are indeed still there, they must be as peaceful as their progeny.

The closest swimming, other than by the pier where there tends to be much broken glass, is at **Espicoco Beach**, which is a few hundred meters along the south road. The pretty beach is backed by a line of coconut trees.

San Joaquin is a pleasant 3-km walk east from Basco, past the airport and across Batan Island, by picturesque farms, farm houses and dory-builders to a tremendous pebble beach. Waves from the powerful Pacific Ocean come ashore with such force that each receding wave moves the rocks and causes a thunderous roll. Sit in the shade nearby, meditate, read a book, watch and hear the power of the sea: an invigorating experience.

If you like your pebble beaches swimmable, walk 3-km along the road north to **Chadpidan Beach**. There are beautiful views of Mt Iraya and its steep foothills along the way, but almost no shade, so bring a hat.

Island Circle

Jeepneys, about 4 a day, ply the Basco-Uyugan route, and it is well worth visiting Mahatao, San Vicente, Ivana and Uyugan, all unique and attractive communities. On Sundays and some "plane days" (when PAL flies in), the jeepneys may go as far as Itbud. The coastline drive is one of the most beautiful anywhere.

The most convenient way to see southern Batan Island is to hire a vehicle, but this costs about $20 and is not always possible. Try Mr Felipe Amboy or Engineer Abad. Public transport does not reach the beautiful interior. If you have lots of time, prefer to conserve money, and are a good walker, you may set out on foot or do the route partly by jeepney. There is a

Mt Iraya from the road to Diojo

campground with water near Ivana.

However you decide to do this trip, bring several rolls of film. Each village has many clusters of attractive houses, each curve in the road breathtaking scenery.

For an idyllic three or four days, bring bedroll and food. Walk or hike to Mahatao, then head inland on the road to Imnajbu and Itbud. Bear right at the first Y-junction, left at the second and you will arrive at **Diojo**, a spectacular pebble beach. There is water at the village to the right of the wharf, and perhaps you can arrange for some fish also. Return to the last junction and bear left for Imnajbu.

From here it is 8-10 km past fabulous views and through steep **pasturelands** where herds of ponies and cattle run free. Be sure to close and latch all gates after you. If there is water at the old Loran Station, where the high road joins the coast road, you could camp there for the night. Otherwise continue to Itbud or backtrack 1 km to Imnajbu.

The road between Itbud and Uyugan passes the **Vanishing Barrio**, ruins of houses abandoned in the mid-fifties, after a tidal wave crashed ashore and wiped out the village.

All the coastal towns are neat, clean and picturesque. **Ivana**'s church was built in 1785, then made smaller in 1844 when the community's population decreased. There are many solid old houses with heavy windows and doors, and 6-century-old bridges. Boats cross from Ivana to **Sabtang Island**, a 35-min passage.

The China Sea coastline, from Maijin point in the south through to Basco has lots of pretty beaches with sandy shores and coral coasts good for snorkelers. One of the prettiest is White Beach, just north of Mabatui Point on the approaches to Mahatao.

Mahatao, too, is a very picturesque village. During fiestas the villagers slaughter as many as 75 cattle to feed revelers, and hold bull fights for amusement.

Itbayat, the Batanes group's other major island is 4 hrs away by boat, and crossing should only be attempted in the best of weather.

Mindoro
Puerto Galera

MINDORO

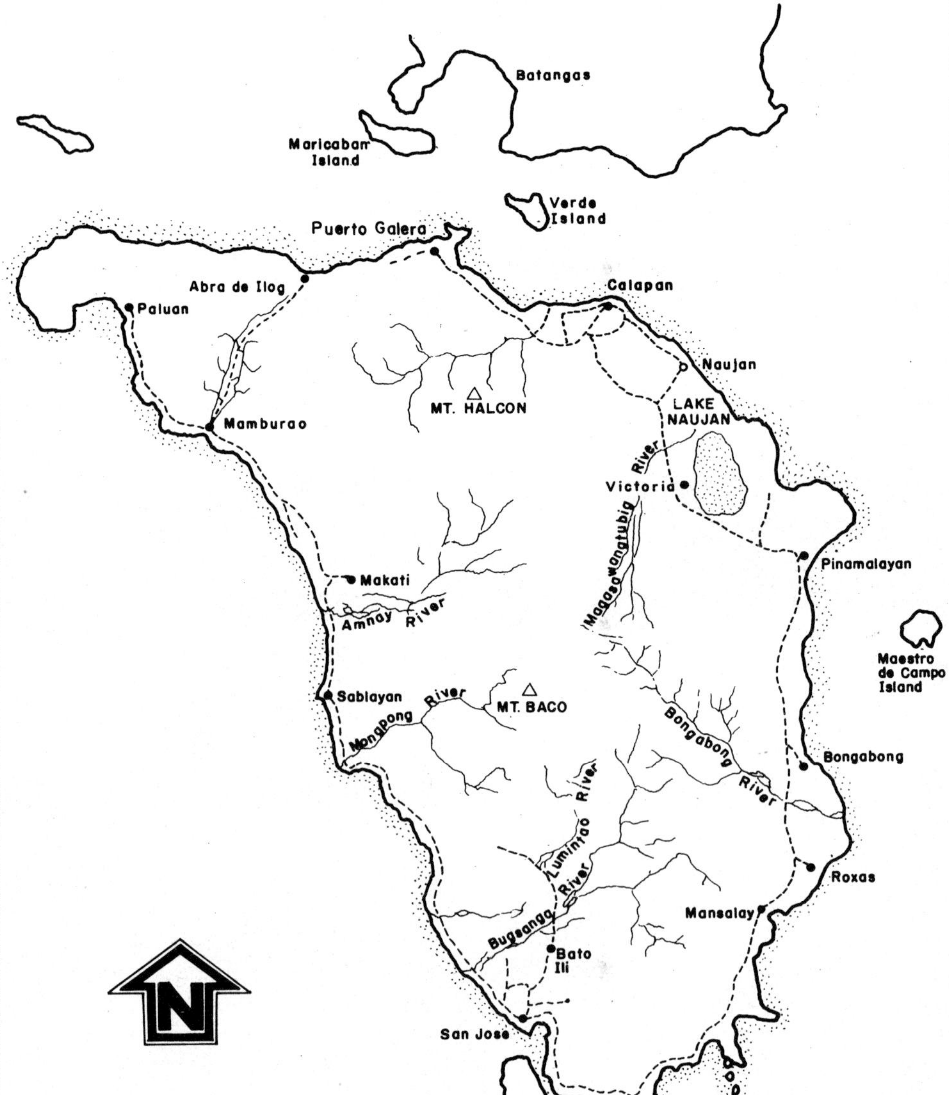
Batangas
Maricaban Island
Verde Island
Puerto Galera
Abra de Ilog
Paluan
Calapan
Naujan
MT. HALCON
LAKE NAUJAN
Mamburao
River
Victoria
Magasawangtubig
Pinamalayan
Makati
Amnay River
Maestro de Campo Island
Sablayan
River
MT. BACO
Mongpong
Bongabong
Bongabong River
River
Lumintao
River
Roxas
Mansalay
Bugsanga
Bato Ili
N
San Jose
Ambulong Island
Ilin Island

Mindoro

access: Puerto Galera: 2 hrs by land plus 2 hrs by ferry from Manila; Mamburao & San Jose: 40 min by air from Manila; p 267
climate: Puerto Galera is fair year round, occasional rains Dec-Feb; San Jose & Mamburao have a marked rainy season June- Nov, especially heavy Aug-Sept.
to do: sun, sand, water sports are the focus, with hiking & visits to Mangyan tribes possible
facilities: myriad huts in Puerto, mostly basic, one better establishment; one up-market place, one lodge in Mamburao; basic lodges in San Jose; pp 285-6

Mindoro is not far from Manila, but is a whole different world of precipitous mountains, primitive tribes and fabulous beaches.

The name Mindoro comes from the Spanish words *Mina de Oro*: gold mine. Panners eke a living from streams, but no viable commercial gold deposits have been found. The island's economy is based on fish, rice, coconuts, some cattle raising and marble quarrying. Tourism is a major industry only in Puerto Galera. A rugged central mountain range divides the island into its two provinces, Mindoro Oriental and Occidental. The highest peaks are Baco (2488 m) in the south, and Halcon (2505 m) in the north.

Puerto Galera is a superb natural harbor, where ships may lie safely even during typhoons. The Spanish arrived to find Chinese traders bartering porcelain, silk, jewelry, and took the goods by force. Consequently the islanders resisted Spanish missionaries and, later, the Americans who followed in their stead.

Today visitors come to enjoy the exceptionally good beaches and reefs around Puerto Galera, where facilities are generally basic and geared towards those who come for sun and fun. A carefree, free-wheeling atmosphere pervades the area.

A few people head for the mountains to visit the tribes and the rapidly diminishing forest habitat of the reclusive tamaraw (a small water buffalo-like animal) and Philippine eagle.

Puerto Galera is accessible by boat from Batangas at all seasons. San Jose and Mamburao should be visited during dry season, unless you don't mind laying over for several days due to inclement weather.

The Tribes

The folk who first settled the lands have been pushed inland by more recent, more aggressive immigrants. In an effort to help the tribes retain some of their ancestral lands, the government has set aside reservation areas. These seldom suffice to allow the tribes to maintain their ancient ways of life, and, as the lowlanders' population continues to burgeon, pressure on tribal lands continues.

Mangyan is the term used to describe the peoples descended from Mindoro's original inhabitants. Alangan, Buid, Iraya, Hanunoo, Tagaydan and Tatagnon peoples are all Mangyan. All are talented weavers, making belts, bags, purses and baskets from *nito*, bamboo, buri and other forest plants. In recent years they have begun stringing beads into necklaces and other ornaments.

The **Hanunoo** have a rich musical heritage. They compose and play music on the *git-git*, a small violin-like instrument with strings made of human hair. They have a poetic tradition which stretches back several hundred years. Poems are etched on bamboo tubes in an Indic script language which differs considerably from that which they use in daily life.

Mindoro highlands

Puerto Galera

The shores of Puerto Gàlera are dotted with many beautiful little white sand beaches, some fringed with reefs teeming with rich and diverse marine life. Puerto has a fine deep water port which has served for many centuries as a haven to ships escaping stormy seas. Puerto's reefs were declared a marine sanctuary in 1974. News of the area's spectacular beaches leaked to the outside world. Puerto's citizens erected little huts to house the influx. Many foreign men stayed, some married local girls and built basic resorts.

Today Puerto is a major destination for low-budget, free-living travelers who come for sun, sand, and other opportunities. Dive shops cater to the visitor who wishes to

Once a friendly, hospitable people, many Mangyan now disappear at the sight of strangers, fearing persecution by lowlanders who have pushed them away from their lands, and ridicule by those contemptuous of their civilization.

All visitors should maintain respect for their way of life, request permission to take photographs, and bring a gift of matches, tinned food, medicine, etc in exchange for the hospitality you will in all likelihood receive.

Nalwak Mangyan family

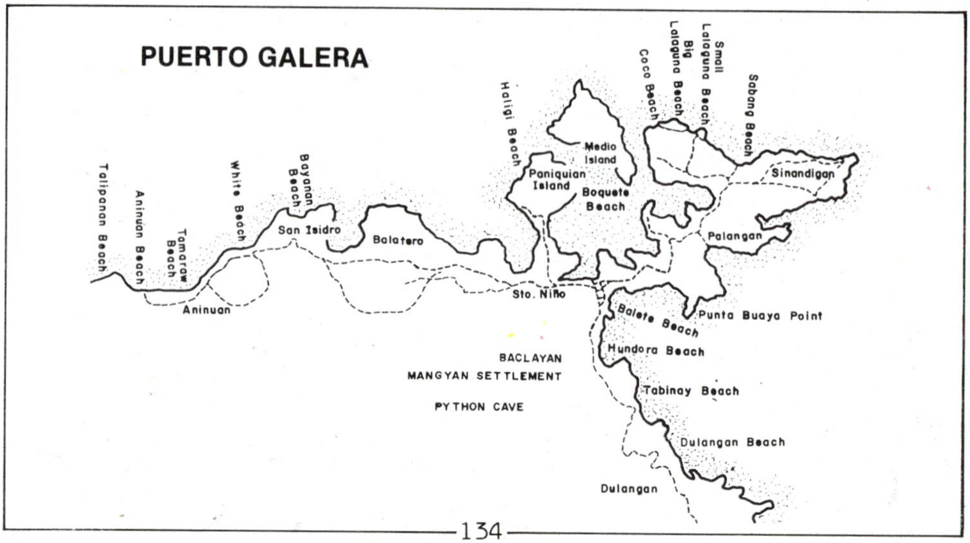

enjoy the reefs, and help enforce a stringent ban on damaging or taking any of the marine life. Numerous beaches are crowded with huts, restaurants, discos, and rental services for water activities.

The easiest **route to Puerto** is an early morning BLTB Bus to the pier in Batangas, then board one of the three ferries, which leave at about 11:30 and 12:30, and charge prices ranging from just over $1, up to $3, depending upon the class and the boat. Local residents fill the inexpensive seats quickly; others are reserved by touts. The fast ferry takes 2 hrs to Puerto, the others take about 3. Touts on board will try to get you to a place they recommend. If you do not have reservations, their services may come in handy. Banca hire from Batangas to Puerto costs about $25, requires some negotiations with the Coast Guard: don't pay anything until you are quite sure clearance from the Coast Guard is forthcoming. Returning ferries leave at 7:30 and 8:00am. During calm seas (usually April and May) there may be an afternoon trip. Manila-bound buses wait for passengers. Be aware of your belongings on the bus and ferry.

Stay on deck for spectacular views while coming into Puerto. The ferry docks in town, where some resorts provide transport to their places. Jeepneys, which pack full very fast, service beaches along the west coast, as far as White Beach, and occasionally 1 km further, and also ply the route to Sabang, from where you may walk to Small and Big Lalaguna. Jeepney service is fairly frequent during daylight. Choose your area, and inspect the digs before settling in.

Most resorts may be accessed by *banca*. *Banca* fees are high, and are set by an association. *Banqueros* usually state a higher rate, and will back into the standard

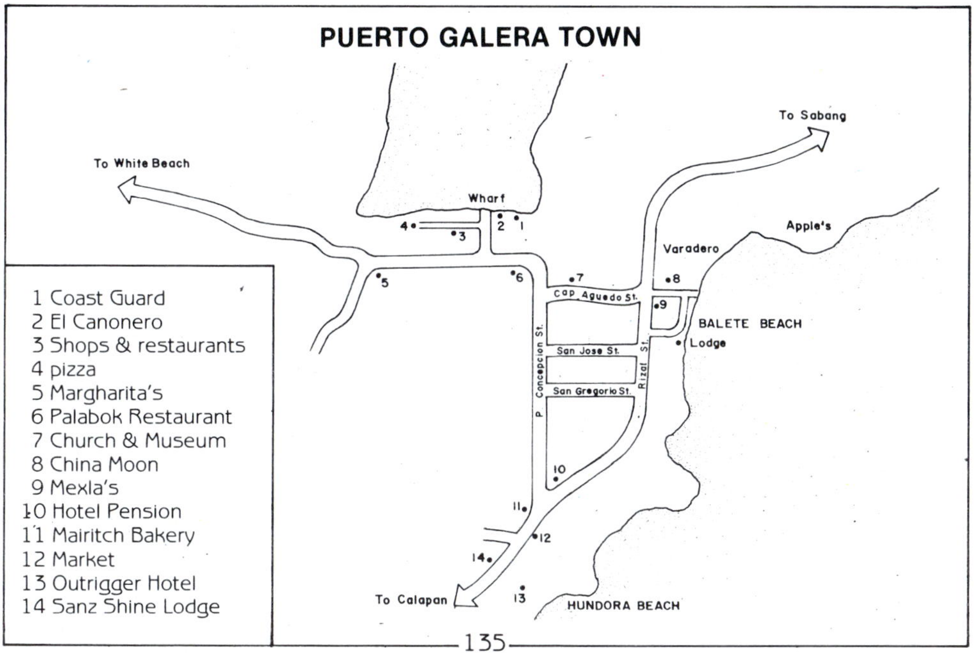

rate with some bargaining.

The center of Puerto Galera has numerous restaurants and inns and a thriving t-shirt and flour-sack clothes industry.

A small **museum** beside the church houses finds of Chinese porcelain unearthed from nearby Bayanan. Inquire in the church school, the *convento*, or the house behind if you would like to see the collection – and leave a small donation.

Beaches **west of Puerto** have good sand and swimming, but not much good snorkeling. **White Beach**, 7 km from town, is very crowded, those further out less so, with nice cottages on **Tamaraw Beach**.

Beaches near **Sabang**, northeast of Puerto, have rocky-corally bottoms, and provide excellent snorkeling and diving. Sabang is very crowded, and noisy with discos. There are two floating bars, the Calapso and Yap- Yum. Capt'n Gregg's has a case of relics recovered from junks claimed by off-shore reefs. **Big Lalaguna** is also crowded, **Small Lalaguna** slightly less so. Nearby Coco Beach, Puerto's up-market establishment, is beautifully landscaped.

Nearby **Paniquian** and **Medio Islands** also have many places, and good beaches. There is good snorkeling off Haligi and Long Beaches, and off **Verde Island**; strong tidal currents off Boquete Beach.

Balete, Hundora and Tabinay Beaches may have rough seas. Encinada Resort, Balete Beach, is very nice; the Outrigger, Hundora Beach, reminds one of Atlantic City.

Walk along the coastal roads for many fabulous views of azure waters, white beaches, boats, all framed by coconut trees.

Mangyan tribes have been settled on two reservations, one at Baclayan, the other on Talipanan. Deep, narrow Python Cave is near the Baclayan settlement. Both settlements are about a 2-hour walk into the mountains. You may also visit a **marble quarry. Tamaraw Falls** are reached by hiking in from the Calapan road. All the hikes require a guide. Arrange fees (about ₱100?) in advance. At **Dulangan**, towards Calapan, you may see gold panning and marble quarrying.

Sustenance

The restaurant at the end, along the harbor front, serves good seafood pizza; tasty wiener schnitzel and wonderful french fries at Harbor Point, good food at Dorothy's, A&L, Bahay Pilipino, China Moon and numerous other places. It is most sensible to ask around when you arrive, as a normally good place may be in a temporary slump if the cook is off, and places come and go with amazing rapidity. Try Capt'n Gregg's and Gigi's at Sabang.

Breakfasts cost from $0.50-2, main meals around $4, mixed drinks around $2.

San Jose

San Jose is Mindoro's largest town, mainly business-oriented, but also a good departure point for visits to Mangyan settlements. Unfortunately San Jose has no going tourist organization, and many of those who come into contact with travelers charge well above what the market ought to bear.

There is some good hiking into the mountains, which are very beautiful, and fair diving. Establish cost in advance. For hiking and visits to the Mangyan contact Mr Vic Victorino, Manila tel 711-4507. He spends part of his time in San Jose and part in Manila and can organize a really nice two or more days trip to the mountains, where you may climb to a waterfall on Mt Tanisan, then hike down to his ranch for one or several nights, and visit the Mangyan who live on or near his property. You may also contact Mr Boni Brillantes, PAL's San Jose Station Manager, for assistance in arranging travels.

It is possible to do one- or half-day visits to the Mangyan, although they may or may not be at home when you get there. Be sure to bring some matches, candy, etc to share. **Bato Ili**, being along the road, is the most accessible settlement. A small store nearby occasionally sells some Mangyan articles. You may also take a jeepney to Paklolo and walk about 20 min to the start of the **Mangyan Reservation**, where it is possible to visit the tribes of the Nalwak area. Most Mangyan are nomadic, so time and patience is needed if you wish to enjoy those who still live in the old way. If you intend to stay in the forest you should be on anti-malarials.

From San Jose it is also possible to visit **tamaraw** country on Mt Iglit. The tamaraw are a small, reclusive and, when cornered, aggressive species of water buffalo which are found exclusively on Mindoro. Owing to destruction of their forest habitat, the species is facing extinction. The government has initiated a tamaraw breeding station not far from San Jose. The herd is small and often hard to find.

Sustenance

Big Newk Restaurant, near the Municipal Building, has an extensive menu, breakfasts around $1.25, lunch and dinner around $2.25. Sikatuna Fastfoods does breakfasts at about 75c, main meals at $1.75. Prices at their beach hotel are slightly higher.

Good, cheap meals may be had in the market, where stalls do individual servings from ₱5, plus rice. In the evenings there are good turo-turo stands in the plaza fronting the *municipio*; vegetable dishes are ₱3, meats are ₱5, tasty *lumpia* is only ₱1. Barbeque stands along the main road before you get to the plaza do chicken, *chorizo*, pork and other meats. The Burger Machine in front of Maan's Pharmacy does hamburgers at ₱4 and ₱7.50, depending upon the size.

Tricycles in San Jose go off duty at around 7 pm, unless you have arranged ahead to have one wait for you. There are several beer and disco joints in town. If you are caught out late without a ride you may be able to catch one near a disco house.

Mamburao

Mamburao, Mindoro Occidental's capital, sits quietly on a long stretch of beach. The town is modest sized, its economy based totally on agriculture. For travelers touring Mindoro's fringes, it is a logical place to break the journey. Jeepneys to San Jose or to Abra de Ilog leave early in the morning.

Vendors meet some morning flights with grapes, fish, shrimps and live crabs to sell to departing passengers.

If you wish to visit the **Mangyan Reservation**, take a jeepney to the Pagbahan River, and follow the road up its southern side to a small barrio. The reservation is a further 3 to 4-km walk.

Traveller's Inn, across from Mamburao market, has 12 basic rooms with bath and helpful people. They can do creditable meals, especially with a little advance warning.

As of this writing there is only one resort, the exclusive Mamburao Beach Resort north of town, with very nice open cottages on a long grey sand beach.

There are also plans afoot to build a simple resort at **Tayamaan Beach**, a very pretty white sand cove 4 km north of Mamburao. In any case it is a lovely place to rest and swim, with shady coconut trees for respite from the sun. Crocodile Hill marks the southern end of the cove, a long pier its northern edge. The sand slopes gradually out to sea providing safe swimming. If you have your own bedding you could perhaps stay at Fiscal Arpato's place, which is intended for daytime use, but has a small cottage and a water pump.

MARINDUQUE

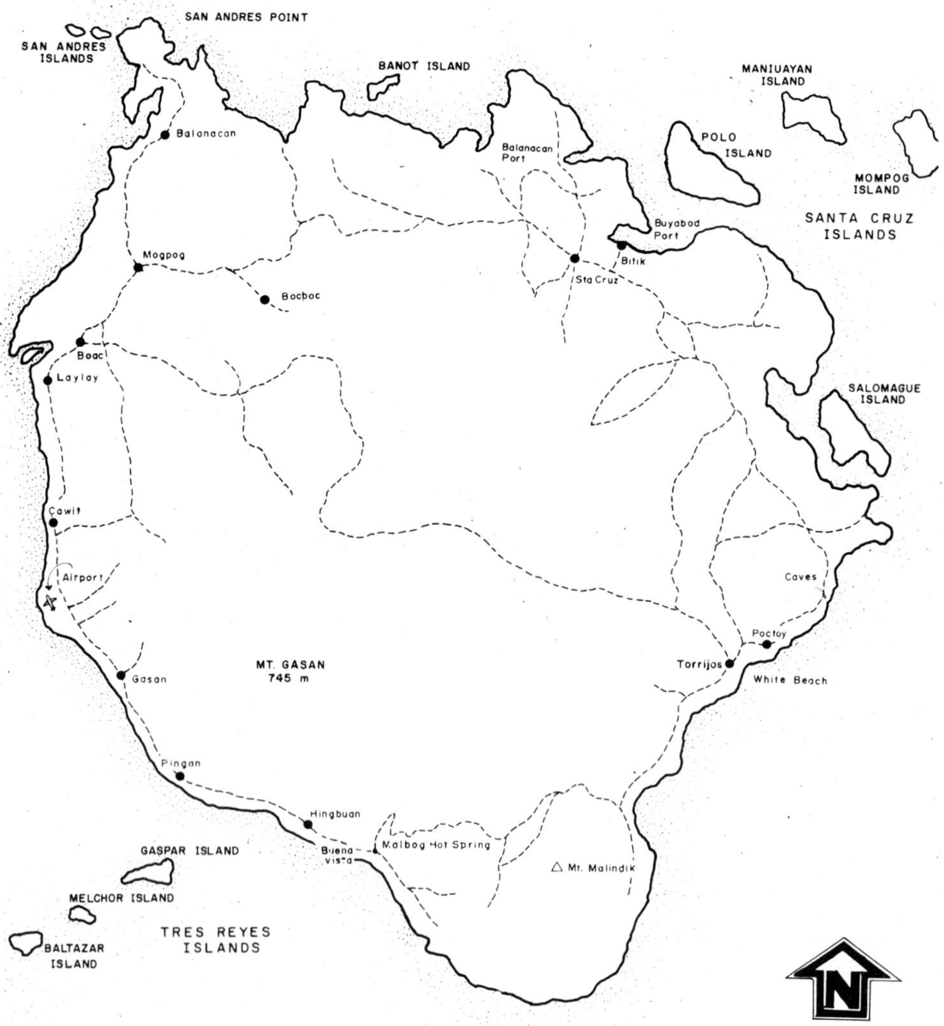
SAN ANDRES POINT
SAN ANDRES ISLANDS
BANOT ISLAND
MANIUAYAN ISLAND
POLO ISLAND
MOMPOG ISLAND
SANTA CRUZ ISLANDS
Balanacan
Balanacan Port
Buyabod Port
Bitik
Sta Cruz
Mogpog
Bocboc
Boac
Laylay
SALOMAGUE ISLAND
Cawit
Airport
Caves
Poctoy
Torrijos
White Beach
MT. GASAN 745 m
Gasan
Pingan
Hingbuan
Buena vista
Malbog Hot Spring
Mt. Malindik
GASPAR ISLAND
MELCHOR ISLAND
BALTAZAR ISLAND
TRES REYES ISLANDS
N

An unusual Morion (Leslie Ann Murray)

Marinduque

access: ½-hr flight from Manila; 2 hrs by *banca* from Lucena, 3 hrs from Mindoro, p 267
climate: driest Nov-May

to do: festival, beaches, snorkel

facilities: seaside rooms & cottages; lodging houses, p 286

Marinduque is a small, round island off the southeast coast of Luzon's Quezon Province. The Easter week Moriones Festival is Marinduque's most glamorous attraction. At this time hotels, private homes and all forms of transport are filled with returning residents, friends and spectators who come to see the imaginatively staged play of a Roman Centurion's conversion to Christianity and his subsequent beheading. Assorted performances unfold over several days, with time to visit the island's beaches and other more constant attractions between. Many of the colorful masks worn by festival participants are purchased by spectators.

At other times, Marinduque is a great get-away, where you probably won't meet too many other tourists and will have the island's sights to yourself. The pace is relaxed. The people seem to manage fairly well. The island is only half an hour from Manila by air, with 10 weekly flights. Accommodations range from one nice seaside resort which has 10 rooms with private bath to simpler cottages by the sea and lodging houses.

Marinduque was originally settled by Mangyan and Malay people. Tagalog is the language spoken. Sung Dynasty pottery finds date trade with the Chinese to between AD 920 and 1289. The remains of a 500-year-old junk rest on the ocean floor off the Tres Reyes Islands.

The name Marinduque probably derives from *malandic*, meaning sloping, but legend has it that two lovers from Quezon, Marin and Garduke, sailed out to sea and drowned themselves when Marin's father, King Batumbacal (literally, ironstone), ordered the poet Garduke slain for pursuing his romantic interest in Marin. Marinduque Island subsequently arose from the spot where the couple died.

Martin de Goiti and Juan de Salcedo sailed up Marinduque's coast in 1571 and claimed the island for Spain. The Spanish settlers had difficulty pronouncing the original name, Malandic, and changed it to Marinduque.

Moriones Festival

In 1870 Fr Pedro Santiago, a Mexican priest, introduced the Moriones pageant in order to dramatize the power of Christian faith. From the simple biblical passage about the Roman centurion who ended Christ's suffering on the cross, Fr Santiago developed the myth of Longinus and week-long Moriones Festival.

Longinus, as the story goes, was a one-eyed soldier who, out of pity, pierced Christ's side. Blood from Christ's wound spurted into Longinus' blind eye. His sight was restored. Because of the miracle, Longinus immediately converted to Christianity, and guarded the body of Christ. For this act of treason, he was condemned to death. Three times he escaped from the centurions and was recaptured before finally losing his head. His three flights are fun for all, as he and others chase willing children and ad lib whatever comes to mind.

Moriones is a Mexican word for helmet. All festival participants wear colorful costumes and masks Most of the masks have helmets and faces with Caucasian features and beards, but some highly imaginative variations crop up as well.

As the Moriones Festival became more well known, commercialism inevitably crept in. Masks made for the performance are often later sold, others are made purely for purchase. T-shirts, hats, souvenirs abound. Several pageants are staged. Some are for the local religious folk and occur at traditional times. Others are scheduled at more convenient hours for tourists. All are great fun. Most sightseers stay in Boac, but the more authentic proceedings in Mogpog are worth seeing because they have retained a close-knit community feeling.

The schedule of activities below is as they occurred in 1985, and may serve as a general guide, but changes may also be expected. On Maundy Thursday the people of Mogpog and Boac roam around their towns wearing the colorful costumes. At 4 pm in Boac Cathedral the religious reenactment of Christ's washing of the apostles' feet takes place. The **Sinakulo,** or passion play, is reenacted by the riverbed, starting at about 8 pm in Boac, and lasting several hours.

In Good Friday the **Way of the Cross** commences from the riverbed in Boac, reenacting Christ's last journey, and finishes at the cemetery where Christ is placed upon the cross (not a crucifixion, although there sometimes are actual brief crucifixions in Mogpog at around noon). During the morning flagellants congregate in the Mogpog town cemetery, maintaining amazingly good spirits as they beat their backs and draw blood from tiny razor cuts made to accommodate the process. When finished, they go to the riverbed to "wash away their sins", and the blood from their arms and backs. In Boac, at 5 pm, the **Santo Entierro** procession, in which all the *santos* are paraded forth from their niches, proceeds from the church, winds through the town and returns to the cathedral.

The **Moriones parade** in Boac commences at about 7 pm. At 8:30 there is a Vigil Mass in the Cathedral, and the scripted version of the beheading of Longinus takes place at around 10 pm at the riverbed. To accommodate the schedules of vacationers the beheading is sometimes repeated at around 10 am on Easter Sunday morning.

On Easter Sunday at 4 am the **Salubong** takes place in Gasan. During the Salubong the community acts out the resurrection and the meeting of Mary and Christ. An angel (child) is lowered from an arch, removes Mary's veil of mourning, and the choir sings the Alleluia.

The original version of the **Pugutan,** or beheading and the events leading up to it, of Longinus takes place in Mogpog at about 8:00 am, followed by a morning of

BOAC, MARINDUQUE

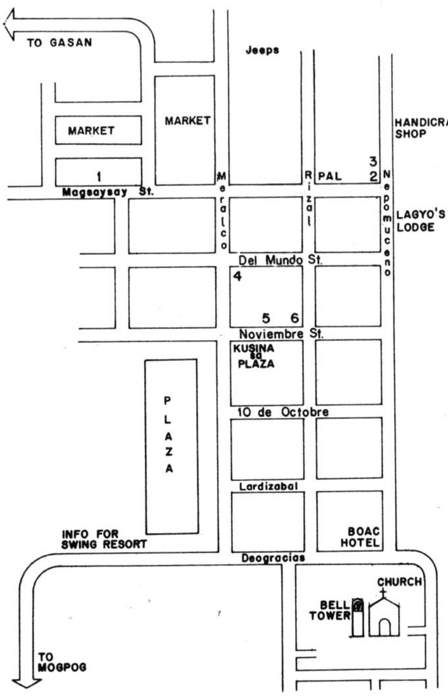

1 Burger stand
2 Bodega Beer House
3 Gift Shop, Ruby's Lodge
4 Marta Go (Paradise Resort)
5 Cely's Lodge
6 Ocampo's (Sunraft Resort)

festivities.

Marinduque also has two festivals in May: the Sta Cruzan on May 3rd and the Flores de Mayo Festival during the 3rd week.

Around Marinduque

A trip around the island is one of the nicest ways to see Marinduque. If time is not a problem and you don't mind very simple accommodation and/or hooked on

MARIA FARR

Morion

spectacular white beaches, take public transport and break the trip in Torrijos. Otherwise hire a vehicle and do the trip in a day. You may also hike inland from Boac and emerge along the coast. Ask Rene Padrigon PAL office, about the route.

For good photos it is best to go south from Boac in the morning and return from the north. The island's points of interest are described below in this order. Set aside a separate half day to see Bocboc Falls in Mogpog, or a day to hike a newly opened trail in Boac.

Jeepneys operate only during daylight hours. They ply the route from Boac to Gasan and Buenavista every hour, but there are only two jeepneys a week from Gasan to Torrijos, one on Monday, one on Tuesday. Jeepneys go from Torrijos to Sta. Cruz every hour, and about every half hour from Sta. Cruz to Mogpog and Boac.

Boac (map, p 141), Marinduque's capital, is on the west coast. Its massive, beautifully restored citadel church is located high on a hill in town, with good views from the bell tower. The original settlement was called *biak* (split) because it was located on both sides of the Boac River. There are several shops in town selling *nito* baskets, decorative wooden birds and, during Easter, *moriones* helmets and T-shirts. Jeepneys wait by the market for passengers.

There are long stretches of pebble beach and several resorts between Boac and *Gasan,* which is 14 km south. The airport is located 2 km north of Gasan. UNI Store, in front of Gasan Town hall, sells decorative birds and basketry, and you can go inside to see the birds being painted.

UNI Store also has a few rooms for visitors, as does Los Amigos Bakery. A few km further south you find Paradise, a pretty, simple resort with cottages by the sea.

Diving, snorkeling and swimming is good off Melchor, one of the **Tres Reyes Islands,** and there is a white coral beach. Remains of a 500-yr-old Chinese junk have been found off shore, but most of its contents have now been removed. At **Pingan** there is a small museum with a few of the pieces found in the junk, and Coast Guard crew that attempts to prevent further pilferage

A few km beyond Buenavista, a track road diverges right to a riverbed. Cross the river on foot to visit **Malbog Hot Springs.** Years ago there was an attempt to develop it, but construction has ceased and the springs flow naturally out from an attractive pool past healthy greenery. I once cured a

Marinduque handicrafts

blistered hand by soaking it in the springs.

The road to Torrijos cuts inland and climbs the northern slopes of **Mt Malindig.** The mountainous, zig-zag drive goes through forested land and mountain life, then descends through great views of the valley, beach and shores of Marlanga Bay.

Continue to **Torrijos,** which was named for a revolutionary general. Turn right beyond town, in barangay Poctoy, to a lovely white sand beach. Great swimming. Fabulous views across the sea to Mt Malindig.

There are a few native cottages on the beach with some basic bathroom facilities nearby. Bring bedding. Buy food in the market and ask someone to cook it for you. Or you could ask the Modesta-Revilla family in town if they have spare rooms, or ask the mayor for assistance.

Talisay Cave, at the BFD Station in Bonliw, may be an interesting stop for children.

Salomague Island has a very beautiful beach, and Willie Red of Sta Cruz has built a resort here, but you need to ask him in advance to have it opened.

Sta Cruz is the hub of activity surrounding Marcopper Mines. Rico's Lodging House offers simple accommodation. Jovilles Resort, on the way into town, is also owned by Willie Red, and again prior arrangement is necessary if you would like to stay here. It has spacious rooms with bath.

Sta Cruz church, built in 1714, is a massive structure with walls 1½ to 2 meters thick, simple line, and a restored façade.

Spelunkers will want to contact the Mendoza family for permission to see **Bathala Caves.** Campers may want to get supplies and head for **Polo** and **Maniwaya Islands,** where beaches and snorkeling are good. Boats departing for the islands leave from Bitik Port at about 7 am. Boatmen live on the islands, so you will have to hire a *banca* to do a round trip.

From Sta Cruz the road winds again into hilly countryside, then descends to **Mogpog.** This town's name is derived from

Door of Boac Cathedral

mag-aapog, meaning lime maker, possibly in reference to a lime kiln the Spaniards found when they arrived here. The Moriones festival originated in Mogpog and is still practiced with much of its original intent (see pp 140-141)

Bocboc Falls outside Mogpog, make a nice half-day trip. Occasional jeepneys ply the Mogpog-Bocboc route (or you can try to hire a jeepney in Mogpog). At the end of the road you alight for a 12-min walk up river. Cross the stream twice, then bear left along an obscure path in order to stay close to the stream. You emerge beside the falls, and can swim in its pool.

On the beach north of Boac, from Swing Resort, you get good views of San Andres Point, where diving is reputed to be good.

Sustenance

Le Baron, which specializes in seafoods, shrimps, crabs but does many things well, is located outside Boac, fronting the municipal building, serves on working days.

Kusina sa Plaza is a local favorite. Beer and some food are available at the Bodega. In Gasan eat at Amigo's, and at Rico's in Sta. Cruz.

Palawan

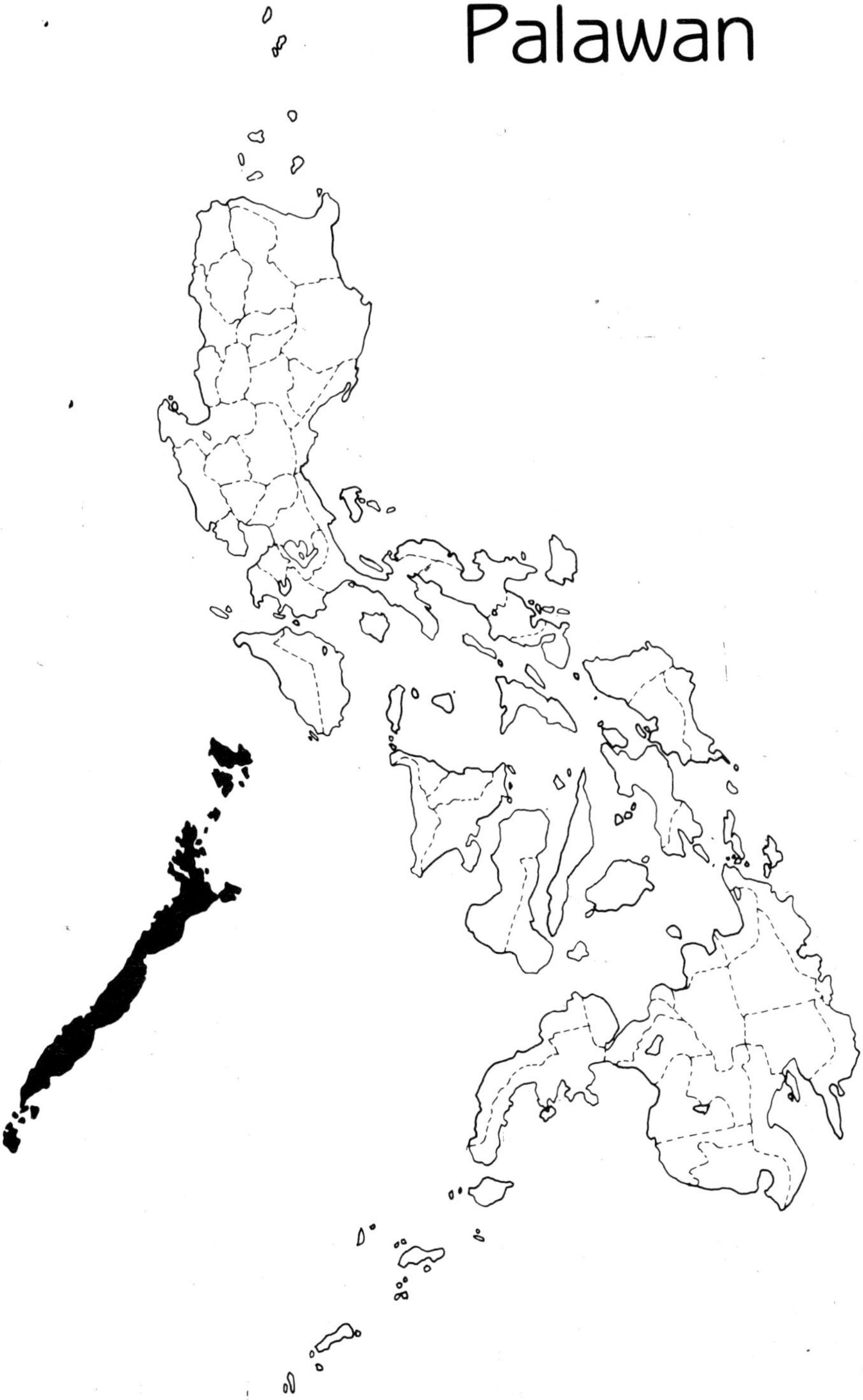

PALAWAN

Linapacan I
El Nido
Pancol
Taytay
Guinlo
San Miguel
Bato
Abongan
SOUTH CHINA SEA
Boayan I
San Vicente
Caramatan Pt.
Dumaran I
Port Barton
Tumarbong
Caruray
Roxas
St. Paul's Bay
Sn.Jose
Caramay
Green Island Bay
Maratapi
Tularquin
Tinitian
North Verde
Buenavista
South Verde
Tanabag
Nagtabon
Baheli
Bacungan
Fondeado I
Honda Bay
Tagburos
Iwahig
PUERTO PRINCESSA
Long Pt.
Table Head
Aborlan
Malanao I
Narra
Quezon
Rasa I
Aboabo
Panitian
Labog
Punang
Karasanan
SULU SEA
Mambalot
Brooks Pt.
Males
Tubbataha Reefs
Batarasa
Bonobono
Malihod
San Antonio Bay
Rio Tuba
Ursula I
Pandanan I
Bugsuk I
Balabac I

Palawan

Palawan

access: 1 hr by air, p 267

climate: dry Dec-Feb, dryest Mar-May

to do: sun, swim, snorkel, dive, hike

facilities: a few hotels, lodges, inns, cottages, sm cabins, p 287

Palawan, the Philippines' last frontier, is a long, narrow island pointing to Borneo. Palawan is an hour from Manila plane, but is otherwise out-of-the-way.

Flora and fauna of Palawan and Mindoro are more related to Bornean life than that of other Philippine Islands. Many species came to the Philippines during the ice ages over the land bridge connecting Borneo, Palawan, Mindoro and Luzon. When the ice receded and oceans rose to their current levels, there were several species which had immigrated to Palawan but had not continued to Luzon.

Among the unique species Palawan hosts are the rare Philippine eagle, scaly anteater, giant turtles, Palawan peacock pheasant, Palawan bear, mouse deer (chevrotain), imperial nutmeg dove, siete colores (seven colors) dove, tabon bird, several orchids, and numerous butterflies. Butterfly collecting is allowed, but most other animals should not be taken off the island.

One thousand years ago Chinese traders named the island Pa lao yu, or land of beautiful safe harbor, in recognition of the many safe havens for ships. The earliest known human remains excavated in the Philippines have been unearthed in Palawan and dated 22,000 years ago, but evidence of human habitation stretch back about 50,000 years.

The Batak, Palawan, Tagbanua and other tribes may be descendants of the original settlers, who came via ice-age land bridges and of later migrants who came on boats. They were followed in the 13th century by Indonesian settlers from the Madjapahit Empire. Tausugs, Muslim tribespeople, inhabit the southern coastal areas.

When the Spanish arrived Palawan was ruled by Borneo from Jolo. The Spanish first occupied northern Palawan and worked their way south from Cuyo and Taytay. When the Sultan of Borneo gave up central Palawan in the 18th century, the Spanish moved their capital from Taytay to Puerto Princessa.

Because Palawan was for many years very sparsely populated in comparison with other Philippine Islands, it has long been recipient of some of Luzon and Visaya's overpopulation. Palawan's delicate ecology and the livelihood of its original tribes is severely threatened by this influx and by the lack of understanding many immigrants have about its environment.

Palawan is now a polyglot mixture of native tribespeople, who have retreated or been pushed to the interior, and of Muslim, Visayan, Tagalog, Ilocano settlers along the edges. There is even a group of Igorots.

The **Batak** are found in several areas of Palawan. They are Negritoes, small, dark, kinky-haired people who sleep in treetops or in hearths to ward off mosquitoes. Men wear g-strings, carry spears. Women usually wear only skirts.

The **Tagbanua** are brown-skinned, slender and have straight hair. The women like brightly colored clothes and ornamentation. They believe in fairies, called *diwata*, which are responsible for their lives. Marriages are arranged when the children are 12. Later, during courtship, the man places a banana stalk by the woman's doorstep. Only if the stalk stays healthy will the marriage be pursued. Polyandry is common; women with several husbands are considered to be in demand, hence worthy of high dowries.

Both the Tagbanua and the Batak have

developed a written language which, like that of the Mangyan of Mindoro, consists of over a dozen gracefully curved letters that are inscribed on bamboo tubes.

The third tribal group, the **Palawans** are a brown, straight-haired people.

There are several smaller tribes, such as the Kanuys of Brooke's Point and the Tao't Bato of the Marcos area. Whether these tribes represent distinct groups which have been in existence for generations is an open question. To restrict outside influence, the Tao't Bato are supposed to be off limits to visitors.

Roads outside Puerto Princessa are unpaved, transport is by heavily laden buses and jeepneys. At the end of a long journey, travelers are often covered with what the locals call "Palawan powder". During July and August roads are often impassable due to heavy rains and flooding in the coastal plains, and seas are rough.

Rains usually last from June through November, with showers continuing as late as February. Palawan's many beautiful beaches, her remaining forests and reefs (logging and dynamite fishing have taken quite a toll) are genuine feasts for the hardy traveler. And, despite the influx of settlers, you still get the feeling of space between towns.

Palawan contains one of the best diving spots in the world: Tubbataha Reef, and about a quarter of the islands in the

Philippines. Some of the northern islands are delightfully unspoilt.

Accommodation in Puerto Princessa ranges from moderate and clean to very basic and sometimes clean. That beyond the capital follows the same pattern.

The low budget traveler can still get by on $3/day in many places. The traveler who needs his own transport will find Palawan very expensive as hire vehicles are pricey. Public transport is available, usually packed, often departing at unscheduled times, and is usually late due to mechanical or tire problems. Should you decide to hire, make it very clear to the owner that he is only getting full price for a relatively trouble-free ride (1 or 2 flat tires may be excusable, more not unless a puncture is the cause). Try the same technique on boat rentals.

Health

Malarial mosquitoes inhabit Palawan's forests. Most travelers who intend to stay in Puerto Princessa and explore other places during the day are not bothered, as the malarial mosquito is a beast of the dusk. Many doctors advise visitors to take preventive medication. This is essential if there is any chance that you will spend a night outside Puerto, unless it is on the beach. Most preventives must be started a couple of weeks in advance of your visit.

If you become ill in Palawan, head for Puerto Princessa and get immediate medical attention. Dr John Mendoza is a wonderful physician, and there are probably other good ones as well.

Travel Assistance

Travel information is available from Ellen Hagedorn, the Tourism Officer, at the capitol (tel 2154) or Kamayan Restaurant. Ask her recommendations for guides and transport.

Baby Baldovieso, who helped gather data for this section, is reliable and nice and can arrange guides and transport. She can be reached at the Badjao Inn. Luis Oliva (look

Beach at St Paul's Bay

for him at Pagitik restaurant/bar) guides and is a good cook. Nancy San Juan of Karla's antiques can recommend reliable guides.

Joe and Cecile of the Duchess Pension are a fund of information. They have a boat in Honda Bay, and offer about the most reasonable rate for the bay tour. Their inn is a gathering place for Peace Corps workers and for many travelers, a great spot for getting up-to-date information on out-of-town places, as well as possibly finding others to share a ride. While gathering information, have a fruit shake - shaved ice and fresh fruit mixed in a blender.

There are other good people, but unfortunately there are a number of locals who treat tourists as milking cows, taking lots of money and giving little service in return.

Puerto Princessa

The capital is a relaxed, spread-out town. Tricycles ply the main roads for ₱1/ride, door-to-door service included. Puerto is mainly a place to rest, eat, and prepare for trips further afield. Stroll along the waterfront, where picturesque houses are built over the water.

Souvenir hunters will want to visit Karla's Etnicraft, Rizal Avenue; the shop in the Rafols; and small shops in several of the lodging places including Mrs Dizon's and the Duchess Pension, where Peace Corps workers sometimes consign items. Karla and Cecile know all about the things they have on hand.

The **museum at Palawan State College** in Tiniguiban, about 5 km south on the main highway, is a good place to get an introduction to the province and some of its tribe's artifacts. Displays of archaeological finds, artifacts, and butterfly and shell collections are well labeled. Bing, the lady in charge, is eager to explain the displays. The museum is open weekdays during working hours, except when Bing is off on an errand. It will cost ₱5-6 to hire a tricycle, only about ₱1.50 if you share the ride. If school is out, have the tricycle wait, or you may have difficulty getting back to town. The campus is very pretty.

Short Tours from Puerto

Beaches in the immediate vicinity of Puerto Princessa aren't wonderful, but the islands in **Honda Bay** are. Don't miss a full or half day cruise with snorkeling, island exploration and, if possible, sun-down drinks on **Cowrie Island** or on **Bat Island**, watching the large fruit bats emerge for

On the underground river

their evening feed.

Snake Island is perhaps the most fascinating of the lot. It is a long tongue of white sand, with a fishing village on the shore and a mangrove which is under water at high tide. Walk the beach, poking in the sand to find, if you are lucky, some large and lovely shells.

You may also want to visit **Canon**, **Pandan and Meara Islands**. A new resort on Meara has cottages, water sports, including diving, restaurant, bungalows.

To get to the islands, hire a tricycle to **Tagburos**, and arrange a pick-up time, or take a jeepney bound for Sta Lourdes, get off at the large Caltex tank, and walk seawards. If you are going to explore the

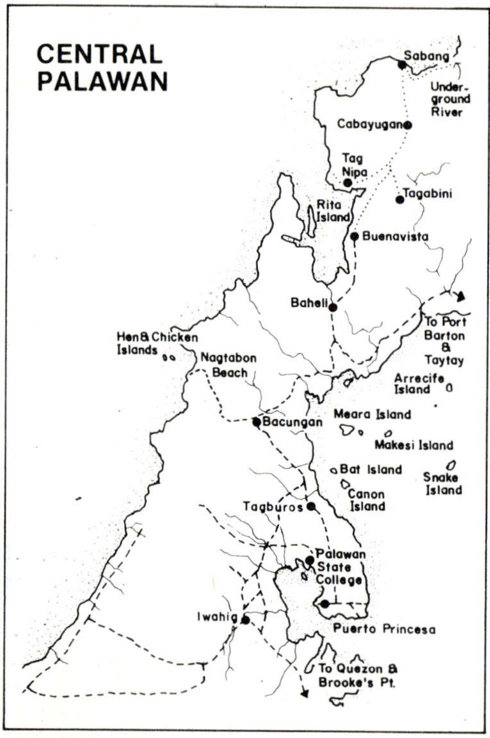

north, have the *banca* drop you off at Tanabag for the night, or longer. Be sure that you have arranged both price and destinations before starting out, as some islands are further out than others. Prices quoted ranged from $12.50 to $17.50. Don't go if seas are choppy.

The wharf at Tagburos is a mercury slag heap: don't eat fish caught nearby.

Nagtabon Beach is a lovely stretch of white sand, with azure waters offshore. You could hire a jeepney to get there (about $25) or take the jeepney to Bacungan, get off at the Nagtabon road, and hike in, about 1-hr walk. The last return jeepney passes by around 5 pm, or whenever it was filled up. The beach has many sand fleas: stay coated with baby oil, through which they can't bite.

Cottages at Nagtabon are owned by Mrs Zenaida Mendoza & Mr Jorge Bummer, who may be contacted in Puerto.

St Paul's Underground River is Palawan's best known attraction and the world's longest known underground river. It exits into a National Park area which is well kept by Mr Vicente Morillo, the ranger. He operates alone and often without encouragement. Do visit him and leave a few kind words, perhaps share a snack. He is happy to tell you about the park and river.

Most people arrive at St Paul's via Baheli from Puerto. The 1½-hr jeepney ride crosses the mountains, with good views back to Honda Bay. *Bancas* are arranged in Baheli, usually costing $45 for large boats, $37.50 for smaller ones for the round trip. The *banca* proceeds down the Baheli river, through remnants of mangrove swamp which is being turned into fish ponds, into the vast bay. The whole journey is picturesque, but takes 2½ to 3 hours each way. Bring cover- ups, lunch, a cushion if you mind hard seats, and a powerful flashlight for use in the cave.

An hour out of Baheli you emerge from the bay into the ocean. Only then will you know if the sea is calm enough to permit passage to St Paul's, although it is often feasible from February to June. Should the *banquero* decide the journey is unsafe, settle for snorkeling at Sta Rita Island, and a picnic before returning.

In good weather you will proceed north along spectacular cliffs, past pretty waterfalls and beaches to a cove where trees drape over a beautiful white beach. Here you can have a refreshing swim before moving through the trees to the mouth of the underground river. Stop along the way to read the signboard about the park and river.

Transfer to the small *banca* to continue upriver 3 km. Only powerful flashes will permit photography. You proceed through several huge domed areas and past some interesting formations to a turn in the river beyond which the *banca* can not go. Explorers have gone 8.2 km into the cave, partly through knee-deep guano, without finding its end.

After returning to the beach, have lunch and a final swim before heading back at 2:30, at the latest.

St Paul's is also accessible via a 2½-hr

banca hire from Port Barton.

Budget travelers with a penchant for hiking may take a jeepney for Baheli from the market early in the morning, then continue overland to Buenavista or Tagbinit, or by boat to Tagnipa, then on foot through Cabayugan and Sabang to St Paul's, asking directions along the way. Find private and very basic lodging at either Sabang or Cabayugan barrios, and you will need a guide for the last part of the walk. Other travelers have hiked in from Tanabag.

Iwahig Penal Colony, established in 1904, is the largest free institution of its nature in the world. On arrival, prisoners are subject to the usual incarceration for several months, complete with chains and hard labor. They are then integrated into the rest of the community - 5000 convicts and their families who lead a fairly normal life farming, etc. The colony is entirely self-supporting, and inmates produce some handicrafts to earn a little extra money. When in uniform, they wear peach-colored outfits.

I have not heard of any other prison in the world where a visiting multinational group of ladies was seen sneaking off around a corner because some felon, murderer or whatever invited them to have a look at the sword he had just made. (Yes, we did buy the thing.)

The handicrafts include some fairly good-sized knives and beautifully inlaid sheaths, woven basketry, walking sticks, etc and it is sometimes possible to buy delicious wild honey at the camp PX. Prisoners are quite amiable, often ask for cigarettes, so it might not hurt to have an extra pack on hand.

Many inmates who have served their sentences choose not to return to their former places and are given instead a small homestead to farm.

The most convenient way to access Iwahig back is by tricycle or jeepney hire. One or more jeepneys leave the market in the early morning for Iwahig, others return in the afternoon, schedules and frequencies uncertain.

Southern Palawan

Quezon is a nondescript town with a market, and a beautiful waterfront. Offshore islands are ideal for sun lovers. It has long been a destination for those interested in the area where the earliest human remains found in the Philippines were unearthed.

The Tabon Caves were first excavated by Dr Robert Fox and staff from the National Museum.

The Quezon branch of the National Museum has exhibits of some finds (the good stuff has gone to Manila), a dilapidated insect collection, some stuffed animals, and good displays of native tribes' handicrafts. The caves are kept locked to prevent damage to remaining contents. Arrange visits through the museum staff, especially Vic, who has a wealth of knowledge about the caves and their history as he was involved with the dig. Set prices for the boat and guide in advance.

The boat ride to the caves area takes 20 minutes, around Albion (Lipuun) Head. Disembark on a beach at the mouth of the first cave, then climb cement stairs to **Tabon Cave**: beautiful views all the way. Here the dig has been left as it was completed so you can see the sites' locations. Continue the ascent to **Diwata Cave**, where the inhabitants buried some of their dead and held religious rites. There are about 200 caves of various sizes in this area Tabon was inhabited for almost 50,000 years, probably during rainy season when the cave offered a hospitable, dry environment. Tool and bone remains demonstrate that the people who lived here were food gatherers, and ate small animals as well as vegetables.

Tabon Cave was abandoned about 9000 years ago, before the land bridges were submerged, when the caves were still 30-35 km inland from the sea shore. Nearby **Guri Cave** was occupied between 8000 and 4000 years ago, yielding evidence of coast-dwelling people with a more advanced civilization.

Until recently, visitors had to use basic

Handicrafts at Karla's

intown lodging or camp in the museum building, which many considered preferable. Now there is a new resort on nearby Tabon Beach, which makes staying very pleasant. Theo, Tabon Resort's Belgian owner, can also help you do a delightful adventure by boat and hiking through mangrove swamp and up the Tumarbon River to a pretty waterfall. You might even see a small crocodile.

Food is good, and cheap (30c for a meal) in small restaurants near the market, and very good at Tabon Resort (about $1.50 for breakfast, $2.30 dinner). Ask what's freshly available and go with it.

There is a very primitive resort (no bathrooms) on Tamlugan Island. Tabon Beach Resort has lovely waterfront property on Sidanao Island, not far from the Tabon Caves, and on Mansarruyan Island, about an hour away by *banca*.

Access to Quezon is by very expensive hire or by crowded public transport. A Charing bus leaves Puerto Princessa daily at 9 am, or whenever it's full (arrive early); fare is $2, the trip takes 5-7 hrs. Puerto Royale has 3-4 daily trips to Brooke's Point. Sometimes you can connect with a jeepney for Quezon at Narra, Aborlan or Aboabo, and jeepneys occasionally go from Puerto.

There is a Tagbanua reservation about 10 km from **Aborlan**. **Narra** is the largest town between Puerto and Brooke's Point, and has a thriving vulcanizing industry, several simple lodging places and restaurants, nearby hot springs, waterfall in the

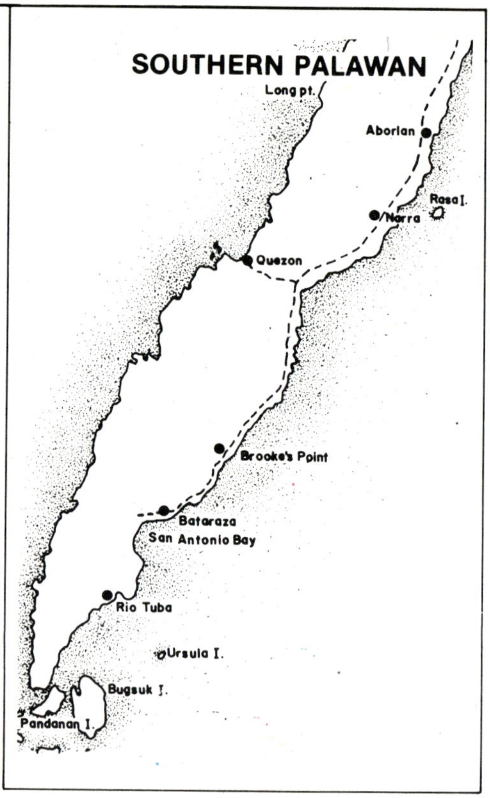

mountains (a good distance) and a pretty island offshore.

Brooke's Point is at the end of Palawan's south road. **Ursula Island,** once the main southern destination, was the nesting place for thousands of birds which returned there each evening from the mainland. Unfortunately the birds were hunted, and have moved elsewhere. A few still come to roost in the evenings, but the long trip needed to get there is not worth the effort. At the time of writing there was some free lance banditry in the southern areas, which have historically been risky to travel.

Northern Palawan

Most travelers head north from Puerto Princessa to the very popular Port Barton and El Nido areas, plus several nice spots in between.

One used to be able to go to **San Rafael**

and visit the Batak, but recent immigrants have pushed them further into the forests, and they are not always readily accessible.

There are cottages on the beach in **Tanabag**, just beyond San Rafael, a coral island nearby for snorkeling, a day trip to a waterfall, a huge cave called Taraw, and a 2-3 km walk along the beach to San Rafael. Inquire for information from the Duchess Pension in Puerto. Visits to the Batak can sometimes be arranged. A trail goes from Tanabag to the Underground River, a 4-day hike.

Miriam Lines has a daily bus, and there are several daily jeepneys which leave Puerto for San Rafael, $.75 and 2 hrs.

Roxas City is the place to change rides for Port Barton. There are a couple of basic lodging places, but it is better to continue to the nearby Coco Loco cottages on a long beach. They also may have a guide to the Batak.

Jeepneys leave Puerto from Malvar St for Roxas City ($2), where you transfer for the 1-hr ride to Port Barton ($1). Puerto Royale buses leave both Puerto and Roxas at 6 and 9 am. Private hire to Port Barton is at least $75, one way. It is sometimes possible to change rides at San Jose for Port Barton, but there is no assurance of a seat from there.

Port Barton and islands nearby have lovely white sand beaches and several establishments which offer lodging. Swissippini and Elsa's are both recommended, rooms by the sea, common baths. You may hire *bancas* for the trip to the Underground River (about $40 for a *banca* for 5) or to El Nido (about $60). Zaccharias Cabungan has had good reports, as do the boats Argentina, Malaya, Neritess and Queen Dolly.

There are several waterfalls near Port Barton, another (Little Baguio Falls) near the airport at Inendeng, beyond San Vicente, which also has a beautiful beach, and lovely areas near Little Baguio Falls. Walk or take a *banca*.

Taytay, the original Spanish capital of Palawan is now a quiet town with a 300-yr-old church and fort. The road from Roxas is not passable during wet season.

Take a jeepney from Roxas to Abongan ($1.50) or Calawag ($3). From Abongan walk 1 km to Taboan, find Lando, who can arrange to hire a boat to Embarkadero,

Iwahig Penal Colony – leading a normal life

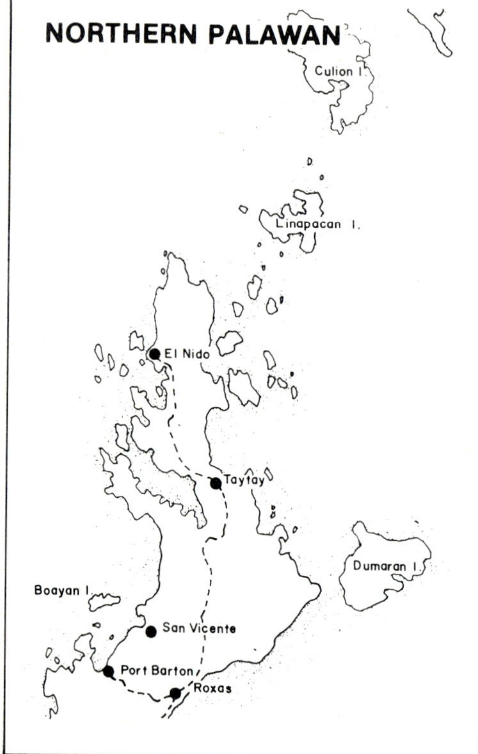

Aside from Ten Knots, Mrs Gloria Fernandez has a cottage for 5, the Lims have a lodging house. An Englishman who is apparently unpopular locally has a place on a beautiful beach on Pangalucian Island.

Distant Islands

Several of Palawan's more inaccessible islands have become special places for travelers who are willing to do the boat rides, although Pacific Air does fly into Cuyo. Accommodation and food in all these places is in private homes.

Coron, where boats plying the Manila-Puerto Princessa route, is reknowned for its fine basketry and delicious wild honey. You may visit Maquinit Hot Springs, bathe in warm sulfuric waters, then swim in the ocean nearby.

Cuyo has a beautiful 300-yr-old church, great diving (bring everything), and a lovely atmosphere.

Cagayan and **Culion**, too, receive high praise.

where you switch to a tricycle to the town. From Calawag you have a 2-hr boat ride to Taytay.

El Nido is even more difficult to reach, unless you charter a flight from Manila or Puerto Princessa. You may find a *banca* going from Abongan (find Lando) or Taytay, or hire one.

Beautiful Ten Knots Resort, **Miniloc Island**, has simple, well done cottages with common bath, good service, sunset dinners served on the mainland, well-run diving, rabbits and ducks on land, and fish come in close to be fed.

The resort staff is actively promoting conservation of the surrounds, and has an on-going turtle raising project in an effort to help the species survive.

Sustenance

A variety of tasty food is available in Puerto Princessa. Tasty native fare is available at Kamayan. Duchess Pension does good snacks, meals (order in advance) and great fruit shakes. Golden Horse serves Chinese food.

Good Vietnamese food and French bread is available cheaply at the refugee camp. ZUM serves German fare. Cafe Puerto serves delicious meals - ask Andrew for his fish in cheese sauce. In the evenings, try Pagitik for a drink and ask for Louis' banana flambe.

Beyond Puerto Princessa there are small *turo-turo* restaurants in larger towns along the road.

Visayan & Central Islands

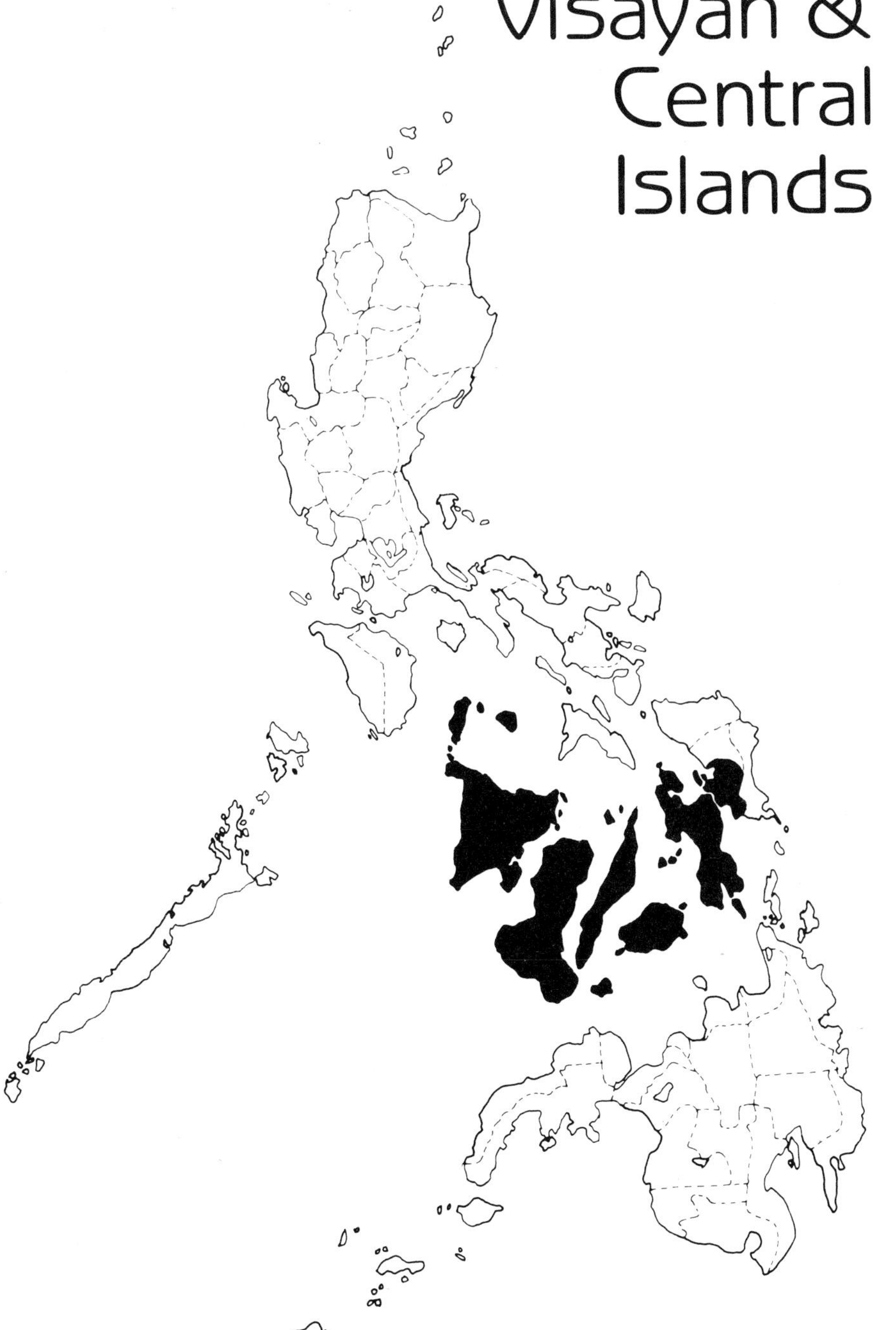

Visayan & Central Islands

Sandwiched between the Philippines' two largest islands, the Visayas are comprised of six large islands (Bohol, Cebu, Leyte, Negros, Panay, and Samar), and numerous small islands and islets, some of significant interest to travelers, such as Boracay, Guimaras, Romblon, Siquijor. The Romblon Islands are not politically part of the Visayas, but they are included here because, geographically, they appear to belong there.

Most of the destinations mentioned are accessible from both Manila and Cebu. They are detailed starting at Romblon, in the northwest, and progressing through Panay, Negros, Cebu, Bohol and finally Leyte. Each area has its own distinct character. Many areas have their own dialects, although Cebuano is widely spoken throughout the region.

Romblon & Tablas

to do: swim, hike
facilities: lodging, p 288

access: 1 hr by air from Manila, p 267
climate: good year round, best Nov-May

Tablas, Romblon and Sibuyan are the largest of the 20 islands comprising Romblon Province. Not frequented by tourists, they have maintained their native charm and remained relatively unspoiled. Reefs have not been overfished. The supply of seafood is abundant and inexpensive. Accommodations and food are simple.

The airport is in Tugdan, Tablas. Every day or so, a *banca* leaves Sta Fe for the 1½ hr trip to Boracay; the crossing should be done only in fair weather. Boats leave to Romblon from San Agustin, passing lovely islets on the way. There is a daily boat from Romblon to Magdiwang, Sibuyan.

Tablas

Tablas is a lush island with gregarious people and many nice pebble beaches. Vegetables are grown on the island.

Tugdan is not much more than an airport with a small hostel, Gutierrez Cool Spot, and a contact for passengers headed for Boracay.

Jeepneys wait for the daily flight to carry passengers to San Agustin ($1.50) or to Looc and Sta Fe. Jeepneys fill up quickly. The journey from Looc to Sta Fe is difficult during rainy weather.

San Agustin, 1¾ hrs north of Tugdan, is a small friendly coastal town. You may want to visit Bitu Falls and Cajbo-aya ruins, although the trails are overgrown. Perez is a great tricycle driver and reliable source of information.

The first jeepney to Tugdan leaves San Agustin at 7am, so if you are staying out of town at the mayor's guest house, arrange transportation the night before to get back into town.

Romblon

The marble carver (Gretchen Hutchinson)

MARINDUQUE
MINDORO ORIENTAL
MINDORO OCCIDENTAL
Roxas
San Jose
Ilin I.
SIBUYAN SEA
Simara I.
ROMBLON
San Agustin
San Andres
Odiongan
TABLAS
ROMBLON
Tugdan
San Fernando
SIBUYAN I.
Cajidiocan
Looc
Sta. Fe
Semirara I.
Carabao I.
Boracay
Caluya
Malay
Buruanga
Sibay I.
Ibajay
Pandan
KALIBO
ROXAS
AKLAN
CAPIZ
Culasi
Dumalag
Sara
PANAY
Barbaza
ANTIQUE
Ajuy
Calinog
Bugasong
Barotac Viejo
Janiuay
ILOILO
SAN JOSE
ILOILO
Miagao
Jordan
GUIMARAS
Tiolas
Anini-y
PANAY GULF
MASBATE
MASBATE
Balud
Jintolo
VISAY
Calagnaan
Sicogon
Bantayan I.
Victorias
Escalan
Silay
Tub
BACOLOD
Murcia
Calatrava
Asturias
Bago
Mambucal
San Carlos
NEGROS OCC.
Toledo
Canlaon
Hinigaran
Himamaylan
Guihulngan
TAÑON STRAIT
Kabankalan
Moalboal
Bulata
Ayungon
Sipalay
Bindoy
NEGROS OR.
TAGBIL
Boljoon
Cagayan I.
Hinoba-an
Bais
Tanjay
Bato
Oslob
Amlan
Bayawan
DUMAGUETE CITY
Zamboanguita
Siaton

VISAYAN AND CENTRAL ISLANDS

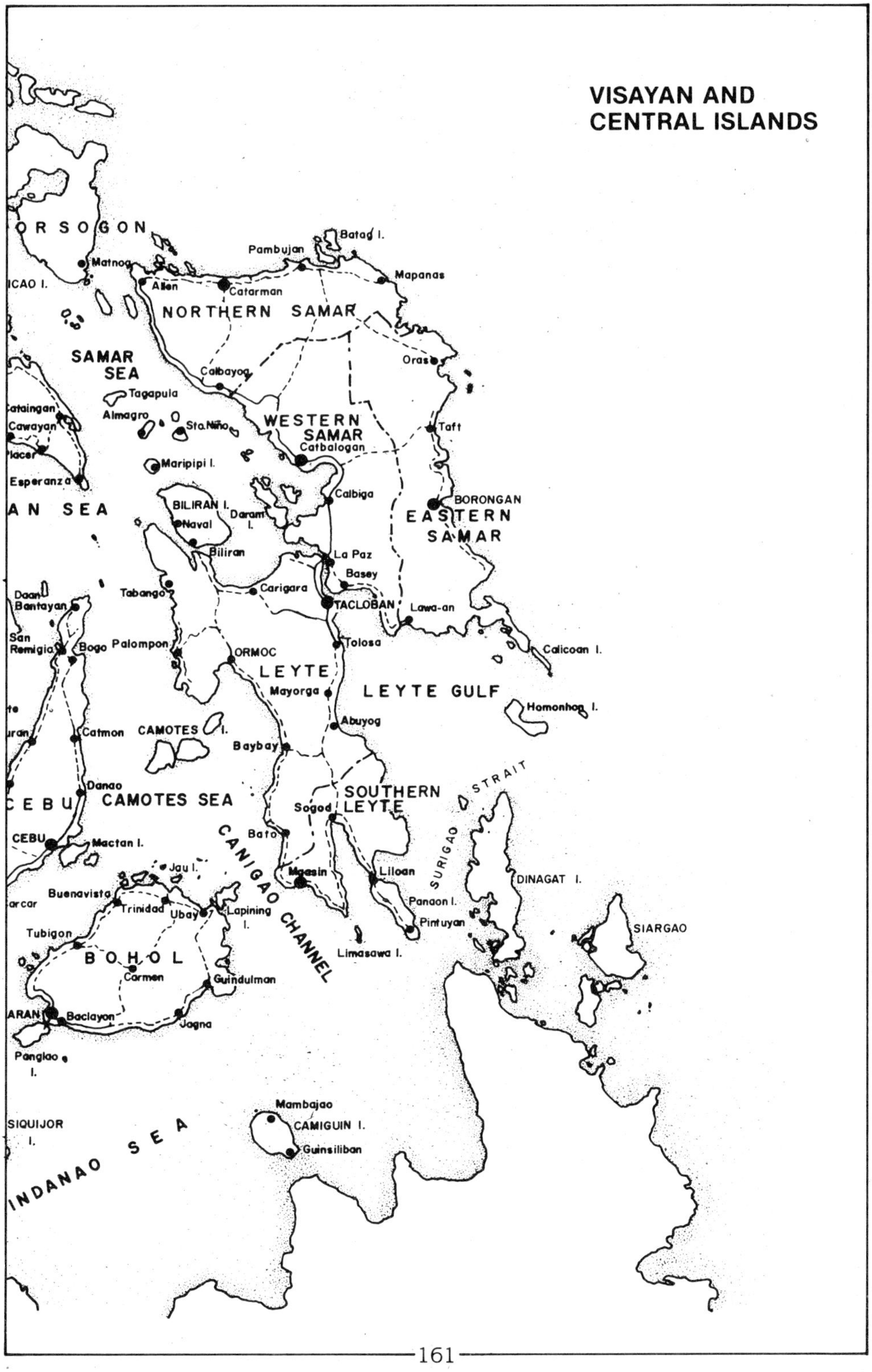

Looc is about ½ hr south of Tugdan. In the town center of **Looc** is a nice plaza, a basketball court and a market area, usually with much fresh fish. A PAL office handles ticketing and reservation.

Santa Fe serves as a jump-off point for transport to Boracay.

Romblon

The lovely port town of Romblon on Romblon island is the provincial capital. Evidence of the island's vast marble supply is everywhere. As you approach the pier by water, quarries are visible above the town, along with the ruins of Fort San Andres, built in the mid 17th Century. From his perch in the town plaza, the statue of a marble carver gazes over crystal waters and harbor activities.

Surrounding the plaza are myriad small shops selling marble eggs, plaques, figurines and mortars and pestles. Salvador Tan's shop across from the post office has one of the better selections. Handwoven *piña* handbags, coin purses and hats are a good buy.

Romblon Cathedral has a beautiful altar and lovely icons. Ask to see the antique collection. Hire a tricycle to explore the island (about $5 for ½ day). Driver Manolo Silverio is reliable, friendly and informative. Enjoy one of the many beautiful beaches, stop to watch the marble hunks being cut into smooth slabs, or hike to a working quarry.

Don't plan to sleeping late in Romblon. Church bells begin to peal, accompanied by crowing roosters and howling dogs, at 5 am and are joined by whisking brooms and shouting children. This cacophany is followed by singing, then mass, generously brought to you by loudspeakers wired to the church.

Sibuyan is a beautiful island with some lovely waterfalls and nice beaches, and rugged Mt Giting-giting to climb. There are no lodging facilities, so plan on camping.

Sustenance

Across from the market in **San Agustin**, Tablas, you can get a good bowl of chicken *mami* at Everybody's Inn for 50c. Meals are available in **Looc** at the Tablas Pension & Plaza Inn. Small shops in **Santa Fe** offer food. In **Romblon**, try the market, small shops, street vendors or bakeries.

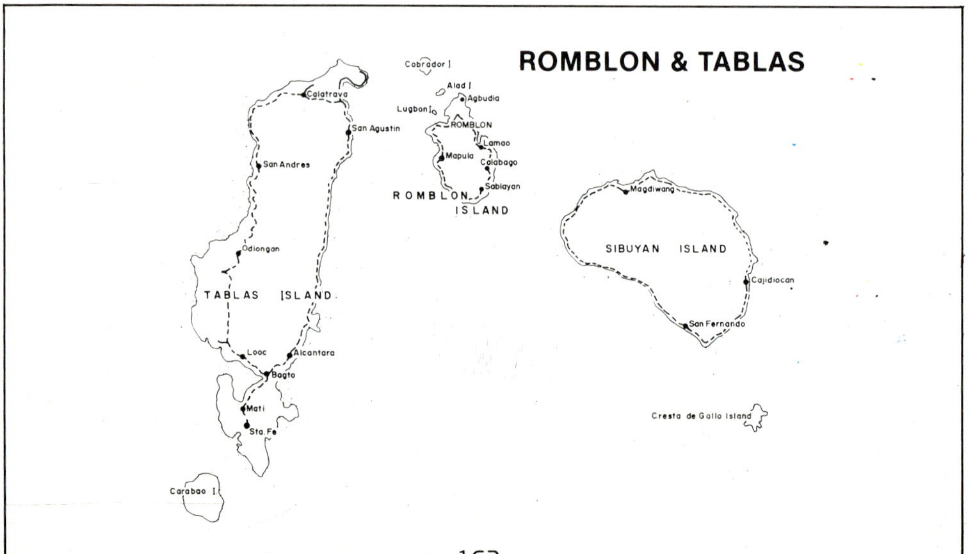

Boracay, Kalibo & Roxas City

Boracay (Maria Garcia Farr)

Boracay, Kalibo & Roxas City

access: 1 hr by plane from Manila to Roxas or Kalibo; 4 hrs by land from Iloilo to Roxas, ½ hrs to Kalibo, 2 hrs from Kalibo to Boracay, p 267

climate: Okay year round, best Nov-June

to do: Ati-Atihan Festival in Kalibo, 3rd weekend of January; beach & water sports in Boracay

facilities: limited lodging & food, p 288

Kalibo

Kalibo, Aklan Province's oldest town and capital, is normally an unpossessing place. But during the 3rd week of January its citizenry and thousands of visitors participate in the famous Ati-Atihan festival. Preparations begin weeks ahead as Kalibo gears up and erupts into an incredible party lasting Friday, Saturday and Sunday.

During the weekend, the legend of Panay's purchase by Bornean Datus from the Negritoes comes to life, with a multitude of colorful, riotous additions. The transaction, in which the Aetas exchanged gold and trinkets for the coastal areas of their island, is acted out, sort of, and like all festivals in the Philippines, many activities are centered around the church.

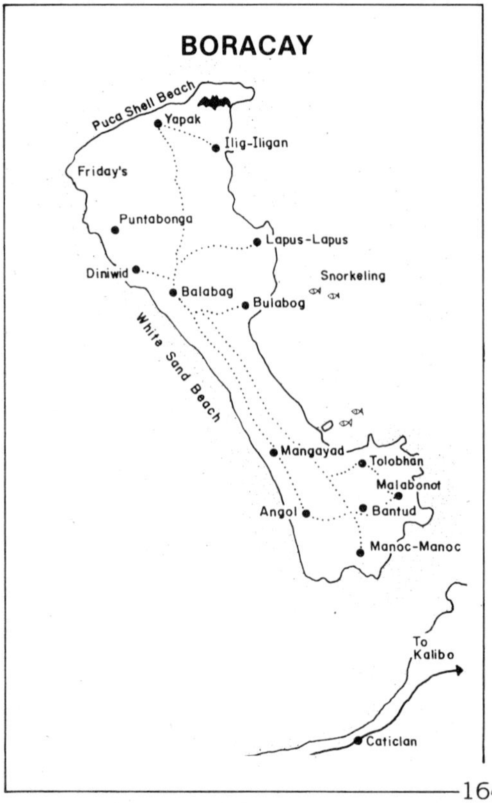

The whole thing is one glorious week-long revel. People don costumes which vary from the artistic to the outrageous, faces are blackened to look like the Negritoes, who come to town and join in the fun which is had in their name, processions and partying take over, nobody is counting how much alcohol is imbibed.

Many other communities have copied Ati-Atihan, but always in a more ordered way, more suited to the temperaments of their citizenry.

Accommodations and transport for Ati-Atihan are booked months in advance. Many visitors camp on the beach. At other times of year most travelers are merely passing through on their way to Boracay.

Try J-Land Native Products, Mabini corner Martyrs, Kalibo, or Roxas and Kalipayan Handicrafts for local products. Accommodation in Kalibo is basic.

Glowmoon Hotel and High Chapparal both offer food. Cafe au Lait on Martyrs St has great fruit shakes at 35c, a delicious mushroom sandwich for 50c, fairly decent schnitzel.

Boracay

Boracay's fabled beaches, with white sand granules as fine as icing sugar, attract scores of tourists. Puka Shell Beach, which suffered from a shell paucity during the puka shell craze, is one of the nicest beaches.

Access is via PAL to Kalibo, then 2 hrs overland to Caticlan; or by charter or Pacificair or Aerolift to Caticlan. From Caticlan there is a short *banca* ride to Boracay. Have belongings well wrapped. When returning to Manila, book the Boracay-Caticlan *banca* the night before you intend to leave.

Although a few resorts have their own generators, there is no commercial electricity on the island. Water supply is inconsistent, and water is not potable. Resorts and restaurants tend to come and go.

Dozens of small establishments have put cottages on the island, and are especially dense along White Sand Beach. Facilities range from very nice cottages with private bath and fan to very rustic indeed. Prices vary widely with the establishment and season. Casa Blanca, Casa Pilar, Fridays (pricey), Lorenzo's, Pearl of the Pacific, Terraces and Tito's have received good comments.

Vendors with an assortment of supplies and foods walk by cottages.

Wind surfing, snorkeling, diving, boating are available in several places. There are a couple of wind surfing schools in Mangayad. *Banca* rentals are about $15 for 3-4 hours for 10 people; sailing *bancas* are $1.25/hr, a bit more with a "driver". Flagged "taxi" *bancas* ferry people from one spot to the next very inexpensively.

Snorkeling is good near Lapuz-Lapuz, Small (Laurel) Island and Yapak. Small Island has a nice beach and a haunted house to explore.

Pony rides are available for children.

Bat caves at Ilig-Iligan are home to large fruit bats which are considered a delicacy.

The Jolly Sailor Bar & Restaurant has safe deposit boxes, is a good place to get information, assistance, help with sending communications, visa extensions.

Manila may be contacted by radio phone from the Red Coconut Restaurant (order food a day in advance), and through Ely Dublin of Pacific Air. Dada's store, Angol, assists with ticketing thru PAL in Kalibo.

A Rock Resthouse has a medical clinic.

Many low-budget travelers come to hang out, hang loose, and hang around for as long as their money permits. Their mores, and those of others who have come in to benefit from the tourist traffic, have often offended locals.

Peace and order problems have surfaced recently. Don't bring valuables.

Niknik (sand fleas) are a rainy season hazzard which is best kept at bay by applying a generous coat of baby oil, through which they can not bite, to the skin.

Sustenance

A wide variety of food is available. Order well in advance, be prepared to wait an hour or two before the meal is produced. Seafoods are best. Ask around for news of the current state of affairs. Many restaurants have only one cook, and food may not be so good when the cook is off.

Chez de Paris' French owner has gained good repute for his food.

Joni's Tex-Mex cuisine is well known, Toby (no sign) does good sausages and Swedish food. Mango Ray and Why Not? also have been recommended.

Lorenzo's holds a cultural show with dinner. For Italian food, try Folemar, Bazura does BBQ. And if you want Filipino food, try Moonlight at Bandida's.

The English Bakery and Marco's make and sell great bread and rolls.

Good food at the Jolly Sailor Bar & Restaurant.

Bars and places for meeting others include Sandbar, Beachcomber, Starlight, and Kontiki.

Roxas City

Roxas City, Capiz Province's capital, nestles peacefully amid a vast expanse of fish

ponds and shrimp hatcheries.
Accommodation in town is simple. Villa Pacita and Marcs, both by the sea, have nice rooms. Marcs also has some less expensive, simple ones.

Beer, barbeque and snacks are available along Baybay Beach, great at sunset. Altacosta does good seafood. The restaurant fronting Marcs, a 15-min walk down the beach, is also popular. All the hotels and inns mentioned on p 288 serve meals and snacks

Although Roxas serves primarily as a junction on the road to and from Iloilo, Boracay and Sicogon, travelers who want a quiet interlude near an 11-km-long beach with several off-shore islands to investigate may well stop a while. **Baybay Beach** is host to sand fleas, so coat exposed skin with baby oil as it will keep them away. There are fishing villages to investigate, and Roxas' new city market is clean, expansive, inviting to wander.

Snorkeling and shallow diving is available at **Mantalinga Island**, directly off Baybay Beach, more off **Mabaay** and **Tuad Islands**, west of Culasi Port. **Olotayan Island** has good white beaches and snorkeling. Roxas isn't set up for tourists, so you'll need assistance from your hotel to arrange transport. Plan to spend the day on Olotayan, as fishermen will take you and pick you up later. Bring food and drink.

Pan-ay town is 7½ km from Roxas City along a bumpy, dusty road. Its huge, massive church (walls 3 m thick) has beautiful retablos, and 8 bells in the tower. One, at 10.4 tons, is the largest bell in the Philippines. It was cast in 1878 from 70 sacks of coins donated by the townspeople.

The people of Panay Island, and especially of this area, hold a number of mystical beliefs and practice rituals harking back to pre-Spanish times. No businessman would consider starting a new fishpond until the local spiritist has performed appropriate rituals. Without them, workers would be convinced that the project would fail. The spirits are taken very seriously here.

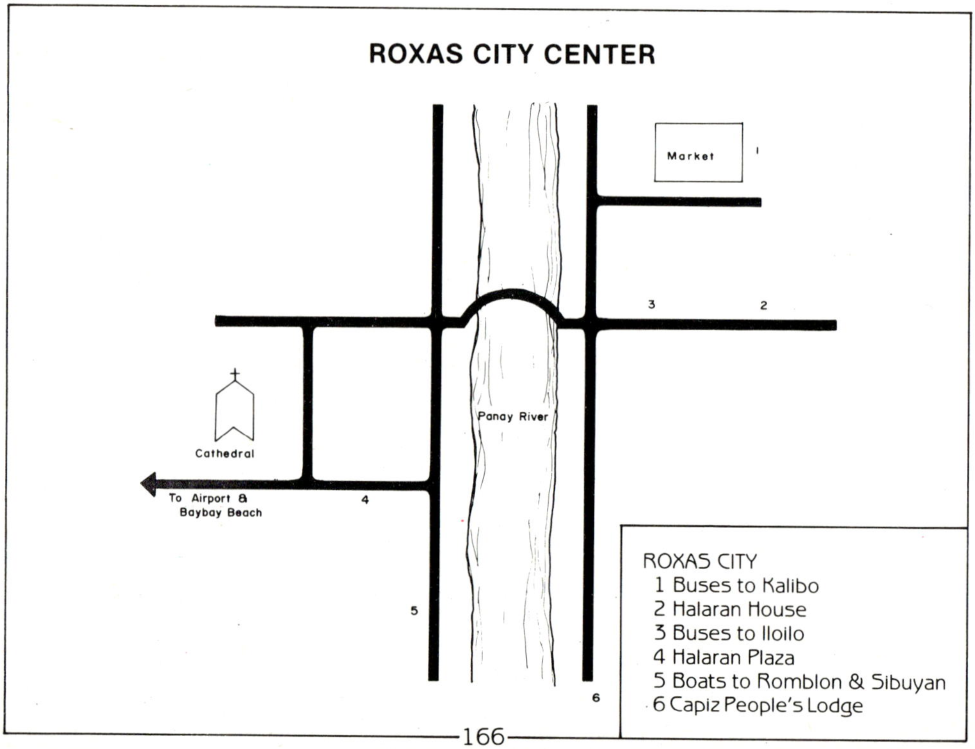

Iloilo

Intricate Embroidery at Asilo de Molo

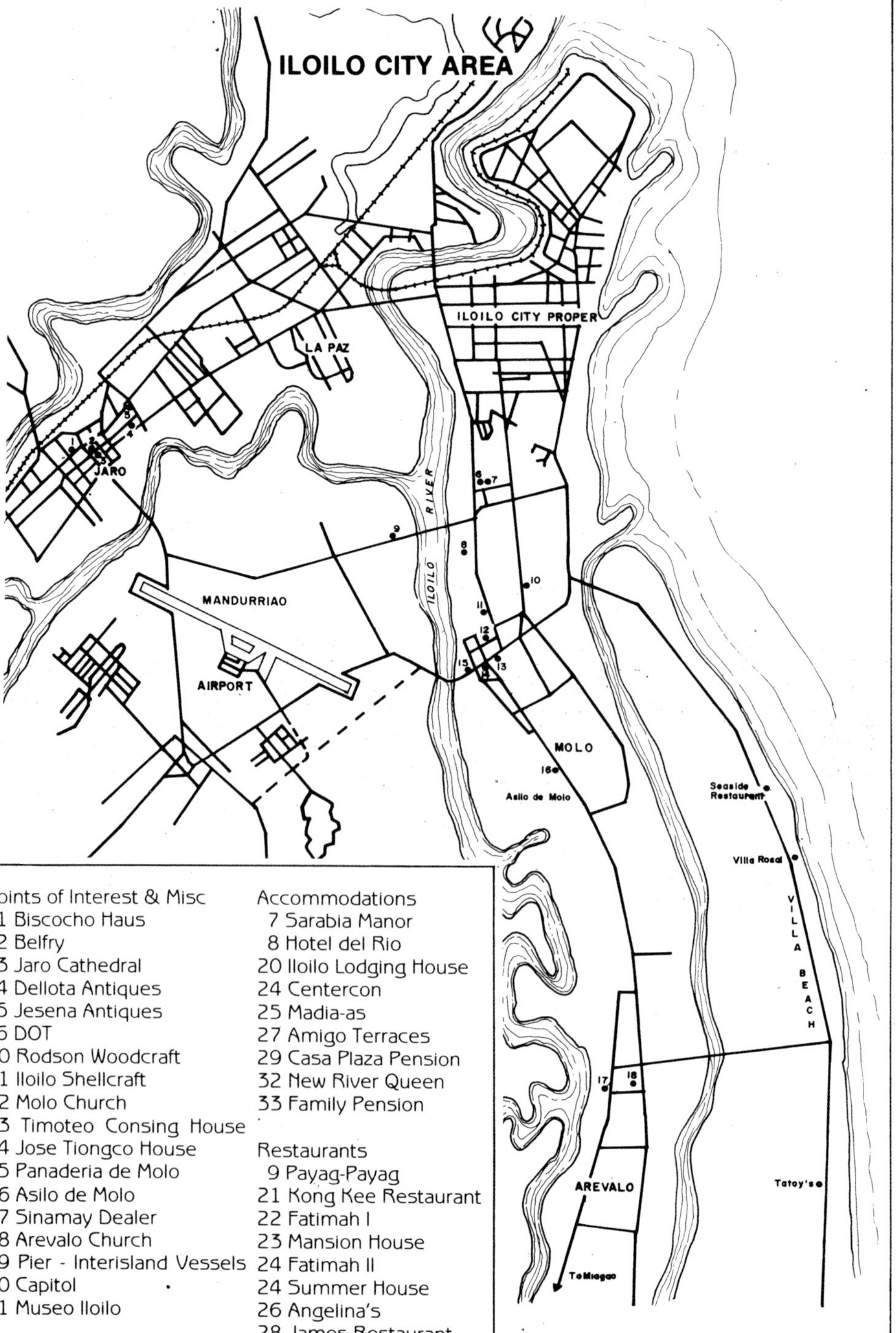

Points of Interest & Misc
1 Biscocho Haus
2 Belfry
3 Jaro Cathedral
4 Dellota Antiques
5 Jesena Antiques
6 DOT
10 Rodson Woodcraft
11 Iloilo Shellcraft
12 Molo Church
13 Timoteo Consing House
14 Jose Tiongco House
15 Panaderia de Molo
16 Asilo de Molo
17 Sinamay Dealer
18 Arevalo Church
19 Pier - Interisland Vessels
30 Capitol
31 Museo Iloilo

Accommodations
7 Sarabia Manor
8 Hotel del Rio
20 Iloilo Lodging House
24 Centercon
25 Madia-as
27 Amigo Terraces
29 Casa Plaza Pension
32 New River Queen
33 Family Pension

Restaurants
9 Payag-Payag
21 Kong Kee Restaurant
22 Fatimah I
23 Mansion House
24 Fatimah II
24 Summer House
26 Angelina's
28 James Restaurant
34 The Tavern
35 La Verandah Fatima
36 Fatima Garden

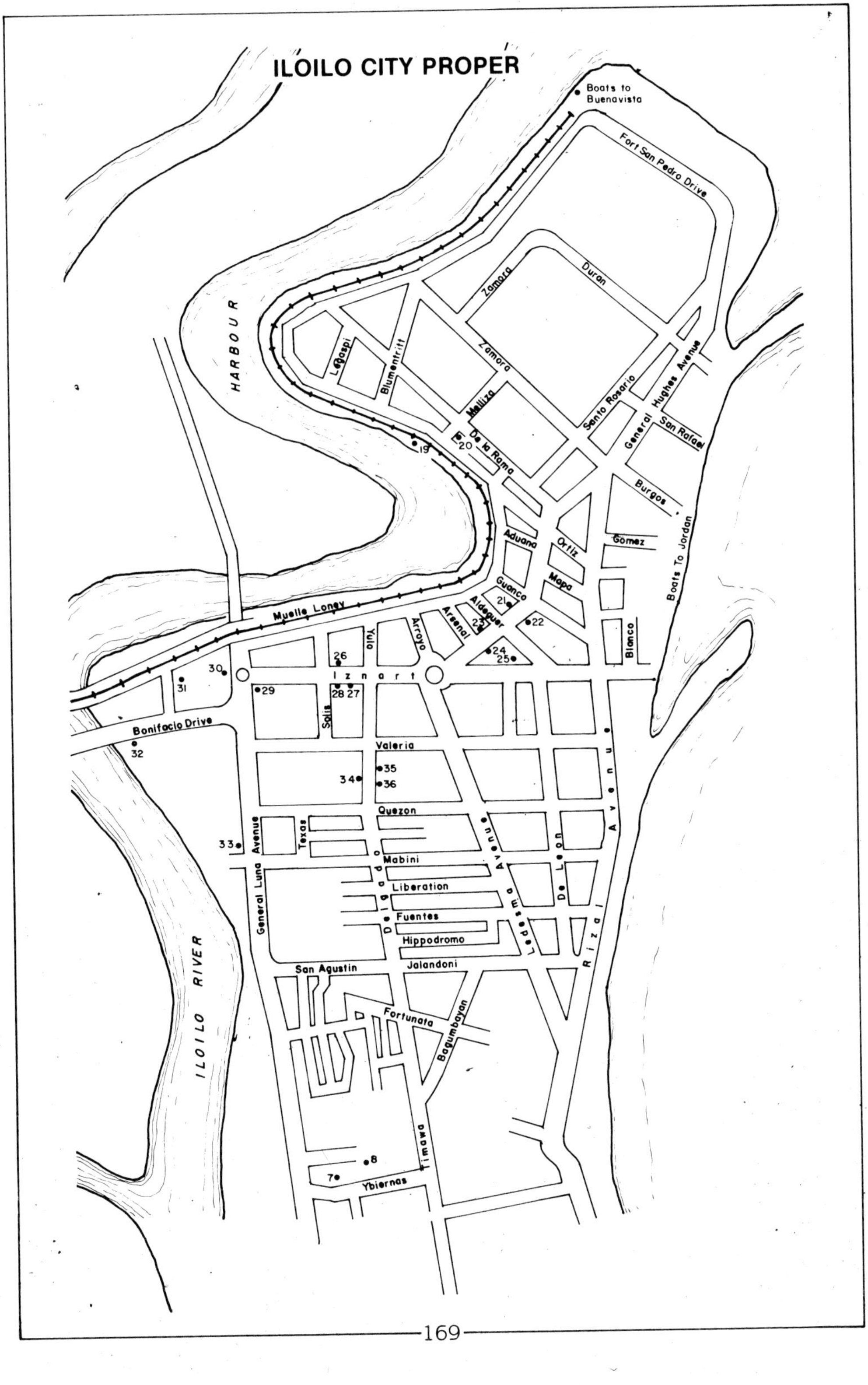
ILOILO CITY PROPER
Boats to Buenavista
Fort San Pedro Drive
HARBOUR
Zamora
Duran
Legaspi
Blumentritt
Melliza
Santo Rosario
General Hughes Avenue
San Rafael
De la Rama
Burgos
Aduana
Ortiz
Gomez
Boats To Jordan
Mapa
Guanco
Aldeguer
Arsenal
Arroyo
Yulo
Muelle Loney
Blanco
Iznart
Solis
Bonifacio Drive
Valeria
Quezon
Texas
General Luna Avenue
Mabini
Delgado
Liberation
Fuentes
Hippodromo
Ledesma Avenue
De Leon
Rizal Avenue
San Agustin
Jalandoni
Fortunata
Bagumbayan
ILOILO RIVER
Timawa
Ybiernas
19
20
21
22
23
24
25
26
27
28
29
30
31
32
33
34
35
36
7
8

Iloilo

access: 1 hr from Manila or ½ hr from Cebu by air; p 267
climate: best Nov-May
to do: swim, handicrafts, dive, visit historic spots, eat
facilities: hotels, resorts, restaurants, p 289

Iloilo, Central Philippines, where the pace is relaxed, hotels clean and gracious; seafood delectable; churches and ancestral houses imposing; beaches many, varied, enjoyable; transportation easy.

Early in the 13th century Marikudo, a native chieftain, sold the coastal shores and lowlands to 10 Bornean datus who fled the repressive Sri Vishayan Empire. Datu Paiburong received the area called Irong-Irong (Iloilo), meaning nose-like, for this is the place where a wide river mouth protrudes proboscis- like into the narrow Guimaras Strait. For three hundred years the islanders lived in relative peace. When Juan Miguel de Legazpi arrived in 1566 he found thriving towns.

Iloilo's south coast

Legazpi settled a governor in Ogtong (Oton). The capital was later moved to Arevalo. Finally, in 1667, it was moved again to Iloilo for safety. The river mouth area provided better protection against raids by Muslim, Dutch and English pirates than the open shores further south.

The Ilongos have a long, genteel, cultured history which is reflected in their ancestral mansions, pleasantly lilting dialect, artistically designed handicrafts, superb seafood cuisine, clean, well managed hotels. The beaches and beach resorts are good, too. There are many festivals in and about Iloilo, and you may time your visit to coincide with them (reservations are needed well in advance for Dinagyang).

The **Dinagyang Festival** is an off-shoot of Aklan's wild Ati-Atihan, but it is refined, ordered, choreographed. Week- long activities culminate in a Mardi Gras-like celebration and parades of costumed "tribes" on the 4th Saturday of January, another on Sunday in which the "tribes" are painted black to resemble the original Negrito inhabitants of Panay.

A colorful **Paraw** (outrigger sailing boats) **Regatta** is held in February, date decided about 6 months in advance of the event. The boats race from Anhawan Resort, Oton, to just north of Iloilo and back. Arevalo District holds its fiesta on the 3rd Sunday of January with a fireworks display, Jaro celebrates on February 2nd, La Paz May 24th, Molo on July 26th, and Mandurriao on November 6th.

San Joaquin celebrates its **Pasungay** (bull fight) festival the 2nd Saturday of

Miagao Church

January with fights between *carabaos*, horses and bulls. The vanquished animal runs away when it is tired. On Good Friday a passion play called **Ang Pagtaltal sa Guimaras** takes place in Jordan, Guimaras. On May 2nd Pavia holds its annual Carabao-Carroza race. A parade of decorated *carabao* sleds is followed by a race among participants.

For a relaxing weekend spend one day doing the fabulous scenery and churches of the south coast, and the city sights and handicrafts. Then relax on a beach at a private island the next day: Isla Naburot, Nagarao, or Sicogon. Or mellow out on one of these beaches for several days.

Iloilo has a helpful, informative DOT office on MH Del Pilar. Do stop in for information and assistance, especially if you are interested in visiting any of the antique collections, as this may require assistance for arranging entry. DOT also has a desk at the airport. Both offices are closed during weekends.

Iloilo City

Iloilo sprawls gracefully over several districts, all accessible by jeepney at ₱1 a ride. Ask at your current stop which jeepney to take for the next destination, and where to alight.

PUs (small taxis) wait for passengers at the airport, and cruise the streets. Hire cars wait at the airport and at the larger hotels for business. Arrange the price in advance.

Jaro District, in the northern part of the city, has several ancestral homes to peer at. Jaro Cathedral is attractive, its bell tower across the street is photogenic. The tower was partly destroyed in the earthquake of 1948.

If you like biscuits, visit Biscocho Haus on Lopez Jaena. They sell *biscocho* (hard toasted buttered bread with sugar), *barquillos* (wafers rolled into round tubes, great with ice cream) and other delicacies. You may visit the **Jesena and Dellota antique collections**. Mrs Dellota also sells antiques, is chatty and knowledgeable about her things, and has a simple cottage

SOUTHERN ILOILO

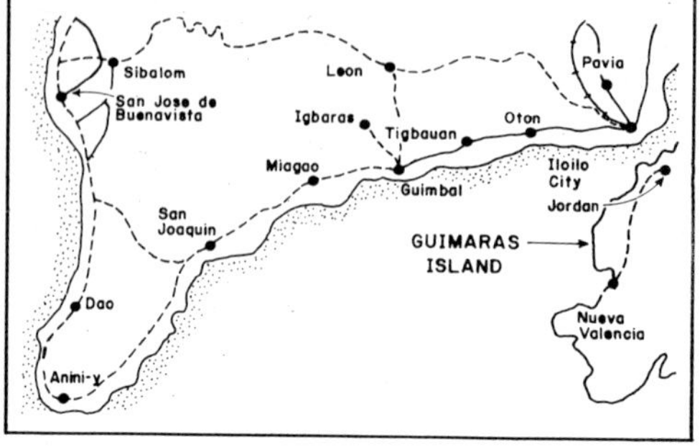

on Guimaras Island which visitors may sometimes use.

On the way back to the city you may want to stop in at CM Bamboocraft, La Paz. Out-of-school youths are employed creating artistic religious and ethnic bamboo articles.

Museo Iloilo, in the **city proper**, houses a well labeled and presented collection of items ranging from pre- historic fossil finds, pottery from sunken ships, secondary and primary burials and photos of the more recent past to a loom on which the delicate *sinamay* fabric is woven, a good collection of *santos* and religious articles, and an exhibit of recent creations of local artists.

The NACIDA display center on JM Basa shows and sells some of the local crafts.

Molo District, which was once the living area for Chinese immigrants, is reputed to have acquired its name when a Chinese resident sighted pirates and shouted excitedly, "Molo, molo!" (eg, "Moro, Moro!"). Its striking Gothic- Renaissance church was finished in the late 1800s. The ornate exterior motif is carried into the interior, repeated and heightened in the five *retablos*.

The nearby **Jose Tiongco Antiques Collection** may be visited by prior arrangement. The Timoteo Consing house fronts the church. **Panaderia de Molo**, where delicious biscuits are made and sold, is just around the corner.

A few shell and furniture products are available at the nearby Iloilo Shellcraft and at Rodson Woodcraft.

Young girls at **Asilo de Molo Orphanage** learn very intricate embroidery, and spend many painstaking hours making religious vestments and other embroidered articles. Watch as their needles go in one thread, out the next, creating designs and flowers so delicate that they appear at first to be water color paintings.

The Sinamay Dealer in **Arevalo District** sells the sheer, delicate *sinamay* fabric for which this area is known. They also have embroidered clothes, linens and other items. Arevalo is also known as the flower district of Iloilo. **Villa Beach** is a very popular nearby getaway for the people of Iloilo, who come to swim and enjoy the food at the many seaside restaurants. A few places also have simple cottages for overnight stays. Food is especially good at Seaside, with a main restaurant and shaded tables on the beach, and at Tatoy's, further south, more native.

South from Iloilo

Iloilo's southeastern coastal towns boast some of the Philippines' most striking Spanish churches and other points of interest, plus a number of good swimming beaches with rustic accommodation. Look for signs along the road.

Anhawan Beach Resort, south of **Oton**, has seen better days and its public facilities leave something to be desired, but there are still some neat, clean cottages on a busy beach.

The interior of **Tigbauan**'s church was destroyed by the quake of 1948, but its façade was fortunately left standing. Decorations around and above the main door look like delicate filigree work carved in stone. The marker to the right of the church commemorates the establishment nearby in 1592 of the first Philippine Jesuit school for boys.

One km south a marker commemorates the American liberation of Panay in 1945.

Guimbal has a simple, solid stone church and the ruins of a seaside watch tower once used to spot incoming pirates. Only the first storey of one of three original towers remains.

A road goes inland from Guimbal to **Leon**, where there are ruins of a huge church. Iloilo's vegetables are grown in Leon's terraced fields.

Miagao, 11 km further south, has Panay's most interesting church. The sandstone facade has been carved into a Philippinized Christian scene in which St Christopher, with the Christ child on his shoulders, plants a coconut tree amid native foliage. The fortress church was built 200 years ago for worship and protection. Each of its massive flanking bell towers is different. They were built by different friars. The inside is totally renovated. Nice view from the bell tower.

Igbaras is 8 km inland from Miagao. Nadsadan Falls is about 4 km from Igbaras by road, then another 4-5 km by foot. The walk takes 1 to 1½ hours. The last part requires negotiating some boulders. Get a guide in town and inquire about the peace and order situation before proceeding. Nadsadan Falls flow like a veil 50′ down a rock face into a deep pool where you may swim.

San Joaquin, 10 min further, was built in 1869 from white coral. Bas relief work on the façade depicts the 1859 defeat of the Moors in the Battle of Tetuan, Spain. Unfortunately, weathering has rendered much of the design difficult to see. The hexagonal chapel of San Joaquin's cemetery, called Campo Santo, is quite remarkable, and easily visible from the road on the way into town.

Cataan Cove, 10 min further along the

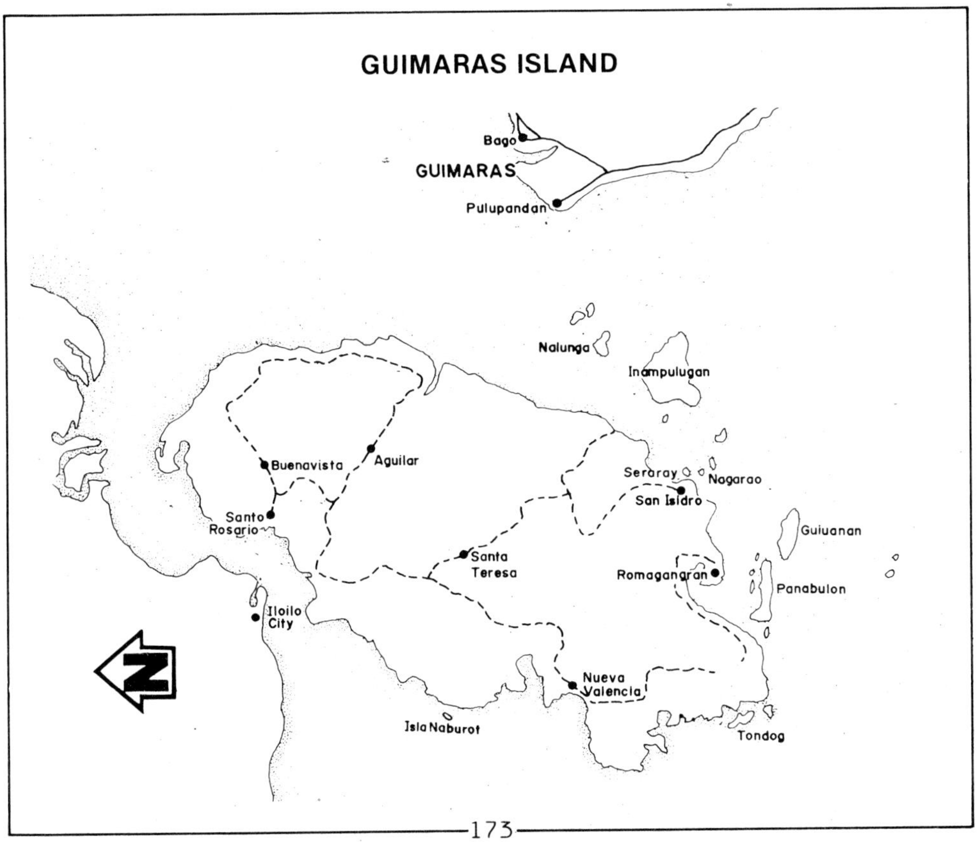

coastal road to Aniny, is the base point for diving activities of Iloilo Scuba Diving Association, where they have a nice clubhouse area. Diving is best December through April, sometimes difficult at other times. Call the ISDA (Iloilo Scuba Diving Association) for information and assistance.

Sta Barbara Church

Guimaras Island & its Islets

Guimaras (map p 179) is Iloilo's largest offshore island, and has a number of good beaches for swimming and snorkeling, two good resorts on small islands around its fringes, and other more basic accommodation such as Mrs. Dellota's cottage in Buenavista may be available.

Holy Week pilgrimages in which the crucifixion of Christ is re-enacted take place on Balasan Bukid (Holy Mountain), a 30-min walk from Jordan. There is a great view of Iloilo from this hill.

Boats cross hourly from Iloilo to Jordan. In the morning jeepneys go from Jordan to Nueva Valencia. Tricycles go to Buenavista.

The wharf in **Buenavista**, 20 min by pump boat from Iloilo, was built by General MacArthur while he was here with the US Corps of Engineers in 1903. There is a nice walk to Daliran Cave. Water collects from several springs and forms a pond. There are formations in the cave.

Siete Picados Islands (Isles of Seven Sins) are a 45-min pump boat ride from Iloilo. The impressive Lopez summer home was built on Roca Encantada in 1910.

There are several beaches around **Nueva Valencia**. Alibuhod Bay, a 45-min walk from Nueva Valencia, has a good swimming beach. There is a marine research area in Igang Bay, interesting to visit. Inquire from the DOT if you wish to visit. Nearby Tiniguiban Island has a white sand beach, with diving off Fiona's Reef. Red shrimps peculiar to this area emerge from their holes only at high tide. They are a protected species.

Catilaran Cave has yielded pre-Hispanic remains. On Good Friday the Pangalap Ritual is enacted, and thousands of people crawl on their knees through the cave in the belief that their ordeal will net them supernatural powers or protect them from evil spirits.

Taklong Island, off Guimaras' southern tip, is a national reservation, the first Visayan Marine Park and bird sanctuary.

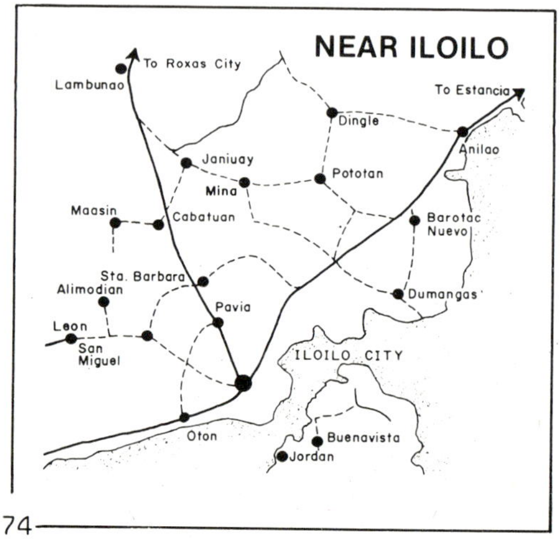

Sicogon

Arrangements to visit should be made through University of the Philippines, Visayas.

Isla Naburot is a 2½ hectare islet with pretty cottages built on the beach and into the hillside, just sufficient to accommodate small groups. Privacy assured, nice white sand beach, a multitude of marine life right off the low water level for snorkelers to enjoy, great food. Owners Pons & Alice Saldaña treat guests as friends. The boat ride to Isla takes 30-45 min from Iloilo.

Nagarao Island Resort is the other side of Guimaras. Several different cottages with assorted facilities are available at assorted rates. It takes about 2 hours to get from Iloilo to Nagarao, 2 boat rides and a jeepney in between. Nagarao has a coral and sand beach with some corals offshore. It is a nice island to walk around, poking into rocks and tide pools. Tennis and boating are available.

North of Iloilo (map p 176)

Although the 19th century churches of the north are distinctive and interesting in their own right, they are somewhat overshadowed by those of the south, and hence are missed by many travelers. You may visit them by jeepney or PU in about half a day. Iloilo Golf & Country Club is also north of the city.

Pavia's unusual Byzantine church is long, low and unfinished. Its warm red brick exterior gives way to a cool, peaceful interior. Holes in the exterior walls were made by bullets aimed by guerrillas at Japanese garrisoned inside during WW II.

Sta Barbara church has a large attached *convento* and delightful interior court. General Martin Delgado launched the Visayan Revolution in this church in 1898. Nearby Sta Barbara Golf course was started in 1907 by 10 Britons and Americans. Its 37 holes are still well kept and guests are welcome to play.

Cabatuan's attractive cemetery is on the way into town. Its solid neo- classical church is being renovated.

Janiuay's century-old church ruins are beside the new church. The original bells are still used, and the whole presents good photographic opportunities. The cemetery,

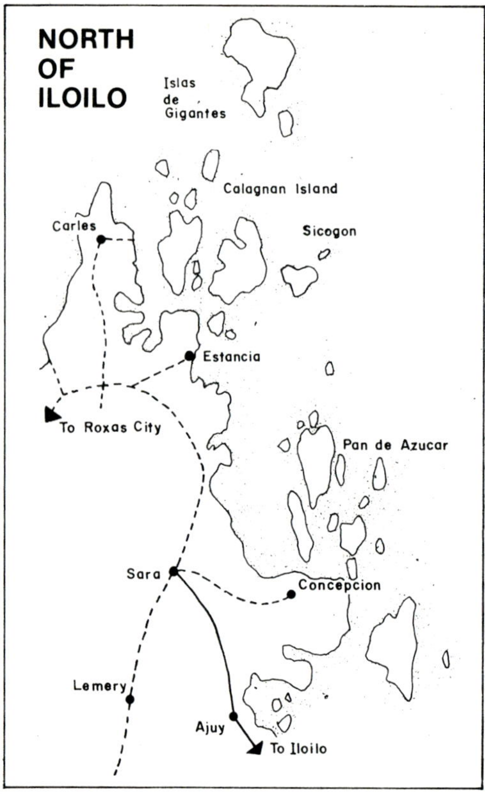

along the road to Mina, has three impressive entry stairways, and a lovely Gothic chapel in the middle. **Pototan**'s cemetery has a Mexican cross in the center.

Dingle's yellow sandstone church has a massive, pleasing facade. **Barotac Nuevo**'s church, on the swing back to Iloilo, shows mixed Roman, Ionic and Doric elements.

The Islands of Northwestern Panay

Several very pretty islands dot the northwestern coast, but only Sicogon is set up to receive travelers. The backpacker may find lodging with villagers on the Gigantes or Pan de Azucar.

Sicogon is a relaxing, private island with nice beaches to swim, comb, wander; windsurfing; some snorkeling; tennis; pretty cottages; good food; Mt Upao (300m) to climb in case you have excess energy; bird watching (hunting is not allowed, so there are many birds). Grey and brown monkeys visit the cove beyond Buaya Beach at sunset. *Banca* excursions can be arranged to Estancia, the mainland town, for market day (Thursday), and to neighboring islands. Sicogon is primarily an up-market getaway for those seeking relaxation. Cottages are spacious, airy, clean.

The island is accessed by air into Iloilo, Bacolod or Roxas City. Charter the resort plane from there. Sicogon is also reached overland from Iloilo (2 hours by taxi or hire car, up to 5 hours by bus, then hire a boat in Estancia to get to the island - they'll ask $25 but don't pay more than $10-15) and from Roxas City (2 dusty, bumpy hours by land). A weekend on the island will cost about US$85, double occupancy, plus optional side trips and transfers.

Gigantes Sur and Norte have numerous caves. You need to be an experienced climber to get to the best known cave, Pawikan (turtle), on Gigantes Sur. Pawikan Cave has a huge mouth with a turtle-shaped rock in the middle, but you have to do some cliff hanging to get there. There are grey monkeys on the island.

Sustenance

Every one of the 10 meals we ate in Iloilo was very good. The Ilongos say its because they like to eat well. They must like to cook well too, especially seafoods. Del Rio's food is outstanding: blue marlin, prawns, smoked bangus, soup of the day, etc., all cooked to perfection, breakfasts $1.50, lunches and dinners about $4.

Several km of beach in Villa, Arevalo, are lined with restaurants, barbeque spots oyster places. Seaside has nice shaded tables by the sea and a restaurant area, very good food: oysters, barbequed chicken, vegetables, garlic fried rice for 2 for $3. Tatoy's, further south, does stuffed chicken, seafoods, all good and served in a native setting, very reasonable. Villa Rosa has a restaurant and 2 cottages. Many other places line the beach.

Good food, too, at the Amigo. Folksy evenings at the restaurants fronting Family Pension and at The Tavern (aircon, too). Payag-Payag on the road to Mandurriao does good fish, but have your taxi wait or walk the meal off on the way back to MH Del Pilar where you can pick up a ride. Try the Regent Garden, 2nd Floor of Amigo Terraces, for Chinese food.

Good reports also on Summer House, Mansiòn House, Kong Kee, Fatima, all along JM Basa, James Restaurant and Angelina's, Iznart, and Chicken House.

Pancit Molo (meat balls wrapped in noodles and cooked as a soup) and La Paz Batchoy (tripe) are local specialities. Try also *biscocho, barquillos* and other biscuits (see p 171).

BACOLOD AREA

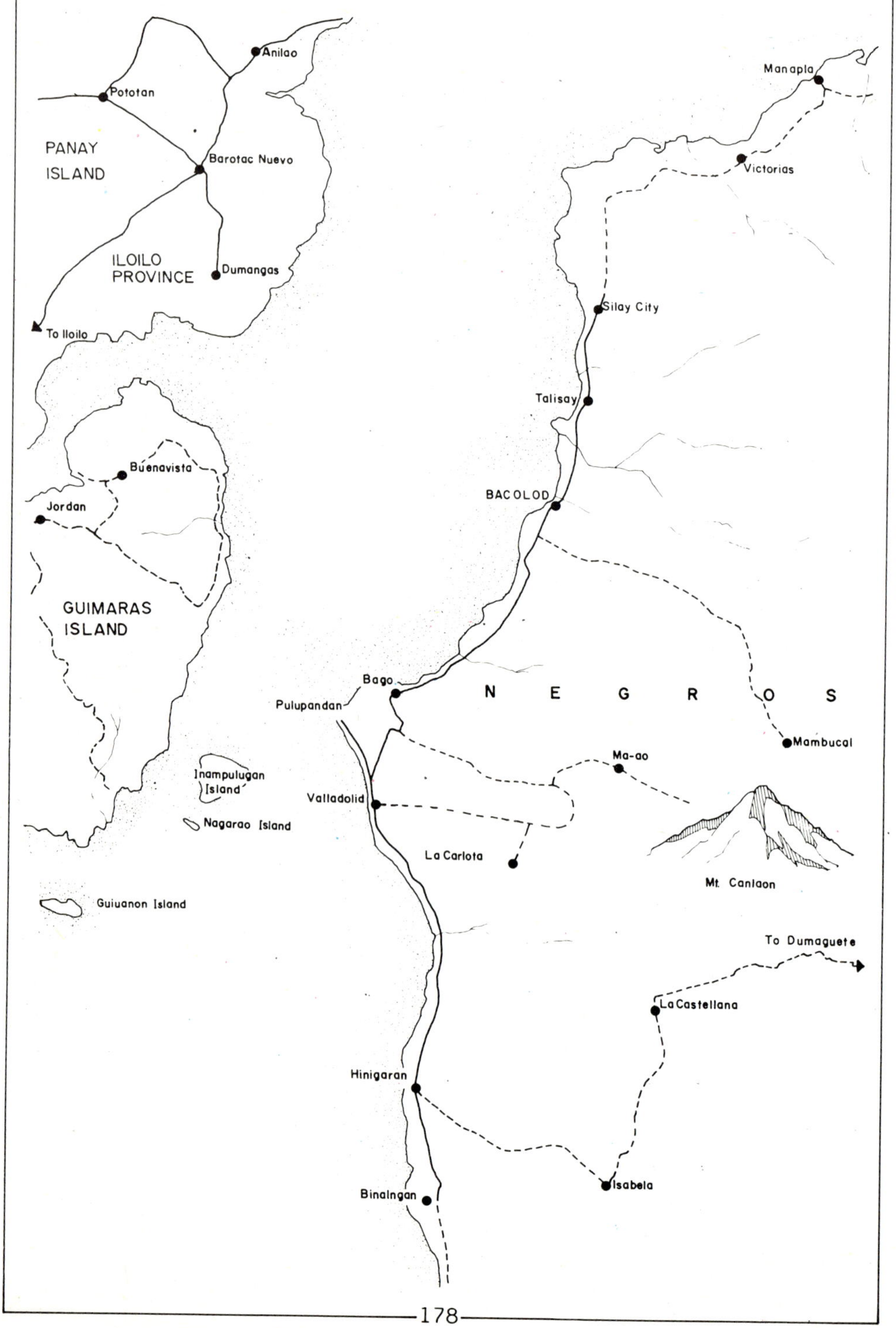

Bacolod

Shell mosaic by Leticia Ledesma, Chapel San [illegible], Bacolod

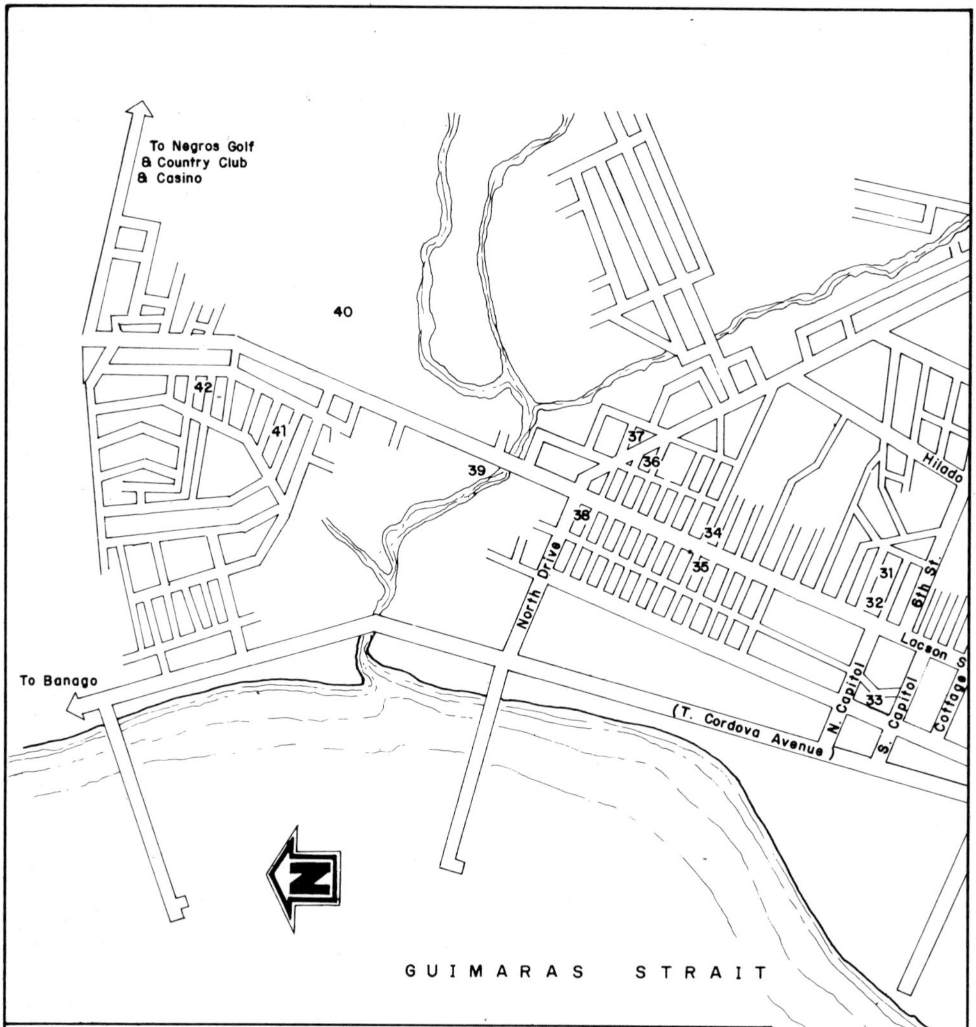

Points of Interest
8 Dept of Tourism
9 City Hall
18 Cathedral
19 City Plaza
29 Luzuriaga Mausoleum
33 Provincial Capitol
41 Chapel San Virgin

Lodging
3 Sugarland
10 Halili Inn
15 Sea Breeze
21 Las Rocas
22 Bascon II
23 YMCA
34 Casa Blanca

Transport
1 Airport
5 South bus terminal
31 Negros Navigation
43 Banago Wharf

Shopping
2 Bacolod Shellcraft
4 Hannah Knitwear
4 Philippine Knit Knacks
6 Libertad Market
7 NDS Ceramics
24 East Market
25 Anaware Ceramics
28 Furniture
30 Samodal
32 Elizabeth's Antiques
38 PSST Antiques
39 Baskets
40 NLS Ceramics
42 Mrs Sarrosa's

Restaurants
11 Ang Sinugba
12 Apollo
13 Popeye
14 Food Fantasy
14 Camillo's
14 Shakeys
16 Jumbo's
17 Manukan Country
20 International
20 Carlos
20 Bibingka
26 Holiday
27 United House
32 Sizzling Inn
34 Cozy Nook
35 Chicken Deli
36 Bob's Big Boy
37 Tita's Food Center

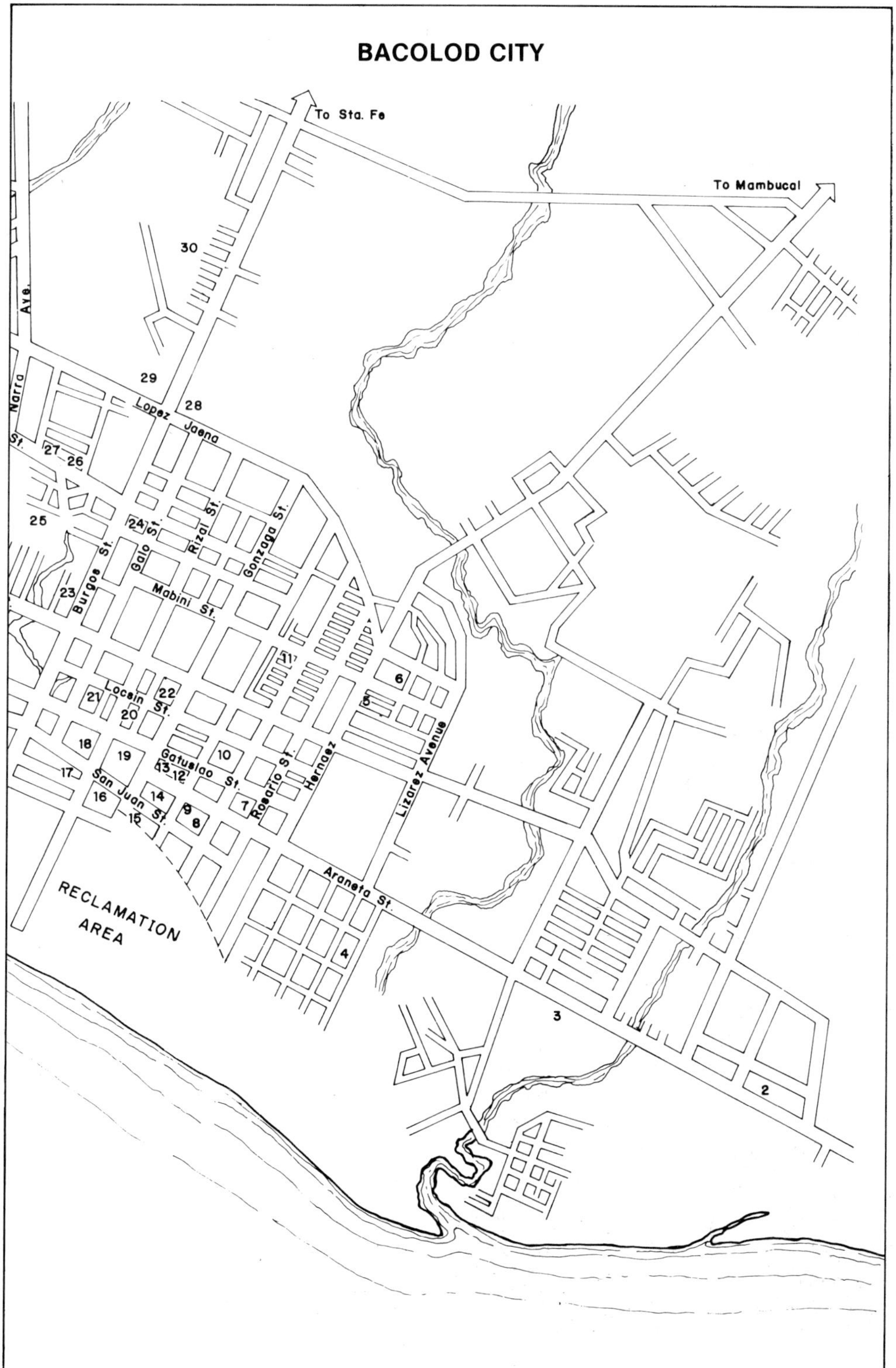
BACOLOD CITY
To Sta. Fe
To Mambucal
Narra Ave.
St.
Lopez Jaena
Burgos St.
Galo St.
Rizal St.
Gonzaga St.
Mabini St.
Locsin St.
Gatuslao St.
San Juan St.
Rosario St.
Hernaez
Lizarez Avenue
Araneta St.
RECLAMATION AREA
1
2
3
4
5
6
7
8
9
10
11
12
13
14
15
16
17
18
19
20
21
22
23
24
25
26
27
28
29
30

Bacolod & Vicinity

access: plane from Cebu, Manila; ferry from Iloilo; bus from Dumaguete p 267
climate: best Nov-June

to do: hike, shop, ancestral houses; sugar centrals, golf
facilities:hotels, resort areas, p 290

During the late 19th century, income generated from sugar made Negros planters fabulously wealthy. They spent their time at ease on huge estates, golfing on one of Bacolod's four courses, gambling at the casino or in the cockpits, attending lavish parties or traveling abroad.

Cane grew lush, green and tall on the plantations, was harvested manually and moved to the mills on steam locomotives built to run on narrow gauge track. Many of these "iron dinosaurs" still ply the same routes, and have been converted back into wood-burners for economy.

Bacolod, Negros Occidental's capital, is a relatively new city, built on the proceeds from farming Mt Canlaon's rich volcanic soil. Estate mansions and monuments built with sugar wealth are still in evidence. As the city came into being its inhabitants could afford the luxury of utilizing space freely. Its roads are generously wide and straight, made to accommodate the elite's limousines and sports cars. The city sprawls easily over 16,000 hectares, giving the whole area relaxed suburban charm. Two decades ago sugar prices began to decline drastically, to a point below most of Negros' sugar centrals' production costs. Bacolod's elite had to trim their budgets. Business was forced to diversify and economize. The halcyon days were over.

Santo in the Montilla House

The gilded life may no longer be visible, and its beaches are not the best, but Bacolod offers great hiking possibilities on Mt Canlaon, good quality handicrafts and antiques to see and purchase, mansions furnished with antiques and art to tour, golf courses to play and antique trains for the locomotive buff.

If you arrive during the 3rd week of October you can enjoy Masskara, Bacolod's Mardi Gras-like festival.

Bacolod City

Bacolod's DOT Office offers a good range of tours for visitors. As they are closed weekends (you can still get maps from the guard, who will ring up an officer in case of need), they should be contacted in advance for arranging weekend activities. Write or call Department of Tourism, San Juan St, Bacolod City, tels 27662, 20772, 23592. Tours offered include a 5-Day Steam Locomotive Tour, 4-Day Canlaon Climb, 3-

Day War Memorial Tour, 8-hour Sugarmill & City Tour, 8-Hour Mambucal Tour, 3-Day Island Hopping Tour, and they are willing to tailor the itineraries to suit your wants and needs.

Additionally, Ramon Hofileña can arrange **art tours** which usually include the extensive and very impressive art collection in his home in Silay City, the pop-art chapel at Victorias, and other points of interest. Contact him well in advance through the DOT.

Transport is not a problem in Bacolod. Jeepneys ply all frequented routes. Ask anyone which jeepney goes your way, and where to find it. Or hire a PU (small taxi) for the ride or the day.

Shoppers and browsers will delight in Bacolod City. **Handicrafts** are available in many shops and in many areas, among them: **baskets** at the central market, along Lacson just before Sunny Village, and at the handicrafts shops mentioned below; **knitwear** from Hannah Knitwear and Philippine Knit-Knacks, both on Lizares Ave; **sea products** at Bacolod Shellcraft and Artwares (the owner/designer, Mrs Leticia Ledesma, has sculpted strikingly beautiful religious works); Nature's Gift, at Sonia Sarraza's home in Sta Clara Subdivision (tel 81134), displays and sells some of the products of the House of Negros, a project aimed at assisting people to increase their income through handicraft production, and she can arrange for visits to the factory; **baskets and other handicrafts** are available at PSST and Sagay Native Products, on Lacson; Samodal's, off Burgos St, and other nearby places do remarkable **shaved wood products** and other items; **ceramics** are available in town at MDS Ceramics, Rosario St, less pricey good quality items at NLS Ceramics, Mountain View Subdivision, inexpensive pottery at roadside stands in the south in Pohonocoy, and in the north before Silay City; and there are several **antique shops** with collections of *santos*, furniture, pottery, etc, most notably the Philippine Arts-Antiques Shop on Lacson St, where you may also arrange to visit the remarkable Montilla ancestral home in Ubay, Pulupandan (see p 185).

Enjoying cane from a disabled truck

Even non-shoppers will enjoy visiting these places to experience the richness of products so intimately tied to Bacolod and the land around. If you have special interest in arts and antiques, inquire from the DOT which collections are available for viewing, and how to go about arranging the visit.

Bacolod also has a wide range of standard articles at good prices. Servandos, on Gatuslao St, is the department store of note.

Bacolod's Cathedral dates from 1882. Cultural performances, impromptu lectures and other activities occur on some Sundays in the spacious plaza fronting the church. And even the cemetery is a curiosity, as

North Drive splits down the middle to accommodate the Luzuriaga Family Mausoleum as its center strip.

The very new **Chapel San Virgin** of Sta Clara Subdivision was originally intended as a ₱7 million extravaganza, but sugar prices fell and consequently funds available for the chapel also shrank. Ingenuity replaced extravagance, giving rise to a remarkable work of art, of native craftsmanship with native materials. The wood and capiz shell chapel is decorated with saints made from intricate shell mosaics. The beautiful mural behind the altar alone has 95,000 pieces of shell, and took 60 men 100 hours of work under the supervision of Mrs Leticia Ledesma.

Visiting **golfers** are welcome at Negros Golf & Country Club, Bacolod Golf & Country Club, and at Vicmico Golf and Country Club, rated in that order for facilities and price. Negros Golf and Bacolod Golf (site of the Casino) are on the road to Murcia. Vicmico is in Victorias Milling's land (below). Bacolod also has 5 tennis court areas.

The Casino is open daily from 3 to 11 pm. Men may wear sports shirts, but they must have collars, thongs are not allowed, nor shorts. Friday and Saturday evenings shuttle buses go from the city plaza, fronting State Theatre, to the Casino and back.

Inland Activities

Sta Fe Resort, a few km from the city, is a bit run down but has a small zoo with birds, a hawk, three monkeys and a crocodile, all in apparent good health, which might be of interest to children and naturalists.

Outdoor enthusiasts will want to head for **Mambucal Resort**. Built to accommodate people who want to bathe in its sulfurous hot springs and cool mountain stream, Mambucal is a convenient base for hikes on Canlaon.

There are lovely walks through the volcano's rich valleys and meadows, and one may follow a mountain stream as it tumbles down a succession of falls, some high and strong, others low and gentle, to its source hours away. Guides are available in Mambucal. If you plan to stay and eat at the resort, book in advance, especially if you want meals. Rooms with bath in the main building are quite nice. Other facilities are rather run down, and the grounds need cleaning up, but this is not a problem for those whose interests lie more in the mountain than the actual resort.

If you would like to climb 2465 meter high **Mt Canlaon**, allow 4 days and contact the Bacolod DOT Office in advance for assistance and guides. Edwin Gatia, one of the tourism officers, is an avid mountaineer and may go with you if he has time. Bring a sleeping bag. The trek goes through mountain rainforest into a dwarf forest and by some small lakes to a beautiful view of Canlaon's quiescent main crater, then descend for a night at the beach. Mt Canlaon is one of the Philippines' many active volcanoes. It was active in 1986, and with luck you will see steam from one of the vents.

The North Coast

Silay City, 18 km north of Bacolod, was the center of Negros Occidental's culture during the Spanish era. The town has many spacious old mansions, and several residents grow lovely orchids. Make advance arrangements with Mr Ramon Hofileña if you would like to visit his home and view his art collection, which includes works from foremost Filipino and European masters such as Goya, Juan Luna and Picasso. If you like Japanese and Korean food, make advance arrangements for a meal at Mr Natalio Velez' Oriental House, a small restaurant which operates by reservation only.

Victorias Milling Corporation (Vicmico) is another 20 km north. Tuesdays through Fridays, 9-12 am and 2:30-4:30 pm, visitors are offered guided tours of the sugar mill and, upon request, of the food processing plant. Locomotives deliver raw cane to the factory. Conveyor belts transfer it to one of three mills, the oldest of which was installed in 1928. Mills crush and wash the cane, turning 70% of its weight into raw sugar. The remaining 30%, bagasse, provides 90% of the fuel for the generators which power the mills.

Vicmico has 365 km of railroad track. Steam engines dating from 1924-1928 have been reconverted from gas to wood-burning in order to economize on fuel consumption.

Vicmico's most striking attraction is its famous **chapel** which has a vivid mural of an angry Christ and saints done as Filipinos in native garb.

Vicmico is partly owned by its employees. Its restaurant and 14-hole golf course are open to visitors.

Llacaon Island, with lovely beaches and reefs, is a further 20 km north.

South from Bacolod

A very good road leads south from Bacolod through Bago City to La Carlota, where it turns inland and crosses Canlaon's southern slopes to Negros Oriental.

Jara Beach Resort, Bacolod's only waterfront resort with modern facilities, is 16 km south. It has cottages, rooms and dorms with tiled baths along the water, and an artificial beachfront area. All the beaches around Bacolod are shallow and corally.

The **Montilla House**, in barrio Ubay, Pulupandan, is an outstanding example of a century-old beautifully preserved ancestral home, restored and furnished with period pieces including Vienna bentwood furniture, Soong and Ming porcelain, Chinese camphor chests and several hundred *santos*, family photographs and portraits. Visits to this house must be prearranged through the Philippine Arts-Antiques Shop. If at all possible, try to arrange your visit when Mr Herbert Montilla Tomkins is at home and can show you around. He belongs to the 7th generation of Montillas who have lived here.

Locomotive enthusiasts will want to visit the **Ma-ao cane fields**, where a long network of track takes early twenties steam locomotives over fantastic bridges as they haul the cut cane to the mills. Check with the Bacolod DOT Office for this and other train visits.

Sustenance

Bacolod abounds with restaurants. For **seafood** try Ang Sinugba (also does other Filipino dishes), the gambas at Sugarland Hotel, and, if you're visiting Vicmico from March through May, there may be lobster available at the country club restaurant (best to call ahead). Local **beef** is very good, and best done at Sizzling Inn and Cozy Nook. **Chicken inasal** is a local speciality: try it at Chicken Deli or Chicken Queen. For Chicken BBQ, beer and a relaxing low-key evening of camaraderie, visit Manukan Country. The best **Chinese** restaurants are Sen Yang, Apollo, United House and Holiday. Sea Breeze Hotel does **Japanese** Misono. Oriental House, in Silay City, does Japanese & **Korean** food, but you must call ahead as they're a very small operation. Carlo's does reasonably good **Italian** fare. There are dozens of **fastfood** and snack shops. Bob's does really good meals and snacks.

International House beside Central Market has a vast range of Filipino dishes, including something called 'drunken chicken'; Roli's is known for its chicken sandwich; try also Snack Plaza and Shakeys.

DUMAGUETE AREA

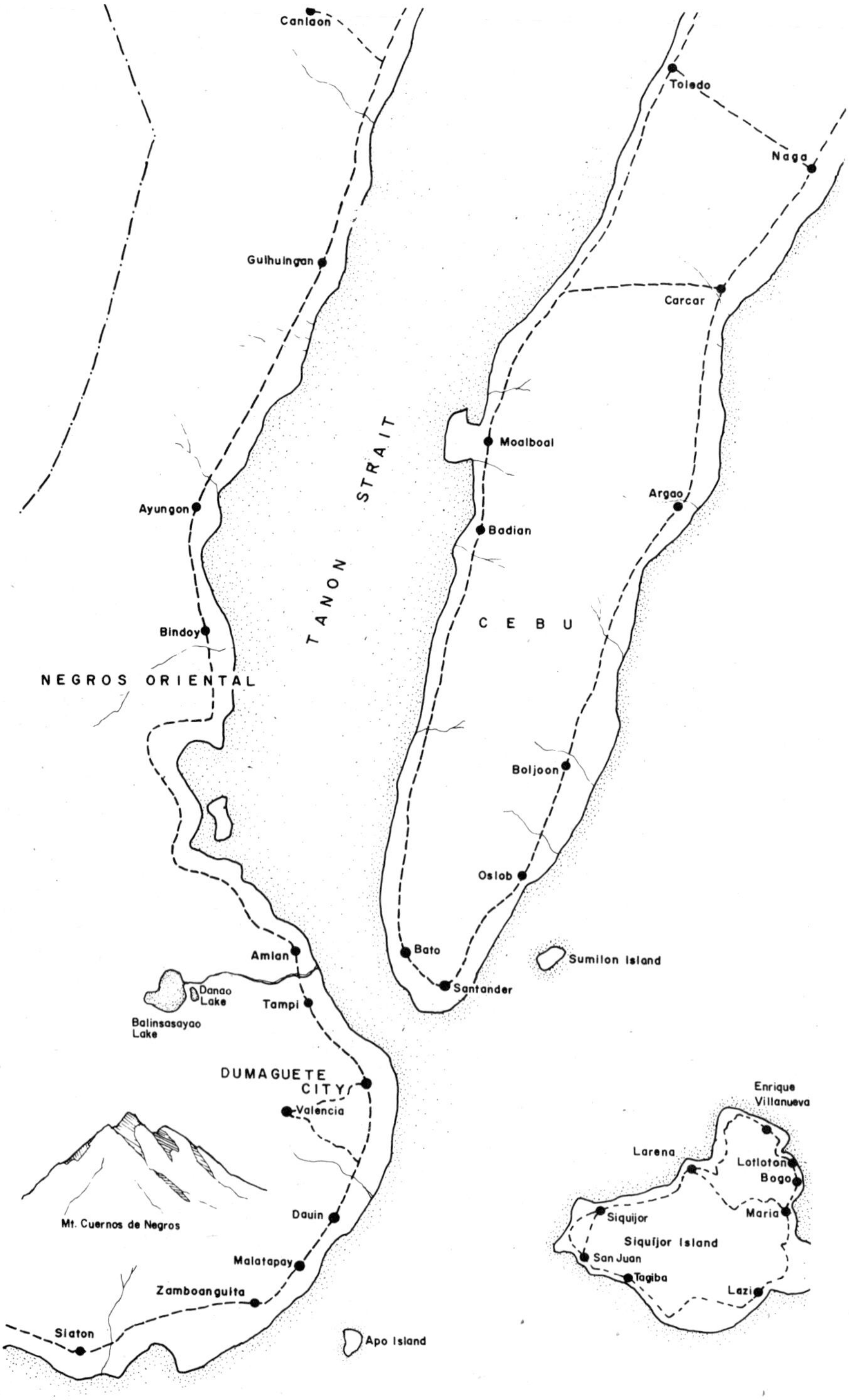

Dumaguete & Siquijor

The market in Dumaguete City

DUMAGUETE CITY

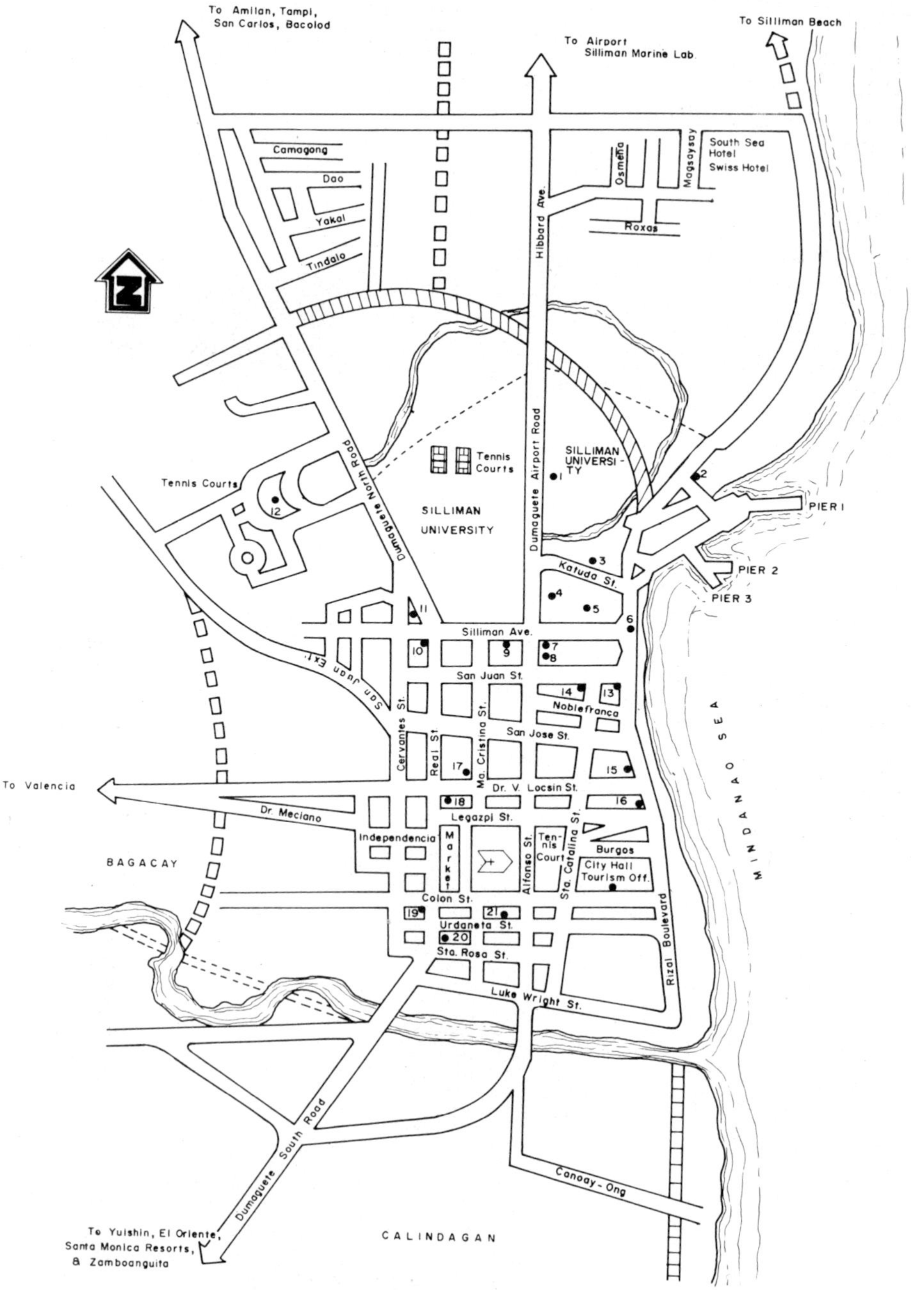

Dumaguete, Negros Oriental & Siquijor

access: 1 hr by air from Manila; bus from Cebu, p 267
climate: best Nov-June
to do: swim, snorkel, dive, museum, handicrafts, market
facilities: lodges & resorts, p 290

Dumaguete City, provincial capital of Negros Oriental, has Protestant **Silliman University** at its heart. Silliman's spacious campus is shaded by magnificent acacia trees. Its academic influence permeates the city. Some residents have established small bird sanctuaries in their neighborhoods. It is a lovely destination, geared to a slow pace, inhabited by hospitable, helpful and often well educated people.

Activities available include swimming on lovely beaches a *banca* ride from the city, snorkeling, diving, hiking, touring nearby towns, handicrafts-hunting, golf, tennis and bird-watching.

Dumaguete is a small city, everything is within walking distance. Tricycles are the most popular form of transport to points within and near the city.

Larger resorts will pick you up at the airport. Inquire before hiring a tricycle, about ₱5 to the city center. To hire a private vehicle, inquire from your hotel or ask for Doming Rubio.

Dumaguete City

The city is easy to see in one day. Maps of the city and province may be available at one of two offices - the provincial tourism office in **Provincial Capitol Building**, a lovely structure with beautiful grounds, or the city tourism office at **City Hall**.

Wander along Lo-oc Rd and Rizal Ave, near the pier. Temporary stalls located at the start of Rizal Ave offer soft drinks, beer, coffee, snacks and the opportunity to sit, enjoy the company of others and exchange information.

Along Sta Catalina St, on the east side of Rizal Park, vendors sell orchids, flowers and plants. Continue through the park and west, across Alfonso XIII St to St Catherine Church, then to the **public market** in the center of town.

The wet market offers freshly caught tuna, most of which is delivered in the early morning. Beautiful jackfish, crabs, lobsters and sometimes *curacha*, a delicious shellfish best described as a sort of

Points of Interest
- 2 Buses north
- 5 Museum
- 11 Vintola's Showroom
- 12 Provincial Capitol & tourism office
- 18 Jeepneys to Tampi & San Jose
- 19 Jeepneys to Valencia
- 20 Buses south

Lodging & Food
- 1 Habitat
- 3 Opena's Hotel & Restaurant
- 4 Silliman Alumni Hall and Cafeteria
- 6 BBQ Stalls
- 7 Jo's Lodge
- 8 Rosalie's and Jo's Bakeries
- 9 Insular Hotel
- 10 Oriente Hotel
- 13 Al-Mar Hotel/Sinugba Restaurant
- 14 Kamay Kainan Restaurant
- 15 Chin Lun Restaurant
- 16 Dumaguete Yacht Club
- 17 Kamagong Restaurant
- 21 Victory Lodge

crab-lobster may be available.

You'll also find an array of fruits in season: mangoes, papaya, jackfruit, and kalamansi, and vegetables, corn and delicious *latu* and *gulaman* (seaweed - give them a try).

If you're hungry (or just curious), have a *Budbud* or *suman* snack - sweetened sticky rice wrapped and cooked in banana leaves. The dry market, to the northwest, displays handicrafts and various paraphernalia used in daily life. Beautifully woven *banig* (sleeping mats, wonderful for sunbathing and picnicking), hats, rubber thongs, baskets, cooking utensils, clothing, tools, hammocks, shoes.

North of the market, at 92 Real St, is Vintola's showroom. They have samples of products made in their factory in Motong - beautiful boxes, jewelry and even furniture made from shell, stone, *carabao* horn, brass and coral. **Think twice before buying coral products – your purchase will encourage further destruction of the reefs.**

A small **anthropology museum** at Silliman has displays of prehistoric finds, including burial remains and Chinese pottery and porcelain, of Philippine tribal relics and artifacts, and of implements used by the sorcerers of Siquijor. Some of Silliman's students help to pay their tuition by selling a few artifacts at the museum

Buri table top

Sumilon Island

shop.

The Luce Auditorium sometimes has evening entertainment. Check for current attractions, usually advertised on banners at the University entrance or ask at the student affairs office.

The Silliman University Marine Laboratory and Farm, between the city and the airport, carries on projects aimed at promoting marine conservation. The marine lab is currently working on a crocodile propagation program in conjunction with the World Wildlife Fund, and on giant clam propogation. It has an ongoing marine conservation program which combines the disciplines of marine biology and sociology to encourage both reef conservation and community development on Apo, Pamilacan and Balicasag Islands. Visitors are usually welcome, but it is best to ask permission if you're interested in exploring either.

Silliman Beach, seaward of the marine lab, is a good swimming beach and has picnic shelters.

Visiting tennis players are welcome at Proxivilla tennis courts by the Provincial Capitol Building. If you're looking for a good game, ask for Jimmy Locsin. There are also two courts in Rizal Park and two on the Silliman campus.

Good golf is available at the San Antonio golf course, north of Sibulan on the San Antonio Road.

Inland from Dumaguete

Valencia, 7 km west of Dumaguete, nestles in the foothills of Cuernos de Negros (Mt Talinis). Residents all seem to have green thumbs, as houses are mantled in lush, beautiful plants, some of which are for sale. At the market you may have a snack of *budbud* or Banana-Q, and thick hot chocolate.

Two km further uphill is a lovely swimming area with a couple of guest houses. Ask at the pool for overnight accommodation.

Camp Lookout, 4 km along another road, offers a gorgeous view of Dumaguete,

Siquijor and Cebu.

The **Philippine Japanese Amity Shrine** is located above Valencia. Contact Boyet Somoza through the Dumaguete Divers' Club for information about the shrine and war memorabilia.

Visits to the geothermal power plant need to be prearranged through PNOC (Philippine National Oil Co) Dumaguete or their Manila offices.

North of Dumaguete

18 km from the city, past Sibulan, just south of San Jose, a trail leads to **Twin Lakes**. A 15-km hike through forests will take you to the two crater lakes Danao and Balinsasayao in lush surroundings. This area has been the site of confrontations between the military, NPA and illegal loggers, so it is best to inquire about security before proceeding. It is also possible to begin the hike from the San Antonio Golf Course Road.

Tampi, 4 km north of San Jose, is known for its cottage industry production of *buri* furniture. It is also the terminal for ferry service to and from Cebu.

There is an interesting boat building industry on a creek on the way into **Amlan**, where several small establishments make and display attractive *buri* furniture.

South from Dumaguete

Signs along the road just beyond Dumaguete announce: "Welcome to Nicaragua", "New York, home of the hoot boys".

There is a good beach at **Dauin**, 8 km south of Bacong, and a market on Saturdays.

Wednesdays at **Malatapay** are market day, when people from neighboring barrios and towns, and from Dumaguete, come to buy, sell, and exchange gossip and news. Temporary barbeques are set up, you may select your fish, have it cooked, and eat it with *pusa* – one serving of rice attractively bundled in a banana leaf package. There are picnic tables by the beach, and, if you're wanting something stronger than a cola, try *tuba* – slightly fermented coconut liquor. The beach is pretty and it's possible to hire a *banca* from here to visit nearby Apo Island.

Zamboanguita, 5 km further south, is a small fishing town with a small zoo and park run by the Lamplighters featuring a collection of native animals, Lamplighter paraphernalia, a stuffed white monkey, (a type reputed to be seen only once a year on Siquijor), and favorite sayings of Fr Tropa, founder of the Lamplighter religious sect.

Just south, along the shore, is Salawaki Beach Resort, a good place to stay or visit for a day.

For nice snorkeling and a good swimming beach try Siyt.

Siaton Bird Sanctuary, created by Silliman University, is 47 km south of Dumaguete, and is reported to be lovely. Twelve km closer is a small, 1 hectare sanctuary run by the Lamplighters. It's well maintained, a beautiful place to picnic.

Apo Island

Apo Island is a lovely day trip, with good snorkeling, swimming and diving, but some strong currents. Residents maintain waters surrounding the island as a marine sanctuary and reserve. They ask for a ₱5 donation from visitors to help with maintenance. Picnic tables rent for ₱5/day, and a small 1-room cottage is available at ₱20 for overnight stays.

Residents are happy to sell you fish, cook it for you on the beach, and stay for a chat. Bring drinking water and beverages.

Women weave and sell beautiful mats from pandan leaves.

Sumilon

A small island at the tip of Cebu, Sumilon was developed by Silliman as a marine preserve, then became involved in a political struggle between two provinces for control, with some greedy fishermen and unscrupulous dive operators benefiting.

Sumilon has lovely beaches and some excellent snorkeling and diving. Bring a picnic lunch and drinks if you intend to stay.

Siquijor

Siquijor, an island shrouded in mystery and mysticism, is said to have arisen from the ocean in a great storm. The Spaniards called it Fire Island, Isla del Fuego. Many of its people take pride in their supernatural powers. They practice a Holy Week Ritual which combines Christian faith with rituals which they believe strengthen their mystical powers.

The island is best known for its *mangkukulam*, healers and/or sorcerers who cure illnesses and cast maleficent spells. For a fee, you may have an evil spell cast on an enemy; or, again, for a fee, you may find the man in Zamboanguita who can reverse a curse someone else has put on you.

Each *mangkukulam* has his or her own technique, but diagnosis is usually accomplished through eye-to-eye contact with the client. Treatment may involve blowing water through a straw onto the affected area, then sucking it back again along with an interesting assortment of objects which have suddenly materialized, and are blamed for the problem. All are blown back into a glass, and the patient is supposed to recover shortly. Many *mangkukulam* also sell *anting-anting* (amulets) capable of endowing the wearer with special powers or protecting him or her from harm.

The best places to find *mangkukulam* are Siquijor town, San Juan or San Antonio.

The best way to tour Siquijor is by tricycle hire from San Juan, Siquijor or Larena. The trip takes a full day and costs roughly $5.

San Juan is a pretty, small coastal town. At the center of town is a fresh water pool and spring which runs into the sea. An old Spanish watchtower is an easy climb up a hill from town. Other remnants of Spanish days are scattered about the island.

Siquijor, the largest town, has the only hospital (travelers may rent a bed in the staff quarters for $1/night). Residents primary amusement comes from VCR tapes, which may be seen for a small fee. The market serves a great cup of thick, rich hot chocolate and rice cake.

Access to Siquijor is via public ferry, which runs twice daily from Dumaguete's main pier to Siquijor town, or through private hire, which may cost as much as $55, depending upon weather and other factors.

Sustenance

South Sea, Yuishin and Sta Monica resorts all serve meals. Dumaguete Yacht Club needs advance notice (the day before for lunch; in the morning for dinner), and specializes in Cajun cooking.

In the evenings by the docks, vendors sell barbequed food. Other places to eat include Kamagong Restaurant; Kamaykainan, for seafood; Opena's Restaurant, with reasonable prices and good food; Rosante; South Sea Beach Resort, is usually good; and there are several places along Quezon Blvd to drop in for a snack or drink.

CEBU

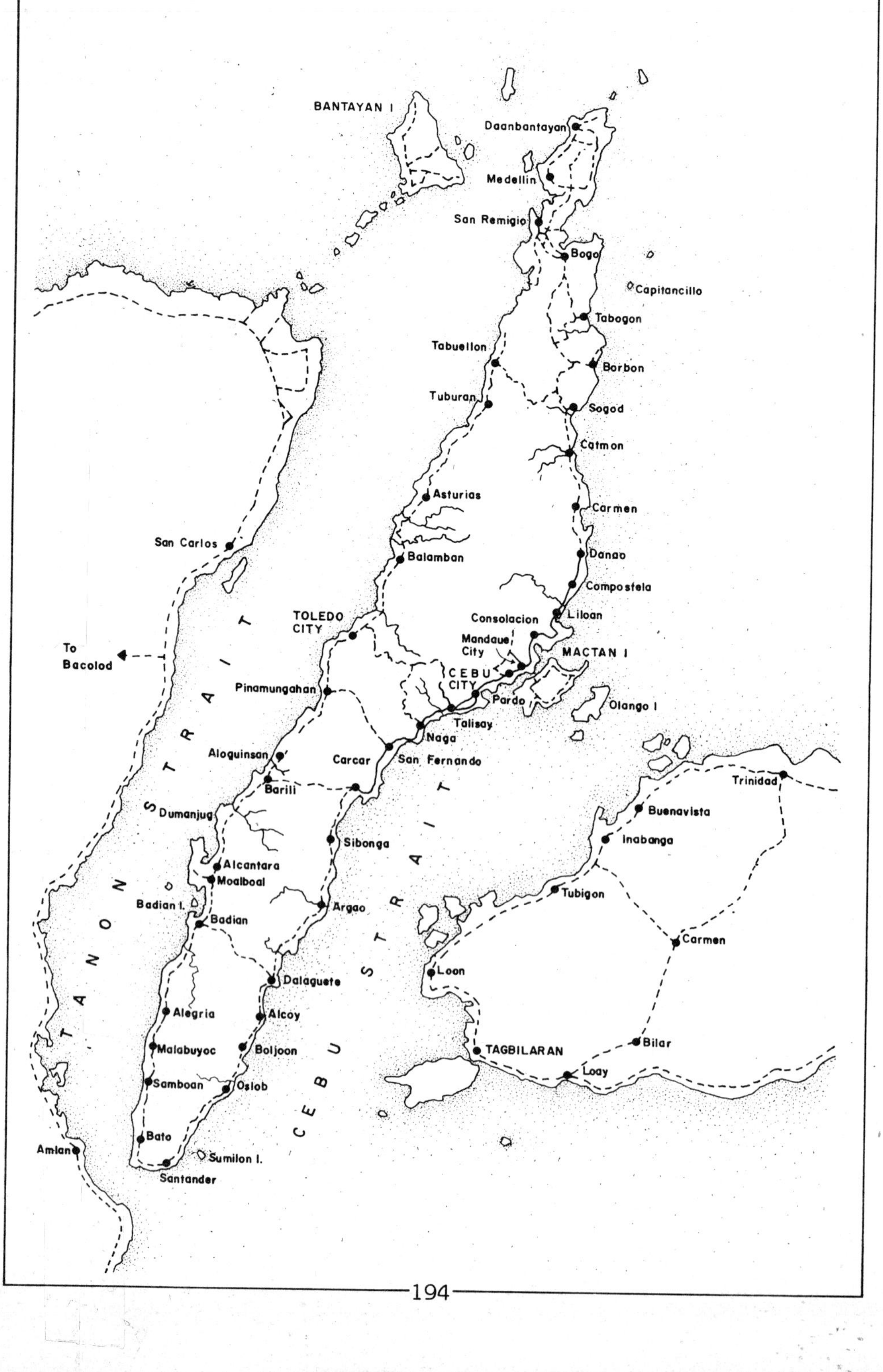
BANTAYAN I
Daanbantayan
Medellin
San Remigio
Bogo
Capitancillo
Tabogon
Tabuellon
Borbon
Tuburan
Sogod
Catmon
Asturias
Carmen
San Carlos
Danao
Balamban
Compostela
TOLEDO CITY
Consolacion
Liloan
To Bacolod
Mandaue City
MACTAN I
CEBU CITY
Pinamungahan
Pardo
Olango I
Talisay
Naga
Aloguinsan
Carcar
San Fernando
Trinidad
Barili
Buenavista
Dumanjug
Inabanga
Sibonga
Alcantara
Moalboal
Tubigon
Badian I.
Argao
Badian
Carmen
Loon
Dalaguete
Alegria
Alcoy
Malabuyoc
Boljoon
Bilar
TAGBILARAN
Loay
Samboan
Oslob
Bato
Amlan
Sumilon I.
Santander
TANON STRAIT
CEBU STRAIT

Cebu

Lapu Lapu Monument, Mactan Island

CEBU CITY

Capitol
N. Escario
Juana Osmeña
Maria Cristina
N. Escario
Don Jose Avila
Kamunung
Don Mariano
Gil Garcia
Orchid
Sampaguita
Jasmin
Osmeña Blvd.
Maria Cristina
Adelf
B. Rodriguez
Happy Valley
San Nicolas Cemetery
E. Pond
Gen. Maxilon Ave.
Queen's Road
Jones Ave.
F. Ramos St.
A. Pond
M. H.
Tambis
Coliseum
Vicente Orguella
Ascencion
Jesus
V. Ranudo
Urguello
P. Del Rosario
V. Rama Ave.
Junquera
Pelaez Ext.
D. Jakosalem
San Jose
Gen. Sepulveda
Sikatuna
Echavez
Gen. Echavez
Gorordo
Pelaez
Don Pedro Cui
Landon
Oreg
P. del Rosario
Sanciangko
Imus
Tupas
Lakandula
P. Balagtas
Borromeo
Leon
J. Luna
Espeleta
Rallos
De la Concepcion
Dimasalang
Colon
Lopez
A. Bonifacio
T. Padilla
4th St.
Alvio
Magallanes
Kalderon
Lopez Jaena
Villagonzalo
6th Ave.
5th Ave.
3rd
2nd St.
1st St.
CITY HALL
Elibusteris
Kawit
Colon
Plaridel
Gomez
Zulueta
Bogumbayon
Don V. Sotto
Briones
Gonzales
Urdaneta
Burgos
Magallanes
Lapu Lapu
2nd Ave.
1st Ave.
Gen. McArthur Blvd.
Palma
Blvd.
CARBON MARKET
Legaspi Ext.
Arellano
Quezon Blvd.
PIER 1
PIER 2
PIER 3
1
2
3
4
5
6
7
8
9
10
11
12
13
14
15
16
17
18
19
20
21
22
23
24
25
26
27
28
29
30
31
32
33
34
35
36
37
38
39
40
41
42

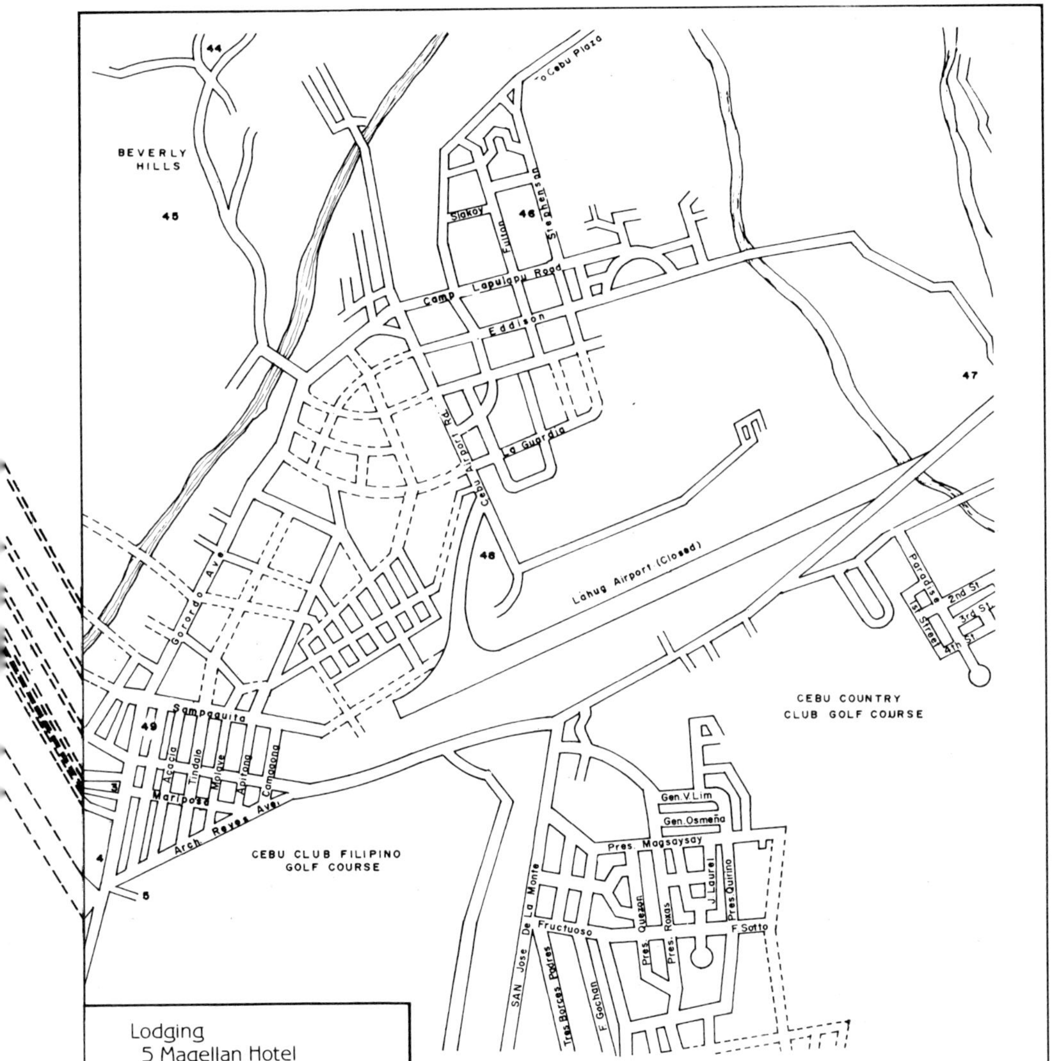

Lodging
5 Magellan Hotel
5 St Moritz
11 Rajah Hotel
13 Kan Irag Hotel
19 YMCA
20 Arbel's
21 Elicon
23 Surigao Pension
24 Tagalog Hotel
25 Mercedes Hotel
26 Century Hotel
28 Queen's Lodge
33 Patria de Cebu
37 Ruftan Pension
38 Sky Vue Hotel
39 Hope Pension
40 Humabon Hotel
41 Lovena's Pension
47 Montebello Villa Hotel

Food & Entertainment
3 Alavar Restaurant
4 Tung Yan II
6 Lighthouse
7 Vienna Caffee Haus
8 Balls
9 Majestic Restaurant
10 Lawiswis Kawayan
12 Before & After 6
14 La Pampangueña
15 Charlie's Piano Bar
16 Beehive
17 Whistler
18 Town & Country
32 Eddie's Log Cabin
46 St Gotthard
48 Golden Cowrie

Points of Interest
1 Provincial Capitol
2 Osmeña House
22 San Carlos U Museum
27 SM Handicrafts Center
29 Casa Gorordo Museum
30 Fort San Pedro
31 Plaza Independencia
34 Cebu Metropolitan Cathedral
35 Basilica Minore del Sto. Nino
36 Magellan's Cross
42 Tabaon Market
44 Taoist Temple
45 Temple of Heavenly Charity

Cebu

access: 1 hr by air from Manila, p 267

climate: dry Nov-June

to do: beaches, dive, snorkel, land tours, handicrafts, resorts

facilities: varied resorts & hotels, p 291-3

Cebu City, the center of Visayan activities and the Philippines' second busiest city, is very popular for its hotels and nearby resorts, beaches and shops. PAL flies daily from Manila to Mactan Island's International Airport. Charter flights arrive directly from Hong Kong, Japan and Taiwan. Planes and boats leave Cebu for most points in the Philippines. Resorts and hotels span a wide range of prices and facilities.

Magellan arrived in Sugbo (the island's pre-Spanish name) in 1521, made friends with Rajah Humabon and baptized him, his queen and many followers. Pigafetta, Magellan's chronicler, reported that Cebuanos lived in stilt houses made of bamboo, wood and nipa. Men were extensively tatooed. Women wore gold jewelry, silks and lip color.

Magellan's Cross

But when Magellan turned his attention across the narrow strait to Mactan Island, he encountered a different reception. Lapu Lapu, the local chief, repelled his entry, slaying Magellan and many of his troops. Cebu's colonization was deferred until Legazpi and Fray Andres de Urdaneta arrived in 1565. Shortly afterwards, they found an image of Sto Niño which may have been left by Magellan. It is now enshrined in the Basilica Minore.

Prior to Spanish colonization Cebu was a hub of trade. Chinese ships arrived with silks and porcelain which they bartered for honey, gold, wood and spices from the Moluccas. Trade restrictions imposed by the Spanish caused the rapid decline of Cebu as a port. During the 19th century many restrictions were lifted and Cebu again became a thriving commercial city.

Cebu Island is roughly 200 km long and a maximum of 40 km wide, hilly, with some good beaches on its peripheral islands and shores. Corn, sugar, mangoes, grapes, coconuts and tobacco are the main crops. The island is too arid to produce much rice. Coastal villagers engage in fishing. Copper, coal and cement are the main industries. Costume jewelry, rattan and *buri* furniture, guitars and porcelain are the primary handicrafts.

Cebu City

Cebu's points of interest are rather spread out. You may elect to see them in comfort and ease by hiring an aircon car or taxi (fix all rates in advance) or do a combined walking-jeepney tour to keep both body and budget fit.

Tours and shopping are described below. DOT personnel in Fort San Pedro can also recommend tour agencies which offer packages such as city, Mactan Island, industrial, diving and night tours.

Hadsan Resort, Mactan Island

City Tour

This tour, designed by Mary Ann Astillero of Cebu's DOT, starts at Fort San Pedro. If you hire a car you can do the entire tour in a day. If you wish to do it in a leisurely manner, or by foot and jeepney, you will probably want to leave your hotel at 8:30 am, plan to have lunch at Fuente Osmeña, and a relaxing sun-downer at the Cebu Plaza or perhaps dinner at the Golden Cowrie and continue the trip the following day.

Ft San Pedro is a lovely, historic spot with a modest entry fee which helps pay for its upkeep. Construction began in 1565, when Legazpi arrived on the ship San Pedro, but was not completed until 1738 Originally intended to repel Muslim raiders, the fort has served many purposes. a stronghold for Filipino revolutionaries; a US army defense post and barracks; a prison camp during the Japanese occupation; the city zoo; and (now) a small park. Over the centuries reclamation has removed the waterfront a couple of blocks from the fort. The two statues flanking the Fort are Legazpi, at the front, and Pigafetta, Magellan's chronicler, on the side.

DOT personnel may provide maps and information, and a bathroom. Other maps may be available at your hotel. If you intend to use at least some public transport, try to acquire the well designed fold-out called "Cebu City Road Maps" that shows all the roads and the jeepney routes.

From the Fort, cross Plaza Independencia and walk up Magallanes St to the gazebo. A box at the base of the present cross houses fragments of the **cross** Magellan and Fray Pedro de Valderrama left to commemorate the conversion of Cebu's Rajah Humabon and Queen Juana. Let your eyes flow to the ceiling mural of the first mass.

Women around the gazebo sell candles. For a small fee they will dance in front of the cross with the lit candles, wishing luck on anyone whom you want to help out, in a short ritual which must predate the Spanish arrival.

Cross the street to the **Basilica Minore del Santo Niño**, which houses the image of the Sto Niño thought to have been left by

Magellan and recovered by Fray Urdaneta 44 years later. Here the faithful wait their turn to file past the statue, and small shops sell religious memorabilia. Lines are longest on Fridays, and the Basilica is closed daily from 12 noon to 2 pm.

The church dates from 1740. Modest attire is required. One sign announces, "This is the plaza of the basilica. Please refrain from any improper acts." And, in case you don't understand, another starts "ACHTUNG!!!"

Exit the Basilica's other side and then head west to Burgos St. Turn left on Burgos and proceed to **Cebu Metropolitan Cathedral**. It closes for lunch from 12-3 pm.

Continue along Burgos 3½ blocks, until you reach a triangle where the road splits in two. Take the right fork and look for a century-old house with a tiled roof. Take the second right after this house, onto Lopez Jaena. **Casa Gorordo** is on the left at the end of the first block.

This house once belonged to Bishop Gorordo and has been restored by the Aboitiz family. It contains historic and cultural relics of old Cebu, a collection of photos, and contemporary art and paintings in a lovely setting. A modest entrance fee includes a guided tour. A must for every visitor who is interested in Cebu's cultural heritage, the museum is open Mon-Sat, 9-12 am and 2-5 pm.

Return to Burgos St. Walk up Colon to the corner of Juan Luna, and board a Lahug-Carbon jeepney going to Lahug. Disembark before the **rotunda** to visit the **Osmeña** house, which holds some MacArthur and **Osmeña** memorabilia. Osmena was the 1st President of the Philippines after WW II.

The many fast foods places on Jones and G Maxillom (Mango) Aves near the circle are a good, inexpensive lunch stop.

Continue to Beverly Hills, a residential section for wealthy Cebuanos. Many residents are Chinese and the area has three temples. Phu Sian (Buddhist) only opens for religious functions. The **Taoist Temple** (which requests no photos of its altars) and the newer **Cebu Heavenly Temple of Charity** (also Taoist) are open to the public. Both temples are attractive and colorful.

Ascend the steps to the Taoist Temple, then continue to the highest shrine. People visit both shrines to pray and seek, through priest intercessors, answers to problems and questions. Ask a temple official for information about the temple or for assistance if you wish to seek the answer to a problem.

Continue up Gorordo to visit the Cebu Plaza.

Return to the city aboard a jeepney to Carbon Market. Get off at the corner of Archbishop Reyes and walk south to visit **Arthaus**, which has a good collection of Philippine and Chinese antiques and perhaps an on-going art exhibit, or to shop at Philippine Treasures for handicrafts (ask for discount). Go back to the corner and get another Carbon- bound jeepney.

Alight again (at the corner of P del Rosario and Gen Junquiera if you took a 4C or 17C jeepney, or at the corner of P del Rosario & Osmeña, if you took a 4B or 17B) to visit the **University of San Carlos Museum**. Enter the main door of the imposing USC building. The Museum is through the first door on the right just as you turn down the first corridor on the right. It houses a well labeled collection of religious carvings, ethnic artifacts, preserved botanical and zoological specimens and archaeological finds. The Museum sells some literature pertaining to its collection and the Visayas. Open weekdays or on Saturdays by appointment, call 72419.

Return to the **Carbon** jeepney again for a look at the market where Cebuanos shop. Bustling with activity, crammed with stalls of handicrafts, fruits, vegetables, meat, fish, flowers, household items and more, it is a fascinating place. But hold your belongings close; Carbon is also happy hunting grounds for thieves.

If you are interested in **numismatics**, ask Mrs Osvel (tel 72450) for an appointment to see her renowned collection. She is off Jones Ave. Ask for directions.

Near the City

Several points of interest lie just beyond Cebu City proper.

If you are interested in **butterfly wing mosaics**, refer to p 203. Take a #9 jeepney from Colon or Carbon.

Mandaue, Cebu's industrial sister city, has two attractions: **Lucky Tableware**, where you may watch beautiful Chinese porcelain being made, and shop (open Monday-Thursday), and, for those of religious inclination, the Chapel of the Last Supper.

To get to Lucky Tableware take a Carbon-Consolacion jeepney (#24), get off at Cubacub and take a tricycle to Lucky.

To visit the **Chapel of the Last Supper**, take a tricycle to Mandaue Highway, then a jeepney marked Manalili or Jones as far as Norkis Cross the street. In front of the BPI Family Bank take a jeepney with Mandaue-Ouano sign or a tricycle. Tell the driver you want to get off at the Chapel of the Last Supper.

The church is a nice restoration. Life-size figures of Christ and the Apostles at the last supper are in an anteroom off the nave. They are redecorated yearly.

Return to Cebu via the same route, stopping at the intersection to Mactan at A Cortes Ave to visit **Cebu Marble** Supply & Shellcraft, or Mactan Island.

Cebu Marble is a supply house for shell, stone and wood products. You may watch necklaces being made and buy some items at reasonable prices.

If you wish to continue to **Mactan** for the beaches, guitar factories and the very attractive Lapu Lapu Monument, take a Cebu-Opon or Cebu-Lapu-Lapu jeepney (from Carbon Market or the corner at Cebu Marble) to the terminal just beyond the bridge. Hire a tricycle and settle the round-trip price in advance. Hadson has the lowest entry fee for day visitors.

Mactan's guitar factories in Abung offer good prices and the opportunity to see how

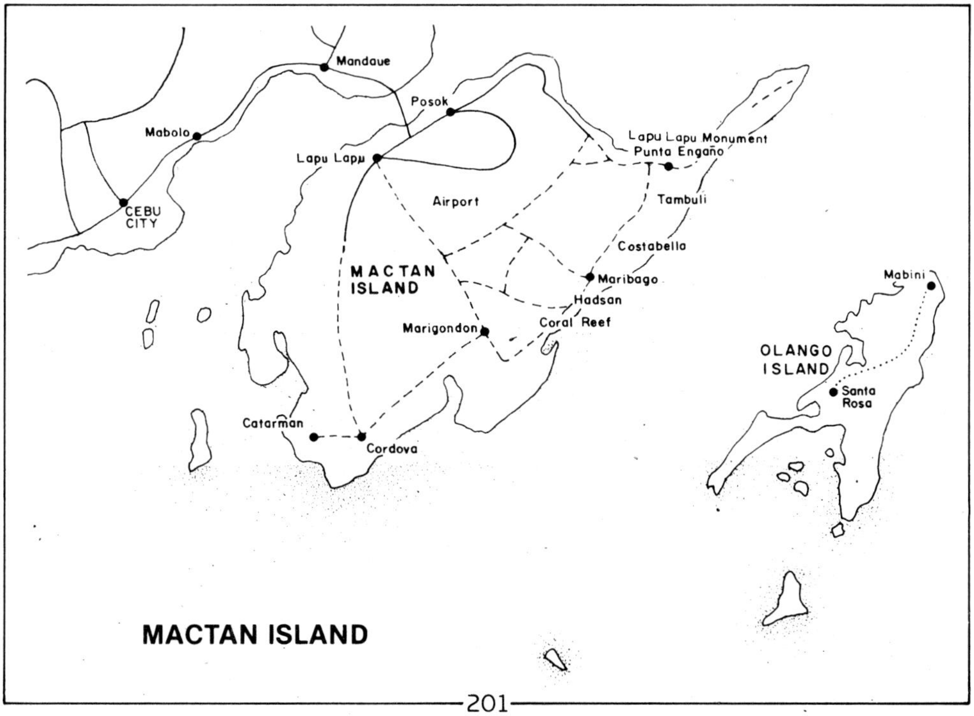

the instruments are made.

Lapu Lapu Monument stands on the beach where Magellan was slain coming ashore (contravening warnings from the natives and orders from the Spanish king). The handsome bronze statue of Lapu Lapu stands in a stunning spot, looking out to sea. Small shops flank the shore, selling inexpensive shell and coral products.

Shopping

No special assistance is needed to spend money in Cebu, where you will find a profusion of shell jewelry, basketry, rattan, arts, handicrafts, almost anything Philippine you desire.

Basilica Minore del Sto Niño

Spread your money wisely. Shops entice tour guides to bring in business by giving them a percentage. A common practice in many places, here it is carried to an extreme: guides, taxi drivers, etc may get 20-50% of your purchase price. You may be able to lop this amount off if you shop unaccompanied.

Shoemart, Robinson's, Rustan's and Tesoro's carry a range of good quality articles. Go to these places to learn maximum reasonable prices.

For a good guitar, go to the factories on Mactan (p 201); for Chinese ceramics, Lucky Tableware (p 201); for shell items at excellent prices, Irfel Trade, Citicenter, Junquiera St, (tels 52807, 90467) and Cebu Marble (p 201), and at Jewel of the Sea where purchases support St Teresa's orphanage; for antiques, Col Roska, Pelaez Ext.; for basketry and fruit, Carbon Market (p 200); for paintings, Arthaus (p 200).

The slaughter of marine turtles is illegal and threatens them with extinction. Please don't encourage poachers by purchasing turtle shell products.

Sustenance

There is a bewildering profusion of places to refuel in Cebu City.

The best seafood is available inexpensively, in a nice native setting, at Golden Cowrie (try the clams). Alavar's, moderately priced, and Lagkaw, inexpensive, also do seafoods well (especially crabs).

Beehive serves Spanish food in a relaxed atmosphere, moderate price. Cebu Bistro Luis is pricier. Continental food, or some variation thereof, is available at many restaurants. Nivel, for steaks and roast, is most expensive, followed by Sizzler; St Moritz and St. Gotthard are next, then Charlie's, moderately priced, great Caesar Salad; First Vienna Cafe for pastries and sausages; Swiss Restaurant, Balls, and Carlo Ristorante.

Majestic has the best Chinese food and is quite reasonable. Tung Yan, better known, is pricier. Ding How has good inexpensive food, and International Rice House is good and cheap. White Gold is fair and moderate.

Ginza (expensive) does the best Japanese food in Cebu. Sunburst has the best chicken.

For lunches, snacks and informal evening meals try Food Street, and the short-order places along Jones Ave near Fuente Osmena. Prices vary from stall to stall, but you can eat cheaply and well.

Nightlife

Cebu's nightlife varies from loud discos to pleasant singalong and piano bars.

Gamblers may enjoy the Casino at Montebello.

Charlie's offers good meals, excellent martinis, easy listening music. St Moritz Pub, with European atmosphere, and Sigay Bar, for singalong, are popular night spots. Eddie's Log Cabin has good atmosphere; there's jazz at Slabadu (Maxillom Ave), disco dancing at the Palace, inside White Gold House (reclamation area). Bachelors Too and After Six are intended for nightowls; Cassanova is a gay bar on Don Mariano Pi.

The South Coast

Southern Cebu has beaches, diving and neat towns with interesting churches, houses and other things to visit. If you are making a day trip, bring a packed lunch. The Philippine Experience (ask Cebu DOT for their telephone number) offers an excellent tour of churches, cottage industries and points of interest.

The southwest coast commenced its cultural ascendancy during the 17th century, when wealthy *mestizo* families began buying sugar land and building beautiful homes and churches in the countryside. Heading south, the first pretty church you pass is **El Pardo**.

Lepido-mosaic art works are created by Professor Julian Jumalon of Basak. In his home nestled amid lush foliage, the Professor collects bits of damaged butterfly wings from all over the world. When he has enough of the correct colors, he lays them over his oil paintings, creating surprisingly alive works of art.

Visits are by appointment only, telephone 91029. To find his house, take the south road to Basak. Turn right at the "Summit Bakery" sign. Follow the wall around one 90° turn to the next. Turn left and stop at the first house on the right.

Continuing south, you pass through Talisay. The **Tabanuk market** spills out into the road, congests traffic and offers some interesting sights.

Lucky Tableware, Cebu

Further on, **Naga Church**, like El Pardo, has an attractive exterior.

Carcar's lovely, quasi-baroque church, was completed in 1876. Its plaza is lined with attractive Spanish buildings, former mansions that are now offices. Carcar is known for the snacks it produces. Ask for directions to an *ampao* factory to see how this puffed-rice sweet is made.

Argao is a charming town. Its superb church has an attached *convento*. Many of the pews are made of heavy, carved wood, and the *retablos* are truly beautiful.

Walk seaward from the church to find Angelita's Holiday Home just beyond the entrance arch.

Argao Beach Resort, exclusive and expensive with watersports facilities, slot machines, rooms and cottages, pool, tennis court and restaurants, is in **Dalaguete**. Next to it is a public beach with shelters for ₱15/day, ₱25 on weekends and holidays. The vendors' association sells souvenirs and rents boats.

From here the road continues through Boljoon, Oslob and Santander, past spectacular views and more lovely churches to Bato, the ferry departure point for Dumaguete.

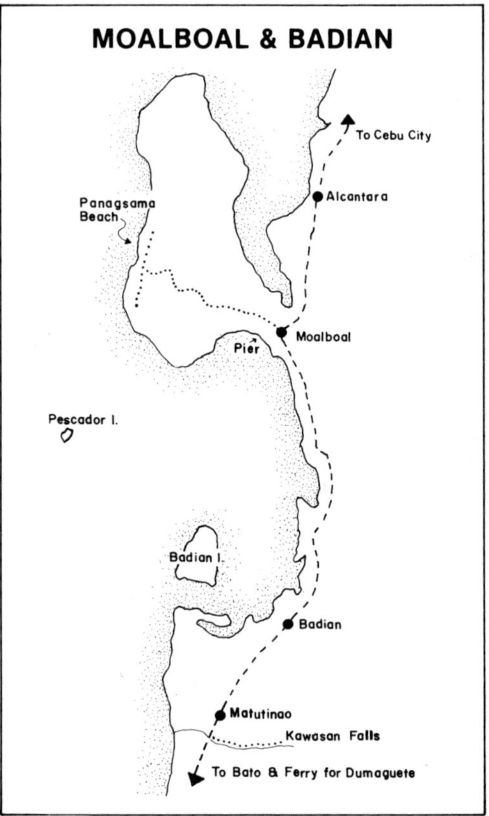

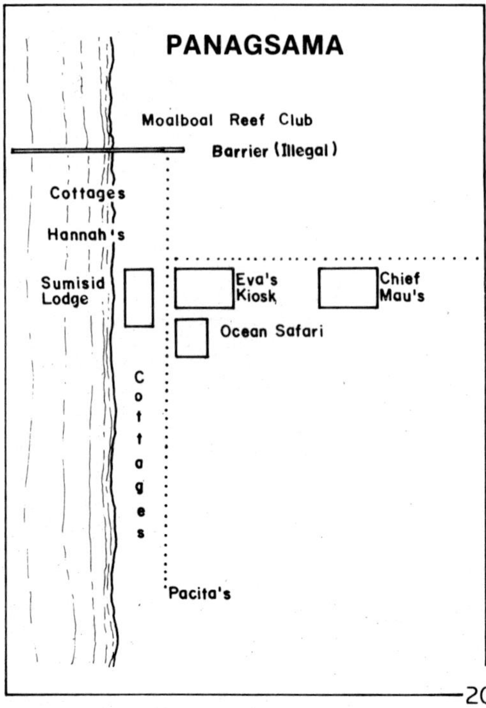

Moalboal & Environs

Moalboal is a tiny town with a market, church, school, cockpit and tennis court, but it is to **Panagsama Beach**, 3 km from town, that vacationers head. Panagsama barrio has become a destination for low-budget travelers and divers, with inexpensive restaurants, nightspots, and clothing made from flour sacks available.

The once spectacular beach was damaged by typhoon several years ago, but is now recovering, as sand is redeposited by tides.

Moalboal aficionados feel Panagsama's atmosphere, its movable discos, Sunday *sabong* (cockfights), and local brews add great color.

Kawasan Falls, at Matutinao, beyond Badian town, offers a half-day away from the beach. There is a small entry fee, which must be paid at the falls.

To get there, cross the bridge in Matutinao, and find the trail at the church. The first waterfall is a 30-min hike, the 2nd is 15 min further.

You may swim in the cool pool at the base of the 12-m tall waterfall.

Badian Island, south of Moalboal, has a very nice up-market resort which can provide helicopter transfers from the airport.

If you are going to Moalboal or Badian, take a taxi or jeepney from Mactan to the bus terminal, then take Philippine Eagle or Villanueva. The bus travels along the south coast to Carcar, then crosses the mountains.

They will, upon request, go to the beach whereas ABC leaves you a 1 km walk. One of ABC's buses does a daily round trip of the southern part of the island.

When departing, ask your resort to arrange a night in advance for a tricycle to take you to the bus.

By private hire, Moalboal is 90 km (2½-3 hrs). Some Moalboal resorts can arrange transport for you if given advance notice.

Should you be arriving or departing by private transport on a Thursday, you may wish to stop at the market in Mantalongon, in the central mountains, for a look at handicrafts, produce and local color.

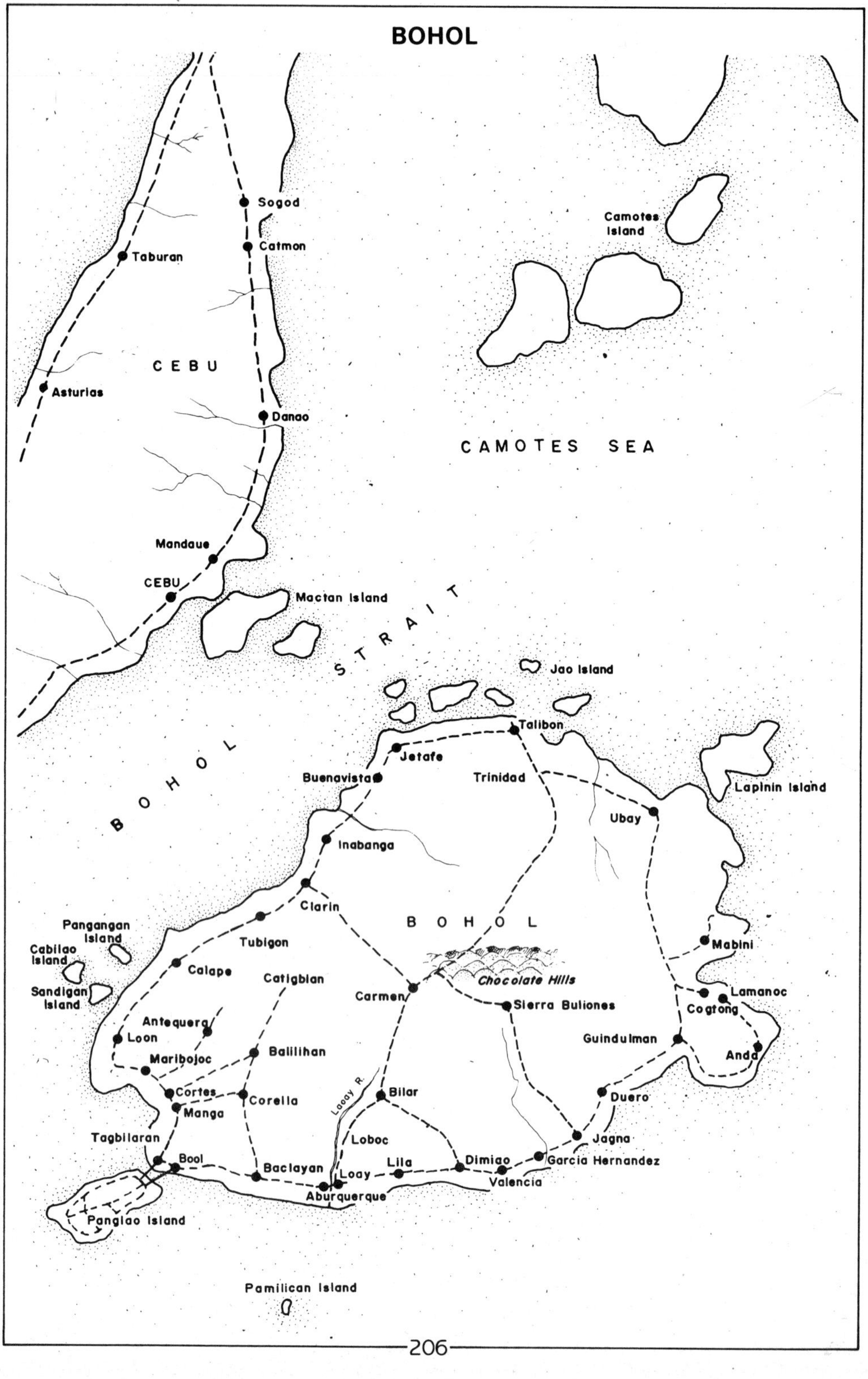
BOHOL
Sogod
Catmon
Taburan
CEBU
Asturias
Danao
Mandaue
CEBU
Mactan Island
Camotes Island
CAMOTES SEA
BOHOL STRAIT
Jao Island
Talibon
Jetafe
Buenavista
Trinidad
Lapinin Island
Ubay
Inabanga
Clarin
BOHOL
Pangangan Island
Cabilao Island
Sandigan Island
Tubigon
Calape
Catigbian
Carmen
Chocolate Hills
Sierra Buliones
Mabini
Lamanoc
Cogtong
Guindulman
Anda
Antequera
Loon
Maribojoc
Balilihan
Cortes
Corella
Manga
Loay R.
Bilar
Duero
Tagbilaran
Loboc
Jagna
Bool
Baclayan
Loay
Lila
Dimiao
Garcia Hernandez
Valencia
Aburquerque
Panglao Island
Pamilican Island

Bohol

Bohol's Chocolate Hills - a verdant green during rainy season

TAGBILARAN

1 Cogon Market
2 Antiques
3 Gie Garden Hotel
4 LTS Lodge
5 City Market
6 Traveller's Inn
7 Mats & baskets
8 Library
9 Provincial Capitol
10 Handicrafts
11 Bistro de Paris
12 Restaurants
13 Cathedral
14 300-year-old house
15 Causeway Bridge Market

Bohol

access: 15 min by air, or 2 hrs by boat from Cebu, p 267
climate: relatively good all year; driest Nov-Jun; hot Mar-Jun
to do: swim, dive, tour towns & chocolate hills, hike
facilities: resorts, lodges, p 293

Although the Chocolate Hills are Bohol's best publicized asset, it is the island's other attractions, the beaches and reefs, people and handicrafts, towns and churches, which entice the visitor to linger.

Long before the Spanish "discovered" the Philippines, Bohol had contact with other civilizations. Remains from Anda Peninsula tell of a people which used gold jewelry and death masks, interred their dead in heavy wood coffins and "enhanced" their women's appearance by flattening and shaping their skulls.

Chinese traders began visiting Bohol and Cebu before the 5th century, bringing wares and collecting goods for their return to the mainland. Boholanos acquired wealth as distributors, taking the Chinese goods as far as the Moluccas, and returning with spices, honey and other items to barter.

Prior to the Spanish arrival the main city may have been on stilts in the shallow harbor between Panglao Island and the mainland. According to legend, Portuguese sailors razed the town and abducted one of the queens, prompting Sultan Sikatuna to move his people to Bool, an area just outside the present site of Tagbilaran City. Some of the other sultans moved their people to Mindanao.

When Legazpi came, he took other places by force, but in Bohol he chose to sign a peace treaty with Sultan Sikatuna. He may have been impressed with Sikatuna's friendliness, but he was probably more impressed with the economic possibilities he saw in developing trade with the Boholanos.

The Spaniards immediately set about building churches and proselytizing. The Philippines' oldest stone church is in Baclayon, and Bohol boasts many other interesting churches three to four centuries old. All show an architectural blend of European, Mexican and Moorish influences. They have ornately carved *retablos*, double façades, and give the feeling of spaciousness and airiness. Many have beautifully painted ceilings.

The treaty between Legazpi and Sikatuna remained in effect for 45 years. Sikatuna chose to be baptized just before he died. Fellow Muslims felt betrayed and turned on Sikatuna's people, frequently raiding Bohol.

Although the Boholanos converted to Roman Catholicism, they refused to put up with friar abuses, and, in 1744, Dagohoy led the people in a successful revolt.

For 85 years Bohol remained an independent island within the Spanish colonial Philippines, but in the interim, the island's importance as a trading center was greatly diminished. Although Bohol was retaken by Spain, the Boholanos have never been easily suppressed. They caused frequent problems for the American colonizers, problems which were exacerbated by violent reprisals.

The Boholanos were equally unwilling to accept Japanese suzerainty in 1941, moving their government away from Japanese control and printing their own money. Rice, vegetables and farm produce from Bohol supplied both WW II protagonists and the island escaped the war relatively unscathed.

Since 1945 Bohol has remained peaceful and pleasant. The way of life is quiet, the pace relaxed. A comfortable feeling of camaraderie results from the relative

Precious shells worth a small fortune, clockwise from top: *Cypraea aurantium* (golden cowrie), *Conus gloriamaris, Cypraea leucodon, Cypraea valentia, Conus excelsus* & *Cypraea guttata* (center)

equality with which Boholanos treat each other. When the Spanish friars were ejected the people retained their farms and a wealthy landed class never arose. There aren't any very rich Boholanos, but there aren't any very poor ones either, and Tagbilaran City is one of the few cities in the world where it is safe to walk around at any time of day or night.

Public transportation serves all towns mentioned. Make advance arrangements with your hotel for private transport. We have found the Laos of Gie Garden and Momo Beach willing to arrange just about anything for guests, so long as they have advance notice and their schedules permit.

When making plans, remember that the Philippines is a very fluid place. You could arrive in Bohol to discover that everything is at a standstill due to a fiesta. Join the crowd. The Boholanos will be delighted to have you, and you'll have a unique experience to treasure.

Tagbilaran (map, p 208)

Bohol's quiet capital has a range of hotels and lodges, a market, several handicraft shops, and numerous small restaurants.

The last Governor, Rolando Butalid G, commenced restoring the capitol building to its original design, making it worth a visit. Tagbilaran's restored, decorative cathedral is another point of interest.

Near **Causeway Bridge** are two ancient houses, remnants of the Spanish days. José Maria Rocha, who was for a long time mayor of Tagbilaran, has restored his **300-year-old house** to its original form, and it is fascinating to see from the outside.

Early in the morning, boats come to the Causeway Bridge market, which buzzes with buying, bargaining and selling activities. Hungry hagglers snack on local *puto* (rice cake), which is brown because it is leavened with froth from *tuba* (coconut alcohol) fermentation.

Tagbilaran's few nocturnal diversions include dancing at Coralandia, bowling at Marbella Leisure Plaza, and having a few beers at a café.

The city market and small nearby shops offer mats and intricate basketry. Persistent market beggars are recent immigrants from troubled areas of Mindanao.

One km south of the city center, on the seaward side of the road, is a marker commemorating the **blood compact**. Here, Sikatuna and Legazpi drew their own blood, mixed it with wine and drank it to seal the pact of peace between their people.

Ilaw Community Center is just beyond and behind the marker. The community development center is run on funds from the United Nations and from countries abroad. It has a canteen, rooms (available when not booked for a conference) and a shop where you may see and purchase handicrafts from projects which they are helping to develop.

Bohol by Land

While it is possible to travel Bohol's circumferential road, most visitors will be content with a trip along the northeast coast from Tagbilaran to Tubigon, or the south coast to Jagna or Duero.

In either case you need to hire a vehicle or go by public transport from one town to the next. The south east coastal exploration could be worked in with a trip to the Chocolate Hills and/or the River Safari, but all three cannot be happily managed in one day. The northeast coastal tour could be incorporated with an arrival by boat from Cebu to Tubigon, as could the Chocolate Hills trip.

Panglao Island, accessible by two bridges from Tagbilaran, offers many activities. You may get around by tricycle from Tagbilaran, but be sure the tricycle waits for you.

Panglao

Panglao Island's main attractions are its beaches and beach resorts, but it also has two towns with interesting churches, shell dealers and a back-yard jewelry industry to visit. Several establishments crowd the fringes of Alona Beach's beautiful white sands, with the up-market Bohol Beach Club nearby. Momo, on the other side, has lovely cottages nestled into the vegetation beside a beach.

Dauis church's ancient structure has suffered extensive renovation. The façade is poorly done, but the two baroque bell towers are interesting examples of the Moorish influence in Bohol's architecture. One unusual feature is a well inside the nave.

A number of jewelers in Dauis' barrios can remodel silver coins into rings and other things. If the timing is right, you may stay and watch, or relax on a nearby beach while the work is done.

The limestone foundations of Bohol and

From a bridge between Panglao and Tagbilaran

PANGLAO ISLAND

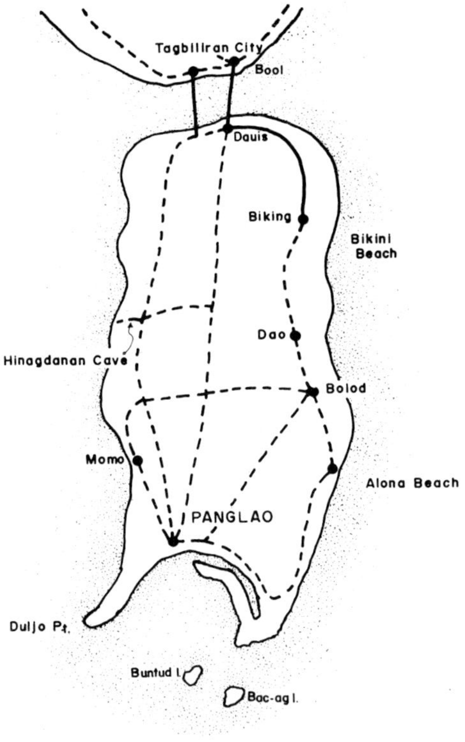

Panglao are riddled with caves. **Hinagdanan Cave** in Dauis is interesting and easy to visit. In the Visayan dialect, Hinagdanan means laddered, and at the cave you ascend steps to a cavern with an underground pond about 50' in diameter. Both ends of the cave are open, and you may see local children diving into the pool.

Panglao town is at the western end of the island. Only a portion of Panglao's original church remains, and it has been incorporated into a grotto. The present 20th century church has been constructed in the old style, using coral blocks and wooden ceiling beams.

The watch tower behind the church affords a pretty view of the bay with **Balicasag, Bacaag and Buntod Islands**. The latter two are within the narrow coastal reef and provide good diving for beginners. There is a deep channel between the nearer islands and Balicasag.

Panglao has two **shell dealers**. Quirino Hora is near the market and Dao Hora is near the town hall. These shops will delight serious collectors as well as casual buyers, for they have both inexpensive and very rare items. Quirino Hora is very candid about the shells he offers.

Northeast from Tagbilaran

The road from Tagbilaran to Tubigon, which is the departure point for the ferry to Cebu, is fairly good. Beyond Clarin the road is less traveled, and there are many bridges to cross at the northern end of the island where the road traverses vast mangrove and nipa swamp. Each town has its own points of interest, usually centered around the church and/or market, and on a clear day along the coast, views across the sea to Cebu are spectacular..

Traveling north from Tagbilaran City, you pass barrio **Taloto**, where the seminary is located. During the afternoons in **Manga**, the next barrio, you may buy fresh fish and have it cooked on the beach.

Continuing, you traverse the winding **Abatan River** three times, and cross a vast nipa swamp. Bohol's nipa swamps have traditionally been community property. Anybody may harvest the nipa, but he is obliged to leave enough of each plant to ensure its survival and regeneration. The *pau* plant (similar to taro) is also treated as community property.

Turn off to **Cortes** for a good view of the river mouth and nipa swamp from behind the massive church.

Antequera is the distribution center for exquisite baskets made from *nito*, bamboo, *sig-id* and other vines. The road to Antequera branches inland on the way to Maribojoc. The pleasant 8-km drive from the coast road to Antequera passes through rice fields, foliage, villages and hills. Sunday is market day and buyers come as early as 4 am to purchase what is available and to place orders. By 8 am much of the better items are taken. Jeepneys ply the Tagbilaran- Antiquera route hourly on Sundays. On other days there may be as few as 3 trips, the bus doesn't leave until it is full, and the last trip back may be as early as 3 pm.

The palanquin inside Antequera church is nice but the church is otherwise unremarkable.

About 1 km before Antequera a road leads off to **Inambacan Falls**. Nearly 2 km along this road is a river. Cross it and head upstream to the falls and cave beyond. You need a local guide. The cave is great fun for advanced, equipped spelunkers.

Back on the coastal road you may

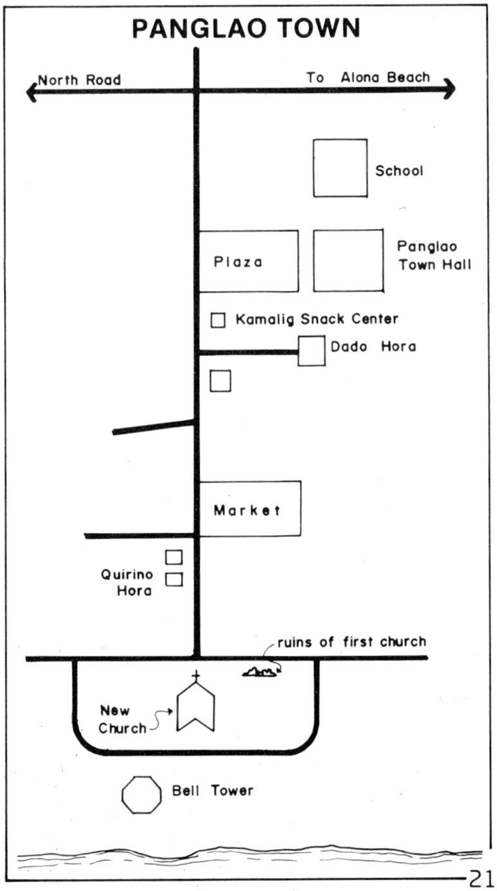

continue to **Maribojoc**. Its church has lovely *retablos* and beautifully painted ceilings.

The *conventos* of many Bohol churches double as high schools. Consequently one sees much educational activity going on in the churches, which are used as extensions of the convent schools.

Punta Cruz watch tower, beyond Maribojoc, was once used as a look-out for marauding pirates. According to legend, the cross at Punta Cruz protected Tagbilaran by extending its arms and blocking the bay. There are good views of Tagbilaran Bay and Panglao's coast from the watch tower's grounds.

Loon, the next town, is Bohol's largest municipality with 60 barrios. Most of the coastal residents are fisherfolk.

Loon's attractive church is made of large coral blocks, has twin bell towers attached to the façade and a massive archway supporting the choir loft. Ceilings are beautifully painted, the *retablos* are very nice, floors are tiled. A long wide staircase leads from the church to the town behind. Across the highway from the church is an attractive hexagonal building which houses the saints' palanquin.

Continuing along the road, one can see across the coastal plain to **Sandigan and Cabilao Islands**, which are accessible by a combination of boat and tricycle. There is a white sand beach on Cabilao.

Calape has a relatively new church, very ornate and beautifully painted with relief work depicting *palay* (unhulled rice) and *lanzones* on the exterior. Its ornate gothic theme is carried over into the interior, with columns and an equally ornate *retablo*. The Moorish influence stands out in the pointed arches. The choir loft extends over the entry arch.

Both Calape and Loon have "miraculous" images: Casila, or the Lady of Light, in Loon and a miraculous virgin and a miraculous St Anthony in Calape. Believers communicate with St Anthony through an interpreter-spiritist for answers to queries. The images are in barrios near the towns, and you need a guide or local assistance to find them.

From Calape through Tubigon you are treated to lovely views of Cebu across the channel. This area produces bananas and red sugar. I stopped to watch *buri* being woven into chairs, and four young puppies chewing on an amiable piglet.

Tubigon is the only area in Bohol where *calesas* (horse carts) are used. Tubigon's old church suffers from lack of maintenance and has bushes and shrubs growing from its exterior. It is a large and breezy church with massive columns down the nave. Continue directly seaward from the church, onto Tubigon's wharf for great views and delicious *alimasag*, the deep sea crab, at small cafeterias. Boats depart Tubigon for the 2-hr trip to Cebu.

Clarin is a pretty town with lots of San Francisco plants along the road and flowering bushes hiding the houses. The church has a central belltower, double façade and attractive exterior. Beyond town an unpaved road goes inland to Carmen and the Chocolate Hills.

Villagers in **Badiang** and **Cogon** barrios weave *buri* chairs and curtains, and there are several interesting houses.

Inabanga has a Spanish church and a market with a primitive toilet and restaurants where you may eat. Watch your belongings in this town.

Beyond Inabanga countless bridges traverse rivers and streams that merge into vast nipa and mangrove swamps along the shore all the way to Ubay. **Buenavista** is a collection of shacks on a picturesque little bay. People from Buenavista go marketing in Cebu, as it is closer than Tagbilaran. Houses and churches in this area are more modest than in towns closer to Tagbilaran.

Jetafe church is small but has a tiled floor and a *retablo* in keeping with its attractively simple facade, and a very handsome brown Sto Nino.

Talibon, President Carlos P Garcia's home town, has a big school and an attractive old church with a convent school at the rear. There is a good view of **Jau Island**. Talibon is another good place to feast on crab. The Jau Islanders weave high quality buntal hats. There is a small resort on Jau, with

Baclayon Church – built in 1595

Momo Beach, Panglao

anchorage facilities for yachts.

From Talibon the road is wide, flat, smooth and straight. In **Trinidad** the more traveled road goes inland to Carmen. On Thursday the island people from Jau paddle upriver to Trinidad to do their marketing.

There is a grass airstrip on the approaches to **Ubay**. The town is the departure point for boats to Leyte, but otherwise isn't much to look at.

The Southeast Coast

The southeast coastal road is a long and pretty drive. The Chocolate Hills are accessible from the coast, as is the River Safari.

An **underground river** flows into the sea 1 km before Baclayon *poblacion*. At low tide people come here to wash their clothes in the freshwater pool; at high tide the water is salty, and people swim.

Baclayon church, the oldest stone church in the Philippines, was built in 1595. Its solid fortress-like structure gives a feeling of permanence. The beautifully ornate *retablos* of the central and side altars still have some of their original gold leaf paint, and the *santos* they house are attractive. The original ivory faces were stolen in 1974.

The convento, a later addition, has a small museum with interesting religious relics. It is not generally open to the public. To gain entry, ask permission from the priest.

Wednesday is market day in Baclayon, when fish, food and handicrafts are traded. The handicrafts consist mainly of abaca and *buri* hats, mats and rope, winnowing baskets and knives.

Mangrove swamps that serve as the breeding grounds for crabs and fish line the coast. Bohol fishermen catch more fish than they can consume. There are no refrigeration facilities, so much of the catch is preserved in brine and vinegar, packed and taken for sale in Mindanao's highlands.

Wednesday is also market day in **Alburquerque**. The church has a central bell tower. The double facade is attached by an arcade to the *convento*. Ceilings are beautifully painted. The columns inside the nave have been resurfaced with tin, and the *convento* is in need of repair.

Clarin Beach, on the approaches to Loay, is a pretty beige sand cove ringed with houses. By the road is a forge and you may see nipa weaving.

Loay church is a massive structure with ceiling paintings and a sculpture over the point of the façade, an ornate choir loft, no pillars inside the church, and an atrocious canopy over the altar. Although the church is not very large, it gives a wonderful feeling of spaciousness and airiness.

The Clarin house near the church is a functioning example of a well-preserved wealthy Filipino home of one or two centuries ago: airy rooms, wide floor boards, pictures and mementos of the past. As this is a private house, you need to ask permission from Ms Inday Clarin if you want to have a look.

Just beyond Loay the road forks, one part going inland to Loboc and the Chocolate Hills (see p 217), the other continuing along the coast.

Lila has a relatively recent church (1925). Maguey cactus beside the road beyond Lila is cut, taken to the sea and pounded on the rocks to remove the pulp. The maguey is left overnight under piles of rock to finish the process, dried and sold for weaving into rope, sacks and doormats. Most buyers come from Leyte.

There is a good view of Mt Hibokhibok and Camiguin Island from here. Camiguin is only 1 hr away by *banca*.

Coming into **Dimiao**, there is a seaside rock known as MacArthur's hat. In the uplands, a mining company is slowly moving an entire mountain of high grade limestone to Japan.

Dimiao church is large, has a double façade and very nice *retablos*.

Valencia has a newish gothic church. Statues of Rizal and the Sacred Heart face each other in front of the church, the Sacred Heart apparently giving the freethinking Rizal a lecture. Roxas Park is about 3 km from the main road. It is a boy scout camp and has two natural swimming pools.

Badiang springs are on the coast beyond Valencia. Here water gushes out from the mountains into a pool and over the hillside. People come to swim and wash their clothes.

Jagna is the departure point for boats to Butuan and Mindanao. There are a couple of restaurants among the collection of rectangular buildings before the pier. If you aren't sure that the food is fresh, have it reheated or go to the market and buy fish for the restaurant to cook.

Jagna church is very beautiful. The church has a high choir loft, semicircular façade, and all over the ceiling paintings done in 1930 by Rey Francia, a Cebuano who painted many ceilings in Bohol.

Just before km 78 the road goes through the pass where Bohol's guerrillas wreaked havoc on the American forces in 1901, and again on the Japanese in 1945.

Just beyond **Guindulman** a road goes right to the **Anda Peninsula**, an unspoilt area with many beautiful beaches and coves, but no facilities. Anda's pretty church and most of the houses in the town were badly damaged during the typhoon of 1984.

The National Museum is conducting a dig in Lamanoc, on the other side of the peninsula. To visit it you must continue from Guindulman to Candijay, then turn seawards to barrio **Cogtong**, but it is necessary first to have made arrangements with the National Museum in Manila, or you may find nobody to accompany you to the dig site. Expect some difficult climbing.

The museum office in Cogtong has some finds on display, including a molave wood secondary burial coffin decorated with a reptile head motif on the lid, and a poster explaining the finds. There are drawings of other types of coffins. Skulls found at Anda had been flattened, a practice which has also been found to have existed in other central Visayan islands and northern Mindanao. Anda finds date man's record on Bohol back to 10,000 BC. The fisheries school next door has an exhibit of fossils, some shell jewelry and neolithic and paleolithic stone tools and some items of biological interest.

The road from Guindulman to Candijay passes through beautiful, precipitous limestone hills.

There is lots of *pau* (taro) growing between Candijay and Alicia. Just beyond Alicia a road goes inland to Sierra Buillones and Carmen. The area between Alicia and Ubay is used for rice farming.

The Chocolate Hills

You usually get a good but rather distant aerial view of the Chocolate Hills flying in from Cebu to Tagbilaran, but most visitors want a closer look. If your hotel arranges trips to the Chocolate Hills, allow half a day and pack lunch. If you use public transport, allow more time. There are two routes from Tagbilaran: by bus to the Chocolate Hills Complex, which is beyond Carmen, and by jeepney to Loboc, where you change for Carmen. Ask the driver to let you off on the road to the complex, and walk up hill about 1 km. Allot 1½ hrs to the hills by private vehicle, at least 2 hrs to Carmen by public conveyance.

If you travel the Loboc-Carmen route to the hills you may want to investigate **Loboc**'s church and furniture maker (below). There are attractive houses on the way into Loboc. A few km further inland you pass the Tontonan hydroelectric plant and park.

On the approaches to **Bilar** you may hear the thump-thump of rice pounding. The families in this town demand a large quantity of rice in return for their daughters' hands in marriage, and so the young men are kept busy.

If you intend to do the Chocolate Hills, then leave for Cebu by boat from Tubigon, plan to spend the night at the Chocolate Hills Complex, then catch an early (7:30) jeepney to Carmen. A bus leaves Carmen at about 8:30 for the 2-hr ride to Tubigon. Conversely you may arrive in Tubigon from Cebu, go to Carmen, then leave for Tagbilaran at 4:00 pm.

The **Chocolate Hills** are at their brownest between February and May, and are green after July, when rain revives the grass cover.

There are many stories about the hills' origins, and some are Boholano legends. One maintains that two giants had a fight here, throwing huge boulders at each other. When they tired of the contest they left, but didn't clean up the battlefield.

Another legend tells of a giant named Arogo who fell in love with a mortal named Aloya. He kidnapped her, but she didn't love him and died. In his grief, Arogo cried many tears, which ran in rivers and eroded the soil to form the Chocolate Hills.

There have also been a number of scientific proposals regarding the formation of the hills, including simple weathering of limestone formed beneath the sea and uplifted; formation of the hills by suboceanic volcanism, then uplift of the sea floor; and a more recent theory, born from observations of similar structures, which maintains that as a massive volcano self-destructed it spewed huge blocks of stone. These were then covered with limestone and later uplifted from the ocean bed

Green or brown, mythical or real, the hills are lovely. The Chocolate Hills Complex has a restaurant, dorm beds and rooms but they have water problems during dry months.

River Safari

One superb way to end a day is to take a boat trip up the Loay River from Loboc to Busay Falls. Be sure to leave time to investigate **Loboc** town and its church before the river trip.

The church is massive and impressive. Lower portions of the exterior relief work have been damaged, but in the upper areas, faces of the pope and angels are intact Ornate paintings on the ceilings date from 1926 and 1927 and are matched in effect by the lovely *retablos*. The organ is unfortunately no longer working.

When Boholanos want new carved wood furniture they come to Loboc to order it. Vigal's furniture shop, where you may see beautifully carved molave pieces or watch the work in progress, is just beyond the plaza.

The Laos of Gie Garden and Momo Beach Resort originated the River Safari, bringing guests to Loboc, where they board a *banca* and go up the Loay River, gazing at the flora, people and little farms along the way. The trip ends at **Busay Falls**, where you can jump in for a refreshing swim before returning downstream into (if the timing is right) the sunset, waving at the river folk who wave enthusiastically back. Utopia.

Bohol Beach Club also does this trip now, and possibly others, but it must be arranged in advance.

Tarsiers, Flying Lemurs & Butterflies

Bohol is still home to some rare fauna, among them the tarsier and the flying lemur and several species of butterflies.

Tarsiers are primitive primates that probably diverged from the root stock which eventually gave rise to monkeys, apes and men. Shy little nocturnal creatures with long tails, large round eyes and fuzzy bodies, they are threatened with extinction due to the destruction of their forest habitat and poaching. They are extremely difficult to keep alive in captivity.

Occasionally a caged tarsier is offered to tourists in Tagbilaran, along with the story that it was born and raised in captivity. A friend purchased one which looked very sad and took it to a patch of forest in Corella where tarsiers are known to live. Immediately upon its release this "tame" creature leapt for the trees and was gone. One tarsier may have been saved. Many more will be caught only to die with unwitting travelers. Please don't buy the stuffed ones either.

Flying lemurs are the size of large house cats. Members of a family of gliding mammals, they are neither lemurs (primates) nor can they fly, but the generous flap of skin between their legs and tail allows them to glide between tree branches. Like the tarsier, their primary enemy is man, who destroys their natural habitat and hunts them for food.

During Nov-May Bohol's forests teem with colorful **butterflies** flitting to and fro. Enthusiasts come from Japan and points beyond to net and preserve specimens. As butterflies hatch, mate, lay their eggs and die within a few days (some within hours), a modest amount of butterfly hunting is unlikely to affect survival of the species.

Hiking

Bohol is great hiking country, and camping can be arranged at the boy scout camps Magsaysay in Bilar and Roxas in Valencia. Contact the Laos of Gie Garden or the office of the Governor.

Sustenance

You can get tasty meals at the Gie Garden Hotel (specialize in Chinese food). Bistro de Paris near the cathedral does hamburgers and, if you order ahead, seafoods. The Garden Cafe on the grounds of the cathedral offers lunch and snacks. It is run by and for the benefit of the deaf. Horizon Restaurant at the market has an extensive menu and there are several small snack shops in and about the market place, as well as some restaurants on Gallares St.

All resorts provide meals.

Leyte

"Pete" Grimm remained in the Philippines during WW II and helped prepare the Tacloban area for MacArthur's return. Decades later his daughter, Linda, wades out to greet her dad's old comrade.

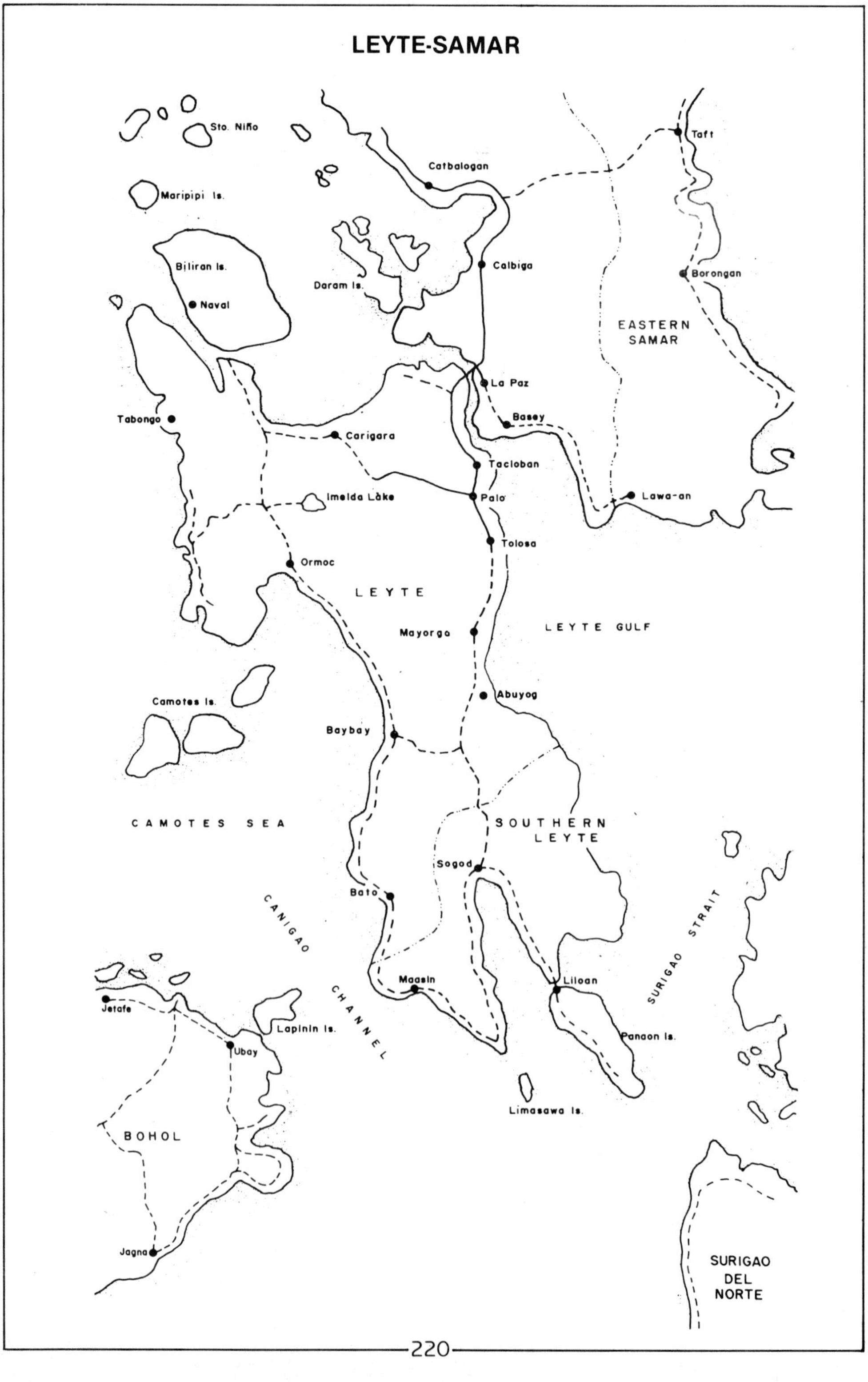
LEYTE-SAMAR
Sto. Niño
Maripipi Is.
Catbalogan
Taft
Biliran Is.
Naval
Daram Is.
Calbiga
Borongan
EASTERN SAMAR
La Paz
Tabongo
Basey
Carigara
Tacloban
Imelda Lake
Palo
Lawa-an
Tolosa
Ormoc
LEYTE
Mayorga
LEYTE GULF
Abuyog
Camotes Is.
Baybay
CAMOTES SEA
SOUTHERN LEYTE
Sogod
Bato
CANIGAO CHANNEL
SURIGAO STRAIT
Maasin
Liloan
Jetafe
Lapinin Is.
Ubay
Panaon Is.
Limasawa Is.
BOHOL
Jagna
SURIGAO DEL NORTE

TACLOBAN CITY

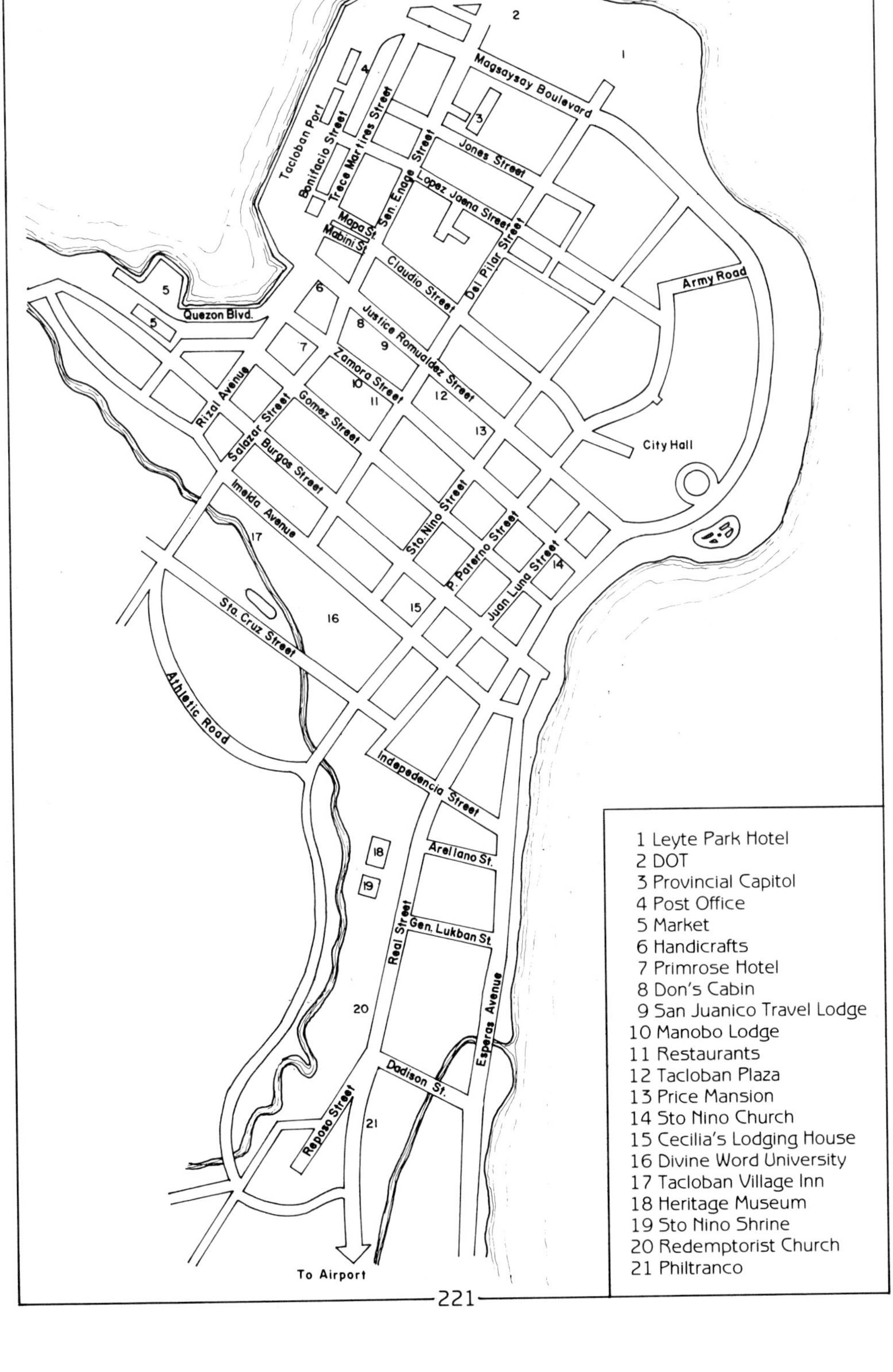

Leyte

access: plane from Manila (1 hr) and Cebu (1/2 hr), bus from Manila, boat from Cebu to Ormoc, p 267
climate: best March-July

to do: WW II nostalgia trip, hike, shop, hiking, spelunking

facilities: hotels, lodges, p 294

Tacloban & Vicinity

Tacloban City, capital of Leyte Island Province, is a focal point for those whose

Mat decorating, Basey, Samar

Philippine ties go back to World War II, for it was to Red Beach, Palo, south of the city that General Douglas MacArthur arrived on October 20, 1944, to fulfill his famous promise "I shall return".

Much of the city's tourism activities are based around this famous event, and many of the protagonists and their families, whether Filipino, American or Japanese, come to Tacloban to remember.

The two top hotels - Leyte Park and MacArthur Park - are quite nice. There is a range of simpler accommodation.

The remembrance route takes you to **Red Beach**, to see where the troops landed, and the larger-than-life-size statues of General MacArthur, President Sergio Osmeña, Carlos P Romulo and several other men wading ashore. Side trips to **Hill 522**, Japanese memorial shrines and other spots where much fighting took place are often included. In Tacloban City one may drive by the **Redoño** House, where President Osmeña was billeted, and tour the **Price Mansion**, where MacArthur stayed and was narrowly missed by a Japanese bomb on the night of his arrival.

The Divine Word University Museum houses a photo-exhibit of the landing and some interesting relics from Sohoton Caves in nearby Samar. The relics include two crania, one flattened in the style of the day (flat-top-skulls were in vogue for some Visayan and Mindanao women in and about the 12th century) and another coated with calcium carbonate, the stuff that stalagmites and stalactites are made of; shards and broken pieces of Ming and Sung dynasty pottery and porcelain which have been donated by wealthy families; some church accoutrements; an exhibit of Mangyan (tribespeople from Mindoro Island) photos and artifacts; and a collection of original historical documents and manuscripts.

Most of Tacloban's points of interest were developed by Imelda Marcos in order to glamorize her origins.

At the **Shrine of Sto Niño and Heritage Museum**, visitors are given a tour of the many bedrooms, each done in a motif representative of a different Philippine region or style, and a diorama depicting some stage in Imelda Marcos' real or imagined life.

The house is an extravagant showpiece for Filipino architecture and materials. Ceilings made of wooden squares give the visual impression of the woven matting the area is so well known for. There is an awesome collection of carved ivory and Chinese porcelain, statues of the Sto Niño and assorted female goddesses, scores of photos of Imelda and a few of Marcos. The Imelda cult was strongly reinforced here and elsewhere in Tacloban.

The **Convention Center and Library** beside the shrine houses an extensive library and 82 dioramas of Philippine cultural minorities.

Another show-piece is the very beautiful 2-km long **Marcos Bridge** which snakes its way over the shallows and then spans the very deep San Juanico Strait between Leyte and Samar.

Tacloban's other attractions include the very well appointed Leyte Park and MacArthur Park Hotels, the city market for fruit and Waling-Waling for very good handicrafts, especially the colorful *banig* (mats) and abaca and bamboo products.

All the above, as well as **Palo church** (for the *santos* and *retablos*) and the NACIDA handicrafts display center in Palo, can be toured in a day. Ask your hotel or the helpful people at the DOT for assistance with transport, or hire a tricycle.

Sohoton Park

Sohoton Natural Bridge National Park, across the San Juanico Strait in Samar, is one excellent reason to visit Tacloban, especially for naturalists and spelunkers. Arrange private hire or take a jeepney to Basey, Samar. Basey is a simple town; no lodges or restaurants. The only possibility for staying over is to find private accommodation or to ask the BFD officers if you can camp in the office building.

Visit Sohoton from March through early August. During rainy season the rivers may be too swift to negotiate, and showers can be expected.

There are numerous caves in Sohoton Park. Panhulugan and Sohoton Caves are accessible by *banca*, then a short walk.

Panhulugan is situated near some cliffs which were used as defense posts by insurgents fighting the Spanish and, later, the Americans. When the regular armies came up the river the rebels rained logs and stones down on their enemies, then disappeared into the rocky area, not to be found.

Panhulugan Cave has numerous chambers and several very interesting formations. Officers in charge of the park can conduct visitors, pointing out formations. Some have signs indicating their similarities to other things: a flow area looks like the Banawe rice terraces; a horizontal ribbon-like formation is compared to the Great Wall of China going past the Chocolate Hills of Bohol; there is a group of elephants, organ pipes, etc.

From Panhulugan you may continue upstream to the junction with the Sohoton River. A few minutes up this river brings

Panhulugan Cave, Sohoton Park

you to **Sohoton Cave**, a long tunnel, and there is about an hour's climb to **Sohoton Natural Bridge**. Flora and fauna abound in the park. Although there has been some poaching, park personnel attempt to minimize it. Both Panhulugan and Sohoton Caves have been inhabited for millennia. Archaeologists have unearthed remains of early dwellers and their belongings as well as a goodly amount of Ming and Sung pottery and porcelain. Some of the finds may be seen at the Divine Word University Museum in Tacloban.

The Basey River emerges from the mountainside a few hundred meters beyond the junction with the Sohoton. Here you may swim, and it is said the waters are pure and sweet.

If you intend to visit Sohoton, inform the BFD head office in Tacloban and ask them to send word ahead to the Parks officer to arrange for your visit so that a boat and experienced guide will be available when you arrive in Basey. *Banca* rentals cost $10-12.50.

Ormoc & Vicinity

Ormoc is a quiet city with a delightfully clean market that offers inexpensive baskets and handicrafts.

Imelda Lake, 20 km from Ormoc, nestles into one of seven National Parks in the Leyte-Samar Region. Wilderness flora and fauna may be seen. There is a 10-km circumferential road and trail as well as other walks. A 3-day hike takes you to Maginhaw National Park, but to stay overnight you need a permit from the BFD Regional Office in Tacloban, and there are periodic security problems. Consequently most visitors stay only during the day.

To get to the lake you can either hire a vehicle or take public transport. One jeepney leaves Ormoc for Ga-as at about 6 am, then returns immediately. From Ga-as there is about a 5-km walk back to the lake. Other jeepneys go more frequently to barrio Milagro, which is about 6 km from the lake.

Sustenance

Tacloban does not have a large range of eating places. Best food is available at the Leyte Park, with Sinugba for seafoods and the MacArthur Park next. Don's Cabin on Romualdez St. does good chicken, fish and steak. The adjacent Mandawe Fast Foods Center does tasty, inexpensive lunches and snacks. Fast foods and turo-turo style meals are available at a number of restaurants along Zamora St. the Asiatic Restaurant does Chinese food, the Hamburger Station, Good Morning Fast Foods, the Silahis Restaurant, Savory Steak House, Chinatown Restaurant, Rovic and a host of others in the vicinity. If you like lechon, try the stand along Enage, between Romualdez and Zamora Sts.

Food is good at Don Felipe and Pongos hotels in Ormoc.

Mindanao

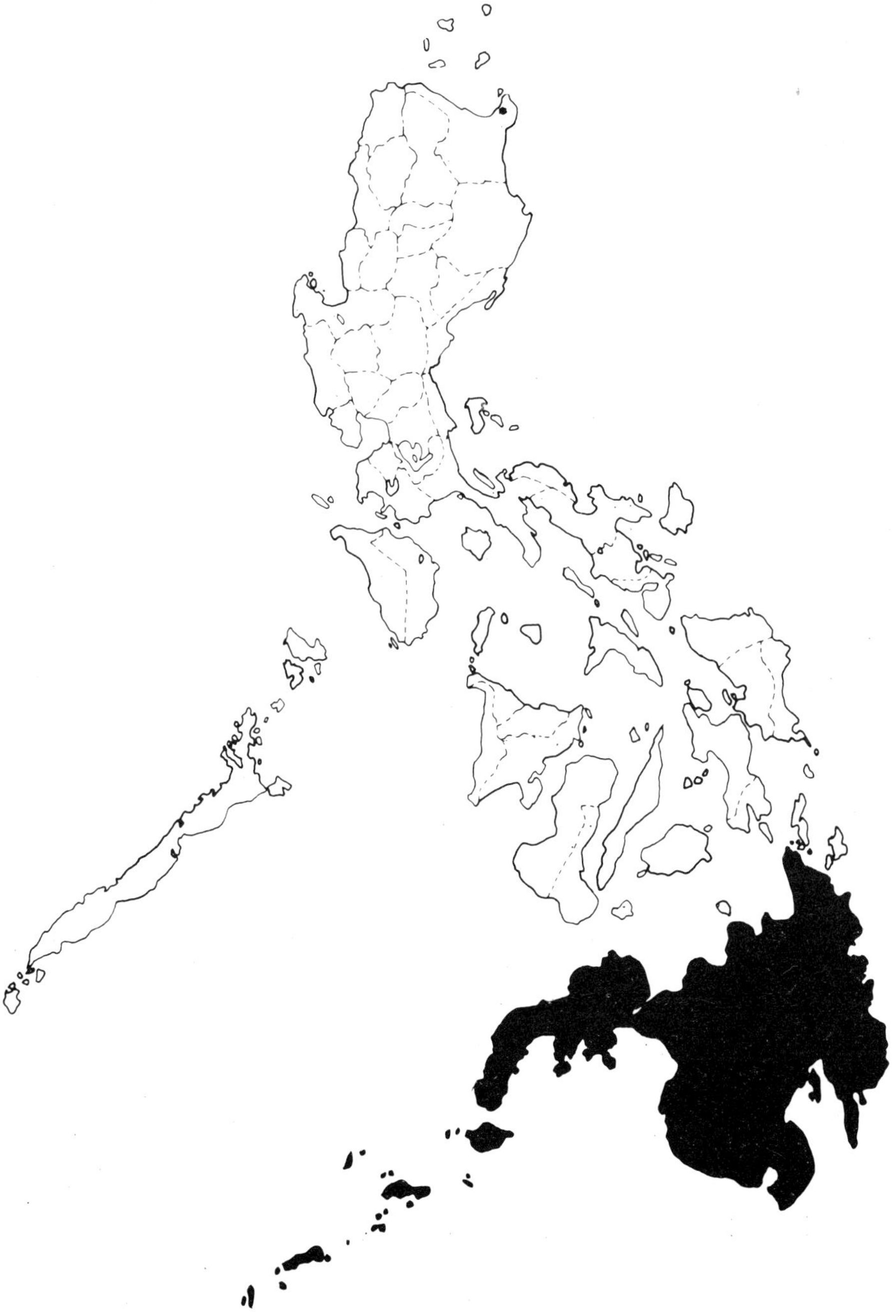

Mindanao

Mindanao, the Philippines' second largest island, is a meeting place of many peoples from many cultural backgrounds.

The original tribal inhabitants, of Malay extraction, were either converted by more aggressive later migrants, or moved successively deeper and deeper into the forests and mountains.

The Muslim influence first came in the 14th century from Malaysia through the southern islands of Jolo, Tawi Tawi and Basilan. For many years the Sultanate of Sulu ruled much of the Philippines and Borneo. By the 16th century the Spaniards were attempting, with little success, to convert Mindanao Muslims to Christianity.

Because Mindanao was less densely populated than the Philippines' more northern islands, settlers were encouraged to go south. They found land which was untitled, and registered it as their own. Original inhabitants felt the land was theirs by rights of inheritance and/or Koranic law. The scene was set for many bitter wars and lasting enmity.

Although considered a Muslim island, many areas of Mindanao, especially those around the coasts, have predominantly non-Muslim populations.

Tribal and Muslim inhabitants feel justifiably bitter about their loss of lands, while Christians feel they and their forebears laid legitimate claim to the property. There is no easy solution to the problem.

Several groups feel the law will not work for them and have united to defend their people or claim power for themselves. Davao, Zamboanga, Cagayan de Oro, all major population centers, are usually quite safe. Ask before venturing beyond them to be sure that the route bears no unpleasant surprises. Bus company operators usually know the score.

Yet it is precisely this mixture of peoples which makes Mindanao such an interesting place to visit.

No shopper can resist the bazaar- like markets of Zamboanga, where you must bargain hard for a reward; the stalls of Aldevinco Market in Davao, where handicrafts from all over the island are available and fruits are indescribably delicious; or the smaller markets and shops.

The people, many of whom still proudly wear their tribal costumes, are fascinating and, once a visitor has been properly introduced by a friend, are hospitable and warm.

The landscape has, for the most part, been stripped of its fabled forests, yet is still lovely.

At the Eagle Breeding Station on Mt Apo you may be fortunate enough to see one of the few remaining Philippine Eagles, a magnificent bird doomed to extinction by man's relentless encroachment on its natural habitat.

Mindanao

Mandaya women at Dabaw Etnica: preparing abaca fiber (foreground); tieing in preparation for dyeing (background); dagmay, abaca fabric, on the loom (right)

MINDANAO

NEGROS
CE
Dipolog
ZAMBOANGA DEL NORTE
Pagadian
ZAMBOANGA DEL SUR
Olutanga I.
San Ramon
Zamboanga
Sacol I.
Sta.Cruz I.
Tictauan I.
Basilan
SULU
Jolo
Tawi-Tawi

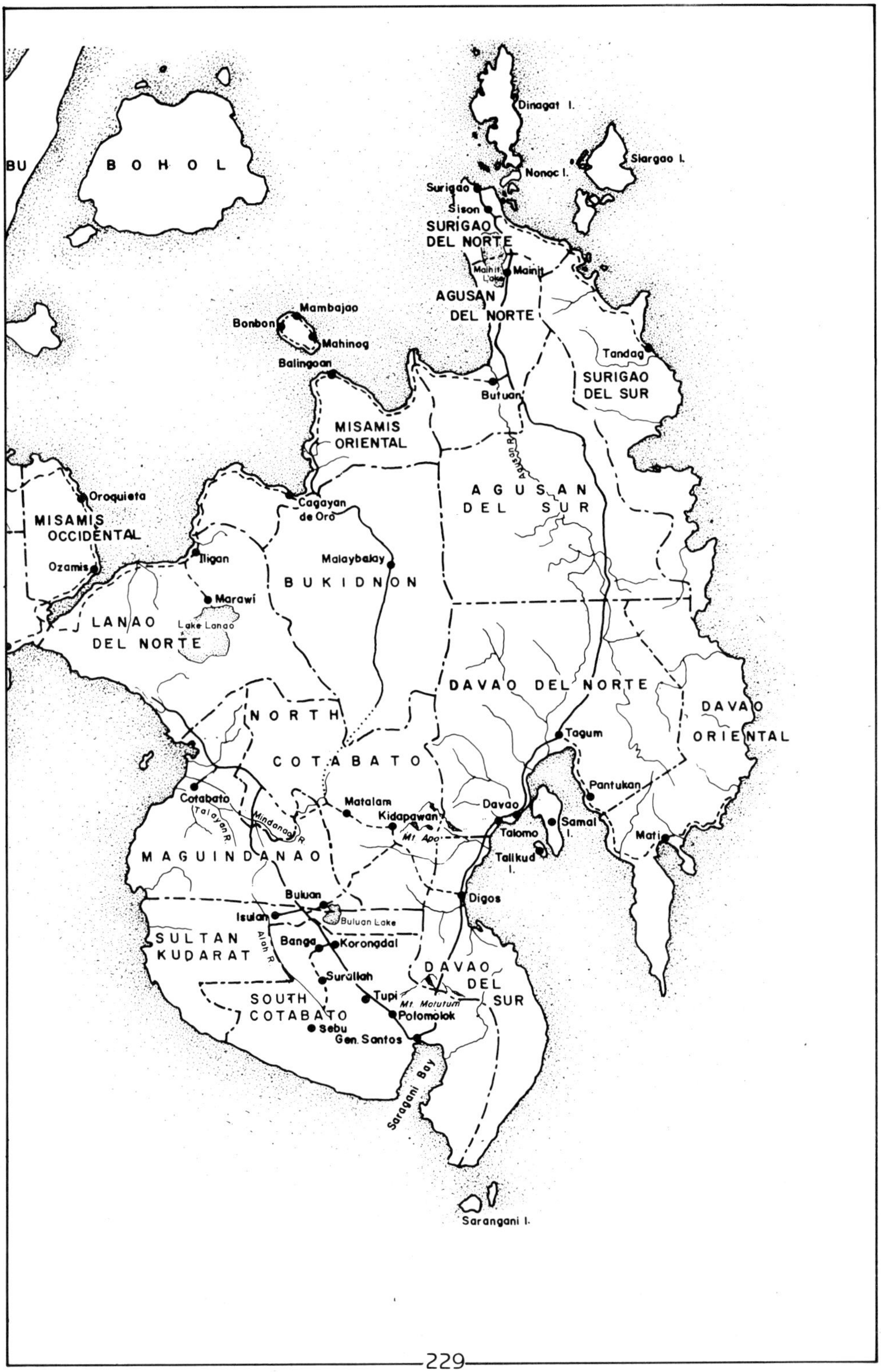
BU
BOHOL
Dinagat I.
Siargao I.
Nonoc I.
Surigao
Sison
SURIGAO DEL NORTE
Mainit Lake
Mainit
AGUSAN DEL NORTE
Mambajao
Bonbon
Mahinog
Balingoan
Tandag
SURIGAO DEL SUR
Butuan
MISAMIS ORIENTAL
Agusan R.
AGUSAN DEL SUR
Oroquieta
MISAMIS OCCIDENTAL
Cagayan de Oro
Iligan
Ozamis
Malaybalay
BUKIDNON
Marawi
LANAO DEL NORTE
Lake Lanao
DAVAO DEL NORTE
NORTH COTABATO
DAVAO ORIENTAL
Tagum
Pantukan
Cotabato
Talayan R.
Mindanao R.
Matalam
Kidapawan
Mt. Apo
Davao
Talomo
Samal I.
Talikud I.
Mati
MAGUINDANAO
Buluan
Digos
Isulan
Buluan Lake
SULTAN KUDARAT
Alah R.
Banga
Koronadal
Surallah
DAVAO DEL SUR
SOUTH COTABATO
Tupi
Mt. Matutum
Polomolok
Sebu
Gen. Santos
Saragani Bay
Sarangani I.

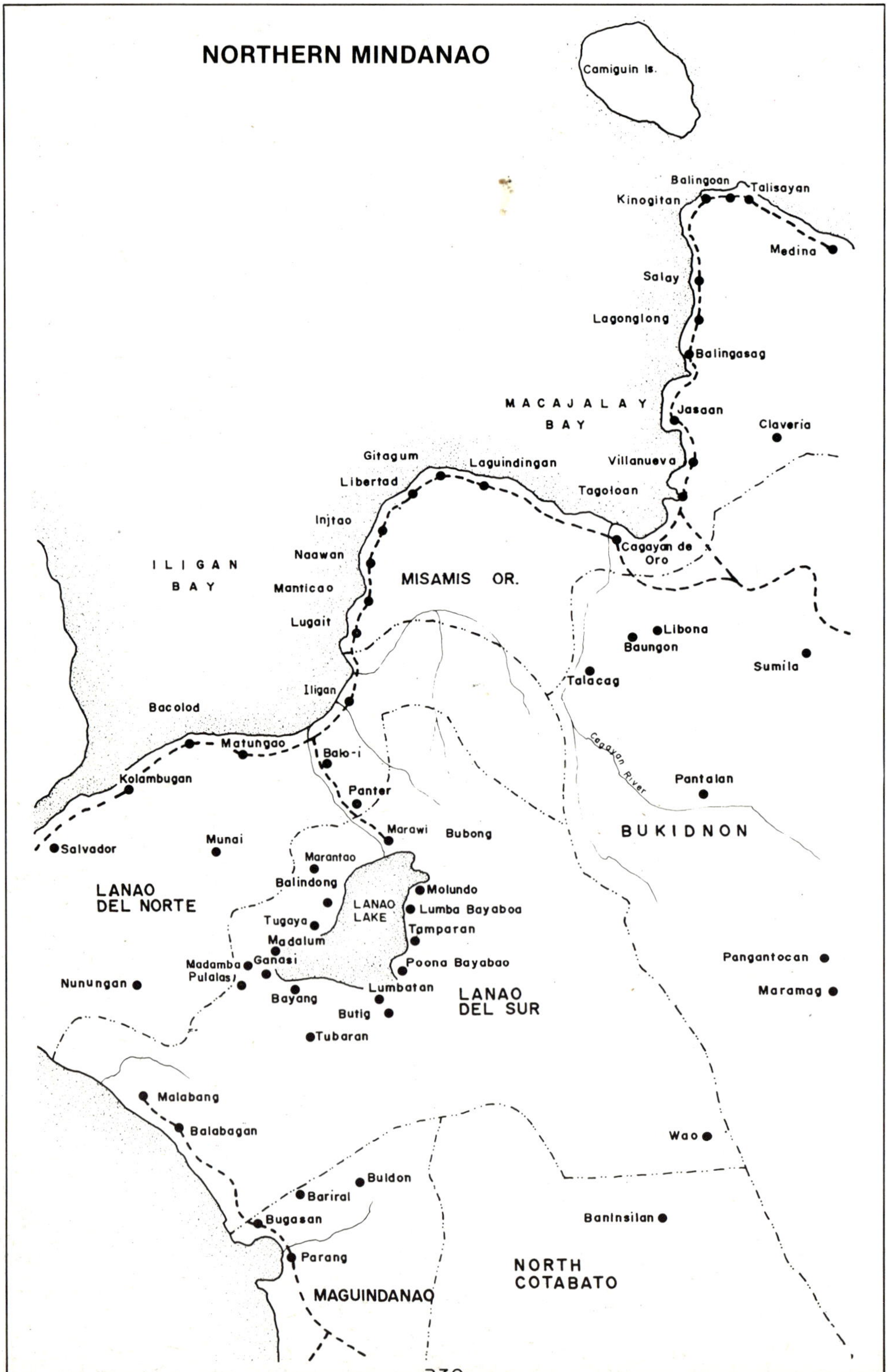
NORTHERN MINDANAO
Camiguin Is.
Balingoan
Talisayan
Kinogitan
Medina
Salay
Lagonglong
Balingasag
MACAJALAY BAY
Jasaan
Claveria
Villanueva
Gitagum
Laguindingan
Libertad
Tagoloan
Injtao
Cagayan de Oro
Naawan
ILIGAN BAY
Manticao
MISAMIS OR.
Lugait
Libona
Baungon
Sumila
Talacag
Iligan
Bacolod
Matungao
Cagayan River
Balo-i
Kolambugan
Pantalan
Panter
Marawi
Bubong
BUKIDNON
Munai
Salvador
Marantao
Balindong
LANAO DEL NORTE
Molundo
LANAO LAKE
Lumba Bayaboa
Tugaya
Tamparan
Madalum
Madamba
Ganasi
Poona Bayabao
Pangantocan
Pulalas
Nunungan
Lumbatan
LANAO DEL SUR
Maramag
Bayang
Butig
Tubaran
Malabang
Balabagan
Wao
Buldon
Bariral
Bugasan
Baninsilan
Parang
NORTH COTABATO
MAGUINDANAO

Cagayan de Oro & Camiguin

Katibawasan Falls, Camiguin Island

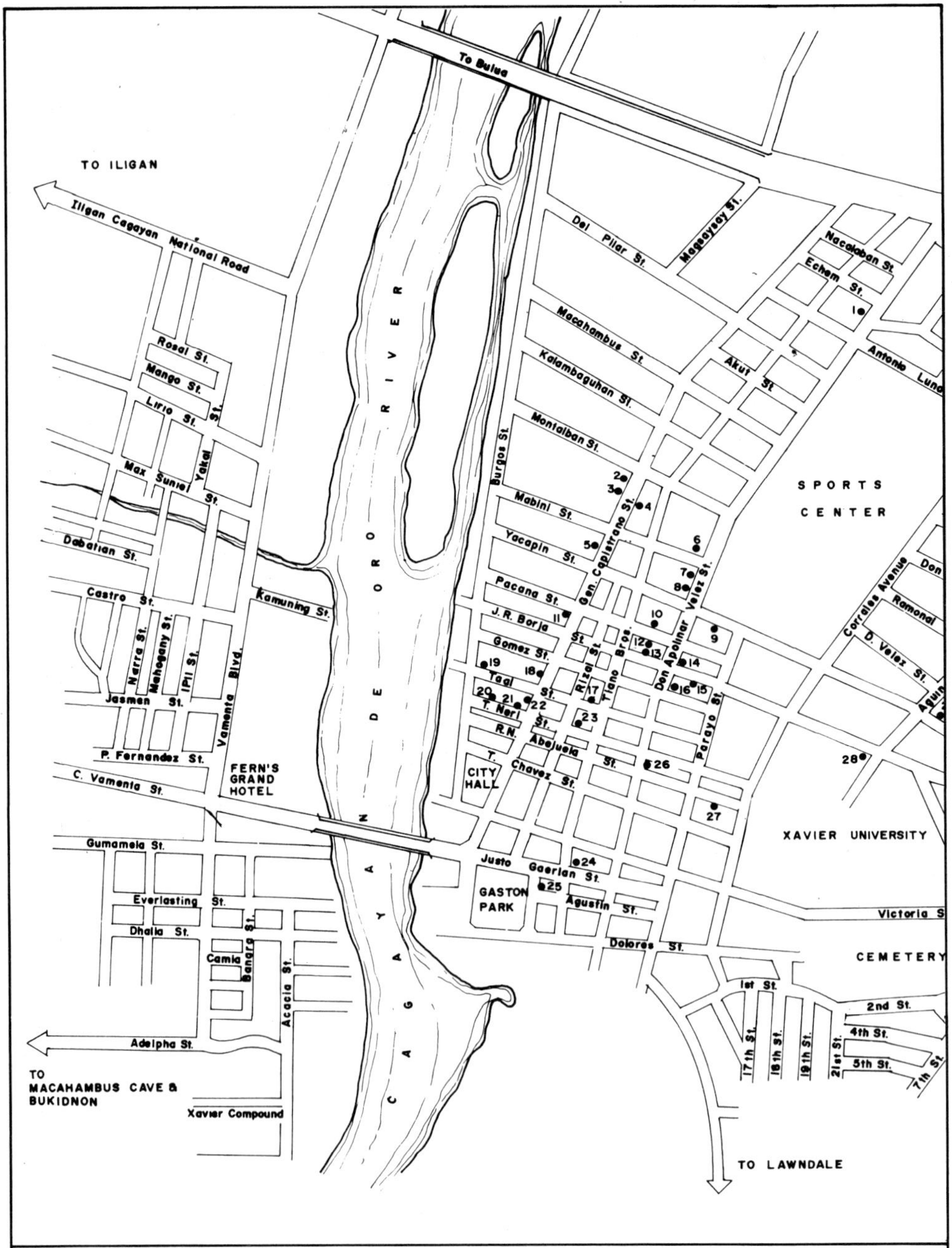

Miscellaneous
10 Brass shop
20 PAL
26 Tourist Information
30 Oro Bohol Trading

Accommodations
6 Mabini Lodge
7 Tropicana Hotel
11 Palace I & II
13 Golden Star
14 VIP Hotel
15 Sampaguita
16 Oro United
17 Satellite II
18 Perlas Inn
19 Satellite I
21 First Parkview
28 Casa Filipina
29 Fem's
32 Golden Star
33 De Luxe

CAGAYAN DE ORO CITY

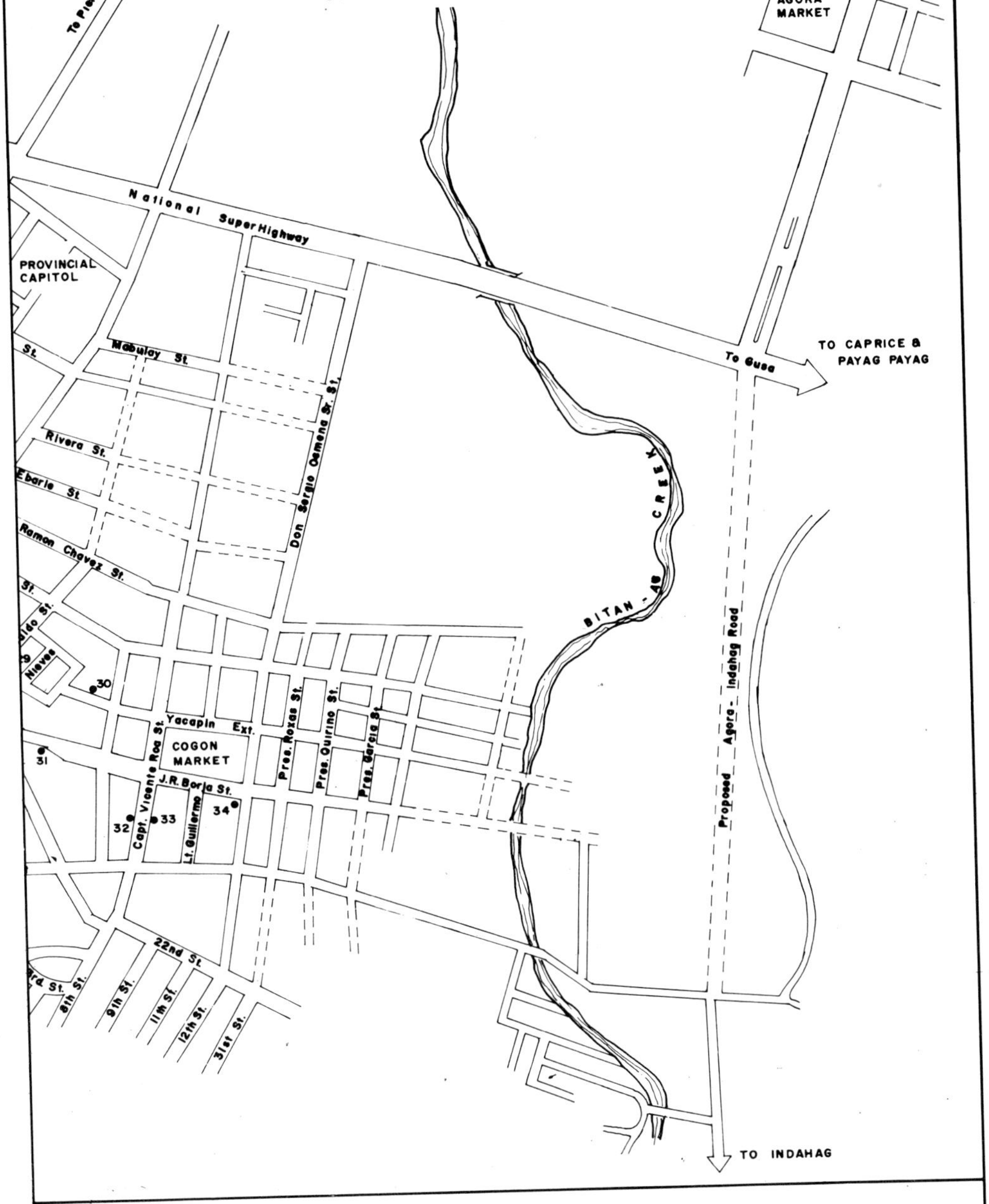

Food
1 Caprice Steak House
2 Sunburst Fried Chicken
3 Amadeus
4 Double E
5 Bungalow
8 fast food (evenings only)
9 Shakeys
12 De Oro Plaza
19 Maya's Fruit Garden
22 Thrive's
23 Fruit stands
24 Consuelo
25 Garden
27 Plaza Divisoria
31 Oro Rama
34 Barrio Gaisano

North Central Mindanao

access: to Cagayan de Oro - 1½ hr by air from Manila, 40 min from Cebu, Camiguin - 3 hrs by land and ferry from Cagayan; Iligan - 40 min by air from Cebu, 1 hr by land from Cagayan, p 267

to do: caves, hiking, beaches, museum
facilities: hotels & lodges in Cagayan de Oro and Iligan; simple resorts in Camiguin, p 294-5
climate: best Nov-April

Cagayan de Oro serves as a jump-off point for excursions in and about north central Mindanao, especially to Camiguin Island, Bukidnon and Marawi City.

Cagayan de Oro City covers a large and varied-landscape. The downtown area bustles with shoppers and traffic, the harbor is filled with shipping activity, and a few industries hug the coastline, but much of the city consists of grassed flatlands and forested canyons. Del Monte has a vast plantation in the uplands, just into Bukidnon. Macahambus Cave and Gorge, Huluga Cave and Catanico Falls are all remote, yet within city limits.

Most of Mindanao is historically restive, and one cannot be sure from afar which areas are quiescent and which are not at any particular time. Check with the Regional Tourism Office in the Marcos Sports Center before venturing into Bukidnon, Lanao or points beyond, and with the City Tourism Office in the basement of the building behind City Hall before visiting the more rural city areas.

If you wish to visit the Bukidnon or Manobo tribespeople, make advance arrangements with the Regional DOT Office.

Camiguin Island seems to be the one traditionally peaceful spot in the area.

Giant tropical foliage in Macahambus Gorge

Cagayan de Oro

Cagayan de Oro, like most of Mindanao, has experienced several waves of immigration. **Huluga Cave**, on the east bank of the Cagayan de Oro River 8 km south of the city, yielded evidence of the oldest known settlers in this area, dating back 2500 years. The cave residents were probably forebears of the Manobo and Bukidnon tribespeople.

You may visit the cave and nearby dig site which gave evidence of settlement between 400 BC and AD 200, but there is not much to see as it has been completely excavated. To get there, take a PU to the Roa Logging Camp, exit the other side, take a *banca* across the river, then clamber up the face of the cliff, using some tree roots as a ladder.

Some of the finds from the cave are exhibited at **Xavier University's Museo de Oro**, an important stop for visitors who are interested in the city's past. The museum displays include exhibits of prehistoric archaeological finds, Spanish-era historical relics, and artifacts of and ethnological information about current Mindanao tribes, mainly the local Bukidnon and Manobo, but also the Maranao, T'Boli and Mandaya.

Xavier University has good archives pertinent to the above fields. For more in-depth information than the museum displays, contact Fr Demetrio, Museum Curator.

The **Bukidnon** (people of the forest) inhabit the eastern Lanao area, number about 50,000 and are known to be fierce and independent. The **Manobo**, who inhabit part of the highlands of Bukidnon and Agusan, have a rich artistic tradition and are respected for their prowess as warriors. They live in village settlements on reservations.

Both these tribes frequently find it necessary to actively resist efforts to take over their lands. Hence, it is necessary to contact the DOT Regional Office in advance of planned visits, and let them prepare your trip, transportation and guides. You could also go to Malaybalay, Bukidnon, and stay overnight, taking the chance that you could proceed to the Manobo settlement 10 km away, again after checking on the situation with the local PC Command. If things are calm, get a local guide, not a military one.

Cagayan River, cradle of civilization in northern Mindanao, taken from Macahambus Cave

The Bukidnon and Manobo were pushed inland from the Cagayan de Oro River valley by the Muslims, who arrived in the 16th century. The Muslims fiercely resisted the 18th century Spanish coming, but were, in turn, pushed inland by the influx of Christian immigrants from the Visayas and Luzon. The Christians successfully, although temporarily, defeated superior American forces in battle at Macahambus Cave in 1901.

Macahambus Cave is 14 km southeast of the city, about 30 min by road. You may hire a PU car or take a Talacag jeepney from Carmen market and tell the driver you want to get off at Macahambus. The jeepneys leave at 1-2 hour intervals. Bring a powerful flashlight.

The cave is of esthetic rather than archaeological interest. A short walk through it brings you to a spectacular view of the Cagayan River hundreds of feet below Walk carefully; the floor is slippery.

Continue uphill on the road past the cave, and turn right on a flagstone path. Walk through the houses to the gorge. Descend steep iron steps, 50 m down to a river which flows through the gorge and gurgles out through a cave. Eons ago the underground river's roof collapsed, creating this massive hole now filled with lush vegetation. One tall tree pokes its way through the top of the gorge.

Although the Americans were originally repulsed here, they quickly established themselves and realized the value of the land. Today the vast **Del Monte Plantation**, with its American-style agriculture and buildings, rests just over the border in Bukidnon. The cannery is at Bugo, 7 km east of the city. You may visit the cannery and venture up to the plantation to see vast fruit fields, play 18 holes of golf, eat a good lunch, and shop at the club house souvenir shop.

To get there, hire a PU car or take a Bachelor, Ceres or Express Royale bus to Camp Phillips, and try to find transport from there to the club.

En route to Del Monte you may take a side trip to **Catanico Falls**. Water cascades over boulders into a pool where you may swim. The falls are 20 min from the city by road, then a 45 min walk. Inquire about the area's security before proceeding.

The last major fork in the road before Camp Phillips leads through Bukidnon. You may continue to **Malaybalay**, the pretty capital, and stay overnight at La Montana, Traveller's Home or Circle Lodge. Sometimes Manobo people come into town in the mornings to sell honey they have collected from the forests.

Other things to do in Cagayan de Oro city proper include visiting **Cogon Market**, which has several handicraft and brass shops. Watch your things here, and on jeepneys. There is also a brass shop on Pacana St near the VIP Hotel. Stroll around **Gaston Park**, which fronts San Agustin Cathedral. Or, if you are interested in **shells**, call Mrs Delicia Sontillana, tel 2411, and make arrangements to see her collection at 26 Fernandez St, Carmen District.

Camiguin Island

Small, pretty Camiguin Island, with friendly, peaceful people, lies off the eastern entrance to Macajar Bay. Its current inhabitants are almost wholly of Visayan and Chinese origin. Their way of life revolves around the land, its coconuts and fishing.

To get to **Camiguin**, hire a car or PU vehicle or take a Bachellor, Fortune or Ceres Liner bus from Cagayan de Oro to Balingoan, about a 1½ hr trip, then a 1 hr ferry ride to Benoni. The ferry is scheduled at 6:30, 7:30, 9:00 am and again in the afternoon, but often doesn't run on schedule. Arrive early and be prepared to wait. In calm weather you can rent a *banca* to take you from Balingoan to Benoni. Ferry passage is about ₱10.75, *banca* hire ₱200. Jeeps frequently ply the Benoni- Mambajao route (₱6).

Accommodations in Camiguin are simple and refreshingly clean. The beach resorts are quieter and more relaxing than in-town lodges.

Camiguin is a volcanic island. In 1871 Camiguin's old capital, Bonbon, was submerged in an eruption. In 1951 Mt Hibok-hibok erupted, asphyxiating 2000 inhabitants. The volcano has been quiescent since then. Volcanic activity is monitored by a Comvol (Commission of Volcanology) station on a mound between Mts Hibok-hibok and Timpo-ong.

Camiguin's shores consist mainly of pebble and dark sand beaches between rocks and lava flow areas. Those who need white sand can go to White Island, a sand bar (no shade) off Kuguita, Mambajao, or Magsaysay (Mantigue) Island off Mating, Mahinog.

Mambajao, Camiguin's post-card pretty capitol has several gracious old buildings with an impressive volcano as back-drop.

For assistance and information see Chit Silva at Mambajao City Hall, the Governor's

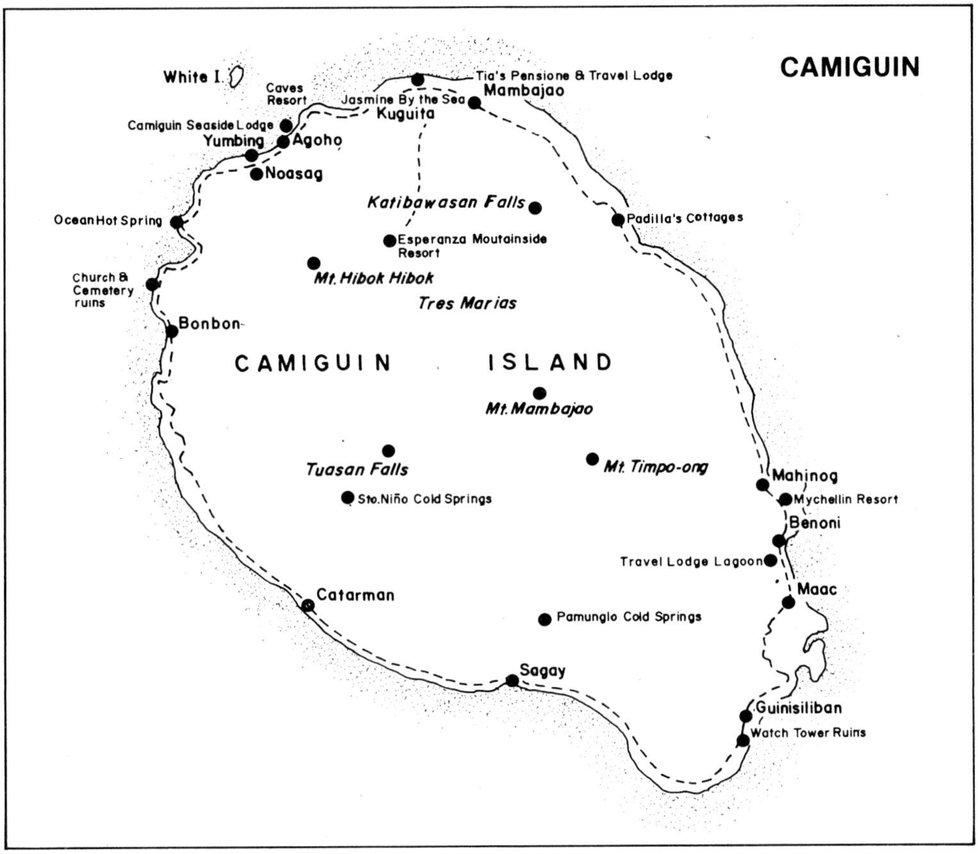

office in the capitol building, Lt Gomez in the DOT Office in PNB, Mrs Tia of Tia's Lodging House, the NACIDA Center between Tia's and the church (all on the main road) or at Camiguin Travel Lodge (opposite the market).

Springs dot Camiguin, and rivers tumble down its volcanic slopes, producing two impressive falls and many lesser ones. The main activities are hiking to these natural phenomena and soaking up the peaceful, relaxed aura. Children everywhere call out, "Hi, friend!" to visitors, and then, if you respond, ask, "What's your name?" Even the police go around unarmed, a rarity in the Philippines.

Allow 2 days to climb **Mt Hibok-hibok**. A guide is essential. You should probably plan to stay overnight at the Comvol station or Ardent Hot Springs. The ascent takes about 6 hrs if you're in good shape.

Katibawasan Falls punctuate a very beautiful, powerful stream which plummets 40 m into a cool pool. The falls are about 4½ km from Mambajao, on the slopes of Mt Timpo-ong. Bring lunch and have a relaxing picnic.

Esperanza Mountain Resort, owned and operated by Mambajao town, has dammed a stream where the **Ardent Hot Springs** bubble up. You may sit and soak in 36 C mineral water. There are dorm rooms for overnight stays, and a German has leased the cafeteria to use as a disco.

At **Naasag** there are coastal hot springs where you may soak in hot fresh water at low tide and warm brackish water at medium tide. Find out when low tide is expected before heading for Naasag, or for **Bonbon**, where the sunken church and cemetery (casualties of the 1871 eruption) are only visible when the waters are low.

Further along, on Camiguin's western slopes, you may hike from Catarman to **Tuasan Falls**. Part of the trail hugs the mountainside. You may also visit the **Sto Niño** cold springs swimming pools and relax under the trees. **Pamunglo**, another cold spring, is located outside Sagay.

You will need to arrange transport to these places, as public transport is not frequently available on the western side of the island. Cost of a jeepney hire to circle the island is $18-20. It is sometimes possible to hire a motorcycle for the day. If you go around the island, stop in **Guinsiliban** to see the 300-year-old watchtower.

Because there is frequent transport from Mambajao to Benoni, sights on the eastern side are more accessible. You need a guide with local knowledge and a good flashlight to find the cave in **Magting** which was inhabited by earlier settlers.

Iligan & Marawi

There is not much to do in Iligan except visit the few Maranao shops (prices higher than Marawi) and **Maria Cristina Falls**, which is interesting but not as full as it was prior to the installation of the hydroelectric project.

Marawi City, capital of Lanao del Norte, is frequently a hot spot. To visit, take public transport from 9-12 am and 2-5 pm only (unless things really cool down). Stay at the Marawi Resort Hotel (if you are on a very stringent budget, you may be out of luck). Be very careful about your goings and comings. Foreign men would do well not to sit down next to local women on the buses. Ask permission before taking photographs of people.

Marawi's **Mindanao State University's** (MSU) Aga Khan Museum has good exhibits of cultural items from Maranao and other Mindanao Muslim tribes. Brass shops line Marawi's wide central road and you may also buy things at Dansalan College's art shop. The market is fascinating. There is an excellent view of picturesque **Lake Lanao** from the site of the old city hall. Don't swim in the lake, or you risk a nasty schistosomiasis (liver fluke) infection.

Sustenance

Cagayan de Oro is littered with little restaurants. Fruit stands on the corners of Gomez & Capistrano or Neri & Taal can provide between-meal nourishment. Tasty little white *puto* (rice cake) is available in the vegetable section of Cogon Market in the mornings until about 11 o'clock.

Relatively expensive restaurants ($3-5/meal) are: Amadeus and Caprice Steak Houses for meat and other dishes; VIP for a variety of tasty meals; and Caprice by the Sea for seafoods. De Oro Plaza serves the best Chinese food in town, and of course Shakey's has pizza, but only after 2 pm.

Moderately priced places include Barrio Gaisano with Filipino and Chinese foods; Bungalow and Consuelo both serve native foods; Payag in Gusa does native seafoods and has huts for trysting; Garden Cafe and Divisoria Plaza serve Chinese food (Divisoria has musical entertainment); and Sunburst Fried Chicken. Oro Rama has inexpensive fast foods.

The Village Den is a good place, a bit out of town, near some putting greens. If you intend to visit the Village Den, Caprice by the Sea and Payag you should arrange in advance transport back to your hotel.

Given advance notice, all resorts on **Camiguin** provide meals, and it is best to have their specialities. You can buy barbequed fish in the Mambajao market for ₱6, and Mrs Tia's tasty food costs $1.25/meal.

Camiguin Traveler's Lodge is a good place to stop for a drink.

Electricity in Camiguin is usually available from 4:30 pm - 11 pm, so drinks may not be cold.

Davao

Tribal designs on modern pottery, Princess Ceramics, Davao

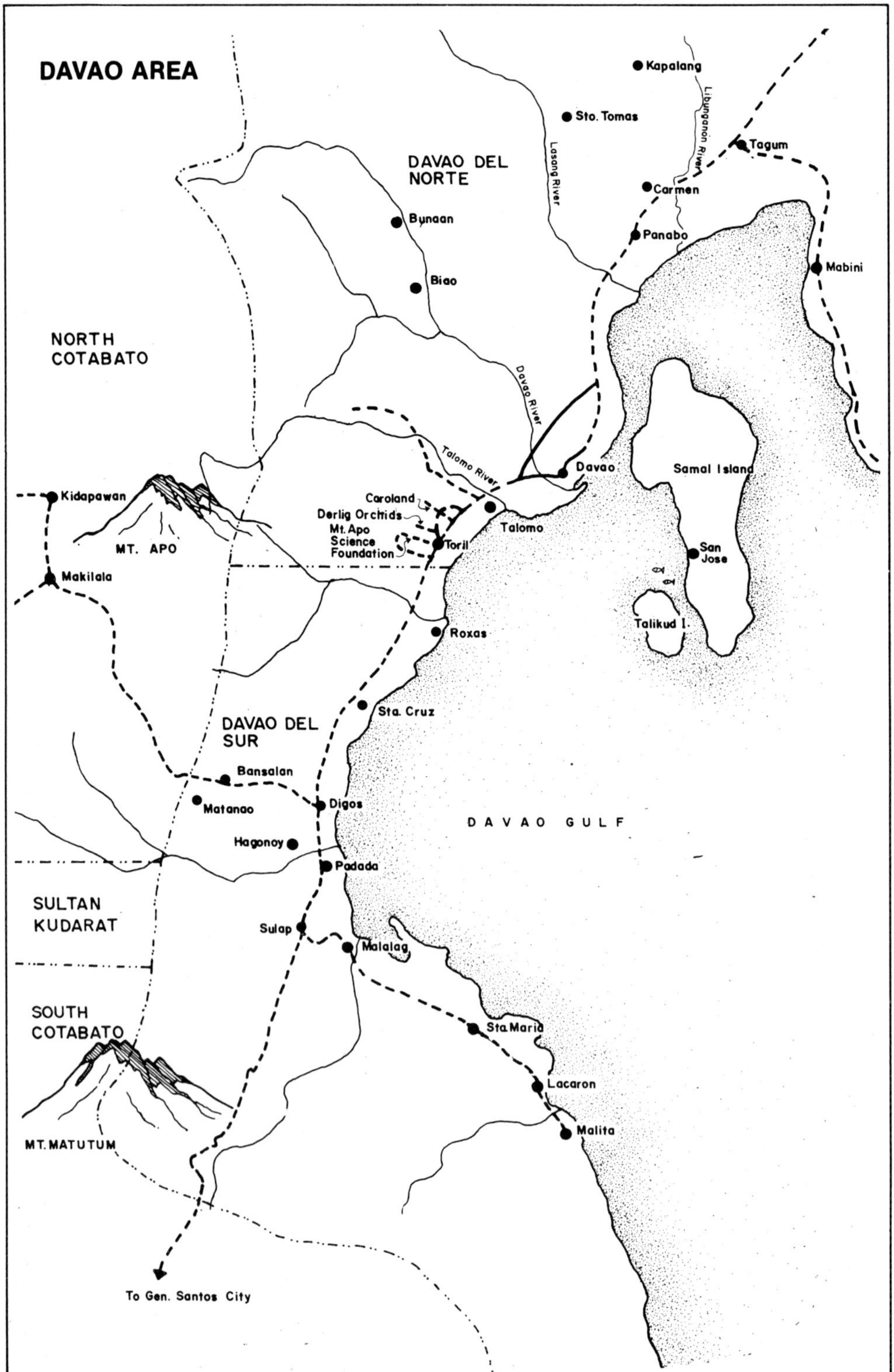
DAVAO AREA
DAVAO DEL NORTE
Kapalang
Sto. Tomas
Libunganon River
Lasang River
Tagum
Carmen
Bunaan
Panabo
Mabini
Biao
NORTH COTABATO
Davao River
Talomo River
Davao
Samal Island
Kidapawan
MT. APO
Caroland
Derlig Orchids
Mt. Apo Science Foundation
Toril
Talomo
San Jose
Makilala
Talikud I.
Roxas
Sta. Cruz
DAVAO DEL SUR
Bansalan
Matanao
Digos
DAVAO GULF
Hagonoy
Padada
SULTAN KUDARAT
Sulap
Malalag
SOUTH COTABATO
Sta. Maria
Lacaron
Malita
MT. MATUTUM
To Gen. Santos City

Davao

access: 1½ hrs by air from Manila, p 267

climate: good year round

to do: swim, golf, shop, island hop, dive, mountain climb

facilities: top resort, hotels, lodges, p 296

Davao comprises three provinces and one of the world's largest cities in land area. Davao's earliest inhabitants were the tribal ancestors of today's Bagobo (Davao City), Manobo, B'Laan and Tagacaoili/T'Boli (all from Davao del Sur), and Mandaya (Davao Oriental) tribespeople. Sama people occupied the offshore islands, Aetas lived in the valleys, coasts and hills. The coast dwellers were displaced inland when the more aggressive Maguindanaos arrived from Cotabato, Zamboanga and Jolo. The Spanish first visited early in the 16th century, but did not obtain the area until the mid 19th century.

Davao's resistance ended with the slaying of the leader Datu Bago. Christian settlers came from the Visayas and Luzon, displacing some earlier residents.

Davao City is the prettiest southern metropolis. Attractions range from islands in the bay to markets, museums, religious shrines, orchid and fruit plantations, golf and mountain climbing. There is a good range of hotels and lodges.

During the monsoon, rains occur mostly at night. There are no typhoons. Davao is an amenable place to visit year-round.

City Center

Because Davao City's land area is extensive, attractions are well spread out. Jeepneys ply main routes. Taxis are available, but not abundant, and hire cars may be found in front of the Apo View and Insular hotels. Fare from Insular to City Center is ₱1.50 by jeepney, $1.25-1.50 by taxi and $2 by hire car. Several tour companies offer city and countryside tours. We found Amity Tours knowledgeable and reliable.

The city is a comfortable place to stroll, enjoy the people, parks and handicrafts. Rizal and Osmeña Parks front City Hall and St Peter's Cathedral, a curious structure which attempts to combine Moorish design and Roman Catholicism, a gesture of reconciliation in an area where Christians and Muslims are often at odds.

Stroll along San Pedro and nearby streets, then up C M Recto to **Aldevinco Shopping Center**, to get a feel for the city and its people. Aldevinco is a shopper's paradise: antiques, excavated pottery and porcelain, handicrafts, artifacts from Mindanao's varied tribes, a profusion of Indonesian batik, traditional Muslim brass items such as betel nut boxes, tribal weavings, T'Boli bronze figurines, bags made from *banig* (woven pandan leaves), clothing, costume jewelry, etc. Bargain well, lop as much as 50% off the Muslim brass, 25% from some other items. Lakambini Crafts, across the street, has more handicrafts.

A visual and gastronomic feast of fruits is available 2 blocks away at the **Madrazo fruit center.** Here's your opportunity to taste a plethora of exotic fruits very cheaply when in season, including the tasty but odiferous durian (NOT allowed in your hotel, nor on the plane!), the delicious and not so smelly *marang*, mangosteen, rambutan, *lanzones*, avocado, *chico*, banana, pineapple, mango, oranges, pomelo, santol, guava, and so much more. A meal or two a day from purchases at Madrazo treats the palate and

Muslim Fishing Village near Santa Ana Wharf, Davao

the pocketbook.

Stroll or take a jeepney to **Sta Ana Wharf**, fronting spacious, green **Magsaysay Park**. Then wander south to a wooden foot bridge which crosses the river to the **Muslim Village**. The ₱0.25 toll supports bridge maintenance. There are picturesque views into the dense shanty area, with a couple of mosque spires poking above the huts.

A few steps further south along the road brings you to several simple restaurants serving *kinilaw* (sashimi made from Tuna), barbequed *bariles pangga at buntot* (tuna jaw and tail) and *pusit* (squid). Luz Kinilaw is the most popular.

Davao's large Chinese community's places of worship are along Cabaguio Ave. The 5-yr-old **Taoist Temple** houses saints representing many religions. Ask Mrs Alvarez, the priestess, if you wish to have your fortune told. **Lon Wa Buddhist Temple** is further along. One per cent of Davao's population is Buddhist. The structure appears to have been transplanted from China. Inside, a large golden buddha sits atop a slab of Italian marble.

Outskirts of the City

More handicrafts are available in places slightly further from the central district. At **Princess Ceramics** you may watch artists as they hand paint intricate replicas of Mandaya, Bagobo, T'Boli and Maranaw designs on pottery. Each piece is signed. **Nieva's Lumad** are doing similar designs on wood for jewelry, desk sets, boxes, etc.

Davao Insular Intercontinental Inn and surrounds is a destination in itself. Relaxing gardens spread over 4 of its 8 hectares, where shrubs are sculptured into animal forms: a *carabao* with its yoke, horse and *calesa*, squirrel, birds, and a fisherman with his *banca*. Twice a day men climb the coconut trees to remove the *tuba* (sap which is fermented into alcohol). Great pool, big enough to really swim in, wind surfing, tennis, several restaurants.

Boats depart from the Insular's wharf for the white beaches of Samal and Talicud Islands.

Just over a bridge behind the Insular is a tiny Mandaya settlement called **Dabaw**

Coconut wood boxes with tribal designs, Aldevinco Market

DAVAO CITY AREA

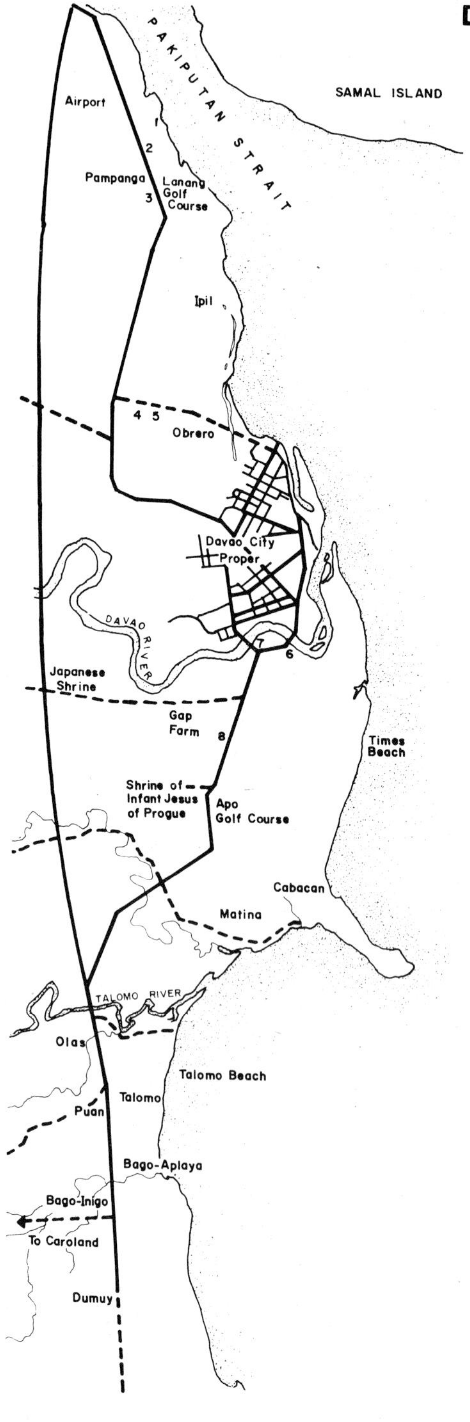

Points of Interest & Misc
2 Dabaw Museum
3 Nieva's Lumad
4 Buddhist Temple
5 Taoist Temple
6 Bus Station
9 Agdao Public Market
10 Magsaysay Park
11 Barbeque *bariles* and *kinilaw*
13 Princess Ceramics
15 Madrazo Fruit Center
16 Aldevinco Shopping Center
20 PAL
22 St Peter's Cathedral
23 City Hall
24 Amity Fruit Center
25 DOT
26 Amity Tours
32 Bus Station

Accomodations
1 Davao Insular Hotel
7 Tourist Lodge
8 Venee's
12 BS Inn
18 Davao Famous Inn
21 Maguindanao Hotel
25 Apo View Hotel
29 El Mimar
30 Men Seng
31 Pension Felisa

Restaurants
11 Barbeque *bariles* and *kinilaw*
14 Harana II & Sarungbanggi II
17 Davao Famous
18 Shanghai Restaurant
18 Cusina Davao
19 China Royale Restaurant
27 Sarungbanggi I
28 Dencia's

DAVAO CITY PROPER

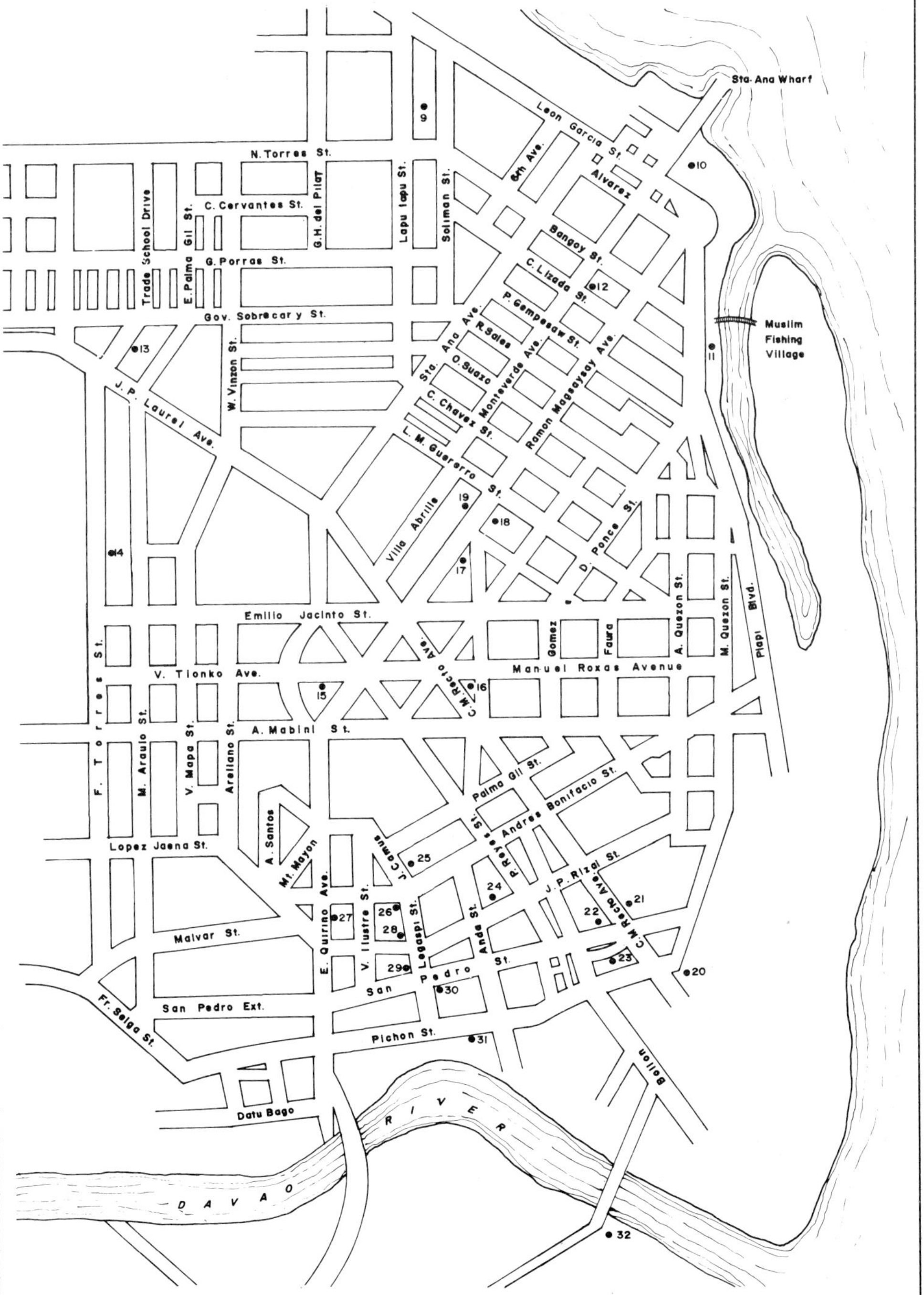

Samal Island

Etnica. One house nestles amid neatly kept grounds. Mandaya residents occupy one small room. The rest of the house is a porch-like display area. Women sit preparing the abaca fiber, tying, dyeing and weaving it into the colorful *dagmay* fabric which they use for clothing, blankets and many other purposes. Young girls embroider intricate designs on pieces of cloth which will be sewn into blouses. Bags, bracelets, household gods, abaca cloth, and items with the Mandaya and other designs painted on them are available.

Dabaw Etnica is a going concern which helps the Mandaya adjust to their greatly reduced tribal lands by providing alternative income.

Dabaw Museum, a project of a local women's club, is a short walk from the Insular. Exit the gate to the village, take your first left on Agusan Circle, and follow the road around a 90° arc to the museum. Displays inside include photos, tribal artifacts and costumes. Everything is well labeled. A few high- priced handicrafts are available. The museum is open from 9-5 daily except Mondays and holidays.

The islands fronting Davao have pretty white sand beaches. **Samal Island**, the larger of the two, has a couple of resorts. Water is sometimes a problem and electricity is newly installed.

Paradise Resort has a nice white sand beach lined with shady Talisay trees, with grass and coconuts behind them. There are beach chairs, bar, and protective flotation around the swimming area. You may rent *bancas* to paddle, mahjong sets and cards.

Nearby Coral Reef Beach Resort also has a nice beach, three rustic cottages with common bath and a house to rent. Barbeque lunches are available weekends, may be ordered a day ahead of time on other days.

Tickets to Coral Reef and Paradise are available at Insular, $1.25 for the day, including transport and entry fee. You may also board the boat from their wharf for ₱8 one way. The fee helps to pay for upkeep and maintenance of the wharf.

It is less expensive, but (at low tide) muddier, to wade onto the *bancas* on the neighboring beach. Transport is ₱15 one way for up to 6 passengers, ₱2.50 each additional person.

Talicud Island is about 50 min further by *banca*. It has beautiful, secluded beaches, but no facilities. Bring everything, including snorkel and a good pair of binoculars if you are a bird watcher.

Shell vendors will approach with corals, shells and dead turtles. Let them know you do not support the imminent extinction of the sea turtle nor reef destruction.

South

Several points of interest line the route south to Mt Apo and beyond, and several dark sand beaches, some with overnight facilities.

Times Beach, 2 km from the city center, is crammed with picnic sheds and barbeque stands. The water is murky with silt from the nearby mouth of the Davao River.

Gap Farming Resort is a little further along in Green Valley, Ma-a. The resort has orchards full of fruit trees and orchids, a pool, a cave which the Japanese used during WW II, and cottages amidst pastoral surroundings.

The **Shrine of the Infant Jesus of Prague**, an open air chapel with a replica of the Prague icon and of Our Lady of Fatima, is on a nearby promontory. Religious folk come to pray. Travelers come to enjoy the view of Davao City, the bay and its islands, and the farmlands and mountains behind. A nearby **Japanese Shrine** commemorates war dead.

Greenhills Orchid Farms has thousands of orchids growing and blossoming in terraces.

Back along the coast, the next point of interest is **Talomo Beach**, a landing site for invading Japanese in 1942, then Americans in 1944. Hulks of several sunken vessels still lie beneath the waters. Salakot Resort maintains a clean area with picnic tables for daytime use. For information see Miss Rosy Dayao, Insular's sales manager.

Apo Golf and Country Club has very well kept 18 holes to play. Visitors are welcome. Arrangements can be made through the DOT or your hotel.

Caroland Resort at Bago Iñigo Farms has picnicking, pony rides, a pond stocked with big carp which come up for bits of bread, fishing, and a flock of wild ducks which have taken up residence. Fruit trees and orchids provide shade and added interest.

Villa Victoria Beach Resort provides overnight seaside facilities. There are clusters of beach cottages, an extensive children's playground, pretty grounds, a large Chinese restaurant, waterfront area for swimming, backed by grassy areas shaded by coconut trees.

Nearby **Derling Orchid Farm** is a great

stop for orchid fanciers: hundreds of rows of many different species of orchids, some for sale.

Several resorts along **Talisay Beach** have rustic overnight facilities. Kalayaan Resort keeps its beachfront clean. The beaches are shaded by large Talisay trees. **Gueno-o** and other beaches line the shore as you continue south.

Mount Apo

Apo, the Philippines highest mountain (2909 m), is an enjoyable climb year round. Apo is a dormant volcano with no recorded eruptions. The forests which once hugged its slopes are being cut down, the land converted to farms, and the habitat of the Philippine eagle is fast disappearing. Nevertheless it is still a mountain well worth visiting.

Mt Apo Science Foundation, Eden, Bayabas, Toril, at the base of Apo offers great views and a cool spot (62°-70°F). The foundation is supported by endowments from Asia Foundation and the University of Mindanao to do research on agriculture and woodlands.

If you wish to visit the **Eagle Breeding Station** in **Baracatan**, you may either hire a vehicle ($20-22.50 round trip) or take a Toril-Baracatan jeepney (₱12-14 one way). There are 3 trips daily. The last one returns to the city at 3 pm. The final 16 km of road is rough. Bring all food and provisions.

At the Station you can see captive eagles which the crew hopes will breed and perhaps prevent extinction of the species. You can hike on the mountain from here.

Early April and May are the best time for climbing Apo, as cloud cover is minimal. Allow 4 days for the climb. Arrange for guides and provisions ahead, or find a guide in Kidapawen, North Cotabato. Kidapawen is 110 km from Davao City. Buses depart the Ma-a station early in the morning for the trip.

At Kidapawen you must go to the Municipal Building to register before proceeding by jeepney to *barangay* Ilomavis. From here it is a 3-hr hike through farms to the first camp at Lake Agco, at 1200 m. Lake Agco is fed by several springs of varied temperatures and there is a cabin by the shores where climbers may spend the night.

The second day is spent climbing from Agko to the Marbel River for a lunch stop and on to Lake Venado (or Maluno). You cross the Marbel River many times along the way, pass hot springs and a couple of waterfall. Camp for the night on the shores of Venado, a small shallow lake at 2400 m.

A 3-hr hike to the summit remains, through rocks, moss and dwarf trees to the rim. You may peer into the sulphurous crater, and out across the land. Enjoy vast panoramas from the top, then return to Lake Venado, or to the hot springs to soak an achy body. On the last day, finish the ascent and return to Davao.

Several other routes are feasible for the more experienced climber. Inquire at Amity Tours or ask Frank at DOT.

Sustenance

There are several good places to eat in Davao.

Harana I and II are known for good **Filipino food** and steaks, native setting, lawns and play area for children, at night bring repellent. Sarungbangi, fronting Harana II, serves the same sort of food in an airconditioned area, is highly recommended. Barrio Palayok, MacArthur Highway, does good native food, and *lechon* is available at Estrella Lechon, also on MacArthur.

Because Davao has a large Chinese population, it has several good **Chinese restaurants**. Luk Tian has good food but closes at 6 pm. Davao Famous, Shanghai and China Royale are all on Magsaysay. Kusina Davao and Dencia's also serve Chinese food - you can get a whole meal at

Dencia's for about ₱22.

For a real treat in native setting, try the restaurants near the Muslim village south of Sta Ana Wharf. Luz Kinilaw is especially well known. Choose your food, limited to *kinilaw* (tuna sashimi), barbequed *bariles pangga at buntot*, (tuna jaw and tail), and barbequed *pusit* (squid). Wash it down with beer or soft drinks. And arrive early if you want to sit by the window overlooking the river and Muslim village beyond. Truly delicious.

Mikado in Apo View serves Japanese food.

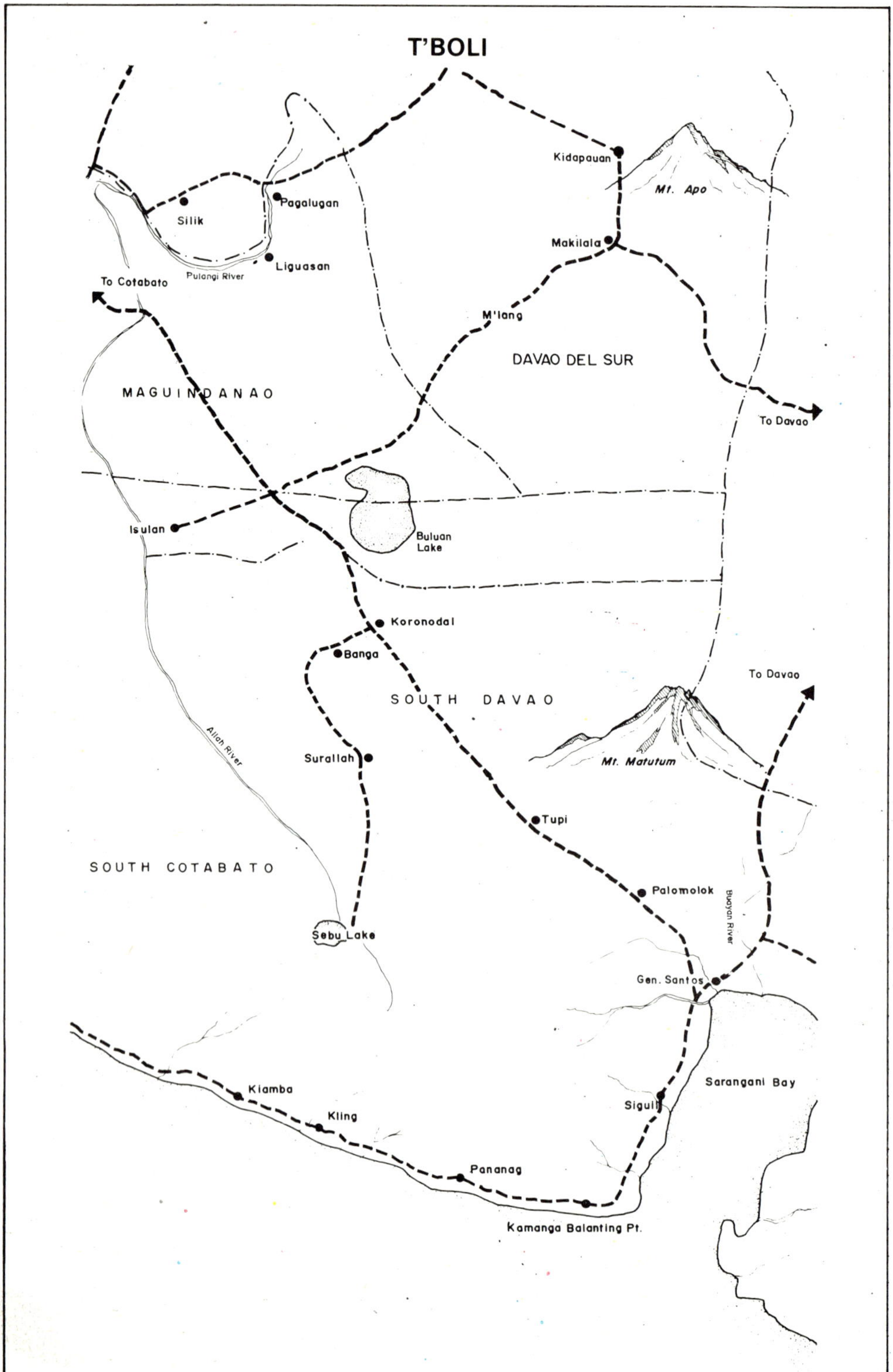
T'BOLI
Kidapauan
Mt. Apo
Pagalugan
Silik
Makilala
Liguasan
Pulangi River
To Cotabato
M'lang
DAVAO DEL SUR
MAGUINDANAO
To Davao
Isulan
Buluan Lake
Koronodal
Banga
SOUTH DAVAO
To Davao
Mt. Matutum
Surallah
Allah River
Tupi
SOUTH COTABATO
Palomolok
Buayan River
Sebu Lake
Gen. Santos
Sarangani Bay
Kiamba
Siguil
Kling
Pananag
Kamanga Balanting Pt.

T'Boli dancer

T'Boli

access: by air into General Santos, Allah Valley or Cotabato City, then land to Lake Sebu, p 267
climate: relatively good all year

to do: visit tribe; hike

facilities: bed space at Sta Cruz mission by prearrangement, or at Antenor's, p 296

Mindanao, the Philippines' second largest island, is host to numerous tribal groups whose cultures antedate the 14th century Arab coming and who, until recently, lived in symbiosis with the forests they inhabited.

The T'Boli are one of those many tribes. Reclusive and gentle, they have maintained and evolved an artistically rich cultural tradition dating back more than two millennia. They weave the beautiful T'Nalak cloth, forge utile and attractive brass-bronze ware and compose hauntingly serene music which blends with their surroundings.

Most people are introduced to the T'Boli through their vibrant T'Nalak, cloth made from abaca fiber which is tie-dyed black and rust using natural plant coloring, then laboriously woven on back-strap looms into one of the loveliest natural cloths available anywhere. It is strikingly attractive, and one cannot help but be curious about its creators.

The T'Boli are also bronze smiths. Through the lost wax process, which makes each piece uniquely individual, they forge bells for their costumes, chain links for jewelry and for their horses, bits for their horses' bridles, and attractive sculptures of their lifestyle

The T'Boli are wonderful musicians, with a wide array of instruments made from the natural products of their world: bamboo tubes, wooden guitar-like instruments, mouth harps, bronze gongs, drums, etc. They are balladeers, singing of their lives and legends, and dance is an important part of their festivities.

Yet, for all their artistic genius, the T'Boli have remained economically naive, losing precious ancestral lands to creditors, politicians and an assortment of sharp operators. All lands abutting **Lake Sebu** are owned by lowland migrants.

Today, and for the past 24 years the **Santa Cruz Mission** has been operating in Lake Sebu. Their purpose is to help the T'Boli become economically self- sufficient once again, to maintain their traditions and to retain pride in their heritage, to educate them so they can farm their remaining land more intensively using crop rotation to maintain the soil's viability, and to deal with outside economic pressures, handle health problems and other programs which assist their livelihood.

While many T'Boli, through the influence of the missionaries, are nominally Christian, they continue, simultaneously, to worship the spirits which they believe to control almost every aspect of their daily lives. Affluent men have several wives. Ancient rituals are still practiced.

Only people with genuine interest in T'Boli culture will want to make the effort to visit them. The visit is best prearranged through the Sta Cruz Mission, (PO Box 7278, Marbel, South Cotabato - write or cable) which can advise on the safest route of access, and can provide transportation, board and lodging.

Spur-of-the moment and low budget travelers will have to go it alone, possibly using spartan accommodation available in Lake Sebu town, such as Antenor's.

The area is poor, most people survive at subsistence level. All food for visitors has to be brought in.

Lake Sebu's waters exit in a small river,

then thunder down seven falls to irrigate lowland crops. Siluton, the highest of the falls, is a delightful 3 km walk from the lake.

Saturday is market day in Lake Sebu town, an interesting time to be present as colorfully dressed T'Boli come in from the hills to barter their produce for supplies.

While in Marbel, on the way to or from Sebu, try the tasty, interesting shakes at the Breeze Restaurant.

GENERAL SANTOS CITY
(Dadiangas)

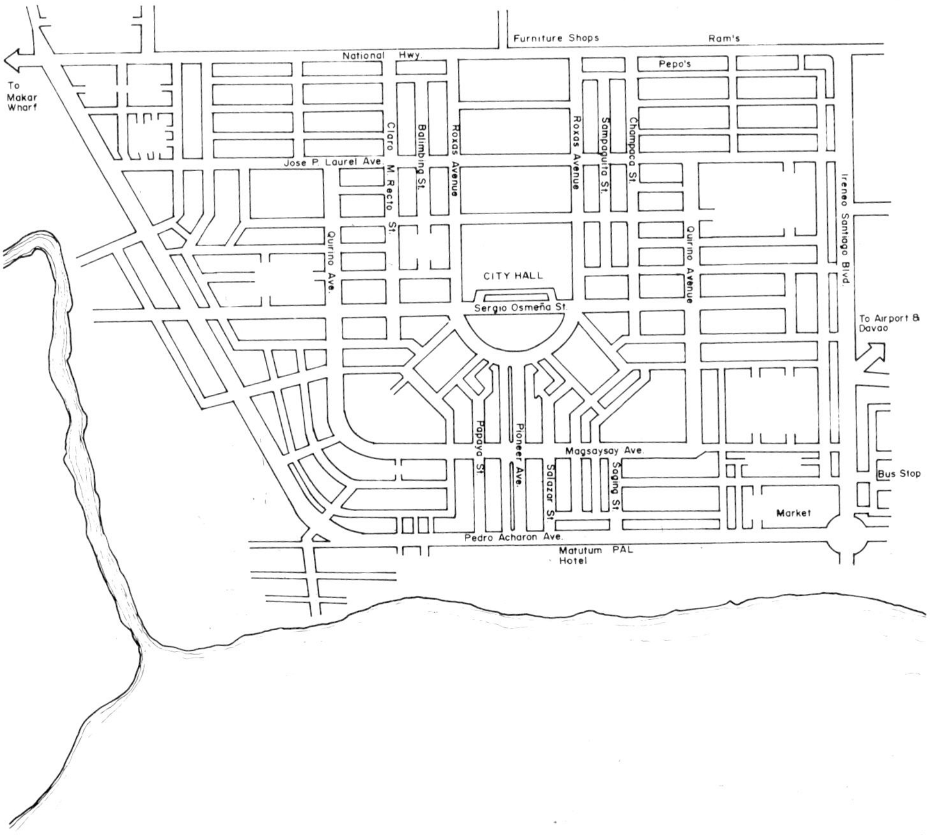

ZAMBOANGA AREA

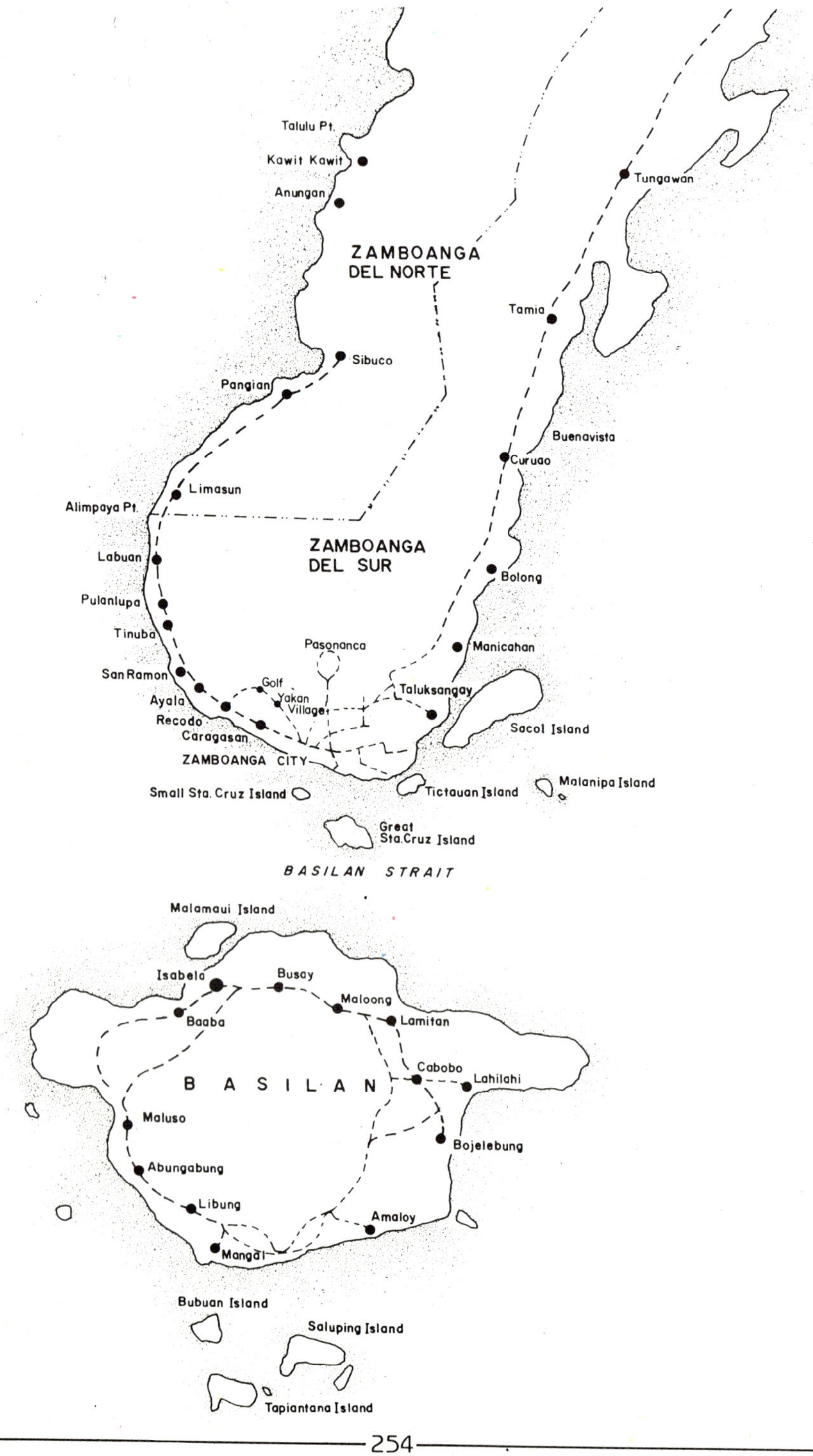

Zamboanga

Taluksangay

ZAMBOANGA CITY AREA

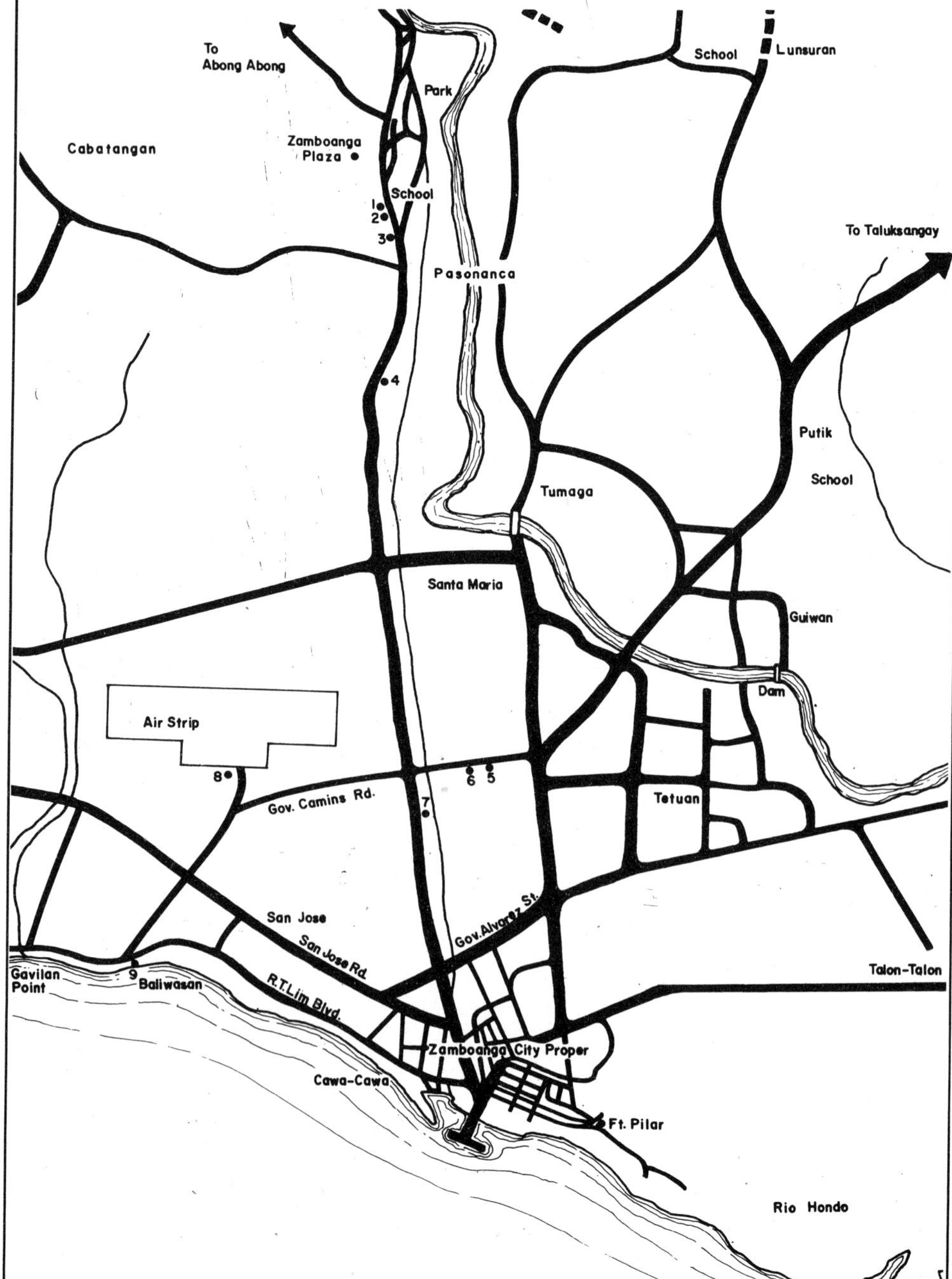

ZAMBOANGA CITY PROPER

Points of Interest & Misc
7 Century Gift Shop
13 Zamboanga Home Products
17 Plaza Pershing
19 Fort Pilar
20 Barter Trade Zone
21 PAL
21 DOT
22 Handicrafts shops
23 City Hall

Accommodations
10 Zamboanga Hermosa
12 Astoria Hotel
15 Paradise Lodge
16 Paradise Lodge
21 Lantaka
23 Unique

Restaurants
1 Antonio's
2 Aldea
3 Country Chicken & Mano Mano
4 Palmeria
5 Atin Atin
6 Bulakeña
8 J's Pad
9 Boulevard
11 Abalone Restaurant
14 Goldirose
15 Fast Foods
18 Swiss Bar
24 Casa de Oro
25 Alavar

Zamboanga

access: 1¾ hrs by air from Manila; boat to Davao, Cebu, Manila, p 267
climate: good year round, driest Nov-Apr
to do: beaches, Muslim & Yakan villages, golf, handicrafts
facilities: hotels, restaurants, p 297

Zamboanga is Mindanao's most popular tour destination for both Filipino and foreign travelers. It has a good assortment of acceptable accommodations and restaurants, a superb beach, excellent diving, a bazaar-like market, weavers, antique and curio shops, walking, a golf course, tennis courts, etc, all of which await your pleasure.

The travel brochures have conditioned people to expect to see *vintas* (boats) with brightly colored sails in the harbor and lots of flowers in the city. In fact the *vintas* use plain sails except on special occasions, and most of the flowers are tucked away in private homes. The expected veneer is not there, but much else is.

You can spend two delightful days in Zamboanga visiting the markets and shops, seeing the Yakan weavers and spending time on Sta Cruz Island's pink sand beach or diving. Longer, or more condensed, stays allow for excursions to Taluksangay, and, politics permitting, Basilan Island, Jolo or Tawi Tawi.

Tribal Groups

Five tribal groups may be found in and around Zamboanga: the Subanon, Sama, Tausug, Badjao and Yakan.

The **Subanon** were among the earliest settlers who occupied much of the

Badjao Burial Grounds, Samal Island

Yakan Village, Zamboanga

peninsula centuries ago and are now thinly spread through parts of Zamboanga provinces to Misamis Occidental. The name "subanon" means "upriver" or "upstream" in reference to the areas they inhabited. The Subanon live in small family farming units.

The **Sama** (commonly called Samal) inhabit the coastal regions of Jolo, Tawi Tawi and Zamboanga. They are a peaceful, sociable people who live in dense settlements of stilt houses over the water's edge or in houseboats, making their living fishing and diving for pearls and shells.

Tausug is the largest ethnic group of this area. They tend to be more aggressive and wealthier than the other minorities. They are farmers and fishermen.

The **Badjao**, or Tau-Laut, are sea nomads who live their whole lives on houseboats, coming to shore only to be buried.

The **Yakan**, who come from Basilan, are master weavers. They are farmers, and wear beautifully woven clothing. The Yakan inhabit the uplands of Basilan. A small settlement of Christianized Yakan live on the outskirts of Zamboanga City (see p 261)

Zamboanga City

The early Subanon settlers called the area Jambangan, meaning land of flowers. Later immigrants, the Badjao and Sama, called it Samboangan, meaning anchorage, and they still call it by that name. Chinese records mention trade with the Subanon, Sama, Tausug and Badjao as early as the 13th century.

Although the Spanish established an early mission at Recodo, they date their founding of the city from the arrival of Legazpi and Fray Urdaneta in 1635. The cornerstone of Ft Pilar was laid in the same year, and the name Zamboanga was first recorded on that cornerstone.

During the Spanish rule people came to Zamboanga from Luzon and the Visayas. Others came from Basilan and Sulo to escape political problems at home. The migrants developed a dialect unique to Zamboanga. Called Chavacano, it is a mixture of unconjugated Spanish and native words. Zamboanga was the seat of the Church for all of Mindanao, and Zamboanga remained Mindanao's capital during the American regime.

City Hall was built in 1907 and housed American military governors, including John (Blackjack) Pershing.

Today 80% of Zamboanga's population is Christian, the remaining 20% mostly Muslim. Although the city has a predominantly Christian character, the Muslim influence comes to the fore in the markets and some villages.

Getting around Zamboanga is easily done by tricycle and jeepney, but it is best to have your hotel recommend a tricycle driver or guide they know, especially in the evening. Negotiate the rate in advance, and arrange for the round trip as it is not always easy to find transportation back.

For trips outside the city you may ask your hotel to recommend a travel agent or use one of the guides with a car for hire outside the Lantaka (ask the hotel first about their reliability).

Markets and Shops

Pearl and gem vendors abound in the town and around the market, and most of the items offered are imitation. Real pearls aren't damaged by flame, so ask if you may test a pearl you like by holding a lighter or match to it. If the vendor declines, the pearl is plastic.

The most accessible shopping area is Valderroza St, between Lantaka and City Hall, where there is a row of shops selling ethnic artifacts. Other shops are scattered throughout the city. Please refer to the map.

Shops selling shells and shell products are located on the San Jose Road. You may visit Laygan, Rocan and San Luis. Rocan is closed during lunchtime.

The city has two interesting markets to poke about in. Some of the vendors come on a bit strong but can be readily managed with firm good humor. It is important to be very careful with your bag and wallet in and about these markets. Keep wallets in front pockets; hold handbags in front of and close to you.

The **City Market** has a large fish and vegetable area which is fascinating and presents great opportunities for the photographer. You can also buy mats here. As soon as you show interest you will be surrounded by women unfolding dozens of them, hoping you will buy them all. Some of the stalls in the flea market area sell brass wares, antiques, shells, Indonesian batik, *malong* (large pieces of decorative material sewn in a circle, in which the women wrap themselves), weavings from Basilan and Jolo, etc. Bargain well, it's part of the game.

The penchant for smuggling things through the Philippines' wide open southern door has never been successfully controlled by the government. The **Barter Trade Zone**, Zamboanga's second market, resulted from an attempt to limit and legitimize some of this trade. There are some good buys here, usually of interest to Philippine residents.

Zamboanga's waterfront is its most important economic district and also its most interesting area. The Badjao stay just outside the Lantaka hotel, selling mats and shells from their boats. Their initial prices tend to be very high. Some of the boat children will ask to dive for coins.

RT Lim Blvd, the other side of the market, fronts the anchorage for *bisligs* and *basnigs*, the fishing boats which come in from the deep seas. This very picturesque area lends itself to superb sunset photos.

Ft Pilar was built in 1635 by Fray Melchor de Vera, abandoned in 1663, and rebuilt in 1718 to fend off attacks from Muslims, Dutch, British and Portuguese. In 1898 it became an American barracks, and is currently a historical shrine on the outside and home to many squatter families on the inside. Climb the ramparts for a good view of the Muslim area beyond and the waterfront. A bronze plaque at the eastern end tells the history of the fort.

Rio Hondo is the Muslim village beyond Fort Pilar. You can get a good view from the river edge, or cross the bridge to the mosque. In either case expect a contingent of children looking for handouts, candy or whatever. Residents are Badjao, Sama and Tausug. If you wish to enter the mosque, remove your shoes first.

Pasonanca Park is about a 15-min jeepney ride from City Hall. There are gardens in and about the park, a freshwater swimming pool kept clean by constantly flowing spring water, a tree house for honeymooners (you may get permission from the mayor to stay for a night, but it is open all day for viewing); a pleasant place for walks.

You may walk or drive from Pasonanca to **Abong Abong**, a park started by the colorful late Mayor Climaco. Abong Abong is in the lower end of the city's watershed area. It has facilities for camping, lots of area to hike, lovely views and a park dedicated to two assassinated modern heroes, Ninoy Aquino and Mayor Climaco, whose grave is here.

The **Yakan Village** 7 km from the city, is settled by migrants from Basilan who are now Christian. Here they weave and sell unique, intricate cloth with colorful geometric designs. Visitors are welcomed by a man playing a xylophone- like instrument, and you may watch the women weaving.

Zamboanga has the oldest golf course in the country, built in 1910. Visitors are welcome to play. There are three tennis clubs.

Yellow Beach, the landing site of US forces on March 10-12, 1945, is just beyond the Yakan Village.

Caragasan Beach, a nice pebble and sand area with shades for day use, is about 10 km from the city, near the Muslim University, and is bordered by a typical Muslim fishing village.

Recodo, site of the first Spanish mission, is 4 km further, and now hums with boat building activities.

San Ramon Penal Colony, a self-contained economic unit where prisoners often choose to remain with their families even after their sentence is served, is located 20 km west of Zamboanga. There is a handicrafts shop along the road, but they also have an outlet at Zamboanga Home Products, in the city.

Taluksangay is 19 km north of Zamboanga, a very pretty drive through farms decorated with flowers and past a boat building industry. The village was originally settled a century ago by a few families, and now has over 800 Badjao, Sama and Maguindanao. It has a very pretty mosque and interesting strolls along the catwalks of the village where you may see women weaving mats, and children playing in the water.

The women and children of this village tend to be very pushy, almost insisting that you buy their mats (all of them), and children swarm about, begging and delighting in peering up the catwalks under visitors' skirts - good reason to wear slacks.

Santa Cruz Island is a 25-min boat ride from Lantaka or from the waterfront in front of Alavar (approximately a $4 round trip from Lantaka, less from Alavar; don't pay until you return; tip if you enjoyed the boatmen).

The island has a long beautiful pink sand beach with shades and a soft drink and beer stand, assorted gem vendors, a few masks and snorkels for rent, and no food. If you plan to stay the day bring a packed lunch.

A stroll northward along the beach will bring you to an interesting burial ground with old and new graves. The boat people come to rest on land only after death, and even then their graves are decorated with replicas of figures in boats.

Sumagdang Beach, Basilan

The Southern Islands

The further south you travel, the further you get from the already tenuous arm of the law. Before setting out, inquire about the safety of the area you intend to visit. Inquire again when you get there, and arrange for a guide who knows the area and is known there.

Basilan is 27 km from Zamboanga. There are four daily trips from Zamboanga to **Isabela**, Basilan's capital. Boats leave Zamboanga and Isabela at 7 am, 10 am, 1 pm and 4 pm. In 1985 the 1 to 1½-hr trip cost ₱18/person, first class, or ₱25 for the aircon room in the boats which have them.

Visitors arriving in Basilan are required to go to the City Hall. The tourism people in the Governor's office will help with advice and will procure military clearances needed for places you wish to visit. Ask also for assistance with transportation, and settle the price before starting out.

Points of interest within the city include **Kuam Purnah Mosque** by the waterfront, Claretcraft Handicrafts Display Center, beside Santa Isabel Cathedral, and the relief map of the islands in the town plaza.

There are some basic hotels in Isabela, the best of which are the Basilan and Clover's Pad, but it is no problem to return to Zamboanga for the night. There are several restaurants in the town.

One easy and fascinating tour is a boat ride across Isabela's harbor for a peek at the **Sama Village** on the other side. The people are friendly, waving and grinning at you as you aim your camera and wave back. Children dive into the swift current for coins. This ride alone is worth the trip to Basilan.

White Beach, on the other side of Malamawi Island from the Sama Village, is very pretty but you should ascertain the political situation before going. The quickest way to get there is to hire a *banca* for the trip around Malamawi Island.

Sumagdang Beach is closer to town, and very picturesque with a white sand shore, but a corally surface under the water.

The **Menzi Plantation** is only a 5-min tricycle ride from the City Hall. Here you are given an interesting and well done guided tour of the rubber plant and of the palm oil processing area, and a lot of information about their products.

Lamitan is most interesting on Tuesdays and Sundays, when the Yakan bring their goods to market, dressed in their colorful tribal costumes.

The main problem with Lamitan is getting there and back. You may go by bus (2 hrs) from Isabela. Or you may go by boat from Zamboanga. The ferry leaves Zamboanga daily at about 4 pm, and returns at about 9 the next morning (not very convenient for tourists). You may have to spend at least one night in Lamitan or in Isabela, depending upon the transportation schedule.

Upon arrival in Lamitan you must check in with the office of the mayor, and ask for accommodation assistance. If you go to Lamitan from Isabela, speak to Ms Damona Saja'il who works in the governor's office. She is a Yakan from Lamitan and goes home often enough to be able to be informative.

Jolo and Tawi Tawi are beautiful, but traditional problem areas, so proceed only after ascertaining safety. Kidnapping for ransom is an occasional occurrence. Jolo is inhabited by Tausug.

Jolo has a number of beautiful white sandy beaches and several mosques. **Tulay Mosque** is one of the prettiest in the country. **Bud-Datu**, just under 2 km from town, is the site of Sulu's first Muslim ruler's tomb. Good views from this hill,

Handicrafts, weaving, fruits are available at the market. Tax free goods from surrounding countries come to the Barter Trade Zone.

There are several lodging houses in Jolo, one in Tawi Tawi.

Tawi Tawi airport is an island away from Bongao town, which has one hotel, a lovely beach nearby, and Mt Bongao behind. Should you decide to climb this holy mountain, be aware that it is highly respected. The monkeys are sacred, and must be treated accordingly. Beware of snakes.

Be sure to ask for assistance and information in the capitol building in Bongao before venturing out from town.

Sunset form RT Lim Blvd, Zamboanga

Sustenance

You won't go hungry in Zamboanga. Seafoods are especially good here, but even meat lovers will enjoy their meals.

For evening dining, there are two restaurants which should not be missed: Lantaka and Alavar. Start the evening with drinks as the sun goes down over the harbor, work into dinner.

At Lantaka you may enjoy your evening by the sea wall looking into the harbor while bargaining and conversing with the Badjao. Order the seafoods platter (even if it isn't on the menu), well in advance.

Alavar is the best house of seafoods in Zamboanga, with an extensive menu. Other places which do seafoods well include Abalone and Bulakeña (also has Filipino dishes & BBQ).

Steak aficionados will want to go to Antonio's. Try the quails' egg soup. Aldea, next door, has a children's playground, and does great paella and sizzling tenderloin. The Peacock, also in Pasonanca, serves great sashimi and hot tuna, inexpensive, and has an active darts group.

Palmeria has quiet music, nice decor. Try the house chicken, spare ribs, arroz a la marinera.

Casa de Oro does German and Austrian dishes as well as seafoods. At Country Chicken & Mano Mano use fingers for chicken & native dishes.

Beer and snacks are available in the evenings at the Swiss Inn & Bar, Atin Atin (native foods - try *papait*, a goat meat dish) and Boulevard (for sunsets, snacks & beer).

Should you need a snack at the airport try J's Pad.

Reference

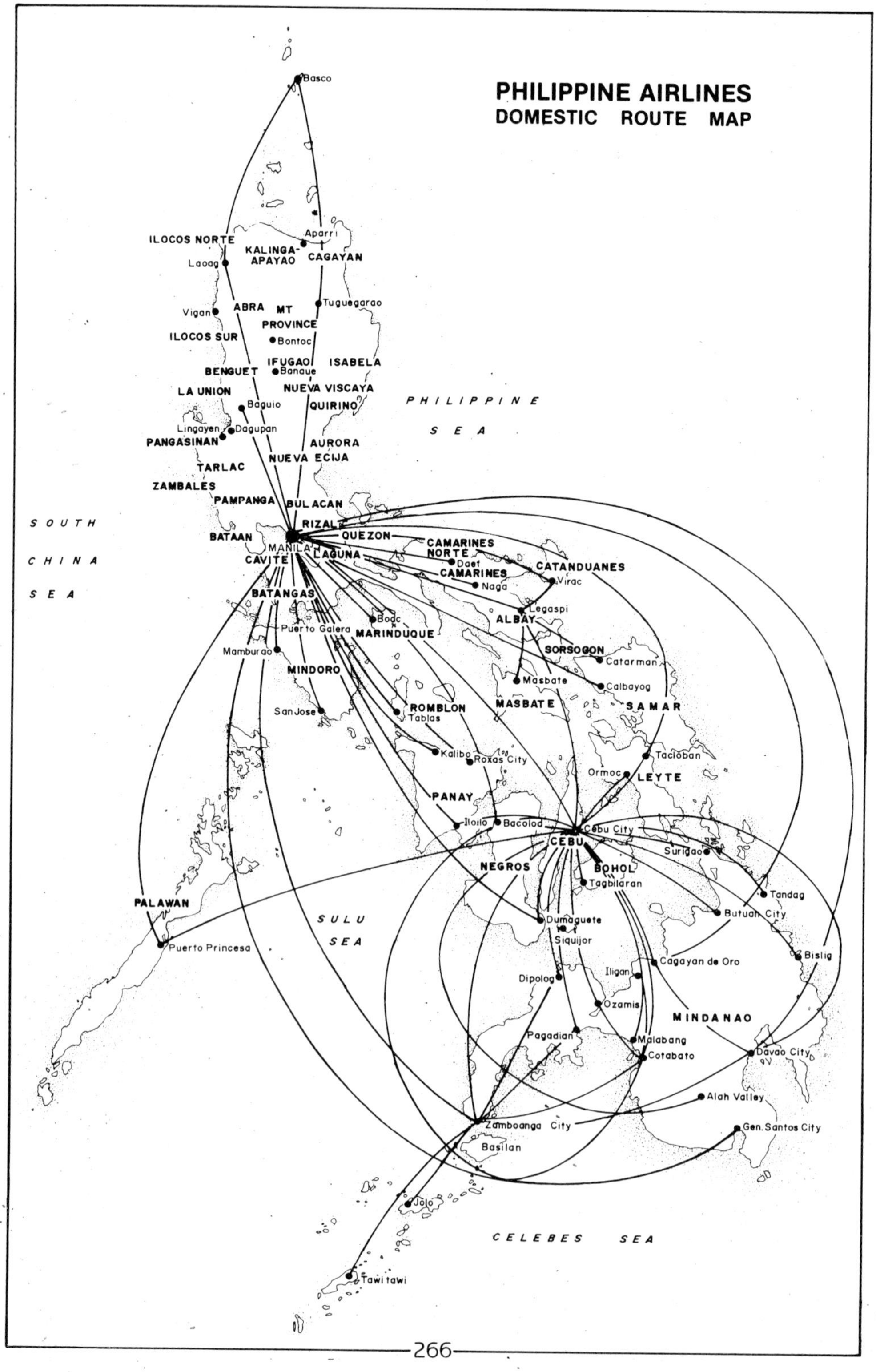
PHILIPPINE AIRLINES
DOMESTIC ROUTE MAP
Basco
Aparri
ILOCOS NORTE
KALINGA-APAYAO
CAGAYAN
Laoag
Tuguegarao
Vigan
ABRA
MT PROVINCE
ILOCOS SUR
Bontoc
IFUGAO
ISABELA
BENGUET
Banaue
NUEVA VISCAYA
LA UNION
Baguio
QUIRINO
PHILIPPINE SEA
Lingayen
Dagupan
PANGASINAN
AURORA
TARLAC
NUEVA ECIJA
ZAMBALES
PAMPANGA
BULACAN
SOUTH CHINA SEA
RIZAL
BATAAN
MANILA
QUEZON
CAMARINES NORTE
Daet
LAGUNA
CAVITE
CAMARINES
Naga
CATANDUANES
Virac
BATANGAS
Legaspi
Boac
ALBAY
Puerto Galera
MARINDUQUE
Mamburao
SORSOGON
Catarman
MINDORO
Masbate
Calbayog
MASBATE
SAMAR
San Jose
ROMBLON
Tablas
Kalibo
Roxas City
Tacloban
Ormoc
LEYTE
PANAY
Iloilo
Bacolod
Cebu City
CEBU
Surigao
BOHOL
NEGROS
Tagbilaran
PALAWAN
Tandag
SULU SEA
Dumaguete
Butuan City
Siquijor
Puerto Princesa
Bislig
Cagayan de Oro
Iligan
Dipolog
Ozamis
MINDANAO
Pagadian
Malabang
Cotabato
Davao City
Alah Valley
Zamboanga City
Gen. Santos City
Basilan
Jolo
CELEBES SEA
Tawi tawi

Transportation

BY AIR

Philippine Airlines (PAL) has regularly scheduled routes, but schedules change 4 times yearly. Check the latest timetable for updated flight times and schedules. The tables below give a rough guide for frequency and flight times.

Routes not pertinent to this book have been omitted.

PAL's information phone, 832-2791, is often hard to reach. It may be sensible to go to one of their offices, such as the PAL Bldg, Legazpi Village, the Intercontinental Hotel, or S&L Bldg, Roxas Blvd.

Jeepneys and buses meet incoming flights at provincial airports. Board promptly. They leave when full, and do not return to the airport until the next flight comes in.

Central Islands

Cebu: A shuttle bus runs between the airport and the Rajah Hotel for about half the price of a taxi.

Use waiting time while in transit to poke around the small market hidden on the first floor, have a meal in the airport, or, if your layover is several hours, go to one of the resorts on Mactan (great food at Costabella) or visit the Lapu Lapu Monument - but be sure to hire transport for the duration, and don't pay until you are back at the airport. Cebu City may be 1 hr or more from the airport if traffic is heavy.

Additionally, PAL flies between Cagayan de Oro and Davao 5 times weekly and between Davao and Zamboanga 3 times weekly.

Charter companies operate to other destinations, and fly to Caticlan, which is close to Boracay. These include:

Aerolift Phils Corp, 851 Arnaiz (Pasay) Rd, Makati, tel 817-2369;

Pacific Airways, Domestic Rd, Pasay City, tel 832-2731

Luzon & Environs

to	from Manila	from Cebu
Baguio	1/day 50 min	
Basco	5/week 185 min	
Laoag	3/week 85 min	
Legazpi	3/day 50 min	1/day 80 min
Mamburao	2/day 45 min	
Marinduque	2/day 50 min	
Naga	2/day 65 min	
Puerto Princessa	2/day 70 min	
San Jose	1/day 40 min	
Tuguegarao	6/week 75 min	

Central Islands

to	from Manila	from Cebu
Bacolod	4/day 60 min	2/day 40 min
Cebu	4/day 65 min	
Dumaguete	1/day 75 min	9/week 40 min
Iloilo	4/day 60 min	2/day 35 min
Kalibo	18/week 80 min	
Ormoc		2/week 35 min
Roxas	1/day 50 min	
Tablas	8/week 65 min	
Tacloban	17/week 70 min	9/week 35/min
Tagbilaran		3/day 30 min

Mindanao

to	from Manila	from Cebu
Allah Valley		4/week 95 min
Cagayan de Oro	3/day 85 min	1/day 35 min
Cotabato		12/week 80-105 min
Davao	3/day 100 min	2/day 50 min
General Santos		11/week 105 min
Iligan		5/week 60 min
Zamboanga	2/day 90 min	18/week 55-130 min

BY WATER

A vast network of boats criss-crosses the waters between the Philippines' many islands. Many of the craft are small outriggered canoes *(bancas)*, but there are also several major shipping lines which adhere to seasonal schedules. The guide given below for times and rates is approximate, and should be rechecked for up-to-date information.

Shipping companies often responded to our queries for schedule information by saying that their schedules were fluid, thus we had to leave many spaces blank.

Within Luzon & Vicinity

from	to	departure	return	vessel	hrs	cost
Batangas City	Puerto Galera	11am daily	7am daily	ferry	2	₱12
Batangas City	Calapan, Mindoro			boat		
Lucena (Kota)	Balanacan, Mdq	tidal, daily	daily	ferry	3-4	
Balanacan & Gasan, Mdq	Pinmalayan, Mindoro	Tu, Fr	We, Sa	*banca*	3	₱40
Caminawit, San Jose, Mindoro	Tablas, Buruanga, near Boracay	1/week	same	large *banca*	24	

Manila to Points Beyond

- Negros Navigation does 6 weekly trips between Iloilo and Manila, has a nice first class section which should be booked in advance;
- William Lines has a weekly boat from Davao to Manila, stopping at General Santos and Zamboanga along the way, taking two days for the journey.
- Sweet Lines has a weekly boat from Davao to Manila via Zamboanga and Iloilo.
- Oriental Maritime, Masagana, and William Lines have weekly boats to Puerto Princessa, taking three days and going via San Jose on Mindoro and Coron.

Addresses and telephone numbers of shipping companies with passenger accommodations from Manila are:

- Aboitiz - Kings Court Bldg, Makati, tels 88-74-51, 816-4875
- Negros Navigation - Negros Navigation Bldg, Arnaiz (Pasay) Rd, Makati, tels 816-3481, 85-69- 86, 818-3804
- Sulpicio Lines, 415 San Fernando, Manila, tels 47-96-21, 47-53-46
- Sweet Lines, Pier 6, tels 20-17-91, 26-35-27
- William Lines - booking office 1508 Rizal Ave Ext, Caloocan, tel 361-0764; Pier 14, tels 21-98- 21, 40-54-58

From Manila to the Visayas and Mindanao

to	departure	return	line	ship	hrs	cost
Bacolod	Tu, 10am	We	Negros Navigation	Don Julio	21	$22/15/9
	Th, 9am	Fr	Negros Navigation	Santa Maria	21	$15/9
	Su, 9am	Mo	Negros Navigation	Don Claudio	21	$20/15/9
Cagayan de Oro	Tu, 4pm	Sa	William	Cebu City	26	$29/20/13
	We, 12mn	Su	Sulpicio	Dona Susana		$26/21/13
	Fr, 2pm		Negros Navigation	Santa Florentina		$22/22/13
Cebu	We, Su, 10am		William	Dona Virginia		$22/12/10
	Th, Su		Sweet	Sweet Roro 2		
	Fr, 10am		Sulpicio	Phil Princess		$21/17/15
	Su		Sulpicio	Davao Princess		
Davao	Fr, 12mn		William	Manila City		$31/27/19
	Su		Sulpicio	Davao Princess		

From Manila to the Visayas and Mindanao, continued						
to	departure	return	line	ship	hrs	cost
Dumaguete	We, 12mn Fr, 8am Sa, 12mn		Sulpicio William William	Dona Susana Ozamis Cebu City	 26 26	$22/18/11 $22/12/11 $15/10/6
General Santos	Tu, 10am Fr, 12mn		Sulpicio William	Don Eusebio Manila City		$40/29/19 $33/28/19
Iligan	Tu, 4pm		William	Cebu City		$29/22/13
Iloilo	Tu, 10am Tu, 3pm We, 12nn Fr, 10am Sa, 3pm Su, 12nn	Mo Mo Tu Th Fr Sa	Sulpicio Negros Navigation Negros Navigation Negros Navigation Sulpicio Negros Navigation	Don Eusebio Santa Florentina Don Claudio Don Julio Dona Marilyn Santa Maria		$19/14/9 $21/15/9 $15/9 $21/15/9 $19/14/9 $20/15/9
Kalibo	Mo, Th		Aboitiz	Aklan		
Malay	Fr, 6pm		William	Misamis Occidental		$15/8/6
Puerto Princessa	Tu, 9am		William	Misamis Occidental		$16/11/10
Tacloban	Mo, 1pm We, 1pm		William Sulpicio	Tacloban City		$15/12/10 $19/11/10
Tagbilaran	Fr, 8am		William	Ozamis		$22/13/11
Zamboanga	Tu, 10am Fr, 12mn Sa, 3pm		Sulpicio William Sulpicio	Don Eusebio Manila City Dona Marilyn		$29/24/13 $26/20/13 $25/22/13

Within the Central Islands

Information below is a synopsis. More information should be acquired at destination before proceeding, especially as to where and when to acquire tickets, actual times and days of sailing. Be prepared to arrive early and wait for departures.

Within the Central Islands					
from	to	departure	return	boat/line	hrs
Cebu City	Bacolod (*3) Dumaguete (*2) Ormoc, Leyte Siquijor Tacloban, Leyte Tagbilaran, Bohol Tagbilaran, Bohol Tubigon, Bohol	We, Fr daily daily Mo, Fr, Sa Mo-Sa 12mn daily 8am daily 4-5/day	Su, Mo daily daily Th, Su Mo-Sa morning afternoon same	Bisaya, Negros Lines George & Peter, Gothong Ormoc/Ramon Aboitiz George & Peter, Sweet assorted Sweet Heart/Sweet Asia China	16 6 5-6 10 12 3-4 3-4 2-3
Argao, Cebu	Loon, Bohol (*1)	2/day	2/day	Kanlaon (ferry)	1¼
Bacolod	Iloilo (*4)	7am & 3pm daily	same	Don Vicente/Princess of Negros (Negros Nav)	2½
Dumaguete	Siquijor	2pm daily	7am daily	St Christopher	3
Ormoc	Bohol	2am daily	daily		

Within the Central Islands, continued					
from	to	departure	return	boat/line	hrs
Romblon	Roxas City Sibuyan Tablas	Fr daily 2-3/day	Su daily same	Aklan *banca* *banca*	
Roxas City	Sibuyan	when full	same	boat	
Sta Fe, Tablas	Boracay/Caticlan	daily	same	*banca* - cross only in calm seas	2½
Tagbilaran, Bohol	Dumaguete Siquijor	12 mn, Tu Th, Fr	 Th, Su	William Sweet Sound/Dona Magna	3 4

*1 Ceres Bus Lines have a bus-ferry package which leaves Cebu Southern Terminal at 8am and takes you all the way to Tagbilaran, a pretty ride.

*2 Travel overland by bus to San Sebastian, Talisay or Bato, then ferry to Tampi or San Jose, then continue by jeepney or bus to Dumaguete, is the route most frequently used.

When returning from Dumaguete, early ferry crossings may connect with an aircon bus.

*3 The more traveled route is overland by bus to Toledo, ferry to San Carlos, then continue overland by bus to Bacolod. Ceres Lines have a package.

*4 This crossing is great fun, lovely scenery. Dockside vendors poke wares to boarded customers, using nets on long handles to deliver the goods and collect payment.

Central Islands to Mindanao

From Cebu there are daily boats to Cagayan de Oro (about 12 hrs - Sulpicio, William, Gothong & Trans Asia); 1 weekly boat to Davao (about 25 hrs – Sulpicio); 6 weekly boats to Iligan (about 12 hrs – Gothong, Sweet, George & Peter); and 1 weekly boat to Zamboanga (about 24 hrs - George & Peter);

From Tagbilaran, Bohol, there are 1-2 weekly trips to Cagayan de Oro (about 7 hrs - Trans Asia and Sweet Lines);

From Bacolod, Negros Navigation goes 5 times weekly to Cagayan de Oro (about 13 hrs);

From Dumaguete, there are 3 weekly trips to Zamboanga (about 20 hrs - George & Peter);

From Iloilo there are 6 weekly trips to Cagayan de Oro (about 15 hrs - Negros Navigation, William), 1 to General Santos (Sulpicio) and 3-4 to Zamboanga (about 21 hrs - Maritime, Sulpicio, William).

Land transport, especially over unsurfaced roads, suffers from frequent flat tires, causing delay and making lengths of journeys difficult to estimate.

Schedules are given where they are fairly reliable; even so, check for latest updates before embarking.

First class buses are more comfortable than regular class, may stop less often, may be airconditioned; regular buses squeeze more bodies into seats, may stop more frequently. Lines which operate some airconditioned buses are marked with an asterisk (*).

Luzon & Vicinity

MANILA TO POINTS NEARBY

Batangas - BLTB Co. For Anilao, change in Batangas City to a jeepney for Mabini and Anilao. Some resorts are accessed by *banca.*

Cavite - buses and jeepneys from Baclaran Market.

Circling Laguna de Bay - hire a vehicle to do the trip in a day. Buses for Antipolo leave near the corner of EDSA and Aurora Blvd, Cubao. From Antipolo buses and jeepneys continue around the bay. Buses for Santa Cruz leave from South Expressway in front of the South Supermarket. Jeepneys go from Santa Cruz to Pagsanjan or Majayjay.

Pampanga River Valley - Baliwag Transit to major towns (about $0.60 to Bulacan); then transfer to jeepneys.

South - Philtranco* and BLTB Co*

Zambales - Victory* has hourly buses to Olongapo.

MANILA TO POINTS BEYOND

Baguio - Dagupan*, Dangwa*, Pantranco*, Philippine Rabbit*, Rajah*, Sarkies*, Sunshine*, Victory*, all do the 5-hr trip for $3-4. Rajah, Sarkies and Sunshine have stops in Ermita and/or Makati.

Banawe - Sarkies* transfers travelers to a minibus in Solano, continues to Banawe (10 hrs total). Buy a round trip ticket to ensure space on the return. Dangwa goes straight through to Banawe (8 hrs). Both have 1 daily trip. Several jeepneys ply the Banawe-Lagawe-Solano route to meet buses on the highway.

Bicol - Philtranco*, Sarkies*, Sunshine*, JV Liner and others make the 10-hour journey to Naga, another 2 hrs to Legazpi, with stops in between outside Iriga. Many travelers prefer the night bus. PNR (train) takes roughly the same time over a more rural route. Philtranco* continues through Sorsogon.

Cagayan Valley - Inland Trailways*, Sarkies*, Dalin*, Dangwa*, Pantranco* take about 11 hours to Tuguegarao. Each has 1 or more daily trips. All buses stop at Earnshaw St, Sampaloc before continuing, except Dangwa, which has its terminal nearby on Dimasalang. Sarkies stops in Mabini before going to Earnshaw. Many buses allow reserved seating. Pantranco has a daily bus to Santa Ana, Cagayan. From Santa Ana you continue by tricycle to San Vicente.

Ilocos Coast - The journey from Manila to San Fernando, La Union, takes about 5 hrs. Vigan is 2 hrs further, Laoag another 2 hrs, for a total of 9. Fariñas*, Franco*, I Aniceto*, Maria de Leon*, Pantranco*, PNR, Philippine Rabbit*, Pioneer Times* and Viron serve all three cities and points between. If you are going to a resort in Bauang, La Union, you may request the bus to stop on the highway near it. Some buses will not stop until they reach San Fernando, in which case you get a jeepney back to the resort.

Pangasinan (100 Islands) - The trip from Manila takes roughly 4 hrs to Lingayen. The route is served by Dagupan Bus and Pantranco. Lingayen is another half hour, plus a 20-minute tricycle ride to Lucap. Bolinao is an hour beyond Alaminos. Both Alaminos and Bolinao are served by Pantranco, but most lines stop in Lingayen, where you transfer to a jeepney for the onward journey.

Times Transit goes to Lingayen from Vigan and La Union.

Dagupan Bus has trips from Baguio.

Philippine Rabbit and Victory Liner have trips to Pangasinan through Zambales.

BETWEEN POINTS ON LUZON

Baguio to Points Beyond:

San Fernando La Union (1 hr), Vigan (3 hrs) and Laoag (5 hrs) – Marcita's Liner (hourly to San Fernando La Union), Philippine Rabbit (hourly), Times, Viron & others.

Kabayan – 3/day, Dangwa, $2.

Sagada – 2/day, Lizardo and Dangwa, $3.

Bontoc – daily, 7am, 8 hrs, Dangwa $3, other lines also.

Banawe – daily, 10 hrs, Dangwa $4 via Bontoc; daily, 8 hrs, Dangwa, $3.50 via Cagayan Valley.

Tuguegarao via Solano – 2/day, Pantranco; other lines also. Tuguegarao via Bontoc & Banawe – Greenland & Dangwa.

Central Mountains

Bontoc to Sagada – jeeps leave late morning, then mid-afternoon

Bontoc to Banawe – Immanuel bus at about 8 am; jeeps at about 10-12 am; bus is more comfortable

Laoag to Tuguegarao

Florida, Pantranco & St Peter's go across the top of Luzon when the road is safe.

LUZON TO MINDORO & MARINDUQUE

Marinduque – Philtranco to Lucena, jeepney to Kota, ferry (daily departure depends on tides and seas) to Balanacan

Mindoro – BLTB bus to Batangas City, ferry (leaves 11 am, returns 7 am). Beware of pickpockets on this route.

Around Mindoro, land transport is not feasible during rainy season, and is very dusty during dry season. Jeepneys frequent the Puerto Galera-Calapan route. Occasional jeepneys ply the poor road between Calapan and San Jose. One daily bus and a few jeepneys go between San Jose and Mamburao. Early in the morning a jeep goes from Mamburao to Abra de Ilog (1 hr), from where a boat may leave for Puerto Galera at 8-9 am.

MANILA BUS TERMINALS:

- Baliwag, 33 EDSA, Quezon City & 2nd Ave, Caloocan, tel 350860, 344478
- BLTB Co - terminal on EDSA, Pasay City tel 833-5301
- Dagupan Bus Co, New York Ave, Quezon City, tel 976123, 995639
- Dalin, 608 F Cayco, Sampaloc, tel 605665, 741-9120
- Dangwa, 1600 Dimasalang, Sampaloc, tel 731-2859
- Fariñas, Laong-Laan St cor M de la Fuente, Sampaloc, tel 731-4507
- Franco, 860 M Earnshaw, Sampaloc, tel 618069, 731-2584
- Inland Trailways - EDSA, Pasay City; stops at 6 Earnshaw cor F Cayco, tel 617925, 617912
- Maria de Leon - Gelinos St cor Dapitan, Sampaloc, tel 731-4907
- Pantranco North - 325 Quezon Ave, Quezon City, tel 997091, 951081
- Philippine Rabbit - 819 Oroquieta St, Sta Cruz, Manila, tel 216996, 711-5811, 711-5819; 256 North Diversion Rd, Balintawak, Quezon City, tel 359574, 346264
- Philtranco, EDSA, Pasay City, tel 833-5061
- PNR, 943 CM Recto, Tutuban Station, tels 216639, 217466, Samson Rd, Caloocan, tel 362-3272
- Rajah - departs from between the Intercon and Shoemart, Makati Commercial Center, and goes to the Parkview Hotel, Burnham Park, Baguio City. Several offices: tel 596626, 592724, 590242, 590254
- Sarkies - buses for Baguio leave first from JP Laurel Bldg cor del Pilar and Pedro Gil, Malate, and stop between the Intercon and Shoemart, then go to the Hyatt Terraces in Baguio, the bus for Banawe and Tuguegarao, depart from JP Laurel Building, then stop at Earnshaw St; the bus for Bicol, departs from JP Laurel. Sarkies offices are at JP Laurel, Malate, tel 508959, 582153, 572250
- Sunshine - departs from the Aloha Hotel, Malate, to the Hyatt Hotel, Baguio; terminal 359 Don Revilla, Pasay City, tels 831-7370, 831-6243, 584248; 776 M Earnshaw, tel 603041; offices 451 MH del Pilar, tel 584787
- Times Transit, EDSA, Quezon City, tel 973570; 1716 Laong Laan, Sampaloc, tel 731-4180;
- Victory Liner - departs from terminal on 651 EDSA, Pasay City, tel 833-5019
- Viron, 1209 Blumentritt, tel 741-0405

Land Transport in the Central Islands

PU vehicles found in the central islands and Mindanao are small taxis. Bargain for the price before you start out.

TO LEYTE

Tacloban, Leyte - Philtranco has daily buses from Manila, taking 24-48 hrs.

Ormoc, Leyte - Express buses take 2½ hrs from Tacloban.

FROM CEBU

Cebu - be aware that all buses in Cebu travel at break-neck speeds.

Moalboal - some resorts will arrange transport. Otherwise hire a taxi all the way, or to the Southern Bus Terminal, then take the Philippine Eagle or Villanueva, which will, upon request, take you to the beach in Moalboal. ABC leaves you a 1-km walk to the beach. When departing Moalboal, arrange the night before for a tricycle to take you to the bus.

Dumaguete - 8 or more buses daily from Cebu City's Southern Terminal to Bato or San Sebastian, where you transfer to a ferry, then to a jeepney for Dumaguete. ABC's aircon bus leaves at about 2 pm for Bato. The whole trip takes about 5 hrs. Return on the early ferry to connect with an aircon bus to Cebu.

Bacolod - 2 daily buses leave Cebu's Southern Terminal early in the morning, Sunshine* ($5) and Ceres ($4.20) for the 8-hr trip to Bacolod via ferry from Toledo to San Carlos City.

Bohol - Ceres liner leaves at 8 am and 2 pm to Tagbilaran via a ferry from Argao to Loon ($2.20). Ferries (about 5 daily) from Cebu to Tubigon allow you to continue overland to the Chocolate Hills en route to Tagbilaran, although you may have to spend the night at the Chocolate Hills Complex.

Buses travel the main road to Carmen. There is a 1-km walk from the main road to the complex.

WITHIN NEGROS

Bacolod-Dumaguete - express buses take about 7 hrs via San Carlos City

Bacolod-Cebu - see Cebu

Dumaguete-Cebu - see Cebu

WITHIN PANAY

Iloilo-Estancia - Garnet Express departs hourly between 2:30 am and 3 pm.

Iloilo-Roxas-Kalibo-Caticlan - Nanduantes has a 2½ hr express run twice daily; R&K has 8 daily buses to Roxas and 4 on to Kalibo (5-6 hrs or more); one goes through to Katiclan. In Roxas City, buses leave from Roxas Ave for Iloilo. Others leave from beside the market for Kalibo.

Roxas-Kalibo - Candido, Kitahon & Obuyes Lines have 6 daily trips, starting at 4:30 am. The journey takes about 2 hrs.

Roxas-Estancia - a few jeeps & buses; the trip is a very dusty 3 hrs.

Kalibo-Caticlan - jeeps and minibuses; about 1½ hrs.

Land Transport on Mindanao

Cagayan de Oro-Camiguin - hire a car or PU vehicle, or take a Bachellor, Fortune or Ceres Liner bus to Balingoan (1½ hrs), then a 1-hr ferry ride (scheduled for 6:30, 7:30 and 9 am, and once in the afternoon) to Benoni, then jeepney to Mambajao. Ferry costs ₱10.50; banca hire about ₱200. Cagayan de Oro-Davao - Bachellor & Fortune*

Cagayan de Oro-Iligan - several daily 2 hr trips on Fortune and on Bachellor lines.

Davao-Kidapawen (for Mt Apo), General Santos, Marbel (for T'Boli) - Mindanao Transport.

Iligan-Marawi - jeeps depart in the mornings and afternoons; it is wisest to take public transport, and to travel only during hours when public transport is going frequently.

Lake Sebu - land transport from General Santos (2 hrs) and Cotabato City (least preferable at the time of writing, due to political situation), to Marbel; buses and jeepneys to Surallah (Allah Valley); change to jeepney for Lake Sebu.

Zamboanga - buses to major cities when the political situation permits.

Lodging

Lodging in the Philippines comes in a wide assortment of types, ranging from tree houses and nipa cottages with outside bathroom and toilet facilities through cottages and rooms beautifully done of native materials yet having all the comforts one could want, to western-style cement hotels and resorts.

Lodging also comes in a wide variety of prices, from less than a dollar a night for bare boards to over a hundred dollars a night for luxuries which would cost much more elsewhere. In general, lodging in the Philippines ranges from reasonable to very cheap by international standards. There is, however, a great variation throughout the country in standard and in the price you pay for essentially the same thing. Prices also vary seasonally, with demand. Easter and Christmas seasons are busy and more expensive, and many places are booked well in advance at these times.

An assortment of taxes and service charges totaling as much as 23% may be added to the room bill, especially in upper bracket places. We have added these into prices published below – which might well change.

In all but the top priced establishments (and even then, sometimes) prices may be negotiable.

In general, cleanliness, as judged by western ideas, decreases with price. We have noted exceptions to this rule. For the very low budget traveler, who runs a slight risk of being attached by ectoparasites, we recommend Pretty Hair Shampoo as a good, strong, fast remedy. It is available in most drug stores.

Codes are used to briefly describe accommodations we have inspected or have on good report from reliable sources.

Please be aware that changes can be expected – prices increase, service varies, managers come and go, taking their styles with them.

It is assumed that all establishments in the B and higher price category have hot running water.

Price Key:

AAA	– over $50	C	– $10 and up
AA	– over $35	D	– $5 and up
A	– over $20	E	– $3 and up
B	– over $15	F	– under $3
*	– full board	pp	– per person

Room type key:

a	– airconditioned	p	– private bath
ctg	– cottage	s	– 1 bath shared between 2 rooms
d	– dorm	c	– common bath
k	– kitchenette		
h	– hot running water		

Credit Cards:

International Cards:

- A – American Express
- D – Diner's Club
- M – Mastercard
- V – Visa

Philippine Cards:

- B – Bankard
- BP – BPI card
- F – Fareastcard
- E – Equicard
- P – PCIBcard
- R – RCPC
- U – Unicard

Metropolitan Manila: Ermita, Malate & Pasay Nb: append -Manila to all cable addresses

name & phone	price	type	location	description	facilities	food
Manila Hotel 470011 cable: MANILHOTEL tlx: 40537 MHOTL PN	AAAA	a,p	Rizal Park, Manila	very nice	tennis; pool; putting green; etc most cards	several rests & bar
Westin Philippine Plaza; 832-0701 cable: PHILPLAZA tlx: 40443 FILPLAZA PN	AAAA	a,p	CCP Complex, Manila	very nice large pool	tennis; puting green; jogging; most cards	several rests & bar
Holiday Inn 597961-80 cable: HOLIDAYINN tlx: 63487 HOLIDA PN	AAAA	a,p	3001 Roxas Blvd, Manila		pool; most cards	several rests & bar
Century Park Sheraton; 501201 cable: CENPARK	AAAA	a,p	Vito Cruz St, Malate Manila	large lobby; friendly staff	pool; most cards	several rests & bar
Hyatt Regency Manila; 831-2611 tlx: 63344 ETPHYA PN	AAAA	a,p	2702 Roxas Blvd, Pasay City, Metro Manila		pool; most cards	
Manila Hilton 573711 cable: HILTEL tlx: 63387 HILTEL PN	AAA	a,p	UN Avenue, Manila		pool; sauna; casino; most cards	4 rests bar
Manila Midtown 573911 cable: MIDTOWN tlx: 27797 MNLMID	AAA	a,p	Pedro Gil cor Adriatico, Manila		pool; most cards	several rests & bar
Silahis International 594891 cable: SILATEL tlx: 63163 SILTEL PN	AAA	a,p	1990 Roxas Blvd, Manila		pool; casino; Playboy Club; most cards	rests, bar
Admiral Hotel 572081-93 cable: ADMITEL tlx: 74240488	AAA	a,p	2138 Roxas Blvd, Manila		pool; most cards	rest
Bayview Hotel 503061 cable: BAYPRINCE tlx: 223311 BAY PH	A	a,p	1118 Roxas Blvd, Blvd, Manila		pool; most cards	rests
Aloha Hotel 599061 tlx: 27668 HAC PH	A	a,p	Roxas Blvd cor Padre Faura, Manila Manila	helpful staff	most cards	rest
Ambassador Hotel 506011	A	a,p	2021 A Mabini,	will discount;lg Chinese hotel	most cards	Chinese rest
Casa Solanie 508641-45	A	a,p a,p,k	1811 Leon Guinto Malate, Manila	nice entry; no elevator; some rms with balcony	most cards	rest
Las Palmas 506661	A	a,p a,p,k	Mabini St, Malate, Manila	helpful staff; roomy lobby; good value & loc	most cards	bar, coffee shop

name & phone	price	type	location	description	facilities	food
Kanumayan Inn 573660-1 cable: 65058 MANF PN	A	a,p	2317 Leon Guinto Malate, Manila	good entry;good English; helpful nice garden; older rooms best	lg, cln pool shop most cards	rest
Jadevine Executive House; 508601-5	B	a,p	UN Ave cor J Bocobo, Malate, Manila	helpful staff good location	some cards	coffee shop w/ extensive menu
Hotel Soriente 599106	B	a,p	A. Flores cor J Bocobo, Malate, Manila	helpful staff lg, bright rms not all w/ window; good location	some cards may discount	next to large coffee shop
Casa Dalco 507558 cable: CASADAL	B C	a,p a,c	1910 A Mabini Ermita, Manila	helpful staff; good location; good place	some cards	rest
Circle Pension 522-2920	B-C D	a,p a,c	Remedios St, Remedios Circle, Malate, Manila	helpful staff; very cln; great location & ambiance		sm dining rm, excellent menu
Casa Dalco 598522	C D E	a,p a,c c	1318 F Agoncillo Ermita, Manila	nice old house; helpful staff; good value;	luggage storage	full meals
Midtown Pension 508780	C D	a,p c	551 Padre Faura, Ermita, Manila	near transport; no towels		coffee shop nearby
Dutch Inn 599881	C B	a,p apts	1034 Roxas Blvd Ermita, Manila		no cards	
Olga Casa Pension	C D	a,p p,c	Vito Cruz St Malate, Manila			shop & bar
Malate Pension 585489; 593489	C D	a,p a,c p,c	1771 Adriatico St, Malate	helpful staff; good location; good contacts; family atm;	garden; locked storage	coffee shop
Eden's Pension 522-2389	C D	a,p p,c	2158 Carolina St, Malate, Manila	helpful staff; clean	limited storage	meals
ECA Pension 595257	C D-C	a,p c	1248 J Bocobo, Malate	family atm; helpful; sm bath rooms		pre-order meals
Lucky Pension	E	c	M Adriatico, Malate, Manila	good location; bring padlock		

AAA – over $50
AA – over $35
A – over $20
B – over $15
* – full board

C – $10 and up
D – $5 and up
E – $3 and up
F – under $3
pp – per person

a – airconditioned
ctg – cottage
d – dorm
k – kitchenette
c – common bath

p – private bath
s – 1 bath shared between 2 rooms
h – hot running water

A – American Express
D – Diner's Club
M – Mastercard
V – Visa

B – Bankard
BP – BPI card
F – Fareastcard
E – Equicard
P – PCIBcard
R – RCPC
U – Unicard

Metropolitan Manila: Makati

name & phone	price	type	location	description	facilities	food
Oriental Mandarin 816-3601 cable: MANDAHOTL tlx: 63756 MANDA PN	AAAA	a,p	Paseo de Roxas cor Makati Ave, Makati	very good	pool most cards	rests; good deli/ bake shop
Manila Peninsula 819-3456 cable: PENHOT tlx: 22476 PEN PH	AAAA	a,p	Ayala cor Makati Aves, Makati	lg lobby with tables, snacks	pool most cards	rests; good deli/ bake shop
Intercontinental Manila; 815-9711 tlx: ACA 33314 ICHPA	AAAA	a,p	1 Ayala Ave, Makati	nice lobby	pool most cards	rests, coffee shop
Manila Garden 857911 tlx: 45883 GARDEN PM	AAAA	a,p	Makati Commercial Center, Makati	least expensive of Makati's top	pool most cards	rests - good Japanese food
Gilarmi Apartelle 857011-19 cable: GILARMI tlx: 22404 GMI PH	AA-A	apts	52 Ayala Ave Makati		pool Cards-A,V,D	coffee shop
Amorsolo Mansion Apartment Inn 818–6811–19 tlx: 66033 AMORMN PN	AA-A	apts	130 Amorsolo St, Makati	lower weekly; pleasant; good location	Cards-A,V,U	nr rests
Charter House Apartelle 817-6001-16 cable: CHARTERHAUS tlx: 22115 CHR PN	A–AA	a,p	114 Legazpi St, Makati	lower weekly; good staff,	pool most cards Cards-M,D, B,R,E	coffee shop
YMCA 817-1229 tlx: ITT 40404 PX 567	A	a,p	7 Dao St, San Antonio, Makati	good staff & service	pool Cards-A,D, B,Bp	
Robelle Pension House; 816-3581 tlx: 63885 ROBELL PN	A	a,p	4402 Valdez St, Makati	pleasant, cln; good staff	pool; billiards Cards-A,D,V	pub; a la carte menu
El Cielito Tourist Inn; 880246	A-B	a,p	804 Arnaiz Rd, Makati	good staff	no cards	breakfast
Pension Virginia 885228	A-B	a,p	816 Arnaiz Rd, Makati		no cards	meals avail
La Ville 856426 tlx: 64010 DELTA PN	B C	a,p p,c	6060 Palma St, Makati	good service hot water on request	no cards	coffee shop
Makati Townhouse 878942	B–C	a,p	100 Gil Puyat, Makati	helpful staff	no cards	coffee shop

Near Manila — Batangas

name & phone	price	type	location	description	facilities	food
Punta Baluarte Intercontinental (MNL 815–9711)	AAAA	a,p p	Calatagan, Bats (Intercon Makati)	ctgs & rms by the sea	pools, sports! beach most cards	rest
Anilao Seasport Ctr (MNL 592615)	AA	p,c	Mabini, Bats (Holiday Inn)	rms by the sea	windsurf, dive, etc no cards	rest – good
Aqua Tropical (MNL 586437)	AA A	a,p p	Mabini, Bats (Midtown Ramada)		water sports Cards–A,V	yes
Ligpo Island (MNL 481985)	B–C		Ligpo, San Luis, Bats	rms by the sea	no cards	yes – good
Seafari (MNL 828–5064)	D,Epp	p	Mabini, Bats (85 Long Beach, Paranaque)	ctgs & rms	water sports no cards	yes
Eagle Point (MNL 703328)	AAA–A	a,p p	Mabini, Bats	asstd rms, some v posh	water sports by sea	yes – good
Bonito Island Resort (MNL 873646; 866334)	AA–A	a,p	Mabini, Bats (2172–B Pasong Tamo, Makati)	ctgs on an island	water sports	yes

Near Manila – Cavite

name & phone	price	type	location	description	facilities	food
Puerto Azul (MNL 574731–9) tlx 64546 AZHOTEL P	AAA	a,p p	Ternate, Cavite (Silahis Hotel, Manila)	ctgs & rms; nice	pool, beach, golf, etc ; most cards	rest
Marbella Marina (818-5021)	AA	a,p	Ternate, Cavite (Islander, 115 Alvaro, Makati)	ctgs & rms; nice	pool, beach; most cards	rest

Near Manila — Laguna

name & phone	price	type	location	description	facilities	food
Caliraya Hilltop (472935; 473106)	C	p	Caliraya, Cavinti, Laguna (747 Muelle de la Industria, Binondo, Manila)		no cards	
Pagsanjan Rapids 645–1258 (MNL 832–0309)	AA–A	a,p	Pagsanjan S–317, PICC, CCP Complex, Manila	newly redone	pool on river	good
Pagsanjan Tropical (828–1646)	C D	a,p p	Pagsanjan, Laguna (Bo Pulang Lupa, Las Pinas)	garden area	no cards	
Club Solviento			Los Banos, Lag	modern club; hot mineral springs		
Villa Pansol (673–2095)	B C	p c	Los Banos, Lag (Kaimo Bldg, QC)	mineral spring spa		
Crystal Springs (859423)	A	a,p	Calamba, Lag (313 Puyat, Makati)	mineral pools	mineral spa	rest
Hidden Valley (509903)	AA–A	a,p	Alaminos, Lag (450 UN Ave, MNL)	rms & ctgs	pools, hot & cool	rest
Villa Escudero (521–8698)	AA	p	San Pablo, Lag (1059 Estrada, MNL)	rms & ctgs, nice	lake	rest

name & phone	price	type	location	description	facilities	food
Villa Escudero (521-8698)	AA	p	San Pablo, Lag (1059 Estrada, Manila)	rms & ctgs, nice	lake	rest

Near Manila – Bataan & Zambales

name & phone	price	type	location	description	facilities	food
Montemar (MNL 815-3453)	A	a,p	Bagac, Bataan (Cacho Gonzales Bldg, Makati Ave, Makati)	rms, nice; pvt club – reservations needed	beach, water sports, pool tennis, golf	yes
White Rock Hotel (721–2099/5238 722–0864)	AAA	a,p	Subic, Zam (1 Industria cor Rodriguez, QC)	ctgs & rms; nice	pool, beach, most cards	rest
Sand Valley (922–2763/1739)	A–B C	a,p p	Iba, Zambales (956 Aurora Blvd, QC)	rms	beach no cards	rest – good

Pangasinan

name & phone	price	type	location	description	facilities	food
Pangasinan Village Inn 2525	C	a,p	Calasiao	large rms	pool	rest
San Fabian Resort (MNL 575846)	A C	p c	San Fabian	good rms	beach	rest
Lazy A 4726	B C	a,p ctgs	109 Cayanga St, San Fabian	rms & rustic ctgs	nice pool, beach	rest
Last Resort	C-B	a,p p	Lucap, Alaminos	some rms nice; on the sea		good food
Ocean View (MNL 731–4029)	E,F	p,c	Lucap, Alaminos	nice rms, nice baths; cln; good value		rest
Maximes	C D	a,p p	Lucap, Alaminos	sm rms, on the waterfront		rest
Gloria's	D	p	Lucap, Alaminos	over the water		rest

La Union

name & phone	price	type	location	description	facilities	food
Agoo Playa Resort (MNL 673–7161/2)	AAA	a,p	Agoo (Strata 100 Bldg Pasig)	lovely place	pool, water sports	great food
Sunset Lanai	A	apts	Agoo	beside Agoo Playa		
Cresta del Mar 413297; 413363	A-AA	a,p	Paringao, Bauang	nice rms	pool, water sports; tennis	rest
Anchorage 413794; 413793	A-B	a,p	Paringao, Bauang	good dk rms		rest
Acapulco 412696; 412697	A	a,p	San Francisco, San Fernando	nice carpeted rms white sand beach		rest
Cabaña 412824	B	a,p	Paringao, Bauang	cln rms	good pool; wind surf; hobies	rest; great daiqueries
Bali Hai 412504	B C	a,p p	Paringao, Bauang	rms & ctgs		rest

name & phone	price	type	location	description	facilities	food
Long Beach 412673; 412674 (MNL 721-0862)	A–B C	a,p p	Bauang (Panmazirk, 2nd flr Virra Mall, Greenhills, QC)	rms & ctgs		rest
Leo-Mar Cottages	D	p	Bauang	basic		
Lourdes Beach Resort	E	p	Bauang	basic		

Ilocos Sur

name & phone	price	type	location	description	facilities	food
Narvacan Bagong Lipunan Lodge		a,p p	Narvacan	nice; lovely setting; need own transport	pool	rest
Cordillera Inn	B-CC E	a,p p	Vigan	rms dk, cln	disco	
Vigan Hotel	C E	a,p c	Vigan	some lovely rms		rest
Grandpa's Inn	D E	a,p p	Vigan			
Venus Inn	D F	a,p c	Vigan	sm rms		rest

Ilocos Norte

name & phone	price	type	location	description	facilities	food
Fort Ilocandia Resort Hotel 221166 (MNL 818-8949)	AA-AAA	a,p	Calayab, Laoag (Islander, 115 Alvaro, Makati)	very nice	sm pool; beach hobie windsurf no access to public trans; cards-A,D,V,M R,P,B	rest - good
Villa Lydia 220540	C	a,p	Highway, San Nicholas		pool, tennis cards-A,B	rest
Pichay Lodging Hse 3568	D	a,p p	Primo Lazaro Ave Laoag			breakfasts
Casa Llanes 221125	D D	a,p p	cor P Lazaro & V Llanes, Laoag			rest
Texicano 220290	C C E	a,p p c	Rizal St, Laoag	dk rms		rest
La Playa Blanca (MNL 521-9731)	B	p	Currimao (MNL - Swagman, 521A Flores St, Manila)	dbl beds; beach		rest, tours
D'Coral Beach Resort; 221133 (MNL 972837)	C D-C	a,p p	Currimao	ctgs	beach	rest

AAA – over $50	C – $10 and up	a – airconditioned	p – private bath
AA – over $35	D – $5 and up	ctg – cottage	s – 1 bath shared between 2 rooms
A – over $20	E – $3 and up	d – dorm	h – hot running water
B – over $15	F – under $3	k – kitchenette	
* – full board	pp – per person	c – common bath	

Baguio prices vary widely with the season

name & phone	price	type	location	description	facilities	food
Hyatt Terraces 442-5670 – 77 (MNL 817-3046)	AAA AA	a,p apts	South Drive (138 HV dela Costa, Makati)	very nice	pool, bar, cards-A,D,V, M,C,U,F,B,BP	several rests
Hotel Nevada 442-2400/ 2369/4572	AA-A	a,p	2 Loakan Rd	some rms sm	cards-A,D,V,M C,U,F,B,BP	rest
Safari Lodge 442-2419	AAA-C	p,h	191 Leonard Wood Rd	stuffed animals in lobby	cards-A,D,V,U R	
Parkview 442-4545/ 3144/3108 (MNL 893696)	AA-A	a,p	45 Leonard Wood (914 Arnaiz, Makati)	various size rms nice decor		
Baguio Park 442-5626 – 8 (MNL 522–0541)	AA-A	a,p,h	Harrison Rd (c/o Rajah Tours UN Ave, Manila)	carpeted, nice decor, some rms have fridge	cards-A,D,V,M R,BP,F,U	rest
Baden Powell Hall 442-5836 (MNL 721-7818)	AA–C E	a,p,h p,h d	Gov Pack Rd (3rd St, Quezon City)	nr transport; v cln; nice suites; good common baths	cards-A,D,M B,U	
Munsayac Inn 442-2451	A-B	p,h	21 Leonard Wood Rd	nice place; helpful people	cards-A,D,V,M R	good food
Mountain Lodge 442-4544	A-C	p,h	27 Leonard Wood Rd	great decor; fam rms; cln	cards-D,V,M BP,U,F,R	rest
Hotel Montecello 442-6566 (MNL 521-4685)	AAA–AA	a,p	Maryheights, Bakakeng, Baguio (Manila Midtown Ramada)	sm rms; nice view thin walls;	can arrange healers visit tennis	rest
Villa Rosal 442-4093	B-A D	a,p c	General Luna St	nice; central; good common baths	cards-A,V,M,F	rest
Mount Crest 442-3324/3325	A	a,p	Legarda cor Urbano Sts		cards-A,D,V B,BP, U	rest
Siesta Inn 442-7066	B-C	p,h	Gov Pack Rd	deluxe rms nice		rest, coffee shop, bar
Sicat Hotel 442-4938 (MNL 833-5019)	A-B	a,p,h	Marcos Hwy (Victory Lines, Pasay City)	all rms have tiled b, verandah dark		rest
Belfrantl 442-5012/4298	A-C	p,h	General Luna St	cln, basic	cards-A,D,V R,B,U,F,BP	
Montañosa 442-7574	A-C	p,h	Bokawkan Rd	bright, basic rms helpful staff; tiled baths	cards-A,D,V BP,B,U,F,R	coffee shop
Kisad Pension House 442-3507	A-C	p,h	24 Kisad Rd	tiled baths; 2 dbl beds; cln; some rms have terrace		rest, bar
Inn Rocio 442-4028 (MNL 997317)	B-C	p,h	68 Kisad Rd (86 Dr Lazcano, Quezon City)	rms dark, apts bright; rate incl breakfast	cards-D,V	rest
Venus Parkview 442–5597/6452 (MNL 816-1452)	B	a,p,h	19-A Kisad Rd (2855 Finlandia, Makati)	nice entry; tubs; needs redoing	cards-A,V,M F,R,U	rest, disco
Burnham Hotel 442-2331/5117	A-C	p,h	21 Calderon Rd	nice lobby, nice baths, no screens	cards-A,D,V B,F,BP	

Baguio prices vary widely with the season, continued

name & phone	price	type	location	description	facilities	food
FRB 442-3539	B,C	p,h	Gen Luna cor Assumption Rds	nice, bright, cln rms		coffee shop, rest
Casa Feraren 442-2680	A-B	p,s,h	7 Outlook Drive	comfy; pleasant decor		
Villa La Maja 442-7239 (MNL 818-6406)	B-C	p,h	Outlook Drive (9776 Kamagong, Makati)	good rms		rest
Corfu 442-2969	C E	p,h c	Leonard Wood cor Brent Rd	not all rms have hot water		
Casa Vallejo 442-3045/4601	C,D D	p,h c,h	111 Session Rd	nice place	cards-D,BP	
Pines City 442-6872	D E,F	p,h c,h	21 Fergusson Rd	sm, cln rms com baths ntg		
Baguio Goodwill 442-6634 (MNL 499770)	C-D D-E	p,h c,h	FRC Bldg (c/o Chinatown Inn, Ongpin cor Tambakan, Manila	basic rms; sm lounge; noisy?		rest
Baguio Veny's Inn 442-2420	C,D	p,h	24 Session Rd	cln, basic		breakfast
Rose Bowl 442-4213	C,D	p,h	7 Harrison Rd	no lobby; bright, cln, cln, basic rms	cards-D,V,M R,BP,B,F,U	good Chinese food
Paredos	B-D	c,h	nice family home			
Baguio Village Inn 442-3901	B-D D-E	p,h c,h	355 Magsaysay	simple, good rms pleasant people	cards-A	
St Mary's 442-6156	C D-E F	p,h c,h d,c,h	16 Manzanillo Subd	many good reports nice old house	cards-V	good bread

Bontoc & Sagada

name & phone	price	type	location	description	facilities	food
Pines Kitchenette	C D,E	a,p p,c	Bontoc			rest
Vista Inn	D,E	p	Bontoc			coffee shop
Bontoc Hotel	E,F	p,c	Bontoc			
Mountain Hotel	E,F	p,c	Bontoc	noisy ams		
Happy Home	F	c	Bontoc			coffee shop
Mt Data Lodge (MNL 818-8949)	AAA	p	Benguet-Bontoc border (Islander, 115 Alvaro, Makati)	very nice		good food
Mapiyaaw Sagada Pension	E,F F	p,s,c d,c	Sagada	great place		good food
Julia's	F	c	Sagada	homey; cln, sm rms (some large)		vegetarian
St Josephs	F	c	Sagada	asstd rms		good food
Daoa's Sagada Pension	F	c	Sagada			good food
Traveller's Inn	F	c	Sagada			
Cangbay's	F	c	Sagada			

Banawe

name & phone	price	type	location	description	facilities	food
Banawe Hotel (MNL 818-8942)	AAA E	a,p d,c	Banawe (Islander, 115 Alvaro, Makati)	very nice helpful staff	sm pool	rest
Sanafe Lodge (MNL 721-1057)	B E	p,s d	mkt; (2nd flr, Virra Mall, Greenhills Com Ctr, San Juan)	nice		rest
Banawe View	B C,D	p s	(Tribal Arts, P Faura Mall, Malate, Manila)	above Banawe; very nice		rest
J&L Lodge	Fpp	c	out of town	nice, cln		no food
Green View Lodge	B–C	p	nr mkt	some nice rms		
Cozy Nook	Fpp	c		cln		rest
Halfway Lodge	Fpp	p,c		cln; friendly		good food
Stairway Lodge	Fpp	p,c		cln; homey; friendly		good food
Brookside	Fpp	c		Hebrew spoken		coffee shop
Peoples	Fpp	c		friendly people		good food
Traveller's Inn	Fpp	c				
Wonder Lodge	Fpp	c		cheap		
Adespa Lodge	Fpp	c		cheap		

Tuguegarao

name & phone	price	type	location	description	facilities	food
Callao Resort c/o Cagayan Tourism Office, Capitol Site, Tuguegarao 446-1087	B,C C,D	p c	Callao, Peñablanca	cottages, rms, some OK, some	hike, cave. swim	prearrange or bring
Delfino 446-1952/1953	C,D	a,p	Bonifacio Ave, Tuguegarao	nice suites		Chinese rest
Casa Ludivina 446-1568	D	a,p p	Ruyu, (highway) Tuguegarao	homey; hard beds		rest
Georgie's Inn 446-1434	D E	a,p p	122 Bonifacio, Tuguegarao	spacious, bright		rms
Crown Lodge 446-1739	D E	a,p p,c	Luna, Tuguegarao	common bath not so nice		rest

Camarines

name & phone	price	type	location	description	facilities	food
Apuao Grande (MNL 521-9731) tlx: 49960	AA	p	Cam Norte (c/o Swagman Hotel, Malate, Manila)	cottages, beach	water sports	rest
Aristocrat Hotel 5230	C,D	a,p	Elias St, Naga	light, airy corri dors; ask for rm with window; cleanest & best value in town		rest
Crown Hotel 2585	C D E	a,p,s a,p c	Burgos St, Naga	nice suites rm w sink		rest – best in town
Fiesta Hotel 2760	D E F?	a,p p c	Panganiban St, Naga			

Camarines, continued

name & phone	price	type	location	description	facilities	food
Moraville	E F?	a,p p	Peñafrancia Ave, Naga			
Peñafrancia Resort	D E	a,p p	Carolina	cottages & dorms some nice	pools, tennis hike	rest
New Kayumanggi Resort	D	a,p	Carolina	rms & cottages	pool	
Peñafrancia Beach Resort		p	San Jose	cottages on beach – some nice		rest
Pongol Resort	F	c	Pasacao	very rustic		
Ibalon Hotel; 353	C	a;p	Iriga	nice rms		rest; BBQ
Park View	Fpp	c	Iriga	budget hotel		

Legazpi, Albay & Sorsogon

name & phone	price	type	location	description	facilities	food
La Trinidad 2951-55 (MNL 503306)	B	a,p	Legazpi (Victoria Bldg, 429 UN Ave, Ermita)	City central; cln carpeted rms		restaurant
Vista al Mayon 4811	C D E	a,p p c	F Aquende St, Albay District	fam run; v cln; great views	pool (charge)	home cooking
Tanchuling Inter national House 2788, 3494	D E	a,p,h c	Imperial Subdv, Legazpi City	v cln, spacious rms; lovely common bath	no cards	rest
Casablanca 3130; 3131; 3133	C	a,p	Peñaranda St Legazpi City	v cln; some rms good view	cards: V,M	
Legazpi Pension (Motel); 3132	C	a,p	Arimbay,	cln; friendly staff		
Legazpi Plaza 3344 3345 (MNL 582144/53/62)	C D	a,p p	Lapu Lapu St (MH del Pilar cor P Gil, Malate)	Sarkies bus off in lobby	cards: A,V,U	
New Al-Bay 2218	D D	a,p p	Legazpi	Peñaranda St		
Mayon 2212	D E	a,p p	Peñaranda & Rizal Sts, Legazpi			
Rex 2743	D E	a,p c	Aguinaldo St, Legazpi			
Ritz 2670	D F	a,p c	Peñaranda St, Legazpi	old bldg; noisy; friendly staff		
Sa Bay Bay 2703	D E	a,p p	Mambucal Dist, Legazpi			rest
Reyes Beach Resort	E		Sto Domingo	rustic cottages		
Sirangan Beach Resort	E		Sto Domingo	rustic cottages		
Casa Mañana 4680	D E	a,p p	595 P Burgos,	family run Daraga		
Marbella 4141	D E	p,k c,h	Doña Maria Subd, Daraga			
Rizal Beach Resort		p	Gubat, Sorsogon	simple rms		pre-order food

Batanes

name & phone	price	type	location	description	facilities	food
Mama Lily's	D*		Basco	cln rm in family home	rm & board	good
St Dominic College	Fpp	d	Basco	school dormitory - inquire if space is avail from Ms E Rebaza or Mons M Baltazar		

Puerto Galera, Mindoro

There is a bewildering profusion of cottages on many of Puerto's beaches. Prices vary with demand and season, but generally start at $3 for a simple cottage with bathroom in the vicinity, and go up from there. Inspect the facilities before committing yourself. During busy season, let one of the touts on the ferry book for you - if you don't like the place, move next day. Beaches northeast of Puerto are best for swimming and in-shore water sports. White Beach, near the end of the line for jeepneys, is very crowded. If you prefer peace and quiet, walk further along or take the occasional jeep as far as Talipanan. Beaches near Sabang are pretty, corrally below the water, near excellent diving and snorkeling. Lalaguna and Sabang are very crowded, Small Lalaguna slightly less so.

name & phone	price	type	location	description	facilities	food
Coco Beach Resort (MNL 816-1965/ 0730) tlx 65697 RKENT PN	B	ctg p	beyond Big Lalaguna (2716-C Gen Capimpin St, Makati)	lovely ctgs; setting; beach rocky	windsurf,	good
Encenada Beach Resort	C		Balete Beach		pretty beach sometimes rough	
Outrigger Hotel Motel Beach Resort	C	p	Hundora Beach	like a US beach motel	darts, pool, etc	yes
Halcon Reef (MNL 827-3622 828-3663)	A* D	p	Boquete Beach (Mrs Garcia, 5 Toledo St, Merville, 1700 Parañaque MM)	nice; good reports	water sports	yes
Cathie's Inn		p	Boquete Beach	good reports		
Kalaw House (MNL 842–3543)			high on a hill above Puerto	beautiful view good reports		good
Tamaraw Beach Resort		ctg,p		nice, uncrowded	good beach	yes

Mamburao, Mindoro

name & phone	price	type	location	description	facilities	food
Mamburao Beach Resort (MNL 815-2733)	AAA*	ctg,p	Mamburao (Cityland III, Makati)	lovely ctgs on beach;	water sports	yes
Traveller's Inn		p	Mamburao	helpful staff		

AAA – over $50
AA – over $35
A – over $20
B – over $15
* – full board
a – airconditioned
ctg – cottage
d – dorm
k – kitchenette
c – common bath

C – $10 and up
D – $5 and up
E – $3 and up
F – under $3
pp – per person
p – private bath
s – 1 bath shared between 2 rooms
h – hot running water

A – American Express
D – Diner's Club
M – Mastercard
V – Visa

B – Bankard
BP – BPI card
F – Fareastcard
E – Equicard
P – PCIBcard
R – RCPC
U – Unicard

San Jose, Mindoro

name & phone	price	type	location	description	facilities	food
Big Newk	D	p	San Jose	airy, cln rms; helpful staff		meals
Sikatuna	D E	p c	San Jose	sm rms; on the beach		meals
Red Baron Lodge	 E	ctg p	San Jose	cln, rustic rms		
Executive Inn	E F,E	a,p c	Pagasa, San Jose			rest
Sikatuna Hotel	E F	p c	San Jose	v basic		rest
AB Traveller's Lodge	F	c	Rizal St, San Jose	v basic		
Mosqueras	F	c	San Jose	v basic		
Kapit Bahay Mini Hotel	F	p,c	San Jose	v basic		

Marinduque nb: prices estimated - many negotiable

name & phone	price	type	location	description	facilities	food
Seaview	C	p	Cawit, Boac	nice rms; beach c/o Mrs Sto Domingo, Boac		home cooking
Sun Raft	C	p	Cawit, Boac	rustic; beach c/o Mrs Ocampo, Boac		yes
Swing Resort	C	s,c d	north of Boac	c/o Chuacocos, Boac		
Pyramid Resort		c	Cawit, Boac	c/o Mrs Go, Boac		
Boac Hotel	C D E	1 a,p 2 p s,c	Boac	run down		
Cely's Place	E,F	c	Boac	cln, basic		
Ruby's	E,F	c	Boac			
Amigo's Lodge		s	Gasan	in-town, basic		
UNI Lodge		s	Gasan	in-town, basic		
Municipal cottages		c	Torrijos	cute; basic; bring bring bedding	nice beach	none
Rico's Inn		c	Santa Cruz	basic		yes

AAA – over $50
AA – over $35
A – over $20
B – over $15
* – full board

C – $10 and up
D – $5 and up
E – $3 and up
F – under $3
pp – per person

A – American Express
D – Diner's Club
M – Mastercard
V – Visa

B – Bankard
BP – BPI card
F – Fareastcard
E – Equicard
P – PCIBcard
R – RCPC
U – Unicard

a – airconditioned
ctg – cottage
d – dorm
k – kitchenette
c – common bath

p – private bath
s – 1 bath shared between 2 rooms
h – hot running water

Palawan – Puerto Princessa

name & phone	price	type	location	description	facilities	food
Rafols 2873	A	a,p	Puerto Princessa	top in its category	pool, tours	rest
Emerald Plaza 2611	AA-A	a,p	Malvar St, Puerto Princessa			
Badjao Inn	C	a,p	Rizal St, Puerto Princessa		nice place helpful people	rest, disco-bar
Palawan Hotel	C-D	a,p	Puerto Princessa	fairly cln;		airy rest
Duchess Pension 2761	E,F	c	Valencia St, Puerto Princessa	pretty, sm, cln rms; good reports	tours	rest; great fruit shakes
Mrs Dizon's	E	c	Puerto Princessa	nice rms, some lg nice people		can do meals
Yayens	C D,E	a,p c	Malvar St, Puerto Princessa			rest nearby
Dynasty Hotel	E-D E	p c	Rizal St, Puerto Princessa			
Civen's Inn	E	c	Mendoza St, Puerto Princessa	peaceful, cln; helpful staff		
Circon			Rizal & Valencia, Puerto Princessa			
Garcellano's	F	c	Rizal St, Puerto Princessa	very basic		

Palawan – beyond Puerta Princessa: see text for cottages at Nagtabon

name & phone	price	type	location	description	facilities	food
Meara Marina Island Resort	C?	ctg	Meara I, Honda Bay Puerto Princessa	nice lg rms on a nice island	diving;fishing sailing	yes
Fabellon's Silayan	F	c	Brooke's Point			
Sunset Garden	E,F	a,p,c	Brooke's Point			
Villa Señor	F	c	Brooke's Point			
Tabon Beach Resort	D-E	p	Quezon	very pretty	beach front	meals – good
Quezon Museum		c	Quezon	adv arrange to camp in bldgs		
Duchess Beachside Cottages	E	c	Tannabag; c/o Duchess, Puerto	ctgs, pretty; good beach		order food in advance
Coco Loco Resort	E	c	Roxas City	ctgs, pretty; good beach; tours		
Swissippini	F	c	Port Barton	good reports		meals
Elsa's	F	c	Port Barton	good reports		meals
Palawan Dive Shop	D		Port Barton			meals
Ten Knots (MNL 810–4101,	AAA*	c	Miniloc Island El Nido (Manila Garden Hotel)	nice ctgs; vg service; water sports, diving		great food
Gloria Fernandez	F	ctg	El Nido			town meals
Lim's Pension	F		El Nido town			meals

Romblon & Tablas

(lodging on Sibuyan must be found in private homes)

name & phone	price	type	location	description	facilities	food
Gutierrez Cool Spot		d	Tugdan, Tablas	hostel		
Mayor's guest house		ctg	San Agustin, Tablas			cook own food on the beach
Tablas Pension			Looc, Tablas			
Plaza Inn			Looc, Tablas			
Felmar Pension House "Marble House"	Fpp	p	Romblon, Romblon	cln; owners hospitable	usually no electricity on Romblon 10pm-morning	
Fish Inn	Fpp	c	Romblon, Romblon			
Seaside Inn	Fpp	c	Romblon, Romblon			
Tree House Beach	Fpp	c	Agnay, Romblon Romblon	tree houses; bring beddings c/o Rey Festino in Romblon		
Chamban Beach	Fpp	1 ctg	Chamban Beach, Romblon, Romblon	c/o F Benedicto, Romblon, Romblon		

Kalibo

Rms with ac and bath are available in the C range at Glowmoon tel 3193 and Casa Felicidad, tel 2676.
E range lodging available at Casa Alba, Green Mansion, Apartel Marietta and CT Lodge.

Boracay

Some lodging establishments in Boracay have been there for several years. Others come and go with great rapidity. Prices vary seasonally and with demand.

Top of the price line are Club Panoly (AAA) and Fridays (AA). Book Panoly thru Citibank Ctr, 8741 Paseo de Roxas, Makati, MNL 818–9985, 815–7475, fax 8160747. Book Fridays thru Galleon Gateway, 1089B Consuelo, Manila, MNL 521–5440.

In the A range is Palm Beach Club, Costa Blanca, and Pearl of the Pacific.

Places in the B–C price range which have received good reports include Casa Pilar, Terraces, Lorenzo's (the newer one), Diniwid's (some cottages have kitchenettes) and Salazar. Book Casa Pilar through Ms Ascano, 608 Cabildo, Intramuros, MNL 461368, 992337. Other places may be boked by writing directly to the establishment, Boracay, Aklan.

D priced places with good mention include Boracay International, Paradise Inn, Villa Mare, Sunshine, Boracay Garden and Willy's Place.

Roxas City

name & phone	price	type	location	description	facilities	food
Villa Patria 210180	B	a,p	Baybay Beach	11 cln, airy rms beautiful garden	nearby beach not so cln	rest nearby
Marcs Beach Resort 211103	D D Fpp	a,p p d	Baybay Beach 2 km from Villa Patria	8 cln, nice rms 4 rms several rms	nearby beach cleaner; bowling, tennis, disco	rest/snack on beach
Halaran Plaza 210649	D D	a,p p	P Gomez, on the town plaza	at the central; best of in-town hotels		rest; no alcohol allowed
Capiz People's Resort, 210873	D D	a,p p	Punta Tabuc	dark rms	pool	rest
Halaran House 210615	D D,E	a,p p,c	Roxas Ave			rest; no alcohol allowed

Iloilo City Lodging

name & phone	price	type	location	description	facilities	food
Amigo Terraces 74810-13 cable AMIGOH	B-C	a,p	Iznart & Delgado Sts, Iloilo	central; new; well apptd; cln	sm pool Cards-D,V,M,R	coffee shop; Chinese rest
Hotel del Rio 75585	C	a,p,h	MH del Pilar, Molo	cln; by a pretty river; helpful staff	pool Cards-D,V,M, BP,F,R	coffee shop good rest
Pension Casa Plaza 73461-67; 76964	B-C	a,p,h	Gen Luna	cln, attractive rms; central	rate includes breakfast	coffee shop
Sarabia Manor 72731 (MNL 502120)	B,C	a,p	101 Gen Luna (c/o Bahay Maynila, J Bocobo, Ermita Manila)	new rms nicely apptd	pool, casino Cards-A,D,V, M,many local	4 restaurants
River Queen 76667; 76443	D D,E	a,p A p	Bonifacio Dr central	basic, cln rms; helpful staff	Cards-D	attractive rest by river
Centercon 73431	D	a,p	JM Basa St	entry thru alley		rest
Madia-as 72756; 70206	D E	a,p p	Aldeguer St	lg bright basic cln rms; entry thru alley	Cards-V,M,F,U	rest
Family Pension 72047; 79208	D E	a,p p	12 Gen Luna	sm simple rms w bathrms separated frm rm by shower curtains	Cards-D,V, M,U	folksy rest & bar
Iloilo Lodging House 72348	D E	a,p p c	by the docks	basic sm rms; helpful staff; walk-up to lobby		

Iloilo Resorts

name & phone	price	type	location	description	facilities	food
Isla Naburot Resort 76616; 75925; 73511 cable: ISLA ILOILO	AAA*	p	Guimaras Island c/o P Saldana, PAL, Iloilo City	lovely islet 45 min by boat from Iloilo	water sports diving	great food
Tatlong Pulo (78297)		ctgs	Guimaras Island (Casa Plaza Bldg, Iloilo City)	45 min from Iloilo		yes
Nagarao Island Resort c/o 76046 tlx 5910 AISC PU	AA–A B–D	ctgs c	Guimaras Island (c/o Iloilo Casa Plaza Hotel)	1 1/2 hrs from Iloilo	water sports diving	great food
Villa Rosa 76953		ctgs	Calaparan, Villa Beach			rest
Sicogon (MNL 817–1163; 818–8711 loc 285) tlx 66319 SCGN PN	AAA– AA	ctgs p	Carles, Iloilo (Chemphil Bldg, 851 Pasay Rd, 851 Pasay Rd, Makati)	3 hrs by land frm Iloilo–best fly in; very nice cottages; private island	pool, tennis, water sports, hiking	rest, bar, good food

AAA – over $50	C – $10 and up	a – airconditioned	p – private bath
AA – over $35	D – $5 and up	ctg – cottage	s – 1 bath shared between 2 rooms
A – over $20	E – $3 and up	d – dorm	h – hot running water
B – over $15	F – under $3	k – kitchenette	
* – full board	pp – per person	c – common bath	

Bacolod City Lodging

name & phone	price	type	location	description	facilities	food
Sugarland Hotel 22462 thru 68	C	a,p,h	Singcang	89 v cln rms	pool; disco	rest - good gambas
Sea Breeze Hotel 24571	C	a,p,h	San Juan	56 cln rms		coffee shop, rest; Misono
Bascon II 23141; 23161	C,D	a,p,h	Gonzaga St	central; 37 rms	some rms w phone	rest
Casablanca 81880	D	a,p s	15 St	1 ac rm; 3 with fan fan; neat, cln, nice decor		rest – good
Family Pension 22647	E	a,p p	Lacson Ext	nice entry; basic rms		rest
Townhouse 81552	E	a,p p	North Dr cor Burgos St	out of town;basic cln rms		
Pension Negrense 22071	E	p c	Kamagong			rest
Las Rocas 23378; 27011	E	a,p p	Gatuslao St	run down		rest
Best Inn 23312		a,p p,c	Bonifacio St	family run, good service;bathrms not good		
YMCA 26919	Fpp	a c	Burgos St			

Bacolod area resorts

name & phone	price	type	location	description	facilities	food
Jara Beach Resort 22054	B,C	ctg,p d	Calumangan, Bago City	by the sea; 2-3 brm cottages		rest
			Punta Taytay	cottages		
Mambucal Health Resort	D,E E,Fpp	p c	Mambucal	cottages, rms, some some OK, some run run down	hiking, hot springs, pool	reservations needed for meals
Santa Fe Resort 29468	E	p	Santa Fe	basic cottages, run down, not convenient to transport	pool, sm zoo	coffee shop

Dumaguete

name & phone	price	type	location	description	facilities	food
Dumaguete Swiss Hotel; 4203	B	a,p,h	Bantayan, Dumaguete	all rms w 1 dbl & 1 sgl bed	pool, scuba, windsurf	rest
South Sea Resort 2857; 3683	C C	a,p,h p,h	Dumaguete	some rms with screened porches; beach		rest – good
Sta Monica Resort 3441	C D	a,p,h p,h	Banilad, south of the city	nice ctgs; beach	water sports Cards-V,M,B,U	rest – good

Dumaguete, continued

name & phone	price	type	location	description	facilities	food
Salawaki Beach Resort		p	Zamboanguita	nice ctgs; beach; isolated & quiet		rest – adv notice needed
Habitat 3134	C D	a,p p	Hibbard Ave	cln	Cards-U	
Insular Flintlock 3495, 4255	C C	a,p p	53 Silliman Ave			
Hotel Oriente	C E,D	a,p p	central			
Silliman Alumni 3220 (MNL 593853 or 596020)	D E	a,p p	central; Manila (c/o rm 308 Trinity Bldg, TM Kalaw St, Ermita)			
Al Mar		a,p p				
Opena's 3462	C D F	a,c p c	18 Katuda St			rest – good, inexpensive
Plaza Inn I 2437, 3103	C D	a,p/c,h c,h	V Locsin St		Card-U	
Plaza Inn – Royal Salute, 3400, 4441	C D	a,p/c,h c,h	Alfonso XIII St		Card-U	
YMCA 2382	Fpp	p	National Hwy			

Cebu City Hotels

name & phone	price	type	location	description	facilities	food
Cebu Plaza 92431; 73181 (MNL 819–2636–49)	AAA	a,p	Nivel Hill,Lahug (DCG Bldg, Makati)	modern, nice hotel	pool, tennis	3 rests
Montebello Villa 85021-29 (MNL 857911)	AAA	a,p	Banilad, Cebu (Manila Garden, Makati)	nice rms, garden	pool, tennis casino	rest, bar good food
Magellan 74613 – 25 (MNL 817-4258) cable Magellan Cebu tlx 24729 MIH PN	AAA	a,p	Gorordo Ave, Lahug, Cebu (Rm 206 Don Pablo Bldg, 114 Amorsolo St, Makati)	central; new rms nice	pool	rests & bar
St Moritz 74371-4; 79338	A	a,p	Gorordo Ave, Lahug Cebu	central; nice rms phone in lobby		pub
Mercedes; 97631	B-C	a,p,h	7 Pelaez	central ac; cln		rest
Rajah 96231	B-C	a,p,h	Osmeña Blvd	uncarpeted rms; best; cln		rest
Kan Irag; 97611	B-C	a,p,h	F Ramos, Cebu	cln		rest
Villa Inez 54079	D D	a,p p	A Abellana St	cleanest of its group; group; airy lobby		interesting breakfast
Tagalog Hotel 72531	C-D	a,p	Sanciangco St	cleanest of its group		
Family Pension 22647	C-D E	a,p c	Lacson Ext	cleanest of its group; good common bath		

City Hotels, continued

name & phone	price	type	location	description	facilities	food
Sky-View 73051; 93577	C-D	a,p,h	Luym Bldg	central		rest
Charter House	C-D E	a,p p,c	rms	airy, cln non-ac rms		
Rajah Soliman 91711; 91526	C-D	a,p,h	V Gulias St			rest
Rajah Humabon 77671	C-D	a,p,h	Juan Luna St			rest
Surigao 97857	D E	a,p p	Gen Junquiera			
Cebu Century 97621-9	D	a,p,h	Pelaez St	"bold models" show		rest
Hope Pension 93371; 78234	-D E	a,p p	V Gulias St	non-ac rms OK		
Lovena's Inn 90028	E	a,p p	144 Juan Luna	some rms dark		
Mayflower Pension 72948	E E	a,p c	capitol site	ac rms good value		
Elicon House; 73653	D	p	P del Rosario	cln		
Royal Pension 53625; 93890	Epp	c	655 Urgello	good, cln, well located		
Ruftan Pension 79138		p	Legazpi St	central; many low low budget		coffee shop
YMCA 72125	Fpp	p c	Jones Ave	rundown		
Arbels; 62393		c	Jones Ave nr YMCA			coffee shop
Patria de Cebu; 72084	Fpp	c	P Burgos	cln but run down		

Cebu Resorts

name & phone	price	type	location	description	facilities	food
Coral Reef Resort 61572 (MNL 815–4819/20) tlx 64481 ISPEN PN	AAA	a,p	Mactan Resort Corp, G–11 Cityland Condo 2, Sedeno St, Makati, MM	beautiful!	pool, beach	rest – good
Costabella 83663; 83749	AA	a,p	Mactan	nice, cln	pool, beach	rest – great
Tambuli 70200; 95957 (MNL 522–2301–4)	AAA AA	a,p p	Mactan (Victoria Bldg, UN Ave, Malate)	nice, crowded	pool, water sports	rest
Hadsan 70247; 72679	B–C	a,p p	Mactan asstd prices	asstd ctgs at	rest	
Kon Tiki	C	p	Maribago, Mactan		for divers	rest
Cebu Club Pacific 79147	AA A	a,p p	Sogod	ctgs; nice; 2 hrs frm Cebu	pool; dive	rest

Cebu Resorts, continued

name & phone	price	type	location	description	facilities	food
Argao 70200; 95957 (MNL 522–2301–3)	AAA–AA		Dalaguete (Victoria Bldg, Malate)	2 hrs frm Cebu nice rms		rest
Angelita's Holiday	B	p	Argao	homey; v cln; 2 hrs Home hrs frm Cebu		home cooking
Badian Island 61306	AAA	p	Badian, Cebu	v nice	water sports	rest
Moalboal Reef Club	A*	c	Moalboal			
Sumisid Lodge	C-D	c	Moalboal	cln, tiled brms,		

There are a number of places with inexpensive basic cottages at Panagsama Beach, **Moalboal,** among them Norma's, Cor Isa's, Eva's and Calypso Inn. Inspect before taking a room. Prices vary seasonally. from P60. In **Santander,** near the ferry to Dumaguete, is Manureva – a charming place. There are rustic cottages in **Daan Bantayan.**

Bohol

name & phone	price	type	location	description	facilities	food
Bohol Beach Club (MNL 522-2301)	AAA- AA	p	Panglao (Victoria Bldg, Malate)	rms on a lovely beach	water sports tennis most cards	rest
Momo Beach Resort c/o 3182, 2031 tlx 00758-6348 GIGH PU	AA*	ctg,p	Bilisan, Panglao	ctgs nr beach, very nice; very hospitable	tours; diving Cards-A,D,V, M,B,U	good home cooking
Alonaville Beach Resort	E	ctg,c	Alona Beach, Tawala, Panglao	crowded; cln		short orders
Alona Kew Beach Resort	C,D	ctg,p	Alona Beach, Tawala, Panglao	nice	diving,car, motorbike, boat	rest, bar
La Playa Blanca Beach Resort	D	ctg,p	Alona Beach, Tawala, Panglao	sm rms	diving	
Diver's Lodge 2663	B,C	ctg,p	Alona Beach, Tawala, Panglao	nice	diving; wind surfing	
Yosts	D		Loay	pvt home		
LTS Lodge 3310, 3082	C,D D	a,p c	CP Garcia Ave, Tagbilaran	nice rms		
Gie Garden Hotel 3182, 3025, 2013 tlx see Momo above	C,D	a,p	CP Garcia Ave, Tagbilaran	dark, homey	diving, tours Cards-A,D,V, M,B,U	good Chinese & native fare
Ilaw Center	C D,E E,Fpp	a,p p d	Bool, Tagbilaran	cln; out-of-town; sea view	diving	coffee shop
La Roca 3179; 3009	C	a,p	Graham Ave, Tagbilaran	new rms OK	tours; pool; Cards-D,U	rest
Coralandia 3445	C	ctg,p,k	Graham Ave, Tagbilaran	overlooks ocean	cards-D,V,U	
Traveller's Inn	E Fpp	p,c d	CP Garcia Ave, Tagbilaran	good, cln, basic lodge	no cards	
Saguise Hotel			Ubay	lodge		
Chocolate Hills Complex	p	d,c	Choc Hills, Carmen			rest

Leyte: Tacloban

name & phone	price	type	location	description	facilities	food
Leyte Park 321-3300 – 05 (MNL 818-8949)	AAA–AA	a,p	(Islander, 115 Alvaro, Makati)	beautifully apptd rms & cottages	pool; tennis; most cards	rest – good food; inexp
MacArthur Park 323-3015/3016 (MNL 521–3911)	AA–A	a,p p	Candahug, Palo (Islander, 115 Alvaro, Makati)	on the beach	windsurfing; most cards	rest
Baluarte San Jose 321-2811	D	p	San Jose	spacious native rms, rms, nice beach	pool	rest
Tacloban Village 321-2926	D	a,p	Imelda Ave			rest
Tacloban Plaza Pensionne Deluxe 321-2444	D	a,p	Justice Romualdez St		bowling	rest
Primrose 321-2248	C,D E	a,p p	Zamora cor Enage Sts	least cln of the in-town hotels		
Manobo Lodge	E,F	p/s	Zamora St	pleasant staff, comfy place		coffee shop
Cecilia's Lodging House	F	c	178 Paterno St	very clean		inexp meals
San Juanico Travel Lodge; 321-3221	E F	p	104 Justice Romualdez St	basic in-town lodge		

Leyte: Ormoc

name & phone	price	type	location	description	facilities	food
Don Felipe 2460; 2007 Don Felipe Annex	B D E	a,p a,p p	Bonifacio St, by the pier	very well apptd great view		rest – good food
Pongos 2481; 2211	D	a,p	Bonifacio St	lg, basic rms		rest – good food
Shalom Pension 2208	Fpp	c	Cata-ag cor Bonifacio Sts	very basic, esp the bathrms		

Cagayan de Oro

name & phone	price	type	location	description	facilities	food
Alta Tierra 3661; 3662	C,D	a,p,h	Carmen Hills	nice rms; not near transport	nice pool	restaurant
VIP 3629; 3829; 3768	B,C D,C	a,p,h a,p,h	A Velez St	good deluxe rms helpful staff		good rest
Tropicana 3494; 3949	B-D E	a,p p	Yacapin cor Velez Sts	good cln rms; helpful staff; intercoms;central		rest
De Luxe 3088; 2812; 4067	C E	a,p c	V Roa St, nr the mkt	at the market		rest
Caprice by the Sea 4880; 4980; 4388	C	a,p	Gusa	out-of-the-way	no beach	good seafood
Mabini 3539	D E,F	a,p c	113 Mabini cor A Velez	cln, cheerful ac rms; helpful staff; central; good, sm rms		rest

Cagayan de Oro, continued

name & phone	price	type	location	description	facilities	food
Oro United 4884	D E	a,p p	Gomez cor Velez Sts	v cln; central		
First Park View	D E,F	a,p c	Neri St	sm rms; helpful staff		
Sampaguita 2740; 2640	E E	a,p p	JR Borja St			
Golden Star 4079	D E,F	a,p p,c	JR Borja St			
Perlas Inn 2136; 2036	D E,F	a,p p,c	340 G Capistrano St	good, cln, simple intercoms;		
Satellite I 2315	E E,F	a,p p	Taal St			
Satellite II 4485	E E,F	a,p p	Taal cor Rizal Sts			
Fems 2470	F	c	Yacapin cor Aguinaldo Sts	bright, sm rms; crs run down		
Casa Filipina 3383	F	c	JR Borja			
Palace I & II	F	dorm	Palanca cor Capistrano			

Camiguin Island, continued

name & phone	price	type	location	description	facilities	food
Camiguin Seaside Lodge	E Fpp	ctg,p c	Agoho, Mambajao	cottages, cln; on beach		yes
Caves Resort	D Fpp	p c	Agoho, Mambajao	cottages & lg rms with bath; beach		yes yes
Jasmine by the Sea	E	ctg,p	Sug-ong, Mambajao	cottages; beach		yes
Mrs Tia's	E	ctg,p	Mambajao	cottages; beach		yes
Padilla's	E Fpp	p s	Magting, Mambajao Mambajao	cottages & rms; beach		yes yes
Mychellin	D E,F	p p	Mahinog	cottages & rms; beach		
Camiguin Travel Lodge	D Fpp	p c	La Laguna, Mahinog	cottages & rms; on a pond		
Camiguin Travel Lodge	Fpp	c	Mambajao	by the market		
Mrs Tia's	Fpp	c	Mambajao	main road		good meals

Iligan

The Al Toro and Maria Cristina Hotels are the best places in Iligan.

Butuan

Almont Hotel, San Jose St., tel 3332, ap, A–C Century Inn, Villanueva St., tel 3126, C Embassy Hotel, Montilla Blvd., tel 3737, ap, C Narra Hotel, Bgy Bading, tel 3145, some ac rms, C–E.Hensonly Plaza, San Francisco St., D

Dipolog

Dakak Resort, Dapitan, is getting very good reports, many facilities, all major cards, AAA–AA, MNL tel 721–0426, 721–2463.

Davao City

name & phone	price	type	location	description	facilities	food
Davao Insular 64778 (MNL 815-9711)	AAA	a,p c	Lanang (Intercon, Makati)	nice rms; ask for verandah; lovely grounds	pool, tennis, jogging, golf putting, beach nearby	rest - good
Apo View, tel 74861 tlx 24853 AVH PH (MNL 851288)	A	a,p	J Camus St (Manila Garden)	dk, carpeted rms	good pool; bar; disco; most cards	rest
Maguindanao 78401	C	a,p,h	CM Recto Ave	lg, cln carpeted rms	tennis; pelota; basketball; cards	rest
D'Fabulous Vennees 78934, 76026	C	a,p,h	McArthur Hwy	dk rms; out-of-town	cards	rest – good
BS Inn 79041	D	a,p,h p	Monteverde St	walk-up lobby; bright, airy, cln rms; good value	no cards	
Royale House 73630	C,D E E	a,p a,c p	CM Recto Ave	cln, dk rms rms w/o toilet larger than other places	billiards; darts; no cards	
Fortune Inn 76688	D E	a,p,h p,c	R Magsaysay Ave	v sm rms	no cards	
Pension Felisa 79937	D E	a,p,h p	Magallanes Ave		no cards	
Men Seng 75185; 73101	D,E E	a,p p	San Pedro St	run down	no cards	
Tourist Lodge 78760	D F	p c	McArthur Hwy, Matina	campy lobby; sm rms	no cards	
El Mimar 78926	E E,F	a,p p,c	Legaspi St	run down	no cards	

General Santos & T'Boli

name & phone	price	type	location	description	facilities	food
Ram's Inn 2313	B	a,p	National Hwy	like a US motel	cards-D	rest nearby
Matutum 4901	B,C D	a,p,h p,h	P Acheron Blvd		cards-D,U,B	rest
Pepo's 4333	C,D	a,p,h	National Hwy		cards-D,U,B	rest
Santa Cruz Mission	*	dorm	Santa Cruz Mission, Lake Sebu, S Cotabato (PO Box 7878, Koronadel, South Cotabato)	very cln; by reservation only		good
Antenor's			Lake Sebu, South Cotabato			yes

Zamboanga

name & phone	price	type	location	description	facilities	food
Lantaka by the Sea 3931 – 34 (MNL 871896 816-1590)	A	a,p	Valderrosa St (c/o 94 Puyat, Makati)	cln; "visitors" not allowed; well located; good staff	pool Cards-A,D,V,M	rest v good
Zamboanga Hermosa 2071; 2072	C,D	a,p,h	Sucabon St	cln, sm, nice rms	Cards-D,U,B	coffee shop
New Astoria 2075; 2076	C E	a,p p	Sucabon St	cln rms, some with fridge	Cards-D,U,B	Chinese rest
Paradise Hotel 2936 – 39	D	a,p	P Reyes cor Mayor Climaco	bright, friendly staff	Cards-D,V,U, B,F	24 hr coffee shop
Paradise Pension 3005 – 08	C,D	a,p	Barcelona cor T Claudio	bright, friendly staff	Cards-D,V,U, B,F	24 hr coffee shop
Imperial Inn 3548	D E	a,p p	P Brillantes St	good value; cln & basic		rest
Unique 3598	E,F	p,c	Curcuera St	airy, nice; nr ferry		

AAA – over $50
AA – over $35
A – over $20
B – over $15
* – full board

C – $10 and up
D – $5 and up
E – $3 and up
F – under $3
pp – per person

a – airconditioned
ctg – cottage
d – dorm
k – kitchenette
c – common bath

p – private bath
s – 1 bath shared between 2 rooms
h – hot running water

A – American Express
D – Diner's Club
M – Mastercard
V – Visa

B – Bankard
BP – BPI card
F – Fareastcard
E – Equicard
P – PCIBcard
R – RCPC
U – Unicard

Glossary

Definitions are given for non-English words used in the book. Although the majority of these words are Filipino, some are of other origin. Although there is no "c" in the Filipino alphabet, words commonly spelled with the c are listed. Purists will want to substitute "k" for the hard "c", and "ts" for the "ch"

adobo . . . sauce of soya, vinegar, garlic, pepper in which foods are cooked
albulario . . . herbalist
alimango . . . large, fat shoreline crab
alimasag . . . deep water crab
ampao . . . sweetened popped corn
anting-anting . . . amulet
atis . . . sweet sop (fruit)

baboy . . . pig; pork
bagoong . . fermented shrimp or small fish
balisong . . . fan knife
balut . . . duck egg with developed embryo
banca . . . canoe
banig . . . mat
bangus . . . milk fish
banquero . . . boat man
barangay . . . community
bariles pangga at buntot . . . barbequed tuna jaw and tail
barong Tagalog . . . Tagalog formal shirt
barquillos . . . rolled wafers
barrios . . . communities
basi . . . cane liquor
basnig . . . fishing boat with long nets for catching anchovies
biak . . . split
bibingka . . . rice cake
biscocho . . . zweibeck-like biscuits
bislig . . . fishing boat
bolo . . . knife; machete
budbud . . . sweetened glutinous rice cooked in banana leaves
bulol . . . rice god figurine
buco . . . young coconut
buri . . . palm species

caimito . . . star apple
calamansi . . . walnut size lemon-lime citrus fruit
calamares . . . fried squid
calesa . . . horse drawn cart
camote . . . sweet potato
carabao . . . water buffalo
caretela . . horse drawn cart
catalon . . . healer/sorcerer
chico . . . small beige fruit with pinkish flesh
convento . . . convent; parsonage
crispy pata . . . crisp pork leg
curacha . . . crustacian shaped like a cross between a crab and a crayfish

dagmay . . . Mandaya abaca cloth
Dambang Kagitingan . . . Shrine of Valor
delicadeza . . . sensitivity to the feelings of others
dinuguan . . . tripe cooked in blood
diwata . . . fairy; spirit
durian . . . strong smelling fruit with custard-like pulp around medium seeds

gabi . . . taro
gigantes . . . giants
guinataan . . . fruits cooked in sweetened coconut milk
gulaman . . . agar-agar
gulay . . . vegetables
gumamela . . . hibiscus

halo halo . . . dessert or snack of sweetened fruits and beans and ice
herbolarios . . . herbalists
ho . . . sir or maam

ihaw . . . barbeque
ihaw-ihaw . . . barbeque
inasal . . . roast
inihaw . . . barbeque
ipon . . . fish fry
isda . . . fish

kaimito . . . star apple
kaingineros . . . slash-and-burn farmers
kalachuchi . . . frangipani
kalaw . . . hornbill
kambing . . . goat
kamote . . . yam; sweet potato
kare-kare . . . oxtail, tripe with heart of banana
kilawen . . . marinated raw fish
kinilaw . . . marinated raw fish
kiping . . . rice flour decorations
kiyapo . . . water lily

la Paz batchoy . . . ravioli-like soup
laing . . . meat and chili in gabi leaves cooked in coconut milk
langka . . . jackfruit – large green fruit with fleshy golden pulp around seeds
lanzones . . . clusters of small beige fruits
lapu-lapu . . . garouper
latu . . . seaweed
leche flan . . . milk custard
lechon . . . roast pig
locos . . . coves
lumpia . . . egg roll

mabolo . . . red fruit
maja blanca . . . coconut pudding
malandic . . . sloping
malong . . . wrap-around skirt
mami . . . noodle soup
mangosteen . . . hard, purple fruit with white, edible flesh around several large seeds
mankukulam . . . sorcerers/healers
manok . . . chicken
marang . . . similar to durian, not so smelly
mechado . . . meat roll
merienda . . . snack
mestizo . . . half-breed; of mixed race
mori . . . tiny fish fry
moriones . . . masked participants in the Moriones Festival

nik-nik . . . sand fleas
nilaga . . . boiled
nito . . . a vine

pabitin . . . hanging; chandelier
pakbet . . . Ilocano vegetable dish (also called ***pinakbet***)
palay . . unhulled rice
pancit . . . noodles
pancit canton . . . dish made from dried noodles
pancit guisado . . . noodles, vegetables, meat
pancit Malabon . . . noodles cooked a la Malabon
papait . . . goat's meat dish
parahilots . . . healers
parol . . . lantern
pastillas . . . sweets made from ***carabao*** milk
pattig . . . fish trap
pau . . . taro
piña . . . pineapple fiber
pinakbet . . . Ilocano vegetable dish (also called ***pakbet***)
po . . . sir
poblacion . . . town center
pulutan . . . wrapped food
pusa . . . cat; or rice cooked in leaves
pusit . . . squid
puto . . . rice cake or bread

queso puti . . . white cheese

rambutan . . . red, spikey-looking fruit
retablo . . . retable

sabong . . . cock fight
sampaguita . . . jasmine
santol . . . hard fruit with yellow exterior and white flesh around large seeds
santos . . . icons of saints
sariwa . . . fresh
sig-id . . . vine
sinamay . . . fine material made from pineapple leaves
sinarapan . . . world's smallest fresh water fish (also called *tabios*)
singkamas . . . jicama
sinigang . . . sour soup

siopao . . . steamed filled bread (dimsum)
so-ot . . . grass headdress worn by Batanes women
suha . . . pomelo
suman . . . sweetened glutinous rice cooked in banana leaves

tabios . . . world's smallest fresh water fish (also called *sinarapan*)
talaba . . . oyster
tahong . . . mussel
tapa . . . dried or marinated meat
tinola . . . lemon-grass soup
t'nalak . . . T'Boli abaca cloth
tuba . . . rice or cane wine
turo-turo . . . canteen-style restaurant
turumba . . . dance of unknown origins

ubod . . . heart of palm
uraro . . . arrow root
utang na loob . . . debt of gratitude

vintas . . . out-riggered sail boats of Mindanao

Index

Map Index